The

Railroads of the South

1865-1900

A STUDY IN
FINANCE AND CONTROL

The Railroads of the South 1865-1900

A STUDY IN FINANCE AND CONTROL

By JOHN F. STOVER

CHAPEL HILL

The University of North Carolina Press

Copyright, 1955, by
The University of North Carolina Press

To MARJORIE

ACKNOWLEDGMENTS

ONE OF THE pleasures associated with the last steps in completing a book is the opportunity to acknowledge publicly the inspiration, assistance, and cooperation of the many people who have helped make it possible.

The original suggestion for this research and study came from Professor William B. Hesseltine, of the University of Wisconsin. I am primarily indebted to him, for his unfailing guidance and inspiration made the task of research and writing much easier. In the early research the respective staffs of the University of Wisconsin Library and the Wisconsin Historical Society Library were generous with both time and assistance. Later during a long hot summer the staff of the Library of the University of Illinois was equally helpful. Special thanks are due Dr. Elizabeth McPherson, of the Library of Congress, for her suggestions and aid in the use of the materials of the Manuscripts Division; Miss Elizabeth Cullen, of Washington, D. C., who made readily available the facilities of the Library of the Bureau of Railway Economics; Colonel Robert Selph Henry, of the Association of American Railroads, for his assistance in gaining access for the author to the source materials of several southern railroads; Dr. Stanley Pargellis, Librarian of the Newberry Library, Chicago, who kindly made the Illinois Central Archives available to the writer; and Miss Margaret Collins, of the Newberry Library, who was most generous with her time and assistance. I also wish to thank Professor John H. Moriarty, Director of the Purdue University Library, for his counsel and advice, and Professor Esther Schlundt and Mrs. Koleen Irvin for courtesies shown the

ACKNOWLEDGMENTS

author in his use of materials in the W. F. M. Goss Memorial Library at Purdue.

I wish gratefully to acknowledge the financial assistance given in the publication grant provided by the Purdue Research Foundation, which in a very substantial sense made the publication of this book possible. No list of acknowledgments would be complete without mentioning Professor M. B. Ogle, Jr., of Purdue, whose counsel and assistance, especially in the revision of the manuscript, has been most helpful. Finally, to my wife, who has helped with every phase in the production of this book, I owe the greatest debt of all.

John F. Stover

West Lafayette, Indiana
April, 1955

CONTENTS

		PAGE
	Acknowledgments	vii
	Introduction	xiii
1	Southern Railroads in the 1850's	3
2	Southern Railroads at War	15
3	Southern Railroad Finance in 1865	23
4	Destruction and Rehabilitation	39
5	The Carpetbaggers Lend a Hand	59
6	Southern Ambitions of the Pennsylvania Railroad	99
7	A Story of Receivership	122
8	The Illinois Central Goes South	155
9	Prosperity, Expansion, and Consolidation	186
10	The Louisville and Nashville	210
11	The Richmond and Danville	233
12	Receivership and Consolidation	254
13	Southern Railroads and Northern Finance in 1900	275
	Bibliography	285
	Index	295

MAPS

	PAGE
Railroads of the South in 1865 and New Construction to 1880	25
Growth of Pennsylvania-Southern Railway Security System in the 1870's	106
Extent of Southern Railroad Receiverships in the 1870's	131
Extension of the Illinois Central Railroad into the Southern States	160
Railroads of the South in 1880 and New Construction to 1890	192
The Expansion of the Louisville and Nashville	216
The Richmond and Danville System	236
The Atlantic Coast Line, Plant System, and Seaboard Air Line in 1900	264

INTRODUCTION

THE PURPOSE of this study is to trace the development of a growing northern financial influence over southern railroads in the generation following the Civil War. Prior to and during the war years southerners, using chiefly local finances, owned, controlled, and managed the great bulk of the southern railroads. A generation later, in 1900, northern men and money exerted a considerable financial influence and control over a much enlarged southern railway network. This transition in financial influence and control occurred in a South arbitrarily defined by the author to include only the eight Confederate states east of the Mississippi plus Louisiana and Kentucky. The development of this northern financial influence came during a period in which the railroads south of the Ohio and Potomac rivers achieved a traffic pattern and a corporate maturity comparable to that of the mid-twentieth century.

Despite the fact that southern rail mileage grew nearly fourfold in the thirty-five years after the Civil War, the typical southern line was still somewhat different from northern railroads. This difference stemmed largely from the fact that the usual southern line often had a more limited route than comparable northern lines and generally was built more cheaply than roads north of the Ohio or west of the Mississippi. This cheapness of construction was due as much to the limited volume of potential traffic as to the sometimes favorable terrain or to nearly invariably skimpy capital structures. Southern lines also generally had shorter equipment rosters with rolling stock and motive power that was often inferior in quality to that used in the North. Railroads in the South were also slower to modernize and improve their

INTRODUCTION

track, bridges, and other right-of-way structures. Only in their proclivity for default, receivership, and foreclosure were southern railroads ahead of their sister lines in the North.

As the research for the present study developed, it became apparent that the scope and span of the intended work might occasion grave procedural and substantive difficulties. Obviously a study covering the financial history of a third of a nation's railways (as of 1865) ran some danger of getting bogged down in a morass of dozens of projected rail systems, hundreds of separate railroad companies, and thousands of directors and top officials of those companies.

The author has endeavored to avoid these perils through the use of three procedures in both research and writing: (1) all detailed research and examination has been limited to railroads of one hundred miles or more in length, (2) several general periods or phases have been carefully delineated in southern rail history, and (3) a detailed examination of four significant railroads or railroad systems, which in general stand as specific illustrations of the phases mentioned in the second procedure, has been presented.

Limiting the study in general to railroads of one hundred miles or more in length resulted in a great saving of time and effort. On the eve of the Civil War, lines of over one hundred miles in length accounted for perhaps a third of the total southern railroad companies. At the turn of the century, such major lines numbered only a sixth of all existing companies. On a mileage basis these lines represented a large preponderance of the southern railroad enterprise. In 1860, lines over one hundred miles in length totalled approximately two-thirds of all southern mileage, by 1873 they represented nearly three-fourths of the total, and by 1900 the thirty-one lines over one hundred miles in length had grown so rapidly that they totalled 87 per cent of all southern rail mileage. In general, the shorter lines conformed to the same pattern of growing northern financial influence as did the longer roads. Where shorter lines successfully postponed, or even avoided, northern financial control, this success was caused as much by a northern preference for larger, more

INTRODUCTION

ambitious roads as by any successful plans of resistance by the smaller companies themselves. Actually few really important railroads in the South long remained under one hundred miles in length. The strategically located, eighty-mile Richmond, Fredericksburg and Potomac was an exception, but shortly after 1900 it became a "union" line and was operated by six larger companies. More often a short line became part of a larger system, or perhaps even created that system, as in the case of the eighty-mile Seaboard and Roanoke, the original company in the Seaboard Air Line.

The organization of the present study was also considerably aided by the division of the thirty-five years after 1865 into four periods or phases, each roughly a decade in length. The first seven or eight postwar years were chiefly marked by two often parallel developments, the necessary rehabilitation of the war-torn southern railroads and the pilfering and swindling activities of numerous carpetbaggers who either were projecting new lines or taking over old ones. Strangely enough, the carpetbag era resulted in few permanent railroad acquisitions by the northern men or their southern associates. The second phase appeared with the severe Panic of 1873 and the long depression which followed. In the years between 1873 and 1880, over half of the southern lines experienced the trying sequence of default, receivership, and either foreclosure or reorganization. As a result of these financial difficulties, many southern roads experienced their first (and often also permanent) northern financial influence or control. Other southern lines succumbed to northern financial management in the third period, the decade of the 1880's, years of rail prosperity, rapid construction, and intensive corporate consolidation. Northern influence and control became nearly complete in the last decade of the century, a period including both extensive receivership in 1892 and 1893, and continued rail consolidation later in the decade.

Detailed reviews of four major rail systems serve as specific illustrations of the four periods noted above. In the early 1870's the Pennsylvania Railroad, and the Southern Railway Security Company which it dominated, built up a southern rail empire of

INTRODUCTION

two thousand miles. As one of America's earliest holding companies, this combine marked the first effort of northerners to acquire a number of southern railroads in a single operation. In total effect, however, this new northern management was only slightly more permanent than the operations of carpetbaggers who were busy in the same years. In the middle and late 1870's another northern road, the Illinois Central, was having a more enduring success in its acquisition of a line that had suffered default and receivership during the depression following 1873. The new possession of the Illinois Central, the New Orleans, St. Louis and Chicago Railroad, was in its earlier corporate history a good illustration of railroad carpetbaggism. A third line, the Louisville and Nashville with its rapid expansion after 1880, well illustrates the period of rail prosperity and consolidation during the decade preceding 1890. As with many other southern roads, northern money and management captured the L. and N. during the decade. The final system reviewed in detail, the Richmond and Danville, also expanded rapidly during the 1880's. Perhaps more important was its receivership in 1892 and its subsequent reorganization into the Southern Railway, a six-thousand-mile system controlled by Morgan men and money.

Naturally the measurement of the presence and degree of northern financial influence was a major problem present both in the treatment of the several phases of southern postwar development and also in the specific reviews of the four important rail systems. The very nature and complexity of this major consideration has precluded any attempt on the author's part to deal with the reactions and attitudes of the local communities (or their press and governing officials) to the shifting financial control. Much northern influence and management appeared and developed through the sequence of receivership and foreclosure sale or in the process of extensive corporate consolidation. In both foreclosure sale and corporate consolidation the growing financial influence of the North was often obvious and publicly admitted. Such was certainly the case in 1870 when General Beauregard's New Orleans, Jackson and Great Northern came under the carpetbag influence of Colonel H. S. McComb and again in 1877 when

INTRODUCTION

McComb's expanded system was sold in foreclosure sale to the Illinois Central. It was also true in 1881 when two roads in receivership, the Atlantic, Mississippi and Ohio and the South Carolina Railroad, were sold without question to northern men. Again in the same year a northern syndicate headed by Samuel Thomas, George Seney, and Calvin Brice openly took control of the East Tennessee, Virginia and Georgia away from Colonel Edwin W. Cole of Tennessee as they announced their expansion plans for the new acquisition. Further north in Kentucky the appearance of northern management of the Louisville and Nashville was acknowledged in 1882 with the sale of a large block of Louisville-owned stock to a New York syndicate headed by Edward H. Green.

But other methods of shifting financial influence can also be seen. Northern financial assistance in the extension of an established road is illustrated in the case of C. P. Huntington and the expanding Chesapeake and Ohio. Henry M. Flagler and his Florida East Coast Railway is an example of northern money financing the original construction of a new line. The outside or northern reorganization of a southern line in financial difficulty is clearly seen in the J. P. Morgan creation of the Southern Railway out of the Richmond and Danville properties in the decade of the 1890's.

Frequently this shift in control was completely obvious, being noted in the press of the day and admitted or proclaimed by both former and new managements. Sometimes the changing ownership and control came more quietly and gradually. In such instances an examination of director personnel from year to year normally gives a fairly accurate indication of the degree of northern financial influence and management present. Of course it is true that the southern roads, like all railroads, often selected certain directors intentionally to represent some geographical region, some financial or economic interest group, or because of some individual talent possessed by the designated director. But for most southern railroads a marked shift toward northern director personnel in the last third of the nineteenth century also indicates a growing northern financial influence. This can clearly

INTRODUCTION

be seen in the more detailed studies of such roads as the New Orleans, St. Louis and Chicago (Illinois Central), the Louisville and Nashville, and the Richmond and Danville (Southern). It can be inferred for most other roads as well when we note the growth from only 4 per cent northern directors (for twenty-five major southern lines) in the late 1860's to 69 per cent northern directors (for the ten major lines totalling 73 per cent of all southern rail mileage) in 1900.

As indicated in the four phases of southern postwar rail development, as illustrated in the detailed examination of four typical southern rail systems, and as substantiated by complete tabulations of over sixteen hundred southern railroad directorships (1870 to 1900), northern financial influence grew steadily through the thirty-five years after the Civil War. By 1900 northern men and money were in positions of dominance in nearly 90 per cent of the mileage of the major southern railroads.

The

Railroads of the South

1865-1900

———•———

*A STUDY IN
FINANCE AND CONTROL*

CHAPTER 1

SOUTHERN RAILROADS IN THE 1850's

No DECADE in the nineteenth century was more important in the history of American railroads than the years following 1850. What had been but a scattering of short lines from Georgia to Maine in 1850 became by 1860 a railway network serving adequately all the states east of the Mississippi. The increase in mileage in the decade was from 8,589 to 30,593 miles.[1] As the only "Big Business" then on the American scene, the railroads participated fully in the business prosperity and optimism that appeared with the discovery of gold in California. No other institutions did business on so vast a scale, financed themselves from such a variety of sources, or employed such numbers of men of varied skills. While the railroad-building mania was prevalent in every state, the most intense activity was centered in the trunk-line territory, especially in Illinois, Indiana, and Ohio. In Illinois alone, as much rail was laid in a single year (1,249 miles in 1856) as had been in operation in all the five states of the old Northwest in 1850.[2] In the Panic of 1857, bankruptcy overtook many of the new lines in the Middle West, as well as in the East

---

1. *Eighth Census of the United States, 1860*, "Mortality and Property" (Washington, 1866), pp. 333-334. Even the most casual study of decennial railroad maps for the period 1830 to 1900 will show the vast construction of the 1850's.

2. The military and economic importance of this construction north of the Ohio to the Union in the Civil War has often been noted. See J. G. Randall, *The Civil War and Reconstruction* (Boston, 1937), pp. 83-84; Carl Russell Fish, "The Northern Railroads, April, 1861," *American Historical Review*, 22 (July, 1917), 778-793; Thomas Weber, *The Northern Railroads in the Civil War, 1861-1865* (New York, 1952), pp. 3-14; George Edgar Turner, *Victory Rode the Rails* (Indianapolis, 1953), pp. 23-28, 33-38; William H. Clark, *Railroads and Rivers* (Boston, 1939), p. 128.

and South. However, while private fortunes might vanish, the rails remained to increase the national wealth.

While the greatest railroad building was in the area north of the Ohio, solid progress was also made in the South.[3] The nine states south of the Ohio-Potomac and east of the Mississippi, with Louisiana, built over seven thousand miles of road in the decade, actually building more rapidly than the rest of the nation. The ten southern states increased their mileage in the decade by 340 per cent while the northern states added less than 230 per cent to their lines in the ten years.[4] The southern states had considerably less railroad mileage than the northern states on a basis of area, but in proportion to population the two regions were about equally supplied with railroad mileage. Virginia, the largest and most populous of the southern states, built proportionately more railroad than either Pennsylvania or New York. The percentage increase for both the Carolinas was as great. Georgia, already quite well supplied with railroads in 1850 (and ranking first in the South and fourth in the nation in mileage), more than doubled her trackage in the decade, building more rapidly than any of the New England or Middle Atlantic states except New Jersey and Pennsylvania. Several of the Gulf and interior southern states, i.e., Florida, Mississippi, Tennessee, and Kentucky, increased their mileage nearly as rapidly (on a percentage basis) as the states just north of the Ohio. The story of southern railroad construction in the 1850's can be seen in the following table.

3. The southern states included in the present study are those of the eight Confederate states east of the Mississippi plus Louisiana. Since the railroads of Kentucky (notably the Louisville and Nashville) also served this region, this state has been included, making a total of ten. The railroads of Texas and Arkansas have not been incorporated in the study since the railroad development of those states, coming later and being more western than southern in nature, belongs to the postwar, trans-Mississippi railroad expansion.

4. *Eighth Census, 1860*, "Mortality and Property," pp. 333-334. The southern increase was from 2,080 to 9,167 miles; that for the northern states, 6,509 to 21,432 miles. In 1860 the railroad mileage in states west of the Mississippi was not significant, since the five states (Iowa, Missouri, Arkansas, Texas, and California) with railroads possessed only 6 per cent of the total for the nation.

State	Mileage in 1850	Built 1850-1860	Mileage in 1860	Per Cent Increase
Va.	515	1,256	1,771	244%
N. C.	248	641	889	258%
S. C.	289	698	987	242%
Ga.	643	761	1,404	117%
Fla.	21	380	401	1810%
Ala.	132	611	743	463%
Miss.	75	797	872	1062%
La.	79	255	334	323%
Tenn.	—	1,197	1,197	—
Ky.	78	491	569	630%
Total	2,080	7,087	9,167	340%

Based on *Eighth Census, 1860*, "Mortality and Property," pp. 327-329.

The American railway system as of 1860 could be divided into nearly equal thirds: (1) the Northeast consisting of 10,000 miles in New England and the Middle Atlantic states, (2) the Middle West consisting of 11,000 miles in the upper Mississippi and Ohio Valleys, and (3) the South, of 9,000 miles. The separation between the first two areas was only an artificial one as together they provided the North with a well-integrated transportation network. Nevertheless, historically, physically, and financially, the three areas had fairly distinct characteristics.[5]

The Northeast, with less than a third of the total mileage, had over one-half of the separate railroad companies in the nation. The average line was less than fifty miles in length and less than a tenth of the roads extended over one hundred miles. However, since the major trunk lines (the Erie, the New York Central, the Pennsylvania, and the B. and O.) were located principally in New York, Pennsylvania, and Maryland, the Northeast could claim most of the really long lines (300 to 600 miles). These older lines of the nation, carrying the heaviest traffic in the country, had been expensive to build and maintain, and were valued in 1860 at an average of $48,000 per mile.

5. The following comparisons are based on *Eight Census, 1860*, "Mortality and Property," pp. 325-334.

RAILROADS OF THE SOUTH

With a large third of the nation's mileage and a small quarter of the individual companies, the Middle West naturally possessed railroads whose average length was quite high (102 miles). Over a third of the 110 railroads of the Middle West had routes extending over 100 miles and more than a dozen could count 200 or more mile posts. The Illinois Central, with a route of over 700 miles, had the longest line in America. Since many of the new middle western lines had been lightly built, the average cost of $37,000 per mile was well under that of the roads in the East.

Over one hundred companies shared the southern mileage; the average line was eighty-five miles in length, shorter than those of the Middle West but twice as long as the average road of the Northeast. Slightly over a third of the southern railroads extended over one hundred miles but only one of this number exceeded three hundred miles. In the spring of 1861, just ten days after the start of the Civil War, the 483-mile Mobile and Ohio was completed from the Gulf to Columbus, Kentucky, a river town just a few miles south of the mouth of the Ohio River. As a group, the southern railways were the cheapest to build, averaging $28,000 per mile according to 1860 valuations. Southern railroads cost little more than half as much to build as those of the Middle Atlantic states ($52,000 per mile) for several reasons: cheaper slave labor, lighter and sometimes inferior rails, easier terrain along the coastal plains of the South,[6] and smaller amounts of rolling stock per mile of road. Against these advantages, however, must be set the handicap of often having to build long stretches of track to procure any sizeable traffic. The New Orleans, Jackson and Great Northern had to build over 150 miles to reach any real source of business.[7]

6. U. B. Phillips, *A History of Transportation in the Eastern Cotton Belt to 1860*, (New York, 1913), p. 386 (hereafter cited as *Transportation in the Eastern Cotton Belt*). Cheaper construction costs in the South did not necessarily mean inferior lines. To prove their point, friendly critics pointed to the twelve-year period in Georgia in which no rail passengers lost life or limb.

7. Thomas D. Clark, *A Pioneer Southern Railroad* (Chapel Hill, N. C., 1936), p. 63. For a general account of southern railroads just prior to the Civil War see Robert C. Black III, *The Railroads of the Confederacy* (Chapel Hill, N. C., 1952), pp. 1-48.

The southerners entered into their new railroad projects with typical gusto and enthusiasm.[8] No projected line was too difficult to the lighthearted, long-winded promoters as they sold their wares at the numerous railroad conventions in New Orleans, Memphis, or St. Louis.[9] The romantic dreamers were obsessed with two ideas: first, the building of *any* line would foster southern success in its race with the North; and second, any railroad, of any length or direction, over mountains or lowlands, was destined to become a connecting link in a great new chain of roads handling a vast cross-country traffic.[10] The city and commercial interests were not too hard to convince, but sometimes these high-flown schemes were hard to sell to the back country folk, as James De Bow discovered in Mississippi. Of an 1851 excursion into Mississippi and Tennessee, De Bow wrote:

... the sturdy farmers of the interior, who clustered together to hear us talk about them [the proposed railroads], evinced by their looks the incredulity of the King of Siam, when assured by the missionaries that in their country water would sometimes become hard enough to walk upon. The treated us with respect ... but made merry enough when they got together ... over our 'iron horse' which was to go galloping over their hills and rivers ...[11]

Railroad interest in the southern states of Louisiana, Mississippi, Alabama, and Tennessee early centered around the construction of north-south lines, stretching off into the interior from such ports as Mobile and New Orleans. Moved by a serious decline in trade, Mobile in 1847 projected a line north to the Ohio River. In the spring of 1850, the venerable William R. King, senator from Alabama, joined with his colleague, Stephen A. Douglas of Illinois, to usher through Congress a Federal land grant intended to aid both the recently chartered Mobile and Ohio and the Illinois Central.[12] Since most of the southern road

---

8. Black, *op. cit.*, pp. 16-17.
9. Robert S. Riegel, "Trans Mississippi Railroads During the Fifties," *Mississippi Valley Historical Review*, 10 (Sept., 1923), 155.
10. Phillips, *op. cit.*, pp. 386-387.
11. *De Bow's Review*, December, 1866, p. 635.
12. The Mobile and Ohio estimated that it received, after expenses and taxes, nearly $2,000,000 from the sale of the land grants. *Mobile and Ohio Valuation Docket no. 149*, Accounting Report, I, 13, Record Group 134, National Archives.

ran through Mississippi and Tennessee, the state of Mississippi lent the new company over $200,000, and Tennessee helped by issuing bonds to the extent of $1,296,000.[13] While President Sidney Smith was in Europe trying to sell the road's bonds, the construction crews started work north of Mobile.[14] The line was finished in time to be used by both armies during the Civil War.

Until the early 1850's New Orleans was content with her river traffic. The New Orleans railroad conventions of 1851 and 1852, however, made it clear that Baltimore, Philadelphia, and New York, through their expanding railroad arms, were becoming real rivals for the traditional New Orleans trade with the upper South.[15] The New Orleans, Jackson and Great Northern was chartered in 1852 by Louisiana and Mississippi. Using iron and credit from England, locomotives from Philadelphia, and coaches built in Madison, Indiana, the new road soon began to build northward into Mississippi. Under the leadership of James Robb, Judah P. Benjamin, and John Slidell, who represented the company abroad, the railroad made steady progress and completed the 206 miles to Canton, Mississippi, before the end of 1860.[16] In conjunction with the Mississippi Central, running north of Canton, the new line served as a second through route from the Gulf to the Ohio.

The merchants of Louisville conceived and projected a third major line with a different purpose in view. The Louisville and Nashville, chartered in 1850 with the express purpose of diverting trade to the North through the river town of Louisville, was rather slow in getting under way.[17] It remained for one of Louisville's first citizens, the lame, uncouth, but highly regarded James Guthrie, to push the project with new vigor upon his return from Pierce's cabinet in 1857. Aided by the customary Tennessee assistance of $10,000 per mile, and by large private and

13. *Ibid.*, p. 7.
14. Robert S. Cotterill, "Southern Railroads, 1850-1860," *Mississippi Valley Historical Review*, 10 (March, 1924), 396-405.
15. *Ibid.*
16. Henry M. Flint, *Railroads of the United States, Their History and Statistics* (Philadelphia, 1868), pp. 348-351. Hereafter cited as *Railroads of the United States.*
17. Cotterill, "Southern Railroads, 1850-1860," *loc. cit.*, pp. 402-405.

public subscriptions in Louisville, Guthrie constructed the road to Nashville, reaching the Tennessee capital in November, 1859. The first through traffic was the shipping of supplies to the drought-ridden South. A branch line in the direction of Memphis gave the road a total line of 253 miles by 1860. The pre-Civil War Louisville and Nashville was one of the few railroads to be built for a sum approximating the original promotional estimates.[18]

The other major roads that were built in the 1850's west of the mountains were east-west lines. The Memphis and Charleston began the decade with but forty-five miles of road near Muscle Shoals. Reorganized in 1850, and aided by Tennessee, New Orleans, and Charleston, the managers of the road completed their line from Memphis to Chattanooga by the spring of 1857. With the aid of connecting lines through Georgia, Calhoun's dream of twenty-five years before became a reality. Three years earlier, in 1854, the completion of the Nashville and Chattanooga gave the latter city a connection with the capital of the state. A third line running east from Vicksburg connected with the New Orleans, Jackson and Great Northern at Jackson, Mississippi, and with the Mobile and Ohio at Meridian.[19]

East of the mountains, Virginia built more railroad in the decade than any other state, even overtaking Georgia, and in 1860 claimed 1,771 miles.[20] She more than trebled her 1850 mileage and increased her total railroad investments sevenfold.[21] Aside from the Baltimore and Ohio, which as a northern corporation was considered by some to be a threat to the commerce of Virginia,[22] most of the new railroads ran parallel to the mountains toward the southwest. The longest of the new lines was the Virginia and Tennessee, built between 1852 and 1857, and running from Lynchburg to Bristol on the Tennessee state line. This route reached Chattanooga via the East Tennessee and Vir-

---

18. The directors estimated the cost in 1851 at $3,000,000. The valuation of the line in 1861 was set at $3,580,826. *Ibid.*, p. 405; Thomas D. Clark, *The Beginning of the L. and N.* (Louisville, 1933), pp. 29-30.
19. Cotterill, "Southern Railroads, 1850-1860," *loc. cit.*, pp. 401-402.
20. *Eighth Census, 1860,* "Mortality and Property," pp. 333-334.
21. Flint, *Railroads of the United States,* pp. 345-346.
22. Charles W. Turner, "Virginia Railroad Development, 1845-1860," *The Historian* (Autumn, 1947), p. 47.

ginia, and the East Tennessee and Georgia, and was the only southern road actually to cross the mountains. Almost as important to Virginia was a parallel line to the east, the Richmond and Danville. The road's able president, W. P. Tunstall, completed the road in the spring of 1856. The line was soon prosperous since it connected two important trade centers.[23] The state subscribed to three-fifths of the stock and the citizens of Richmond also generously supported the project.

Further south, the state of North Carolina subscribed to three-fourths of the capital stock of the North Carolina Railroad.[24] Built between 1851 and 1856, the line curved 223 miles through the central part of the state from Goldsboro via Raleigh and Greensboro to Charlotte. Georgia, unlike her sister states, was opposed to a general system of aid to internal improvements,[25] and thus most of her railroad construction in the 1850's was financed through city and private subscriptions. Savannah capital was very important in building the Southwestern Railroad of Georgia which branched out from Macon into the southern part of the state and toward Alabama with some two hundred miles of track.[26] The line, though economically built ($18,000 a mile), was a first-class road and earned good dividends before and during the war.[27] Most of the railroads in the state were already paying a certain tribute to the growing rail center of Atlanta, especially after Georgia in 1850 opened the strategically located and state-owned Western and Atlantic from Atlanta to Chattanooga. Other southern cities were quick to note, and envy, Atlanta's rapid and flourishing growth.[28] Even before the war, a growing portion

23. *Ibid.*, pp. 50-52; Henry V. Poor, *Manual of the Railroads of the United States for 1877-1878* (New York, 1877), p. 354.
24. Cecil Kenneth Brown, *A State Movement in Railroad Development: The Story of North Carolina's First Effort to Establish an East and West Trunk Line Railroad* (Chapel Hill, N. C., 1928), pp. 72-80.
25. Frederick A. Cleveland and Fred Wilbur Powell, *Railroad Promotion and Capitalization in the United States* (New York, 1909), p. 214.
26. Phillips, *Transportation in the Eastern Cotton Belt*, p. 279.
27. *Merchant's Magazine and Commercial Reveiw*, 56 (January, 1867), pp. 25-27.
28. Phillips, *op. cit.*, pp. 390-393. From a hundred or so shanties in 1848 Atlanta had grown by 1860 to a prosperous city with "thousands of fine substantial, and costly houses."

of Atlanta's energetic population were northern men who had come south to develop the money-making possibilities.

The principal lines in the ten southern states offered by 1861 five major through or "trunk" routes: (1) Charleston to Memphis, via Augusta, Atlanta, and Chattanooga, 755 miles, opened in 1857; (2) Alexandria to Mobile, via Charlottesville, Lynchburg, Bristol, Knoxville, Atlanta, and Montgomery, 1,215 miles, opened by 1861; (3) Louisville to Charleston, via Nashville, Chattanooga, Atlanta, and Augusta, 782 miles, opened in 1859; (4) the Gulf to Columbus, Kentucky, via Jackson, Tennessee, from either New Orleans or Mobile, 472 miles, opened in 1859; and (5) an indirect seaboard route from the Potomac to the Gulf at Cedar Keys, Florida, via Richmond, Weldon, Wilmington, Florence, Charleston, Savannah, Waycross, and Jacksonville, 978 miles, complete with but a few gaps by the time of the war.[29] While these routes gave the South a fairly integrated system, the entire network had not a single connection with railroads to the North.[30] The long bridge at Washington was not strong enough to bear trains, and the Cairo-Columbus connection consisted of a two-hour steamboat trip. Louisville had a railroad connection with the North only with the completion of her bridge over the Ohio in February, 1870.[31]

Aside from increased mileage and the creation of through routes, the decade of the 1850's was also a period of experimentation and solid achievement, for both the North and the South, in matters of railroad construction, equipment, and general service. In the construction of the roadbed and track real advances were made. While eleven different gauges still existed in the North (from 4 feet, 4½ inches to 6 feet), by 1860 the general

---

29. Fairfax Harrison, *A History of the Legal Development of the Railroad System of the Southern Railway Co.* (Washington, 1901), pp. 15-18. These five routes accounted for nearly half of the total southern mileage. Three of the five routes passed through Atlanta.

30. Robert Selph Henry, *The Story of Reconstruction* (Indianapolis, 1938), pp. 423-424. Including the Kentucky Blue Grass region with the North, and ignoring the lack of a bridge at Louisville, some people claimed Bowling Green as a railroad connection between the two sections.

31. *De Bow's Review*, March, 1870, p. 316. The bridge had been originally planned forty years earlier, but insufficient finances had delayed construction. Chief Engineer Albert Fink of the L. & N. was the builder.

RAILROADS OF THE SOUTH

favorite was the present standard, 4 feet, 8½ inches. In the South the five-foot gauge was by far the most common.[32] All over the country iron T-rails were in general use by 1860, although on a few southern roads iron-capped wooden rails were still found.[33] The roads universally used the oak or hard pine crosstie or sleeper and some lines were already experimenting with creosote to lengthen the life of the tie.

Railroad superintendents and engineers in the decade were ordering more and more of the new American-type (four drivers with four-wheeled bogie truck in front) locomotives with balloon stack, large headlight, and functional cowcatcher.[34] Especially in the North the first-class passenger train by 1860 included a smoking car and might also include one of the new "sleepers." The new cars, definitely pre-Pullman, were ordinary coaches with the seats replaced by long shelves, three decks high, divided by partitions into bunks.[35] Night travel had become the accepted thing but Sunday trains were matters of dispute, especially in the South, until well after the Civil War.[36] The best chair cars now came equipped with water tank, corner toilet, and newsboy. No restaurant or dining cars were yet available and travelers bought hurried snacks at railroad eating houses during scheduled fifteen-to-twenty-minute stops. By 1859 a passenger could buy a through coupon ticket from New Orleans to Bangor, Maine, and check his baggage the entire distance. Railroad guides and time tables

---

32. Fish, "The Northern Railroads, April, 1861," *loc. cit.*, p. 785. Eight changes of cars, due to gauge, were still necessary for a Philadelphia to Charleston trip. One result of the gauge variation and lack of transfer facilities was that nearly every car belonged to the road on which it was running.

33. *Ibid.*, p. 786. Steel rails came in only after the war.

34. The typical American-type locomotive in 1860 had a name rather than a number, cost $8,000 to $10,000 new, used wood for fuel, cost less than $1.00 a mile to operate, and was the pride and joy of the engineer assigned to it.

35. Fish, "The Northern Railroads, April, 1861," *loc. cit.*, pp. 787-788; Clark, *Railroads and Rivers*, p. 136. The passengers were required to remove their boots before going to bed, but they probably removed little else as the berths were not equipped with curtains. In the South, the "sleepers" were rarely seen. Black, *The Railroads of the Confederacy*, pp. 19-20.

36. *Railroad Gazette*, October 8, 1870, p. 37; *Commercial and Financial Chronicle*, December 26, 1868, p. 833. The Postmaster General in 1868 reported that 124 railroads less than half ran Sunday trains, and half of the railroads offering such service thought it unprofitable. As late as 1870 the upper house in Georgia passed an act prohibiting Sunday trains during daylight hours.

were also in general circulation before the war.[37] Most companies increased the speed of their passenger trains during the 1850's and by 1861 one could travel from Boston to St. Louis in forty-eight hours, from New York to Chicago in forty hours, from New York to Charleston in sixty-two hours, or from Charleston to Memphis in forty-two hours. These schedules were above the average, however, as revealed by the then current habit of smoking on the open car platforms. In the South main-line fast trains seldom exceeded twenty-five miles per hour, excluding stops.[38] In the South the speed, quality, and comfort of the passenger service was of real concern before the war, since passenger revenue in the 1840's and 1850's often exceeded the freight business. By 1860 this was no longer true.[39]

While both northern and southern railroad systems advanced in the decade, 1860 found the southern lines lagging behind in several respects. In every respect except actual length of line, the typical southern railroad was a smaller organization than its northern counterpart. The South was behind in the amount of business and traffic available because the railroads served an area of sparse population with few manufacturing centers. Also, many of her planters and merchants still depended on the smooth highway of the Mississippi. With a smaller volume of business, the average southern railroad naturally had a smaller roster of employees. Although nearly a third of the nation's mileage in 1860 was in the South, that section employed only a fifth of the total railway employees. The four major trunk lines of the North together possessed roughly as much rolling stock and motive power as could be found in all the states south of the Ohio. The Memphis and Charleston had no more equipment than the Philadelphia, Wilmington and Baltimore, a line only one-third as long. In general, the southern roads also had inferior equipment. This, plus lighter rail and lower volume of business, meant that southern trains as a rule were slower and offered poorer service than

---

37. Fish, "The Northern Railroads, April, 1861," *loc. cit.*, p. 785.
38. *Ibid.*, pp. 788-789; Phillips, *Transportation in the Eastern Cotton Belt*, pp. 382-383.
39. Howard Douglas Dozier, *The History of the Atlantic Coast Line* (New York, 1920), pp. 86-87.

those of the North.[40] In short, at the conclusion of the decade the southern railroads were not too well prepared to meet the tasks that lay ahead.

40. Fish, "The Northern Railroads, April, 1861," *loc. cit.*, pp. 781-790.

CHAPTER 2

SOUTHERN RAILROADS AT WAR

MOST OF THE southern railroads during the Civil War experienced a sequence of prosperity, inflation, deterioration due to abuse and lack of material, and finally capture or destruction by invading Union forces. Some roads never enjoyed the prosperity, but all of them sooner or later felt the wear and tear of war. When the war ended the railroad owners and managers almost without exception found their buildings and bridges burnt, their rolling stock scattered, and much of their line stripped down to the roadbed.

Prosperity came first. The first revival of business as the war started affected the lines leading toward the Virginia and Tennessee fronts.[1] Especially the carriers of eastern Tennessee found themselves nearly overwhelmed with a flood of excited soldiers and ancient ordnance moving northward. The East Tennessee and Georgia retired some of its bonds and paid a number of dividends, in Confederate money, of course.[2] Up to 1863 the lines leading toward Richmond were especially prosperous. The Petersburg line doubled its gross revenue between 1861 and 1862 and in the latter year had a record-breaking operating ratio of less than 28 per cent.[3]

---

1. C. W. Ramsdell, "The Confederate Government and the Railroads," *American Historical Review*, 22 (July, 1917), 795-796, hereafter cited as "Confederate Railroads." See also Robert C. Black III, *The Railroads of the Confederacy* (Chapel Hill, N. C., 1952), pp. 134-135.
2. Fairfax Harrison, *A History of the Legal Development of the Railway System of the Southern Railway Co.* (Washington, 1901), p. 657.
3. Howard Douglas Dozier, *The History of the Atlantic Coast Line* (New York, 1920), pp. 106-108. During the same period, 1861-1863, the Georgia Railroad reduced its operating ratio from 57 per cent to 42 per cent. These

The Wilmington and Weldon had a large enough income in the first two war years to pay a 31 per cent dividend in 1863.[4] As the war came to the no man's land of Kentucky in 1861, the L. and N. experienced a different sort of prosperity. The road valiantly strove to cope with the huge traffic moving south as the Confederacy bought more and more goods in the North. Finally company officials imposed a ten-day embargo late in April to permit the road to clear its lines.[5]

Much of the prosperity was unreal and false. As the rates increased and the paper profits rose, in terms of Confederate currency,[6] so too did the expenses and costs of railway operation rapidly mount. Between 1861 and 1864, nails rose from 4 cents to $4.00 a pound, lubricating oil from $1.00 to $50.00 a gallon, mechanic's wages from $2.50 to $20.00 a day, car wheels from $15.00 to $500.00 each, coal from 12 cents to $2.00 a bushel, and shovels from $10.50 to $300.00 per dozen.[7] While wages went up more slowly than material costs, the roads soon found it difficult to raise rates rapidly enough to meet their mounting costs. In 1864 the old senator, John P. King, president of the Georgia Railroad, complained that his road had been running at a loss for two years, due to inflation. King wrote of his road: "The more business it does, the more money it loses, and the greatest favor that could be conferred upon it—if public wants permitted—would

---

marked reductions were, of course, as much due to inability to maintain the road properly as to higher revenues.

4. *Ibid.*, p. 113.

5. George R. Leighton, *Five Cities, the Story of Their Youth and Old Age* (New York, 1939), pp. 62-65. James Guthrie played a cagey game during the summer of 1861, striving to serve two masters at once. Finally, in September, he broke with the South, refusing further cooperation. Part of his line was in Confederate hands, but on the northern portion of the line he received special treatment from the Union, obtaining higher than usual rates for his Federal business.

6. Ramsdell, "Confederate Railroads," *loc. cit.*, pp. 795-796. Special railroad rates for Confederate business were first fixed at Montgomery and Chattanooga railroad rate conventions early in the war in 1861. For a complaint by the public concerning the large profits made by the Confederate railroads see George Campbell, *White and Black, the Outcome of a Visit to the United States* (New York, 1879), pp. 366-367.

7. Dozier, *op. cit.*, p. 114; Charles W. Turner, "The Virginia Central Railroad at War," *The Journal of Southern History*, 12 (November, 1946), 520; Black, *op. cit.*, pp. 127-128.

be the privilege of quitting business until the end of the war!"⁸

As the war started, it was evident to any Confederate strategist that the Confederate railroad map showed several glaring gaps, the filling of which would greatly strengthen the entire system. Jefferson Davis, one of the chief patrons of the Pacific railroad, early recommended the completion of the missing links in the railway system.⁹ The Confederate Congress early in 1862 appropriated $1,000,000 to build the forty-mile gap from Danville, Virginia, to Greensboro, North Carolina, but the line was not completed until in 1864. Though flimsy in construction, the new line gave Richmond three major lines to the south and was a big help in Lee's supply problem. The other major project was to complete the one-hundred-mile line from Meridian, Mississippi, to Selma, Alabama. When the Confederacy finished this road late in 1862, it provided an all rail route (with the exception of a steamboat connection on the Alabama River between Montgomery and Selma and a ferry crossing of the Tombigbee River) from Vicksburg to Richmond, entirely south and east of the mountains.¹⁰

Even with these gaps filled, there still remained the problem of transfer points. City governments, at such points as Chattanooga, Knoxville, Bristol, Lynchburg, Savannah, and Augusta, had been slow to permit the building of terminal facilities because of the opposition of the local hotel and transfer interests. Even where the tracks of two railroads made physical connection, few railroad managements would willingly permit their cars to get out of sight.¹¹ The total result was frequent delays of days or weeks in the shipment of men and supplies.

Even more damaging to the Confederacy than gaps in the rail network or inadequate transfer points were the twin problems of shortage of equipment and difficulty of track maintenance. For several southern roads there can be no doubt but that excessive

8. *Reports of the Directors of the Georgia Railroad and Banking Company* (Augusta, Georgia, 1864), p. 5.
9. Carl Russell Fish, "The Northern Railroads, April, 1861," *American Historical Review*, 22 (July, 1917), 780.
10. E. Merton Coulter, *The Confederate States of America, 1861-1865* (Baton Rouge, 1950), pp. 270-271.
11. Ramsdell, "Confederate Railroads," *loc. cit.*, pp. 796-798.

loading of cars, constant use, lack of time, material, and labor for repair work, and the abuse of rolling stock by Confederate troops was far more responsible for their undoing than the destruction created by Union forces.[12]

The problem of equipment and rolling stock appeared first. Originally lightly equipped with cars and locomotives, most of the newly built southern lines found it impossible to cope with the volume of business offered. As early as the spring of 1862, southern railroad men were predicting the complete breakdown of their service due to rolling stock shortages. Southern railway officials were unable to augment their worn-out equipment because they had always purchased their cars and locomotives from the North. The states north of the Potomac had a dozen locomotive plants for every one in the South. While Tennessee, Virginia, and South Carolina produced a fair number of railroad cars, the state of Pennsylvania could make twice as many annually as the entire South. Some of the company shops, such as those of the Central of Georgia, claimed the ability to make both cars and engines, but the government pressed many of these establishments into ordnance production. Railroad managers, and sometimes state governors, always resisted the efforts of the Confederacy to equalize the supply of available equipment by borrowing from one line to supply another, but as times grew more desperate, the rolling stock of individual companies became widely scattered throughout the southern states.[13]

The maintenance of the track likewise soon became a pressing problem. Most of the iron on southern roadbeds had come from England. Heavy English investments in southern railroad bonds accounted for part of this, but many railroad managements pre-

12. Dozier, *op. cit.*, pp. 106-108.
13. Coulter, *op. cit.*, pp. 274-277; Fish, "The Northern Railroads, April, 1861," *loc. cit.*, pp. 789-790; Ramsdell, "Confederate Railroads," *loc. cit.*, pp. 798-799; Robert S. Cotterill, "Southern Railroads, 1850-1860," *Mississippi Valley Historical Review*, 10 (March, 1924), 404; Robert C. Black III, "The Railroads of Georgia in the Confederate War Effort," *The Journal of Southern History*, 13 (November, 1947), 516-517. The southerners' traditional dislike for mechanical pursuits left much of the actual railroad operation in the hands of northern train men in 1861. Some of these returned home with the outbreak of war. Those that remained on the job were often viewed with suspicion, and sometimes rightly so.

ferred English rails, claiming them to be both superior to, and cheaper (even with the tariff) than, the northern product.[14] The South could, and did, produce some of its own rails, but its 1860 production of 26,000 tons was only a ninth of that of the North. With both sources of supply cut in 1861, railroad presidents at once began to hoard iron and buy everything in sight. Late in 1861 the Georgia-owned Western and Atlantic stumbled upon 1,100 tons of new rail, which it quickly bought up for $50 per ton.[15] After all such sources were exhausted the railroads started to strip the rail from branch lines to maintain their main stems. The Confederate government was soon doing the same thing with whole railroads, seizing lines in Georgia, Florida, and Texas.[16] Such solutions brought new problems, for as branch roads or lines were dismantled the available sources of provisions and supplies for the Confederate armies correspondingly declined. Had the Confederate government early faced up to the problem of its rail transport and instituted a vigorous policy of control and management, as it did in the field of ordnance, the southern railroads might have furnished a more adequate support for the military effort.

Obviously, worn-out equipment and a disintegrating roadbed early created an indifferent railroad service. James De Bow, travelling in the service of the Treasury Department and the Produce Loan Office, had excellent opportunities to note the deterioration in service. He felt that up to mid-1862 the railroads were still in pretty good shape, but even then passenger travel was so plagued by crowds of women and children, wounded and furloughed soldiers, and speculators that seats were never available.[17] A stockholder of the South Carolina Railroad, riding on his road from Charleston to Columbia in July, 1862, complained of the long, slow journey caused by the constant lack of wood and water along the route.[18] The army use of passenger coaches was

14. Cotterill, "Southern Railroads, 1850-1860," *loc. cit.*, p. 404.
15. Black, "The Railroads of Georgia," *loc. cit.*, p. 519.
16. Black, *The Railroads of the Confederacy*, pp 200-214; George Edgar Turner, *Victory Rode the Rails* (Indianapolis, 1953), pp. 314-315.
17. *De Bow's Review*, August, 1866, p. 199; Black, *The Railroads of the Confederacy*, p. 136.
18. Samuel M. Derrick, *Centennial History of the South Carolina Railroad*

often claimed to be responsible for the broken or missing seats, windows, lamps, stoves, and water coolers when the equipment was finally returned.[19] By the end of 1863, there was no room, except at intervals, for other than government goods or troops on the main lines. By the next year, only two or three trains a day were moving from Georgia to Richmond, and, in spite of a speed of no more than one hundred miles per day, frequent wrecks delayed even these. After stripping Virginia and North Carolina of provisions, General Lee was forced to cut his army at Richmond to shorter and shorter rations because of the poor transport from the South. When Sherman reached Georgia and South Carolina, the supply problem was impossible.

As the Union forces carried the war into the South, and especially as the campaigns reached a climax in Georgia and South Carolina in 1864 and 1865, more and more southern railroads suffered destruction at the hands of one military force or the other. The East Tennessee "Bridge Burners" in early November, 1861, caused some of the earliest railroad destruction when they destroyed five railroad bridges around Chattanooga and Knoxville.[20] A month later, the Confederacy had its turn at railroad pillage when Stonewall Jackson removed most of the double track on the B. and O. between Harpers Ferry and Martinsburg. Jackson kept the rail straight as he was saving it for the South. Earlier he had purloined over a dozen locomotives from the same road and managed to drag several of them by horse and man power to Confederate railheads further south.[21] Further west, in the first year of the war, Colonel Morgan's raiders captured trains on

---

(Columbia, S. C., 1930), pp. 224-225. During the war, keeping wood lots filled with cord wood was a constant worry, because of the large amount of manual labor involved.

19. Dozier, *op. cit.*, pp. 108-109.

20. E. Merton Coulter, *William G. Brownlow* (Chapel Hill, N. C., 1937), p. 170.

21. Festus P. Summers, *The Baltimore and Ohio in the Civil War* (New York, 1939), pp. 99-119; Edward Hungerford, *The Story of the Baltimore and Ohio Railroad* (New York, 1928), II, 7-14. While several of the locomotives never reached southern roads, but rusted to scrap in Winchester, one of the finest was reconditioned for passenger service and named the "Lady Davis." In a later raid on the B. and O. in October, 1862, Confederate troops didn't try to salvage the rails but used a tree encircling technique much like the Sherman method of 1864-1865.

AT WAR

the southern lines of the Louisville and Nashville and often sent driverless locomotives northward, hoping to create further havoc.[22]

But Union forces inflicted most of the damage as they invaded the South. The Confederates always tried to destroy their railroads as they retreated, and succeeded fairly well in destroying much of the mileage coming under the jurisdiction of the Union Military Railway Department in 1862 and thereafter. Most of the 2,600 miles (embracing 45 railroad lines) administered by this Department during the war were ex-Confederate lines. Since the fighting frequently shifted back and forth some of these lines were destroyed and then rebuilt several times.[23] Until Sherman was well stocked with supplies in the fall of 1864, his soldiers generally repaired captured Confederate railroads as soon as possible.[24] However, after Sherman cut himself loose from his northern supply lines in November, 1864, the emphasis in the states from Georgia northward was pure destruction.

Sherman's handiwork in Georgia and South Carolina was complete. He destroyed hundreds of miles of track in his march toward Savannah.[25] Marching into the Carolinas, and following Grant's orders,[26] he was just as thorough. After three destructive months in the two states he left his troops to report in person to Lincoln and Grant in a conference at City Point, March 27, 1865. He satisfied both Lincoln and Grant that the railroads of

---

22. John H. Kennaway, *On Sherman's Track, or the South After the War* (London, 1867), p. 28.

23. Robert S. Riegel, "Federal Operation of Southern Railroads," *The Mississippi Valley Historical Review*, 9 (September, 1922), 127-136.

24. *Memoirs of General W. T. Sherman* (New York, 1891), II, 150-152. Sherman tells a story of the Confederate respect for Union railroad reconstruction gangs. One rebel remarked to his fellows: "Well, the Yanks will have to git up and git now, for I heard General Johnston himself say that General Wheeler had blown up *the tunnel* near Dalton, and that the Yanks would have to retreat, because they could get no more rations." "Oh, hell!" said a listener, "Don't you know that old Sherman carries a *duplicate* tunnel along?"

25. *Ibid.*, p. 201, W. T. Sherman to E. M. Stanton, December 13, 1864; p. 228, W. T. Sherman to General H. W. Halleck, December 24, 1864. In passing through Milledgeville Sherman discovered that Gov. Brown had been prudent enough to retain some freight cars for the hurried flight from the capital. Brown stripped the Governor's mansion of carpets, furniture, and vegetables, but left behind muskets, ammunition and the public archives.

26. *Ibid.*, p. 238, U. S. Grant to W. T. Sherman, December 27, 1864.

RAILROADS OF THE SOUTH

the Carolinas could not be used again by the Confederacy.[27] Sherman's work was over. The Confederacy was defeated and soon was to admit as much. The railroads of the South lay in ruins.

27. *Ibid.*, pp. 329-330. In Admiral Porter's account of the conference Grant asked: "What is to prevent their [Johnston's troops] laying the rails again?" "Why," said General Sherman, "my 'bummers' don't do things by halves. Every rail, after having been placed over a hot fire, has been twisted as crooked as a ram's horn, and they can never be used again."

CHAPTER 3

SOUTHERN RAILROAD FINANCE IN 1865

SOUTHERN RAILROADS were wrecks in 1865, but at least the destroyed railroads belonged to the southerners. Southern states, cities, or individuals held practically all of the capital stock of the railroads built before the war.[1] Construction and operation from city to city was the rule in the South. The West had its St. Joseph and Western, Chicago and Northwestern, and Union Pacific. The South was content with its more modest Columbia and Greenville, Charleston and Savannah, or Nashville and Decatur. Serving local interests in general, the original financing of a railroad was normally accomplished by the cities and state served, and by the planters and merchants living along the line of the road. Nothing happened during the war years to change this local control. Other sources supplied a considerable portion of the borrowed money or funded debt, however. The North furnished some, but many of the bonds sold outside of the South were disposed of in England, France, or Germany. Railroad stocks, northern or southern, found little favor in Europe.[2]

1. U. B. Phillips, *A History of Transportation in the Eastern Cotton Belt to 1860* (New York, 1913), pp. 14-15; George R. Leighton, *Five Cities, the Story of Their Youth and Old Age* (New York, 1939), p. 60 (hereafter cited as *Five Cities*); Cecil Kenneth Brown, *A State Movement in Railroad Development: The Story of North Carolina's First Effort to Establish an East and West Trunk Line Railroad* (Chapel Hill, 1928), pp. 72-80 (hereafter cited as *A State Movement in Railroad Development*); John W. Du Bose, *Alabama's Tragic Decade* (Birmingham, 1940), p. 172.

2. A report by the Treasury Department in 1853 revealed that returns from 222 railroad companies (probably the majority of those then in existence) showed $43,000,000 of railroad securities held abroad, of which only $7,000,000 were railroad stocks. Frederick A. Cleveland and Fred W. Powell, *Railroad Promotion and Capitalization in the United States* (New York, 1909), p. 196 (hereafter cited as *Railroad Promotion*). The total American railroad in-

A promoter or promoters usually carried out the original planning of any railroad project. As such, a promoter had of necessity to be an enthusiast. Being himself convinced of the extraordinary profits and advantages to be derived from a new project or venture, it remained for him to convince others. In nineteenth century railroad history generally, the typical promoter and the typical investor were different individuals. The mental attitude that fitted one man for promotional activities often made the same man unfit for certain investment decisions or for the long pull of management. Hannibal I. Kimball, Col. Henry McComb, and John Stanton from Boston (all Yankees who came South after the war to help themselves as they helped the South build railroads) were promoters. But many of the prewar railroad builders, like James Guthrie of the L. and N., were both promoters and investors.

As Guthrie and his contemporaries planned and built the railroads that existed in 1865, they made a variety of appeals for support. The popular canvass for subscription, sometimes house to house, was, of course, a basic approach. The results in the South, as elsewhere, were usually a number of very small subscriptions.[3] These individual appeals were given more weight if the would-be subscriber could read of the project in the local press. Local editors were usually generous with space for editorials, general comment or the reprinting of pertinent material found in other papers. Such a paper as the *American Railroad Journal* for many years was little more than a collective prospectus.[4] Built in an age of pamphleteering, the railroads were also boosted by a countless stream of reprinted addresses, public memorials, and popular petitions and resolutions. Such materials were often first presented at public meetings or at county, state, or sectional con-

---
vestment in 1853 was around $550,000,000, of which perhaps $120,000,000 were invested in southern roads. Well over half of the total was in stocks. *Historical Statistics of the United States* (Washington, D. C., 1949), p. 201.

3. Phillips, *op. cit.*, p. 387; Harry H. Pierce, *Railroads of New York, A Study of Government Aid, 1826-1875* (Cambridge, Mass., 1953), pp. 8-9 (hereafter cited as *Railroads of New York*); Winthrop M. Daniels, *American Railroads, Four Phases of Their History* (Princeton, 1932), pp. 8, 23-24 (hereafter cited as *American Railroads*).

4. Cleveland and Powell, *op. cit.*, pp. 187-196.

ventions.⁵ Actually such conventions seldom resulted in little more than favorable resolutions, the generation of abundant good will, and the fervent hope that other people would step forward with the necessary capital. A succession of such meetings, however, had an inevitable political effect in helping produce financial assistance from city, county, and state governments. Few of the share takings in the South were speculative in nature and stockholder lists changed little from year to year.⁶ In many subscrip-

  5. *Ibid.;* Thomas D. Clark, *A Pioneer Southern Railroad* (Chapel Hill, 1936), pp. 16-17.
  6. Phillips, *op. cit.*, p. 387.

tions even the investment feature was secondary to the motive of providing local transportation facilities or promoting the general prosperity of the region. This impulse, of course, was much stronger in the municipal, county, or state stock subscriptions than for the private individual.

From the earliest railroad construction in the South, the individual stock subscription had been of paramount importance. The citizens of Charleston had chiefly financed, with stock subscriptions, one of the oldest lines in the nation, the Charleston and Hamburg.[7] For the next thirty years, as railroads were built throughout the South, heavy reliance was placed upon the private stockholder. Built just a few years after the Charleston and Hamburg, the Petersburg Railroad sold half of its stock to individuals living near its line.[8] While the state of North Carolina was very liberal with stock subscriptions to both the North Carolina Railroad and the Western North Carolina Railroad, local residents in each instance were also heavy subscribers.[9] Further south the citizens of South Carolina subscribed hundreds of thousands of dollars to three roads, the Louisville, Cincinnati and Charleston, the Charlotte and South Carolina, and the Greenville and Columbia.[10] In the 1830's and 1840's the local residents of cities to be served by the Georgia Railroad and the Central of Georgia were buying hundreds of shares in the new ventures. The trustees of both Mercer University and Emory College had substantial holdings, the latter college having endowed a chair with forty-two shares of stock.[11] Local capital also owned most of the 743 miles of road found in Alabama at the time of the Civil War.[12] In the early 1860's most of the railroad stock originally purchased by the southerners was still in that area. In 1861 less than 3 per cent of the individual stockholders of the Knoxville

---

7. *Ibid.,* pp. 140-147. This road was chartered in 1827 and completed by 1833.

8. The rest was subscribed by Virginia and the city of Petersburg, Howard Douglas Dozier, *The History of the Atlantic Coast Line* (New York, 1920), p. 25.

9. Brown, *A State Movement in Railroad Development*, pp. 72-80, 133.

10. Phillips, *op. cit.,* pp. 168-220, 339-345.

11. *Ibid.,* pp. 227-258.

12. Du Bose, *Alabama's Tragic Decade,* p. 172; James F. Doster, *Alabama's First Railroad Commission* (Tuscaloosa, Alabama, 1949), p. 105.

FINANCE IN 1865

and Kentucky Railroad lived in the North and they held less than 2 per cent of the total outstanding shares.[13] In the same year only nine of the 1,300 Nashville and Chattanooga Railroad stockholders were from the North.[14] Less than 0.5 per cent of the 16,000 shares of the Atlantic and North Carolina were held in the North. In the same year, 1861, at least two-thirds of the shares of the Richmond, Fredericksburg and Potomac were held by southerners. A year later only 12 per cent of the stock of the Florida Railroad was held in the North. Earlier, in 1851, less than 2 per cent of the shareholders of the Southwestern Railroad of Georgia were non-residents of the state.[15]

Even immediately after the war, De Bow seemed to think that the projected 170-mile Tennessee Pacific from Knoxville to Nashville could be financed chiefly with southern money. He also believed the Chesapeake and Ohio might be completed with purely local capital.[16]

Some of the individual railroad holdings paid very well in the prewar years. This was especially true of the lines in Georgia where the Georgia Railroad before the war had more than repaid in dividends its whole capital, the Atlanta and West Point had paid 7 to 8 per cent from the day the line was opened, and the Central of Georgia had paid up to 10 per cent per year.[17] The Georgia Railroad by 1850 had itself subscribed to nearly $1,000,000 of stock of new adjacent lines to the west. The Southwestern Railroad of Georgia had paid good dividends from the beginning, in the early 1850's, down to 1866.[18] It had a very small bonded debt and the bulk of its stock subscriptions had been paid for

---

13. *House Reports of Committees, 2nd Session, 39th Congress*, no. 34 (1866-1867, serial 1306), pp. 560-561.
14. *Ibid.*, pp. 581-602. The nine holdings, however, accounted for 5 per cent of the outstanding shares. The American Bible Society of New York with 4 ¾ shares was the smallest investor of the nine. Several of the other northern investors, however, held from 200 to 1000 shares each.
15. Robert C. Black III, *The Railroads of the Confederacy* (Chapel Hill, N. C., 1952), pp. 40-41.
16. *De Bow's Review*, December, 1866, pp. 628-639; July, 1867, pp. 117-119.
17. Robert Somers, *The Southern States Since the War, 1870-71* (London, 1871), pp. 87-88.
18. *Commercial and Financial Chronicle*, December 29, 1866, p. 817.

RAILROADS OF THE SOUTH

at once with cash.[19] Some other early stock subscribers did not find it so easy to pay for their stock. Farmers in Kentucky who subscribed for early L. and N. stock paid for it by doing the roadbed grading themselves.[20] When the Wilmington and Weldon was organized and built back in the late 1830's the organizers in Wilmington made personal subscriptions that totalled more than the entire taxable property of the town.[21] In some cases private capital held back completely. When the people of Virginia wanted a railroad across the Blue Ridge no private money could be obtained. Most of the work, therefore, was done at state expense. When the war came Virginia possessed a unique railroad, consisting of a series of long high embankments and four tunnels.

Not quite all the southern railroads were locally owned before the war. The exception that proved the rule was the Macon and Western. In 1848, shortly after its completion, capitalists from New York City chiefly owned this one-hundred-mile line from Macon to Atlanta and held half of the ten directorships. By 1859, local interests had managed to capture the board of directors but northern men still held the bulk of the stock. Looking upon their investment as a speculative venture, they insisted in 1859 that an additional 5 per cent be added to the normal 4 per cent dividend. The southern managers resisted but did vote a larger dividend the following year.[22] The Central of Georgia, locally controlled for many years after the war, took over the Macon and Western in 1872.

The individual with a large railroad investment before the war was often discriminated against in matters of control by the original charter of the company. A variety of methods served to safeguard the man with but few shares and to hold in check the large investor. In both the Nashville and Chattanooga and the South Carolina Railroad large holders received only approx-

19. *Merchant's Magazine and Commercial Review*, January, 1867, pp. 25-27.
20. Leighton, *Five Cities*, p. 60.
21. The population of Wilmington was about 3,000, of which a majority were negro slaves. On one occasion the credit of the new railroad was so poor that a stockholder added a hardware branch to his business in order to provide the construction crews with a hundred dozen shovels. Dozier, *op. cit.*, pp. 57-58.
22. Phillips, *Transportation in the Easter Cotton Belt*, pp. 270-271, 296-297.

FINANCE IN 1865

imately one vote for every ten shares, while the small holders had nearly one vote per share.[23] Often a graduated scale was used, as in the case of the Atlantic and North Carolina where the large investment of the state of North Carolina of 12,666 shares was entitled to but 350 votes in stockholder meetings. Large holders sometimes tried to evade the rule by assigning and parcelling out portions of their stock, but in North Carolina court injunctions were used against this device.[24] After the Civil War as northern investors with large holdings grew more interested in the southern lines, they often succeeded in amending the original charters to remove the graduated voting feature.[25]

In the years before the war, state assistance of various sorts was nearly as important in most states as individual stock subscriptions. The typical southern state government was friendly and anxious to facilitate the new railroad projects. It granted charters permitting the railroads to incorporate, subscribed to the stock issues with state funds, lent money, and sometimes even granted special money-making privileges such as banking, as in the case of certain railroads in Georgia.[26] Unlike the Reconstruction years, the state assistance granted prior to the war was normally honestly administered and unaccompanied by any serious charges of fraud or corruption.

Among the southern states, Virginia had the most generous policy in regard to stock subscriptions. Virginia early determined to subscribe to three-fifths of the original stock of any railroad within her borders, when the remainder of the stock had been taken.[27] However, the state was not interested in lending money to railroads and her holdings of railroad bonds as of 1865 were insignificant. In 1851 the state held nearly half of the sixteen million dollars invested in Virginia railroad stock. The state's

---

23. *House Reports of Committees*, 2nd Session, 39th Congress, no. 34 (1866-67, serial 1306), pp. 581-602; Samuel M. Derrick, *Centennial History of the South Carolina Railroad* (Columbia, S. C., 1930), p. 21.
24. Brown, *A State Movement in Railroad Development*, pp. 245-246.
25. Fairfax Harrison, *A History of the Legal Development of the Railroad System of the Southern Railway Co.* (Washington, D. C., 1901), pp. 664-665 (hereafter cited as *Legal Development of the Southern Railway*).
26. Phillips, *op. cit.*, pp. 14-15.
27. Cleveland and Powell, *Railroad Promotion*, pp. 213-214.

share declined to 36 per cent of the nearly thirty millions of railroad stock in existence in 1855.[28] In some railroads the state held even more than three-fifths of the capital stock. She held, after the war, two-thirds of the common and preferred stock of the Virginia and Tennessee Railroad.[29] In the summer of 1865, of the $65,000,000 invested in the 1,771 miles of railroad in Virginia,[30] the state still held railroad stock valued by Governor Pierpont at $22,000,000.[31] Half a dozen years later Virginia's finances were in such condition that the state legislature decided to liquidate the state's holdings. An act approved in March, 1871, provided for the immediate sale of Virginia's railroad stock.[32] While Virginia's railroad investment thus disappeared, the aid of the state to her railroads in the decade before the war had contributed much to her rapid rail expansion.

North Carolina officials were also generous with state aid in building a rail transportation system. Like Virginia, North Carolina was much more interested in stock subscriptions, which gave a modicum of control, than in lending money to railroads. Throughout the ante bellum period, North Carolina had fewer miles and they were more cheaply constructed than in Virginia,[33] and, therefore, never possessed railroad holdings as large as those of the state to the north. In 1836, North Carolina made her first stock subscription when she agreed to take two-fifths of the capital

28. William Couper, *Claudius Crozet, Soldier, Scholar, Educator, Engineer* (Charlottesville, Va., 1936), pp. 133, 146. The state's portion was less than three-fifths of the total because she normally subscribed to only the original stock issue. As successful railroads expanded they often issued additional stock, none of which was taken by the government. For the story of state railroad aid in a northern state in the same decade see Pierce, *Railroads of New York*.
29. Henry V. Poor, *Manual of the Railroads of the United States for 1869-1870* (New York, 1869), p. 89.
30. *Eighth Census of the United States, 1860*, "Mortality and Property" (Washington, 1866), pp. 327-328.
31. Based on a speech made in September, 1865, by Gov. Pierpont and reported in J. T. Trowbridge, *The South: A Tour of its Battlefields and Ruined Cities* (Hartford, 1866), p. 191.
32. *Commercial and Financial Chronicle*, December 16, 1871, p. 806; Harrison, *op. cit.*, p. 475.
33. *Eighth Census of the United States, 1860*, "Mortality and Property," pp. 327-328. In both 1850 and 1860, North Carolina's rail mileage was only half that of Virginia. Also the roads in North Carolina cost little more than half as much per mile to build.

stock of the Wilmington and Raleigh (later the Wilmington and Weldon) when the remainder had been subscribed by cities or individuals.[34] When completed in March, 1840, the new line of 161 miles was reported to be the longest railroad then in operation in the world. The state government was still more generous with a series of roads which she hoped to weld into a route running the entire length of the state from coast to mountains. By 1854 the state had subscribed to three-fourths of the $4,000,000 capital stock of the North Carolina Railroad, serving the middle of the state. In the same year she agreed to take two-thirds of the stock of the eastern link in the system, the Atlantic and North Carolina, running from Morehead City to Goldsboro where it connected with the North Carolina Railroad. The western extension of the system, the Western North Carolina Railroad, also sold in 1858 an equal share of its stock to the state.[35] After the war, the divisions of the state system, one by one, passed out of the hands of the original projectors.[36] Nevertheless, state aid in the prewar years had been of vital importance in giving North Carolina nine hundred miles of line before the war.

South Carolina also aided her railroads, the first assistance being given in 1837 to the Louisville, Cincinnati, and Charleston project, but her aid was much less generous than that of Virginia, and without the over-all planning of that of North Carolina. Most of the prewar railway projects in South Carolina received some stock subscriptions from the state, but the amounts taken were usually small and never were sufficient to give the state any control over the roads. The state's holdings in the stock of a dozen different railroads after the war amounted to only $2,754,660 (par value), or little more than a tenth of the total cost of the

---

34. The state's portion was paid for out of her share of the 1837 surplus from the Federal Treasury. Brown, *A State Movement in Railroad Development*, pp. 36-37.

35. *Ibid.*, pp. 72-80, 117, 133.

36. *Commercial and Financial Chronicle*, September 23, 1871, p. 402; Brown, *op. cit.*, pp. 148, 237-238. The North Carolina was leased in 1871 to the Richmond and Danville and the state's interest in the Western North Carolina was sold in 1880. The Atlantic and North Carolina was retained by the original company until 1904.

RAILROADS OF THE SOUTH

roads and much less than a controlling majority of the stock.[37] The final stock holdings of South Carolina were also lessened by the fact that after 1848 stock subscriptions in new lines were often paid for with railroad stock taken at an earlier time.[38] The state also endorsed the bonds of several railroads before the war, amounting to about $4,000,000, and chiefly aiding the South Carolina Railroad and the Greenville and Columbia.[39]

Further south in the two coastal states of Florida and Georgia there was considerably less state aid. Florida in the years before the war guaranteed the interest on several railroad bond issues and also purchased small amounts of railroad stock.[40] With a modest rail network of not over four hundred miles in 1860, state aid in Florida was small as compared to some of the other southern states. Georgia, before the war, was opposed to any general assistance to railroads, preferring instead to aid specific projects. Her major rail investment was in the 137-mile line from Atlanta to Chattanooga, the Western and Atlantic, which was constructed and owned by the state.[41] When private capital seemed reluctant to build such a road, the state stepped in, investing nearly five million dollars in building the line in the 1840's. Without this connecting rail link to the northwest, the entire railroad development of Georgia would have been slowed and stunted.[42] Georgia also owned seven thousand shares in the Atlantic and Gulf, a line running from Savannah into the southern part of the state.[43]

State aid was no greater in the three Gulf states. The states of Alabama, Mississippi, and Louisiana possessed less than three hundred miles of line in 1850 so of necessity any real aid given came in the decade just before the war.[44] Alabama made a small

---

37. *Commercial and Financial Chronicle*, March 6, 1869, p. 295. The state did hold a majority of the stock of the Blue Ridge Railroad, a mountain project aiming at Knoxville, Tennessee. Edward King, *The Great South* (Hartford, 1875), pp. 448-449.
38. Cleveland and Powell, *Railroad Promotion*, pp. 215-216.
39. *Commercial and Financial Chronicle*, March 6, 1869, p. 295.
40. Black, *The Railroads of the Confederacy*, pp. 42-43.
41. *Commercial and Financial Chronicle*, May 19, 1866, p. 612.
42. Phillips, *Transportation in the Eastern Cotton Belt*, p. 334.
43. *Commercial and Financial Chronicle*, May 19, 1866, p. 612.
44. *Eighth Census of the United States, 1860*, "Mortality and Property," pp. 328-329.

stock subscription to the Alabama and Tennessee River Railroad in 1850 and about the same time lent the Mobile and Ohio $400,000.[45] Alabama became much freer with her aid after the war, endorsing railroad bonds on every hand. Before the war Mississippi also aided the Mobile and Ohio with a $200,000 loan and subscribed $600,000 to the stock of the New Orleans, Jackson and Great Northern.[46] Louisiana in 1853 initiated a system of subscribing to one-fifth of the stock of any railroad projected within the state.[47] Under this act the state subscribed to a total of about $2,000,000 of the stock of the four major lines in the state, the New Orleans, Jackson and Great Northern; the New Orleans, Opelousas, and Great Western; the Vicksburg, Shreveport, and Texas; and the Baton Rouge, Grosse Tete, and Opelousas.[48]

Tennessee, without a mile of railroad in 1850,[49] built nearly 1,200 miles before the Civil War. An ambitious and expanding system of state railroad assistance made this rapid construction possible. Tennessee first aided railroads by purchasing their stock,[50] but soon shifted in 1852 to a plan of lending state bonds directly to railways within the state at the rate of $10,000 of bonds per mile of completed track, the bonds being delivered as each ten-mile section was completed.[51] Practically all of the fourteen lines in Tennessee received this aid in the 1850's and the state railroad debt October 1, 1861, stood at $13,959,000,[52] an amount equal to almost half of the cost of railroad construction up to 1860. This generosity continued after the war, and of the $34,500,000 state debt in 1869, over 90 per cent was due to the railroad as-

45. Robert S. Cotterill, "Southern Railroads, 1850-1860," *The Mississippi Valley Historical Review*, 10 (March 1924), 396.
46. *Ibid.*, pp. 396-397.
47. Cleveland and Powell, *op. cit.*, pp. 214-215.
48. Poor, *Manual of the Railroads of the United States for 1869-1870*, p. 456.
49. *Eighth Census of the United States, 1860*, "Mortality and Property," p. 329.
50. The principal road thus aided was the East Tennessee and Georgia, the state holding $225,000 of stock. Most of this stock found its way into the hands of private holders early in the Reconstruction. Harrison, *Legal Development of the Southern Railway*, pp. 664-665.
51. Cleveland and Powell, *op. cit.*, p. 220. A temporary intermediate plan of state aid was to endorse the bonds of railroad companies.
52. *Commercial and Financial Chronicle*, February 8, 1868, p. 168.

sistance program.⁵³ To the north, the state of Kentucky gave little aid to her railroads, although city and county governments were often generous.⁵⁴ The state debt of Kentucky in 1868 was only one-eighth that of Tennessee—and in the 1850's Kentucky built much less than half the railroad mileage built in Tennessee.

In addition to individual stock subscriptions, and the varied aid furnished by the several state governments, assistance provided by city governments was also important in building ante bellum railroads. City governments and the commercial interests that stood behind them often had the first and generally the keenest interest in seeing some favored railroad project prosper. Norfolk, Wilmington, Charleston, Savannah, Mobile, and Louisville were all interested in one, or several, rail routes to the interior. Often the willingness of a municipality to back a new railroad with cold cash was greatest in those cities whose state governments had modest or stingy internal improvement programs. Charleston, Savannah, Mobile, and Louisville were all in such states. When the Charleston and Savannah Railroad was being financed in the 1850's the city of Charleston took a quarter of the capital stock.⁵⁵ The South Carolina Railroad was also the child of Charleston money. The city of Charleston as of 1861 held 21,500 shares (or a quarter of the total) in the Nashville and Chattanooga Railroad, a road further to the west.⁵⁶ It also had a million dollars invested in the Blue Ridge Railroad.⁵⁷ Further south the Savannah city council was empowered to subscribe to 5,000 shares of Central of Georgia stock when that road was started in the mid-1830's.⁵⁸ A little later, Augusta was a big backer of the Georgia Railroad, and she also had investments further west, having 10,000 shares of the Nashville and Chattanooga.⁵⁹ Mobile aided

53. Poor, *op. cit.*, p. 467.
54. *The Railroad Gazette*, March 18, 1871, p. 583.
55. Phillips, *op. cit.*, p. 363.
56. *House Reports of Committees*, 2nd Session, 39th Congress, no. 34 (1866-67, serial 1306), pp. 581-602.
57. King, *The Great South*, pp. 448-449; James S. Pike, *The Prostrate State, South Carolina Under Negro Government* (New York, 1874), p. 172.
58. Phillips, *op. cit.*, pp. 257-258.
59. *House Reports of Committees*, 2nd Session, 39 Congress, no. 34 (1866-67, serial 1306), pp. 581-602.

her northbound road, the Mobile and Ohio, with a special five-year city real estate tax of 2 per cent. Louisville issued bonds in support of the L. and N. to the extent of $2,000,000.[60] Louisville continued to be liberal with her bounty, until by 1876 she had spent over $8,000,000 in support of tributary railroads.[61]

The average railroad, in the North or South, through the Civil War had a capital structure that consisted of about 60 per cent stock and 40 per cent funded debt.[62] In the South, up to the Reconstruction, individuals, state governments, or cities locally held nearly all the capital stock. Outside capital before the war seemed generally reluctant to invest in southern railroad stock until the roads had clearly proven themselves financially successful.[63] Northern and European investors, however, were willing to risk their money in buying the more secure railroad bonds and especially the state bonds that were being issued to provide money for state railroad assistance programs. English investors held many of the railroad bond issues, but the northerners also held some. Often, however, even for northern railroads, the European was a reluctant investor in the years before the Civil War.[64]

Thus the missions of southern railway agents abroad were frequently unsuccessful. The Natchez and Jackson Railroad in 1839 naturally found European investors unfavorably disposed toward all American railway securities since state credit had been severely damaged in the Panic of 1837. In England the House of Baring in 1839 was especially critical of the securities of southern states.[65] Later in the 1850's it was still sometimes a chore

60. Cotterill, "Southern Railroads, 1850-1860," *loc. cit.*, pp. 402-405.
61. Ellis Merton Coulter, *The Cincinnati Southern Railroad* (Chicago, 1922), p. 10. By the late 1870's the tax payers were trying to call a halt to such largess.
62. *Historical Statistics of the United States, 1789-1945* (Washington, 1949), p. 201. A study of the capital structures of thirty-seven major southern lines (for the years 1866-1868) having nearly two-thirds of the total southern mileage showed a total of $89,000,000 capital stock and $67,000,000 funded debt. Poor, *Manual of the Railroads of the United States for 1869-1870*.
63. Phillips, *op. cit.*, pp. 14-15.
64. Cotterill, "Southern Railroads, 1850-1860," *loc. cit.*, p. 405; Robert Selph Henry, *The Story of the Confederacy* (Indianapolis, 1938) pp. 122-123; Pierce, *Railroads of New York*, pp. 5-10; Daniels, *American Railroads*, pp. 23-24.
65. Ralph W. Hidy, *The House of Baring in American Trade and Finance*

for even well-established northern lines to secure ample foreign credit. John Murray Forbes, able and sober executive of the well-run Michigan Central, frequently complained of the tightness of the foreign money market.[66] In the early 1850's Sidney Smith, president of the Mobile and Ohio, and James Robb, president of the New Orleans, Jackson and Great Northern, both found it difficult to sell their bonds in London. They had better luck once the Crimean War was over.[67] The South Carolina Railroad, the oldest railroad in the South, had not too much trouble borrowing $2,000,000 in "Sterling Bonds" in London.[68] However, Sir Morton Peto, an English M. P. visiting America in the autumn of 1865, was still critical of investments in railroads of the South.[69]

During and just after the Civil War it was very difficult to obtain accurate information on the exact amounts of total foreign investments in American railroads.[70] From 1850 to 1870, however, for all American railroads, never more than a tenth of the total capital stock and no more than a sixth of the total funded debt was held abroad. These estimates are based on the following table.

The southern roads were not heavily represented in the foreign portfolios. In fact, in the *Commercial and Financial Chronicle's* estimate in 1868 only two of the nineteen roads listed as having large amounts of bonds held abroad were southern lines.

(Cambridge, 1949), pp. 263, 430. This English banking house was still cautious in its American railroad investments in the 1850's, generally preferring northern or Atlantic Coast railroads to those of the South.

66. Henry Greenleaf Pearson, *An American Railroad Builder, John Murray Forbes* (New York, 1911), p. 45. In May, 1852, Forbes wrote to a Hamburg merchant who three years earlier had turned him down: "As money seems to be a drug on your side, while we have still use for it here at a fair price, I cannot help repeating the suggestion which I then made for your consideration. When I see quotations on your side and on ours for money, I feel just as you would if old *Java Coffee* were selling here at 4c, and a drug at that, while 15 days distant it was worth 8c in your market." During the same decade the Pennsylvania Railroad found a fairly good market for its bonds in Europe until the crisis brought on by the Crimean War. George H. Burgess and Miles Kennedy, *Centennial History of the Pennsylvania Railroad* (Philadelphia, 1949), pp. 61-74.

67. Cotterill, "Southern Railroads, 1850-1860," *loc. cit.*, pp. 396-397.
68. *Commercial and Financial Chronicle*, April 18, 1868, p. 488.
69. *Ibid.*, August 11, 1866, pp. 165-166.
70. *Ibid.*, September 12, 1868, p. 326.

FINANCE IN 1865

TOTAL RAILROAD INVESTMENT AND PORTION HELD ABROAD
(In millions of dollars)

Year	Total[a] Investment	Capital Stock	Bonded Debt	Stock Held Abroad	Bonds Held Abroad
1872	3159	1647	1511		
1871	2664	1481			
1870	2476				
1869	2041	(1200)	(841)	113[b]	130
1868	1869	(1100)	(769)	56[c]	74
1867	1172	756	416		
1866	(1160)	(750)	(410)	48	50
1860	1149				
1855	763	424	299		
1853	(550)	(330)	(220)	7[d]	36
1850	318				

a. Total Investment, Capital Stock, and Bonded Debt figures are from *Historical Statistics of the United States, 1789-1945* (Washington, 1949), p. 201. The figures in parentheses are arbitrary estimates of the author.

b. The foreign holdings in 1869 are from an estimate of Jay Cooke and Company, Cleveland and Powell, *Railroad Promotion*, p. 196.

c. The foreign holdings in 1866 and 1868 are from an estimate made in the *Commercial and Financial Chronicle*, September 12, 1868, p. 326.

d. The estimates for 1853 are from a special Treasury Department report, Cleveland and Powell, *Railroad Promotion*, p. 196.

The South Carolina Railroad was listed at $2,275,000 and the Mobile and Ohio at $4,593,000.[71] While the *Chronicle* probably lacked complete information on the finances of the southern railroads, there is no evidence to indicate that southern lines were appreciably more in debt to Europe than were the railroads of the North.[72]

The actual control of railroads, in 1865 and today, rests basically with the current stockholders and not with those investors who have lent the railroads money or bought their bonds. The stockholders in southern railroads in 1865 were, with but few exceptions, southerners. In the lists of directors of southern lines

71. *Commercial and Financial Chronicle*, September 12, 1868, p. 326.
72. For foreign holdings of New York railroad securities in the 1850's see Pierce, *Railroads of New York*, pp. 3-25. Foreign holdings of rail securities in this northern state in the prewar years are generally in line with the national estimates given in the above table.

RAILROADS OF THE SOUTH

in early postwar years, few northerners are found. Of 280 directors of 25 major southern lines in 1867-1868, only 11, or less than 4 per cent, were from the North.[73] Less than 10 per cent of the major southern roads listed fiscal or financial agents with offices in the North.[74] Crippled and disabled as the southern railroads were in the early Reconstruction, they were still locally owned and operated.

73. Poor, *Manual of the Railroads of the United States for 1869-1870*. Ten were from New York City and one from Philadelphia.
74. *Ibid*. Three out of thirty-seven companies had such agents, all of them in New York.

CHAPTER 4

DESTRUCTION AND REHABILITATION

IN THE LATE spring of 1865 Confederate railroads were in as crippled and defeated a condition as the armies they had vainly sought to support during the war years. Originally ill-prepared for their vital part in the conflict, by 1865 most southern railroads faced an uncertain future with no resources other than a war-scarred right of way and broken down rolling stock scattered from Virginia to Louisiana. The war had completely destroyed or crippled well over a half of the South's railroads. Twisted rails, burnt ties, disintegrating right of way, destroyed bridges, and dilapidated or lost rolling stock was the normal heritage of the war for the typical southern line. Depots, shops, and other buildings were likewise casualties of the war. Some lines appeared to have vanished completely. As a travelling acquaintance told Sidney Andrews of the railroads of South Carolina, one week they had passably good railroads, the next they were "just gone."[1] Some of the lines were gone for a long time. The 104-mile rail link between Savannah and Charleston was out of operation for five years, until March 2, 1870.[2] In 1867 conservative estimates of only a portion of the damage inflicted upon southern roads by the ravages of war ran as high as $28,000,000.[3]

---

1. Sidney Andrews, *The South Since the War* (Boston, 1866), p. 31. Andrews spent fourteen weeks travelling through the Carolinas and Georgia during the late summer and fall of 1865. He was a correspondent for the Boston *Advertiser* and the Chicago *Tribune*.
2. Henry V. Poor, *Manual of the Railroads of the United States for 1877-1878* (New York, 1877), p. 626.
3. Carl Russell Fish, *The Restoration of the Southern Railroads* (University of Wisconsin Studies in the Social Sciences and History, Number 2, Madison, 1919), p. 7.

RAILROADS OF THE SOUTH

While there was much railroad damage (in other states and at other times) that could not be blamed on Sherman's troops, the climax of destruction clearly came with the five-month scourge through Georgia and the Carolinas. Sherman attached extreme importance to railroad destruction, issued frequent orders on the subject, and often gave the execution of such orders his personal attention.[4] While the "bummers" worked with enthusiastic imagination, they had specific orders from their commanding general to burn and destroy bridges, water tanks, trestles, and depots, to break switches, and utterly to destroy all railway property.[5] In marching through Georgia, Sherman invariably chose to move with the column of his troops actively engaged in rail destruction.[6] Sherman's Chief Engineer, Colonel Orlando M. Poe, had designed and provided special tools for ripping up and later twisting the hot rails. Bonfires of ties and fence rails heated the rails until they bent of their own weight. The troops then twisted the hot rails or curled them around telegraph poles or nearby trees in every imaginable shape, though "hairpins" predominated. Travellers after the war noted a great variety of twisted rail shapes, frequently remarked on the positive destructive genius of the troops, and often noted the differently styled handiwork of several destroying parties.[7] Sherman's troops also sometimes filled in deep railroad cuts with mixtures of trees, brush, earth and loaded shells, being sure that a single explosion would demoralize any gang of Negroes trying to clear the cut.[8] Sherman relied almost exclusively on infantry for his railroad destruction. Back in Atlanta he had discovered that his cavalry were either unable or unwilling to destroy track effectively.[9] He had no higher

---

4. *Memoirs of General W. T. Sherman* (New York, 1891), II, 180.
5. Orders of Sherman to General Howard, February 16, 1865, *ibid.*, II, 277.
6. W. T. Sherman to General H. W. Halleck, December 24, 1864, *ibid.*, II, 228.
7. Andrews, *op. cit.*, p. 215. John H. Kennaway, *On Sherman's Track; or the South After the War* (London, 1867), p. 86 (hereafter cited as *On Sherman's Track*). An Englishman, Kennaway made an extensive tour through the South in the fall of 1865. J. T. Trowbridge, *The South: A Tour of Its Battlefields and Ruined Cities* (Hartford, 1866), pp. 501-502 (hereafter cited as *The South*). Trowbridge made two trips into eight southern states in the fall and winter of 1865-1866.
8. *Memoirs of Sherman*, II, 105.
9. *Ibid.*, II, 104. On August 22, 1864, Kilpatrick reported to Sherman that

DESTRUCTION AND REHABILITATION

regard for the destructive ability of such Confederate raiders as Forrest.[10] The Confederate forces, generally, both infantry and cavalry, never acquired the destructive skill of the more mechanically minded northern soldiers. An ex-Confederate Captain remarked to Sidney Andrews about rail destruction: "We could do something in that line, we thought, but we were ashamed of ourselves when we saw how your men could do it."[11]

While all the Confederate states suffered damage, the destruction was greatest between Mississippi and Virginia. In Virginia the war wrecked most of the lines, with the exception of those around Lynchburg.[12] In the summer of 1865 the lines of the state were in bad condition both physically and financially, none of the operating lines grossing more than enough to pay bare operating expenses.[13] The Norfolk and Petersburg Railroad had hardly a sleeper or rail remaining on its roadbed in the summer of 1865 when William Mahone came back from the war to become once more the road's president.[14] The connecting line to the west, The South Side, had not been out of operation any appreciable time, but the war had destroyed several of its bridges and ruined its rolling stock.[15] Six times during the last year of the war, raiders had damaged the western line running to Bristol, the Virginia and Tennessee Railroad, and it was in operation only about half the time. Only three bridges and as many depots were left standing at the end of the war.[16] South of Richmond both the Richmond and Petersburg, and the Petersburg had suffered considerable damage. Company officials estimated the damage suffered by the short, twenty-three-mile line from the state

---

in a complete circuit of Atlanta his cavalry had so badly wrecked three miles of track near Jonesboro that it would take ten days to repair. On August 23, however, the Confederates were running trains over the line.

10. *Ibid.*, II, 152-153. Forrest's cavalry, however, had earlier (December, 1862) destroyed enough track and bridges on the road north of Jackson, Tennessee, to disrupt Grant's supply lines. Robert Selph Henry, *The Story of the Confederacy* (New York, 1936), pp. 218-219.
11. Andrews, *op. cit.*, p. 32.
12. Fish, *op. cit.*, p. 6.
13. Trowbridge, *op. cit.*, pp. 234-235.
14. *Ibid.*, p. 212; Nelson M. Blake, *William Mahone of Virginia, Soldier and Political Insurgent* (Richmond, 1935), p. 73.
15. Blake, *op. cit.*, pp. 74-75.
16. *Merchants Magazine and Commercial Review*, November, 1865, p. 398.

capital to Petersburg (much of the damage being due to the fire in Richmond set by the Confederates on April 2, 1865) at $254,-000, a sum considerably larger than the company's gross revenue in any prewar or postwar year down to 1868.[17]

In North Carolina, except in the eastern part of the state, the dilapidation of the railroads in 1865 was more the result of wear and tear than of any systematic destruction. In November, 1865, John Kennaway, traveling at night on the Wilmington and Weldon towards Petersburg, found the rails so worn and the track so shaky that he was awakened time and again, thinking that the train was on the ground.[18] Further west, Sidney Andrews, in September, 1865, found the rolling stock on the North Carolina Railroad repaired and repainted, with the track badly worn but better than average for the South.[19]

By 1864 the railroads of South Carolina were nearly worn out. All sorts of old iron had been used to keep the track in repair and the old rolling stock was literally ready to fall apart.[20] Then Sherman came. One of the cardinal aims of Sherman in his fifty-day, four-hundred-mile march from Savannah to Goldsboro, North Carolina, was to break up the rail system of South Carolina.[21] Columbia was at the hub of this ruin. Destruction of the four lines serving the capital city to the east, north, and west ranged for distances of from thirty to fifty miles.[22] The General gave special attention to the South Carolina Railroad, 242 miles in length (and constituting a quarter of the state's total mileage).[23] After the war, the auditor of the company estimated the loss in property due to military destruction to be $1,438,142.[24] Federal troops

---

17. Howard Douglas Dozier, *The History of the Atlantic Coast Line* (New York, 1920), pp. 103-104; Henry V. Poor, *Manual of the Railroads of the United States for 1869-1870* (New York, 1869), p. 83.

18. Kennaway, *op. cit.*, pp. 193-194.

19. Andrews, *op. cit.*, p. 108.   20. Trowbridge, *op. cit.*, p. 566.

21. W. T. Sherman to U. S. Grant, March 12, 1865, *Memoirs of Sherman*, II, 297, 307.

22. Andrews, *op. cit.*, p. 29. Columbia had no rail connection directly to the south.

23. *Memoirs of Sherman*, II, 273-274.

24. Samuel M. Derrick, *Centennial History of the South Carolina Railroad* (Columbia, S. C., 1930), pp. 231-232 (hereafter cited as *South Carolina Railroad*). Losses due to unpaid transportation for the Confederacy amounted to twice as much. The loss due to 111 freed Negroes was $190,973.

DESTRUCTION AND REHABILITATION

were able to use part of the line in May, 1865, in a trip to Orangeburg. Where the track was in place much of it was so weed-choked that the engine drivers slipped as though greased.[25] Four months later, when Sidney Andrews was going over the same route, local residents informed him that miles and miles of iron rail had physically disappeared. The obliteration of the Savannah and Charleston Railroad was so complete that for some time the company made no serious efforts to restore service.[26]

In Georgia, Sherman left the railroads through the heart of the state in tatters. The chief demolition fell on those lines running from Chattanooga through Atlanta and Macon to Savannah. As Sherman captured the line of the Western and Atlantic (Chattanooga to Atlanta) in his push into Georgia, he repaired the track and used the road as his main supply line to support his Atlanta campaign.[27] Before leaving Atlanta in November, 1864, he literally burnt his bridges behind him, for he ordered the destruction of the railroad back to Chattanooga.[28] Before leaving the city Sherman also destroyed and burnt the depot, roundhouse, and machine shops of the Georgia Railroad.[29] Most of the line of the Georgia Railroad was not in the direct path of Sherman's march, although the company itself had acquiesced in October, 1864, to a Confederate destruction of forty miles of the road between Atlanta and Social Circle, Georgia.[30] In his march to Savannah, Sherman could boast of destroying two hundred miles of railroad,[31] chiefly

---

25. *Ibid.*, p. 230.
26. Trowbridge, *op. cit.*, p. 511; Kennaway, *op. cit.*, p. 162.
27. *Memoirs of Sherman*, II, 398-399. Sherman's army in Georgia, before he started on his march to the sea, was dependent for supplies upon a 473-mile single track line from Louisville via Nashville and Chattanooga. The normal daily flow of supplies southward to the 100,000 men and 35,000 animals consisted of 16 trains of 10 cars (10-ton capacity) each, or a total of 1,600 tons.
28. The Confederates, once Sherman had left the vicinity, were only able crudely and partially to restore the road.
29. *Memoirs of Sherman*, II, 177. While the fires were burning the night of November 14, 1864, live Confederate shells that had been stored in one of the machine shops began to explode over the flaming city. Sherman reported that some of the fragments "came uncomfortably near Judge Lyons' house, in which I was quartered."
30. Mary G. Cumming, *Georgia Railroad and Banking Company* (Augusta, Georgia, 1945), p. 80.
31. W. T. Sherman to E. M. Stanton, December 13, 1864, *Memoirs of Sherman*, II, 201.

RAILROADS OF THE SOUTH

that of the Macon and Western, and the Central of Georgia. Sherman's troops demolished the Central of Georgia with such conscientious thoroughness that when J. T. Trowbridge traveled through Georgia in January, 1866, there was still a one-hundred-mile gap of twisted rails and broken bridges east of Macon.[32]

Destruction was nearly as great in the Gulf states of Alabama, Mississippi, and Louisiana. Wilson's raiders severely damaged the Montgomery and West Point, the only road connecting the lower South with Georgia.[33] The road, one of the best equipped before the war, was able to salvage only a single locomotive from its wreckage, and that one was saved only because it had earlier been discarded as worn out. Further south, burnt bridges, twisted rail, and especially the lack of rolling stock almost completely isolated Mobile from the back country.[34] Mobile's line to the north, the Mobile and Ohio, suffered heavily. War havoc destroyed all the bridges, trestle work, depots, and warehouses from Okolona, Mississippi, to Union City, Tennessee, a distance of 184 miles. Sherman, in an early raid at Meridian, Mississippi, had also destroyed twenty-one miles of track.[35] By November, 1865, however, Whitelaw Reid found the road in fair shape from Meridian down to Mobile.[36] Soldiers destroyed portions of the line of the New Orleans, Jackson and Great Northern early in the war, and in 1865 about half of the two-hundred-mile line had been out of operation two years or more.[37] At the end of the war

---

32. Trowbridge, *op. cit.*, p. 501.
33. *Ibid.*, pp. 451-453. Trowbridge reported that the depot at West Point, Georgia, was saved from burning when a lady resident protested to the Yankees that the fire would easily spread to her home. The raiders did burn over a hundred cars, however.
34. Whitelaw Reid, *After the War: A Southern Tour* (Cincinnati, 1866), p. 212. Whitelaw Reid accompanied Chief Justice Chase on a southern trip in the late spring and early summer of 1865. He later returned by himself in the autumn.
35. From the Annual Report for 1866, quoted in Fairfax Harrison, *A History of the Legal Development of the Railroad System of the Southern Railway Co.* (Washington, D. C., 1901), pp. 1433-1434.
36. Reid, *op. cit.*, p. 401. Reid noted on this trip, as elsewhere through the entire South, a high degree of carelessness in the handling of U. S. mail.
37. Henry M. Flint, *Railroads of the United States, Their History and Statistics* (Philadelphia, 1868), pp. 352-354. Losses in rolling stock had also been heavy. From 1861 to 1865 the reductions were: locomotives, 49 to 4; passenger cars, 37 to 4; freight and baggage cars, 550 to 35.

DESTRUCTION AND REHABILITATION

the connecting line just to the north, the Mississippi Central, was in little better shape.[38]

In Tennessee few miles of railway escaped military destruction at some time during the war. The longest line, the Memphis and Charleston, running from Memphis through northern Mississippi nearly to Chattanooga, was especially hard hit. Running east and west through the battlefront, both sides captured and lost it, in whole or part, several times during the war. It was difficult for either side to maintain and protect such an exposed line.[39] After the Federal forces had captured the bulk of the road in the spring of 1862, most of the rolling stock was moved south on other roads and the Quartermaster General of the Confederate Army distributed it to needy roads, many of the cars going into Georgia and the Carolinas, where Sherman's forces later destroyed them.[40] At the end of the war the middle third of the road, running west of Decatur, lay entirely destroyed.[41] The road to the north from Decatur, the Nashville and Decatur, had also lost much of its rolling stock.[42] Further east the Nashville and Chattanooga was more fortunate. While Bragg's retreating army had treated it rather badly, once it became part of Sherman's life line of supply the Federals more properly maintained it, and it was capable of being operated when returned to its owners at the end of April, 1865.[43] The two East Tennessee lines connecting Chattanooga and Bristol had suffered especially from bridge destruction. By the fall of 1865 the owners restored some sort of operation, but anxious passengers often felt that the temporary trestle work actually swayed with the passage of trains.[44] Sufficient rolling stock was on the road in November, 1865, for refugee families to be living in boxcars on side tracks.[45]

38. Reid, *op. cit.*, p. 425.
39. Robert Selph Henry, *The Story of the Confederacy* (New York, 1936), p. 317.
40. Flint, *op. cit.*, pp. 361-362.   41. *Ibid.*, p. 363.
42. Trowbridge, *op. cit.*, pp. 290-293.
43. Robert Selph Henry, *The Story of Reconstruction* (Indianapolis, 1938), pp. 21-22; the restored company officials were still in bad shape, without a dollar in their treasury and without even the barest of shop or office equipment.
44. Reid, *op. cit.*, p. 350.
45. *Ibid.*, p. 348. Perhaps some of the extra rolling stock on roads near

RAILROADS OF THE SOUTH

Railroad service in the South in mid-1865 was poor even on the strongest of the remaining lines. The experiences of Whitelaw Reid in his southern travels from May to December, 1865, well illustrated this fact. In May, 1865, when Chief Justice Chase and his party (including Reid) disembarked at Beaufort, North Carolina, the military authorities provided them with a special train for the trip inland. It consisted of a wheezy locomotive and a worn-out mail car with half the seats gone and all the windows smashed.[46] Later in Virginia, Reid rode in an old coach that boasted seats, and even window glass—seven-by-nine-inch panes in many small sashes to fill the original larger frame.[47] J. T. Trowbridge had similar experiences on the railroads of the coast—on one occasion in an old car filled with wooden chairs, and often in boxcars lined with pine benches.[48] Reid also travelled in boxcars, usually with seats of some sort, although in Opelika, Alabama, the Macon train consisted of two boxcars, without seats, into which were crowded passengers, baggage, freight, and fuel.[49] As the Englishman John Kennaway entered Kentucky in October, 1865, he encountered for the first time racial segregation on American railroads.[50] As soon as a southern road could furnish more than a single passenger conveyance, one of them, always the crudest and usually next to the engine, was designated the "nigger car." The Negroes paid full fare, instead of the half fare previously charged slaves, and relished fully their new freedom to travel.[51]

Chattanooga could be accounted for by a practice of the L. and N. James Guthrie realized early in the Sherman campaign against Atlanta that the army was retaining his cars. Sherman urged Guthrie to do likewise with this connections to the north and soon Sherman was seeing cars in Georgia from almost every road north of the Ohio. *Memoirs of Sherman,* II, 11-12.

46. Reid, *op. cit.,* p. 28.   47. *Ibid.,* p. 339.
48. Trowbridge, *op. cit.,* pp. 215, 506.
49. Reid, *op. cit.,* pp. 365-368. The rusty engine was in no better shape with a battered stack, no headlight and a broken bell.
50. Kennaway, *On Sherman's Track,* p. 18.
51. Trowbridge, *op. cit.,* p. 333; Reid, *op. cit.,* p. 386. Reid reported that whenever a Negro objected to the inferior service at full fare he was always silenced by the argument: "You're free, ain't you? Good as white folks, ain't you! Then pay the same fare, and keep your mouth shut." Before the war, Negroes had not been permitted to travel freely on trains. U. B. Phillips, *A History of Transportation in the Eastern Cotton Belt to 1860* (New York, 1913), pp. 395-396.

DESTRUCTION AND REHABILITATION

Much of the discomfort of travel was due to the rough track. Often the railroads could straighten the bent rails and re-lay them, but the improvised surface was far from smooth.[52] Reid wrote of a trip from Lynchburg to Bristol where the passengers complained of the slow speed, until a glance back at the track quieted the growlers. Occasionally stones had been inserted between short gaps in the crooked rails.[53] Because of the poor track condition, the Georgia Railroad tacked up in each car a printed notice prohibiting people from riding upon the tops or platforms of cars.[54] Wrecks were not infrequent on many of the southern lines and were usually blamed on the general dilapidation of rolling stock and track.[55]

Frequent gaps in the track also made travel exasperatingly slow and painful. Since track could generally be relaid more rapidly than bridges could be rebuilt the usual trip was punctuated with ferryboat crossings at unbridged streams, often at night and sometimes even without benefit of a boat.[56] Overland gaps between rail heads were both more troublesome and more expensive. Spring wagons, old military ambulances, or other vehicles called stage coaches only through courtesy were available at fantastic prices to cross such gaps.[57]

Depots were also slow in being replaced. This was no great change in Richmond, for there many of the trains had always started from the middle of the street, the waiting passengers congregating in corner shops until train time.[58] In country towns at night, however, the lack of a waiting room was a real inconvenience. Reid, Trowbridge, and Kennaway all experienced cold, wet waits for trains. The depot at Corinth was just a ticket shanty, a little frame box no larger than an ordinary privy. Reid and some fellow passengers spent a cold December night at Grand

---

52. Trowbridge, *op. cit.*, p. 501. Trowbridge was told of a recent trip by General Grant over such a relaid road. Grant was supposed to have greatly enjoyed his boxcar ride over "Sherman's hairpins."
53. Reid, *op. cit.*, pp. 339-340.
54. Kennaway, *op. cit.*, pp. 116-117.
55. *Commercial and Financial Chronicle*, September 2, 1865, p. 313.
56. Trowbridge, *op. cit.*, pp. 290-293; Reid, *op. cit.*, p. 425. On one occasion Reid and his fellow passengers had to cross a burnt bridge on foot to reach a waiting train on the other side.
57. Kennaway, *op. cit.*, p. 155.   58. Reid, *op. cit.*, p. 328.

Junction, Tennessee, waiting for the Memphis train and finally built themselves a bonfire out of railroad lumber. Even the bustling Atlanta was without depot facilities in the winter of 1865-1866, passengers getting off the trains often in a quagmire of mud, and always in a labyrinth of sidetracks and freight cars.[59]

Rail travel in the South in 1865 and 1866 was not only slow but expensive. Sidney Andrews paid $5.00 for a seventy-seven-mile, seven-and-one-half-hour trip out of Charleston on the South Carolina Railroad in September, 1865.[60] A little later down in Georgia, he paid as much for service as slow. Few southern trains could go in safety more than fifteen miles per hour, and the elapsed time for long trips generally cut the average down to ten miles per hour.[61] Immediately after the war the passenger fare per mile ranged from six to ten cents, with the Montgomery and West Point charging ten cents in hard money or twenty cents in greenbacks. Many railroads, however, offered destitute ex-Confederate soldiers free transportation back home.[62] As business slowly improved and competition increased in the late 1860's passenger rates declined to a more reasonable figure of four to five cents per mile.[63] They were still far too high for James De Bow, however, who compared them unfavorably with the low passenger rates existing on Belgian railways.[64]

Freight rates were also higher in the South than on most of the northern lines. In the late 1860's, the Chesapeake and Ohio,

---

59. *Ibid.*, p. 425; Trowbridge, *op. cit.*, pp. 290-293, 330, 451; Kennaway, *op. cit.*, pp. 107-108. Any kind of baggage checking was generally lacking in early postwar travel. Ladies, and the gentlemen who accompanied them, sometimes fared better than the average, for often the conductor let all the ladies aboard first. In passenger trains of three or more cars, one car, always the best, was often designated as the "Ladies Car."

60. Andrews, *The South Since the War*, p. 11.

61. *Ibid.*, pp. 230, 288-289; Trowbridge, *op. cit.*, pp. 272-273; Kennaway, *op. cit.*, pp. 105, 234. The slow speed was due in part to the absence of bridges and also to the still imperfect system of fuel provision at the wood lots. At the end of his slow southern trip Kennaway was amazed at the speed of trains north of Baltimore as he returned to New York.

62. P. G. T. Beauregard to C. A. Whitney and Co. (agents of the Morgan Line of Steamers), May 14, 1868, in Letter Book no. 40, Beauregard Papers, Manuscripts Division, Library of Congress.

63. *Merchants Magazine and Commercial Review*, December, 1866, p. 431; October, 1868, p. 287.

64. *De Bow's Review*, March, 1870, pp. 237-253.

DESTRUCTION AND REHABILITATION

the Georgia Railroad, the L. and N., and the Richmond and Danville, all had freight rate structures two to three times as high as that of the Pennsylvania Railroad. This freight rate differential continued into the decade of the 1870's when the typical southern railroad had a four to five cent per ton-mile rate as contrasted to a two cent ton-mile rate generally typical in the North. In testifying as to the cause of high freight rates, General Manager Herman Haupt of the Richmond and Danville, and former Governor Joseph E. Brown, president of the Western and Atlantic, blamed the condition upon: (1) the postwar financial difficulties of southern lines, (2) the paucity of business and traffic in the South, and (3) the comparatively small amount of return freight from southern seaports to the interior. In the postwar years down to 1873, however, the river carrier competition continued to afford a restraining influence upon high railroad freight rates. This was especially true for those railroads running parallel to the Mississippi River. President Abraham Murdock of the Mobile and Ohio claimed the Mississippi River was the most active competitor of his line. As railroad rehabilitation progressed in the late 1860's several railroads sought to create a more efficient freight service through cooperative efforts. Following the lead of the earlier northern Blue Freight Line, the L. and N. and the Western and Atlantic early in 1868 perfected an agreement establishing the Green Line Transportation Company. The most important objectives of the new Green Line (which soon included over 20 companies and 3,300 miles of line) were: (1) to control freight rates, and (2) to facilitate the movement of through traffic by using a system of exchanging freight cars. By 1873, southern railroads were thus providing a more efficient and rapid freight service, even though it was still expensive.[65]

The rehabilitation of southern railroads came slowly but steadily in the postwar years. The restored managers did not save all

---

[65] Fred A. Shannon, *The Farmer's Last Frontier* (New York, 1945), p. 296; William H. Joubert, *Southern Freight Rates in Transition* (Gainesville, Florida, 1949), pp. 17-23, 31-34; Edward King, *The Great South* (Hartford, Connecticut, 1875), p. 54; *Commercial and Financial Chronicle*, January 6, 1866, p. 6; July 21, 1866, p. 66; February 15, 1868, p. 215; *De Bow's Review*, September, 1870, pp. 781-783.

RAILROADS OF THE SOUTH

the individual railroad companies, but the system, as a whole, was restored and put back in operation. A number of factors were responsible. Of primary importance was the aid given by the United States Government. Bond holders, naturally interested in rapid restoration, generally cooperated by approving refunding operations for the unpaid interest on railroad bonds. Some cautious northern capital was also available in small amounts. Basic to the whole endeavor, of course, was the determination of the southerners themselves. Most railroad companies faced their tasks with full vigor, and by 1866 there was even some talk of building several new lines.[66]

Without the assistance of the Federal government the restoration of transportation in the South would have been much delayed. The aid given was of two kinds: first, the actual construction and repair of railroads during the war itself, and second, substantial credits granted in the first months after the war. By the end of the war, the Military Railway Department was in possession of nearly three thousand miles of road, embracing some forty-five lines, most of which were in the South.[67] The Department had restored and repaired many of these lines for at least minimum operation and thus when they were turned back to the owners in mid-1865, they formed at least the bare beginnings of a southern rail network, especially in the area west of the mountains. The actual surrender of the Federally operated roads to the former owners was based on an order from Washington, dated August 8, 1865, which provided that the lines were to be transferred as they stood and that the former owners were to agree to make no claims for damages.[68] The bulk of the government-owned rolling stock was also made available for purchase by southern railroads at an appraised value, on short-term credit.[69] With-

---

66. *De Bow's Review*, April, 1866 p. 442; Fish, *Restoration of the Southern Railroads*, pp. 19-21.

67. Fish, *op. cit.*, p. 11; R. E. Riegel, "Federal Operation of Southern Railroads," *The Mississippi Valley Historical Review*, 9 (September, 1922), 126-138.

68. Fish, *op. cit.*, p. 14. All rolling stock and other property which the roads could identify was to be granted them, regardless of where it was found.

69. The military lines had been operating 433 locomotives, one-quarter of which had been captured. Only a tenth of the 6,605 cars used by the army were captured. *Ibid.*, p. 10.

DESTRUCTION AND REHABILITATION

out this windfall in equipment, many southern railroads would have been unable to furnish any transportation service in 1865.

The first job of a southern railroad president in the summer of 1865 was to get formal possession of his road. Sam Tate, president of the Memphis and Charleston Railroad, went to Washington to procure a special pardon. President Andrew Johnson granted Tate his pardon, and told him the road would be returned by the government as soon as a board of directors of undoubted loyalty had been chosen.[70] The same general procedure was followed in the case of the East Tennessee and Georgia Railroad, and the New Orleans, Jackson and Great Northern.[71] U. S. military authorities operated the crudely rebuilt Western and Atlantic from April to September 25, 1865, when they restored it to the commonwealth of Georgia.

Railroads in nearly every southern state purchased the government-held rolling stock.[72] Railroads west of the mountains bought most of the equipment, with those in Tennessee alone accounting for over a third of the total purchases.[73] A number of Virginia companies purchased small amounts of cars and engines. The total government sales amounted to $10,773,000, of which about a third were for cash, and the remainder on credit.[74] At the end of 1867, the railroads had liquidated only 40 per cent of this debt and the government was finding it increasingly difficult to collect the remainder.[75] Congress passed several acts in the 1870's relieving the roads individually and collectively of portions of the

---

[70]. Flint, *Railroads of the United States*, pp. 362-364. The company got possession early in September. It purchased from the government 10 locomotives, 14 passenger cars, 226 freight cars, shop tools and fixtures, and a large amount of road material, promising to pay the government $491,920.

[71]. The East Tennessee and Georgia found rolling stock and other equipment on its line to the value of $371,000, but being claimed by the government, the company was forced to give a bond for its purchase.

[72]. *De Bow's Review*, April-May, 1867, pp. 489-490. A list of twenty-five roads still indebted to the government in the spring of 1867 included lines in every state but Florida.

[73]. The Nashville and Chattanooga was the largest debtor in 1867, still owing the government nearly $1,500,000.

[74]. Fish, *op. cit.*, p. 25.

[75]. The railroads owed about $5,000,000 in 1867 and still owed $4,646,000 three years later, *De Bow's Review*, April-May, 1867, pp. 489-490; *Commercial and Financial Chronicle*, January 7, 1871, p. 18.

debt. When the government finally closed its books it had lost about $3,000,000 in delinquencies.[76]

Many of the delinquent roads felt their course was just, since they claimed that the appraisals of rolling stock in 1865 had been excessively high. Colonel Edwin W. Cole, president of the Nashville and Chattanooga, complained to the War Department in 1868 that the prices his road had paid for government locomotives were too high and that, therefore, the debt owned the government should be adjusted downward.[77] Most roads pointed out that rail equipment prices had generally declined from 1865 to 1868. Some railroads, such as the New Orleans, Jackson, and Great Northern, also insisted on making large claims against the government for railroad iron and other equipment confiscated during the war.[78] Georgia claimed that her state-owned Western and Atlantic had not been given the same consideration as other southern lines at the time of the equipment sales in 1865. Senator John B. Gordon interested himself in the claim and finally succeeded in securing for the state of Georgia a refund of $152,000 from the War Department.[79]

But the aid of the government, valuable as it was, was not in itself enough. Heavy floating debts, long overdue bond interest payments, and costs of rebuilding that could not be met by purchases from the government required cash or at least credit. Conditions varied from state to state, and from company to company, but the general picture for the whole South was one of a great hunger for capital.

Some few railroads were still fairly well situated financially. While the North Carolina Railroad in May, 1865, had a cash box filled almost entirely with worthless Confederate currency

76. Fish, *op. cit.*, pp. 26-27.
77. E. W. Cole to the War Department, November 18, 1868, in The Library of the Bureau of Railway Economics, Washington, D. C. Cole pointed out that his company had paid $15,000 for inferior locomotives while new ones before the war cost only $9,000 to $13,000. He also charged that some of the rail placed on his road during the war by the army and charged against the company by the government had been taken from other southern lines who were now threatening to sue the Nashville and Chattanooga.
78. Flint, *op. cit.*, p. 357.
79. James H. Johnston, *The Western and Atlantic Railroad of the State of Georgia* (Atlanta, 1931), p. 60.

DESTRUCTION AND REHABILITATION

($356,000 Confederate, $3,600 United States money), it also held eight hundred bales of cotton.[80] In 1865 cotton was as good as cash. Though some of the bales were stolen, the North Carolina reported in 1866 that its remaining cotton, plus its damaged iron, would about re-lay and stock its line.[81] Down in Georgia the Central of Georgia Railroad had earlier had the foresight to reserve large portions of its earnings which at the war's end were chiefly invested in London.[82] It relaid its demolished road with English rails and soon resumed its large and profitable traffic. The relatively greater vigor of Georgia in restoring its rail system was caused in part by the fact that the strongest of the Georgia banks were closely connected with railroads.[83] Even in defeat the bills of the Georgia Railroad and Banking Company were selling at 95 per cent of their par value, and those of the Central Railroad and Banking Company were about as high.[84] The Louisville and Nashville, prosperous throughout the war, had only minor problems of restoration and, in fact, in 1866 was contributing thousands of dollars of free freight service in hauling relief supplies into the South.[85]

Other railroads were not so fortunate. With losses totalling nearly $4,000,000 due to the war, the South Carolina Railroad needed credit badly. Efforts made in the North to obtain money to purchase new rails were abandoned when it was found that the best offers were to take the company's securities at 35 per cent discount. The officials purchased new rails, therefore, only as the revenue of the company permitted.[86] Whitelaw Reid found the railroads of Alabama utterly impoverished unless they could obtain outside financial aid.[87] The Petersburg Railroad managed

---

80. Cecil Kenneth Brown, *A State Movement in Railroad Development: The Story of North Carolina's First Effort to Establish an East and West Trunk Line Railroad* (Chapel Hill, 1928), p. 149; Henry, *The Story of Reconstruction*, p. 123.
81. Fish, *op. cit.*, p. 20.
82. Robert Somers, *The Southern States Since the War, 1870-1871* (London, 1871), p. 72. Somers spent the five months, October, 1870, to March, 1871, travelling through the South.
83. Andrews, *The South Since the War*, p. 365.
84. Trowbridge, *The South*, pp. 458-459.
85. Henry, *The Story of Reconstruction*, p. 201.
86. Derrick, *South Carolina Railroad*, pp. 231-236.
87. Reid, *After the War: A Southern Tour*, p. 212.

to get a $70,000 loan from the Adams and Southern Express Companies, the loan to be repaid in four years by giving the express companies special traffic rates.

What the southern railroads needed was a substantial amount of northern capital. There was an early and a nearly universal acceptance of this financial diagnosis. As early as July, 1865, the *Commercial and Financial Chronicle* saw southern railroad rehabilitation requiring immense amounts of northern money and predicted the requirement would be readily fulfilled.[88] In September, 1865, Governor Pierpont of Virginia publicly invited northern men and northern money to help Virginia rebuild her railroads.[89] In January, 1866, James De Bow made an eager bid in an editorial for northern money. De Bow wrote: "What the South now needs is capital, and if the immense accumulations of the North could only be diverted in that channel, something like the old days of prosperity would be revived, . . . Will not these rich capitalists pause and consider? Never before was so inviting a field opened."[90] Later in the year, after visiting New York City himself, he felt that $50,000,000 to $100,000,000 sent south would double itself within three years.[91] In New Orleans, Beauregard, busy rebuilding the New Orleans, Jackson and Great Northern, wrote that little local capital could be found in the South and that reliance on the North was necessary.[92] Many southern papers, such as the *Memphis Appeal* and the *Charleston Mercury*, added their voices to the growing plea for money from the North.[93] The requests for financial assistance brought forth a modest response. The early appeal of Governor Pierpont may have had an effect, for observers especially noted the presence of northern money in Virginia, the state closest to the financial sources of the North. Whitelaw Reid attributed the marked improvement in Virginia rail transport between May and November, 1865, to

88. *Commercial and Financial Chronicle*, July 8, 1865, p. 57.
89. Trowbridge, *op. cit.*, p. 191.
90. *De Bow's Review*, January, 1866, p. 105.
91. *Ibid.*, February, 1867, p. 216.
92. P. G. T. Beauregard to Col. Blanton Duncan, June 2, 1867, in Letter Book no. 40, Library of Congress.
93. Quoted in *De Bow's Review*, April, 1866, p. 428; June, 1867, pp. 574-575.

northern loans made to several of the state's railroads.[94] Borrowed capital also aided in the recovery in the city of Richmond.[95] Reid heard that Boston money was ready to build a new railroad for Port Royal, South Carolina.[96] Most of the money made available came from New York City, which was already out in front as the nation's financial center.[97] The investments of Henry Clew's banking firm in the South were probably typical. Up to 1873 he had purchased about $3,000,000 of securities in Georgia and Alabama. Many of them were railroad bonds endorsed by state governments.[98]

The northern money that was invested in the South was welcome, but during the first decade after the war it never appeared in the volume anticipated. Early in 1866, De Bow blamed the slow restoration of South Carolina railroads on the lack of northern money.[99] In the next two years he continued to plea for northern money as a hope of the future, not as an accomplished fact.[100] Northern capitalists were still reluctant to invest any large sums in southern ventures in the early 1870's.[101] Contemporaries gave several reasons for the relative failure of northern money to flow south. Primary factors were the general lack of financial security in the South and the presence of more golden investment opportunities in other portions of the Union.[102] In

94. Reid, *op. cit.*, pp. 316-332. Reid reported that Lynchburg was swarming with men who represented northern capitalists.
95. *De Bow's Review*, December, 1867, pp. 595-596.
96. Reid, *op. cit.*, p. 125.
97. *Commercial and Financial Chronicle*, May 11, 1867, p. 587. A report from the Comptroller of Currency, dated December 3, 1866, reviewed the operations of the National Banks in the principal northern cities. New York City with 58 National Banks had them capitalized at a total almost equal to the total of the 129 National Banks in Boston, Providence, Philadelphia, Pittsburgh, and Baltimore. The aggregate deposits in the New York City banks were nearly double the total for the other five cities.
98. Henry Clews, *Fifty Years in Wall Street* (New York, 1915), pp. 278, 548-551. Clews lost heavily on his investment.
99. *De Bow's Review*, February, 1866, p. 217.
100. *Ibid.*, January, 1868, p. 105; August, 1868, p. 691.
101. King, *The Great South*, p. 793. King made an extensive journey in the southern states in 1873 and 1874. The record of his trip appeared in a series of articles in *Scribner's Monthly*.
102. During this period at least one southerner, General John C. Breckinridge of Kentucky, had some investments in northern railroads. Breckinridge was interested in a new railroad being built west from Superior, Wisconsin. After his return to Lexington in 1869, Breckinridge was also connected with

the first eight postwar years, while southern rail mileage expanded by only a third, northern and western rail mileage more than doubled in amount. Some blamed the lack of northern money on the disturbed political and social conditions prevalent in the South, the critics believing that the region would have to mend its ways if it expected more substantial northern financial aid.[103] Others claimed that northern hesitance was due to the Negro supremacy during the Reconstruction.[104]

In rebuilding their lines the southern owners had one asset no enemy could destroy. The laying out and the grading of the average railroad constituted about a third of the total original cost. Another asset that most destroyed lines possessed was the twisted and bent rail itself. Most of this was along the right of way, festooning trees and telegraph poles, or fused together over burnt out bonfires. The Central Railroad of Georgia estimated that its extensive collection of twisted iron was worth two-thirds as much as new rail.[105] Either as scrap sold to the producer of new rails, or straightened out and relaid, the old rails had real value. Trowbridge reported that in the four-month interval between two of his visits to North Carolina, the Petersburg and Weldon Railroad had straightened and replaced miles of bent rails. The result was hardly a smooth track, but at least the trains were running.[106] Some railroads, where the twisted rail was bent beyond redemption, or where the rail was actually gone (as in parts of South Carolina), had to resort to other methods. The South Carolina Railroad, finding the cost of new rail prohibitive, borrowed a page from an earlier Confederate improvisation, and robbed the upper branch lines to re-lay the more important route south of Columbia. In this way Columbia regained

---

railroads in his native state. By 1871, he was vice-president of the 120-mile Elizabeth, Lexington and Big Sandy Railroad. He was also a counsel and lobbyist for the Cincinnati Southern during the latter road's long struggle to gain a right of way across Kentucky. H. J. Wolbridge to General J. C. Breckinridge, November 29, 1871, in Breckinridge Papers, Manuscripts Division, Library of Congress; Henry V. Poor, *Manual of the Railroads of the United States for 1871-1872* (New York, 1872), p. 626; E. A. Ferguson, *Founding of the Cincinnati Southern Railway* (Cincinnati, 1905), pp. 34, 54-55.

103. King, loc. cit.; *De Bow's Review*, June, 1867, p. 607.
104. *De Bow's Review*, January, 1868, p. 105.
105. Trowbridge, *The South*, p. 502.   106. *Ibid.*, pp. 212-213.

DESTRUCTION AND REHABILITATION

rail service again in October, 1866.[107] The Federal-built rolling mills in Chattanooga produced much of the new rail laid on southern lines after the war.

In repairing the track the procurement of an adequate labor force was often a problem. Construction costs generally, both labor and material, were high by prewar standards.[108] Most of the track work before the war had been done by Negroes, many of them railroad-owned slaves. With the war over, many of the freedmen were not inclined to settle down to steady work. The complaints of railroad managers in this respect were numerous. The Atlantic and Gulf Railroad, building through southern Georgia, reported that no Negro that they hired stayed out his whole month to collect his wages.[109] Some white labor was also used. In fact, in rebuilding the South Carolina Railroad, a Confederate Lt. General, Richard H. Anderson, worked for a season as a common day laborer.[110] In Virginia, Whitelaw Reid reported that track gangs of Rebel soldiers and Negroes were working harmoniously together.[111]

But in spite of all the handicaps, shortcomings, and difficulties, the railroad companies rebuilt their lines and put them back in operation between 1865 and 1870. The recovery was unusually rapid in Virginia, as Whitelaw Reid discovered on his second postwar visit to Richmond in November, 1865.[112] The Orange and Alexandria Railroad was soon back in reasonable shape, starting daily mail trains on their way from Washington towards New Orleans.[113] Further south the entire main line of the Memphis and Charleston (except for the bridge at Decatur) was open for

---

107. Henry, *The Story of Reconstruction*, p. 123. Even then, of course, many of the bridges were still not rebuilt.
108. *Commercial and Financial Chronicle*, October 13, 1866, p. 450.
109. Kennaway, *On Sherman's Track*, p. 52. Ten years later, Negro railroad workers were highly regarded. See George Campbell, *White and Black, the Outcome of a Visit to the United States* (New York, 1879), pp. 253, 381; Charles Nordhoff, *The Cotton States in the Spring and Summer of 1875* (New York, 1876), p. 72. The Negroes in the middle 1870's were receiving from 60 cents to $1.50 per day.
110. Henry, *op. cit.*, p. 20.
111. Reid, *After the War: A Southern Tour*, pp. 329-331.
112. *Ibid.*, p. 316.
113. Flint, *Railroads of the United States*, p. 373; *De Bow's Review*, February, 1866, pp. 217-219.

business on November 6, 1865.[114] Beauregard restored the major line out of New Orleans, the New Orleans, Jackson and Great Northern, sufficiently so that by the end of 1866 trains were running to Canton, Mississippi (206 miles) on a thirteen-hour schedule.[115] By 1866 southern rail recovery was so advanced that nearly every state had new railroad projects in mind and in some cases work had actually begun.[116]

The recovery in Georgia, especially Atlanta, was particularly marked. Less than a year after Sherman had left the city in flames, Atlanta had all five of her railroads in active operation, and business men were erecting frame buildings on main street frontage costing $40 a foot. Sidney Andrews felt that Chicago in her busiest days had not seen such activity. In December, 1865, travelers reported that Richmond was not half as far rebuilt as Atlanta. In spite of a small-pox epidemic drummers from every northern city crowded the hotels. The railroads had built Atlanta and after the war Atlanta returned the favor with a vast flood of business.[117]

The trips through the South of James De Bow, as reported in his paper, give a good account of the process of the railroad restoration. In 1866 he found the trains running, accommodations terrible, and the rates twice as high as prewar. By 1867 he reported the railroads in as good a condition as before the war, with comparable schedules and rates only a quarter higher. He also noted that some companies were paying dividends and that many were meeting interest payments on time. In 1868 his successors at the *Review* were arguing for such further improvements as gauge standardization, better rails, consolidation of lines, and better terminal facilities.[118] By 1870 the physical restoration and rehabilitation of southern railroads was practically complete. Southern railroads could turn to new problems.

114. Flint, *op. cit.*, p. 365 115. *Ibid.*, pp. 355-356.
116. *De Bow's Review*, April, 1866, p. 442; Henry, *op. cit.*, pp. 201-202.
117. Kennaway, *op. cit.*, pp. 115-116; Andrews, *The South Since the War*, p. 340; Reid, *op. cit.*, pp. 355-356. Reid reported that the railroads were taxed to their top capacity without filling the city's demands. The trade of Atlanta was a third larger than in the best days before the war.
118. *De Bow's Review*, February, 1866, pp. 217-219; February, 1867, p. 216; June, 1867, p. 597; March, 1868, pp. 264-269; July, 1868, pp. 607-611.

CHAPTER 5

THE CARPETBAGGERS LEND A HAND

THE RELATIVELY rapid restoration of southern transportation facilities in the early postwar years indicated an inherent vitality in the railroads of the ruined land. Although aware of the aid given by the United States Government and by lenient bondholders, travelers and visitors in the South commented favorably on the native recuperative strength of southern railroads.[1]

The vitality and strength was, however, largely expended in the restoration of old lines. As compared to the rest of the nation, new railroad construction in the ten southern states was extremely slow and cautious. In the decade after the Civil War southern railroads increased their mileage by only 46 per cent, adding only 4,187 miles of track to the 9,135 miles of line existing in 1865.[2] The rail network for the entire country more than doubled during the same period and every New England state matched or exceeded the rate of southern construction. Illinois alone built as much railroad in the decade as the entire South and by 1875 had a mileage totalling well over half that of the ten states south of the Ohio River.[3]

Slow southern rail construction was a direct result of the war, both in the ruined railroads calling for immediate attention and in the general loss and destruction of all property. Assessed val-

---

1. Robert Somers, *The Southern States Since the War, 1870-1871* (London, 1871), pp. 86-87 (hereafter cited as *The Southern States*).
2. Henry V. Poor, *Manual of the Railroads of the United States for 1877-1878* (New York, 1877), p. ix; Henry V. Poor, *Manual of the Railroads of the United States for 1885* (New York, 1885), p. xiv.
3. Poor, *Manual of the Railroads of the United States for 1877-1878*, p. ix. Railroad mileage for the nation increased from 35,085 to 74,614 miles in the decade, an increase of 113 per cent.

uations in the ten southern states declined over 50 per cent in the decade of the 1860's, dropping from $4,413,000,000 to $2,190,000,000.[4] Of the ten states, Kentucky, the state that suffered the slightest drop in assessed valuations, built proportionately the most railroad in the decade after the war. Railroads in Kentucky added 759 miles to their 1865 mileage, an increase of 134 per cent.[5] Maryland, another border state that had escaped much of the violent sweep of the war, also built railroads rapidly in the decade, increasing her mileage from 466 to 1,077.

Southern railroad promoters and builders in the decade after the war laid most of their extensions and new lines in the half dozen years from 1868 through 1873. In the first two postwar years the ten states, naturally preoccupied with rail restoration problems, constructed only 440 miles of new line. In the next six years, 1868 through 1873, they built 3,500 miles. In the first two years after the Panic of 1873 they added but 247 miles.[6] With most of the ruined roads back in operation by 1867, the year 1868 marked the beginning of a slowly mounting rail fever in the South. Both travelers in the South and northern financial organs noted the change.[7] Southern railroad stocks that had been infrequently quoted in 1865 and 1866 were being quoted regularly in northern papers by 1869 and 1870 at respectably high figures.[8] The highest quotations appeared in 1871, the year southern railroads out-

---

4. *Commercial and Financial Chronicle*, July 13, 1872, p. 50. The property losses from 1860 to 1870 were most severe in Georgia, Alabama, and Mississippi, where 1870 figures were little more than a third of those of 1860. Virginia and Tennessee suffered much less than the average.

5. Poor, *Manual of the Railroads of the United States for 1877-1878*, p. ix. The Kentucky construction was relatively more rapid than the national average for the period and three times the rate of the ten states here considered.

6. *Ibid*. The year by year building was: 1866, 223 miles; 1867, 217 miles; 1868, 519 miles; 1869, 402 miles; 1870, 733 miles; 1871, 1,094 miles; 1872, 261 miles; 1873, 491 miles; 1874, 177 miles; and 1875, 70 miles.

7. Somers, *op. cit.*, p. 165; *Commercial and Financial Chronicle*, May 9, 1868, p. 584; October 3, 1868, p. 422.

8. Based on a study of southern rail stock quotations taken from the *Commercial and Financial Chronicle* for the years 1865 through 1875. The nine southern lines, Atlantic and Gulf, Central of Georgia, Georgia Railroad, Mobile and Ohio, Macon and Augusta, Macon and Western, Memphis and Charleston, South Carolina Railroad, and Southwestern, were quoted from 1869 to 1875 as follows (average of one share from each of the nine lines):

January 1869, 65; January 1870, 64; January 1871, 70; January 1872, 63; January 1873, 55; January 1874, 47; January 1875, 39.

did themselves with a record 1,094 miles of new construction.

The rate of new rail construction in the South varied a great deal from state to state. Motivated by an overly generous legislature, Alabama outbuilt all her sister states, adding 927 miles to her rail network by 1875 and shooting up from seventh to second place in amount of total line. However, Georgia, with 844 miles of new line, easily retained her position of rail primacy in the South and at the end of the first postwar decade possessed 2,264 miles of railroad. Kentucky was the third state to construct well above the average for the region. The two Carolinas, Tennessee, and Louisiana constructed new road at only a moderately rapid rate. The three remaining states, Virginia, Florida, and Mississippi, constructed very little new mileage and proportionately trailed all the rest of the states in the Union in new trackage for the decade. The construction state by state is shown below:[9]

State	Mileage Dec. 31, 1865	Mileage Dec. 31, 1875	Increase in the Decade	Per Cent Increase
Virginia	1,407	1,638	231	16%
North Carolina	984	1,356	372	38%
South Carolina	1,007	1,335	328	32%
Georgia	1,420	2,264	844	59%
Florida	416	484	68	17%
Alabama	805	1,732	927	115%
Mississippi	898	1,018	120	13%
Louisiana	335	539	204	61%
Tennessee	1,296	1,630	334	26%
Kentucky	567	1,326	759	134%
Total for ten southern states	9,135	13,322	4,187	46%
U. S. total	35,085	74,614	39,529	113%

The late 1860's and the early 1870's were also years of intense and profitable railroad activity by carpetbaggers and their white and colored resident collaborators. Some northerners, such as John T. De Weese, the right hand man of General Milton S. Littlefield in North Carolina, were hitting pay dirt as early as

9. Poor, *Manual of the Railroads of the United States for 1877-1878*, p. ix.

1867.[10] Most of the lush railroad grafting, however, started in 1868 or 1869. The really profitable stealings took place in the next three or four years, and by 1872 to 1873 the conservatives in many states were in the process (or had already finished it) of thoroughly investigating and uncovering the saga of corruption. Opportunities for free and easy economic gain seemed best in the states south of Virginia and east of Mississippi. Organized and legalized railroad corruption was made thoroughly obnoxious in four states, North Carolina, South Carolina, Georgia, and Alabama. But legitimate business men of the North were also investing in the South during these same years. Henry Clews, the New York banker, made heavy investments in the bonds of Georgia and Alabama.[11] Ben Butler saw North Carolina and Florida as states where northern money could be profitably invested.[12]

Carpetbag railroad activity was most evident in the years of relatively rapid southern railroad construction and in those states where that construction was chiefly concentrated. The railroads in the two Carolinas, Georgia, and Alabama added nearly 2,500 miles of line in the decade after Appomattox or about 60 per cent of all new construction in the period.[13] There was, however, no significant connection between the presence of extraordinarily active carpetbaggers in these states and their relatively rapid railroad construction. In all four of the states, with the possible exception of Alabama, the railroads were built in spite of the carpetbagger, rather than because of him. Most carpetbaggers were more interested in milking a railroad exchequer or raiding a state treasury

---

10. John T. De Weese to E. B. Washburne, October 30, 1867, Elihu Washburne Papers, Manuscripts Division, Library of Congress. Already high in Republican circles in North Carolina, De Weese was boasting to Washburne that as a register in bankruptcy he was "making it pay."

11. Henry Clews, *Twenty-eight Years in Wall Street* (New York, 1887), pp. 549-551.

12. O. H. Peck to Ben Butler, December 1, 1868, Ben Butler Papers, Manuscripts Division, Library of Congress. Peck from Boston and "full of Yankee enterprise and grit" asked Butler for advice as to where one could profitably locate in the South. Butler suggested Florida or North Carolina.

13. Poor, *Manual of the Railroads of the United States for 1877-1878*, p. ix. These four states built 2,471 miles in the decade or an increase of 59 per cent over the mileage of 1865. The other six states built new mileage equal to only 35 per cent of their 1865 network.

than they were in the hard work of actually laying track or operating a railroad. Many states paid hundreds of thousands of dollars for railroads that were never completed or put into full operation.[14]

The several programs of state railroad aid in the South after the Civil War were a natural continuation of a prewar development. In the first decade of railroad construction, the 1830's, state debts (both northern and southern) totaling $43,000,000 were attributable to railways. Some estimates for the prewar South indicated that over half of all railroad capital came from local or state governments. Northern and southern railroads alike benefited from the generous federal land grants, a program which between 1850 and 1871 gave over 131,000,000 acres to the railroads. State land grants added another 48,000,000 acres to the railroad bonanza. Both before and after the war, northern and western states, as well as those of the South, were generous in their various railroad aid programs.[15]

In the years before the Civil War, the administration of the various programs of state aid in the South had generally been sober, honest, and economically beneficial. The transportation policies of Reconstruction governments were less successful. Though often sound in theory, the typical postwar state railroad assistance program broke down before the triumvirate of low political and commercial moral standards, a largely illiterate electorate susceptible to manipulation, and the nearly universal presence of elected political representatives with large appetites but few principles.

14. Myrta L. Avary, *Dixie After the War* (New York, 1906), p. 156; Walter L. Fleming, *Civil War and Reconstruction in Alabama* (Cleveland, 1911), p. 604.
15. Winthrop M. Daniels, *American Railroads, Four Phases of Their History* (Princeton, 1932), pp. 33-46; George Rogers Taylor, *The Transportation Revolution, 1815-1860* (New York, 1951), pp. 92-97; Caroline E. Mac Gill, *A History of Transportation in the United States Before 1860* (Washington, D. C., 1917), p. 418; *Public Aids To Transportation* (Washington, D. C., 1938), II, 5-33, 105-115. In the region covered in this study, four states, Alabama, Florida, Louisiana, and Mississippi, participated in the federal land grants to railroads. For state aid to railroads in New York and Nebraska see Harry H. Pierce, *Railroads of New York, A Study of Government Aid, 1826-1875* (Cambridge, Mass., 1953) and Addison E. Sheldon, *Land Systems and Land Policies in Nebraska* (Lincoln, Nebraska, 1936).

Virginia experienced only a small amount of carpetbag railroad activity during Reconstruction. Soon after the return of his "restored government" from Alexandria to Richmond, Governor Francis Pierpont indicated a real concern over the future of the railroads of the state. Following a mild policy of reconciliation between his state and the North, Pierpont in September, 1865, issued a warm invitation for northern men and their money to assist in the rehabilitation of the railroads of the state. Pierpont's interest in railroads was a natural one, for Virginia held a large financial stake in its railroads, owning railroad stock with a par value of $22,000,000.[16] Striving to avoid unnecessary irritation of the dominant northern forces, and strengthened by the state's possession of three-fifths of the company's stock, Pierpont intervened in the Richmond and Danville's presidential election in 1865.[17] The Governor persuaded a majority of the stockholders that the selection of the Confederate hero, General Joseph E. Johnston, would be untimely. They elected instead A. S. Buford of Richmond, a man who continued to hold the position for over twenty years.[18]

A variety of factors contributed to the relative absence of carpetbag activity in Virginia. The moderation of Pierpont plus the early appearance of quite substantial amounts of northern capital aided in a rapid economic rehabilitation.[19] Virginia's escape from pure Radicalism was also partly due to an early split within the Republican ranks. The conservatives supported a more moderate faction, and in July, 1869, helped to elect the mild Republican, Gilbert C. Walker, to the governorship.[20] Six months later Reconstruction ended in Virginia with the seating of her congressmen and senators in Washington. Virginia's extensive railroad construction in the 1850's gave the state a postwar rail network

---

16. J. T. Trowbridge, *The South: A Tour of Its Battlefields and Ruined Cities* (Hartford, 1866), p. 191; Nelson M. Blake, *William Mahone of Virginia, Soldier and Political Insurgent* (Richmond, 1935), p. 79.
17. *Commercial and Financial Chronicle*, April 13, 1867, p. 456.
18. H. J. Eckenrode, *The Political History of Virginia During the Reconstruction* (Baltimore, 1904), p. 32.
19. Whitelaw Reid, *After the War: A Southern Tour* (Cincinnati, 1866), p. 332; *De Bow's Review*, December, 1867, pp. 595-596.
20. Blake, *op. cit.*, p. 101.

that was generally adequate for immediate needs.[21] The average Radical or carpetbagger thus found few favorable railroad opportunities in Virginia.

More respectable groups, however, were interested in the railroads of Virginia. Both the B. and O. and the Pennsylvania Railroad had an interest in the railroads of Virginia.[22] The Baltimore and Ohio Railroad had been interested in Virginia railroads since the late 1850's.[23] As early as March, 1866, John W. Garrett, president of the B. and O., started to buy stock in the Orange and Alexandria Railroad. By 1872 he was able to announce control of what had since become the Orange, Alexandria and Manassas Railroad, a 250-mile line running from Alexandria to Charlottesville and Harrisonburg.[24] As early as 1870, Virginians were claiming that all the roads from Washington to Danville, and from Harpers Ferry to Salem, were essentially B. and O. property.[25]

The Baltimore and Ohio people were also interested in building new lines to fill in their growing system. On February 23, 1866, they incorporated the Valley Railroad, a line that proposed to connect Harrisonburg and Salem, Virginia.[26] Threatened by the rival Shenandoah Valley, a line supported by the Pennsylvania Railroad, the city of Baltimore backed up the Valley Railroad with a $1,000,000 stock subscription in September, 1869, matching in amount an earlier stock subscription made by the parent company, the B. and O.[27] In the same year, General Robert E. Lee became enthusiastic over the possibilities of rail service for his college town,

---

21. *Eighth Census of the United States, 1860*, "Mortality and Property" (Washington, 1866), pp. 327-329; Somers, *The Southern States Since the War, 1870-1871*, p. 27. Virginia built more new line in the 1850's than any other southern state and in 1860 (before West Virginia broke away) she also led the South in total mileage.

22. For an account of the Pennsylvania Railroad's interest in the state see Chapter 6, "Southern Ambitions of the Pennsylvania Railroad."

23. Festus P. Summers, *The Baltimore and Ohio in the Civil War* (New York, 1939), p. 40.

24. Edward Hungerford, *The Story of the Baltimore and Ohio Railroad* (New York, 1928), II, 112-113.

25. George C. Wedderburn to William Mahone, March 30, 1870, Blake, *op. cit.*, p. 114.

26. Hungerford, *op. cit.*, II, 117-118.

27. *The Railroad Gazette*, August 6, 1870, p. 441; J. H. Hollander, *The Financial History of Baltimore* (Baltimore, 1899), pp. 316-318.

and even journeyed to Baltimore to help obtain subscriptions with which to build it.[28] A year later, August 30, 1870, the road elected Lee its new president, succeeding Col. M. J. Harmon. However, the Confederate hero died only six weeks after his election, without seeing a single rail actually laid in the road's construction.[29] The real control of the projected road became more apparent with the selection of Robert Garrett, son of the B. and O. president, to succeed General Lee.

Having no general railroad aid program after the war, and already possessing an adequate network, Virginia's postwar rail construction was exceedingly slow.[30] The state's chief railroad interest in the late 1860's lay in consolidating what lines she already possessed. Local interests, as well as those from Pennsylvania and Baltimore, were in creating new rail combinations. Chief among these was William Mahone, the poker-playing "railroad Bismarck" of Virginia. At the end of the war Mahone quickly exchanged his major general's stars for a return to the presidency of his old road, the Norfolk and Petersburg.[31] His wholehearted restoration of the line soon gained the favorable attention of the stockholders of an adjoining line to the west, the South Side, and on December 7, 1865, the latter road unanimously elected him president. Taking the personal advice of J. Edgar Thomson, president of the Pennsylvania, Mahone proceeded to buy up sufficient stock in a third line still further west, the Virginia and Tennessee, to gain for himself another presidency by November, 1867.[32]

Mahone next desired the legalization of his coup through the passage of a consolidation act in the state legislature. The financial provisions of an earlier consolidation act (1867) could not be met, but a later act approved by the Governor June 17, 1870, permitted

28. Hungerford, *op. cit.*, II, 119.
29. *Ibid.*; *The Railroad Gazette*, August 6, 1870, p. 441. The road finally reached Lexington in 1883.
30. Of the ten southern states, only Mississippi added new trackage more slowly. Only a third of two hundred odd miles built in the first postwar decade was added during the five years of Reconstruction, 1865-1870.
31. Blake, *op. cit.*, p. 72.
32. *Ibid.*, pp. 76, 85-86. A correspondent from New York City wrote Mahone that New York considered him one of the biggest railroad men in the country, even rivaling Vanderbilt.

the consolidation of the Norfolk and Petersburg, the South Side, the Virginia and Tennessee, and the Virginia and Kentucky (a projected line to run west from Bristol) into a new company to be called the Atlantic, Mississippi and Ohio.[33] Mahone was not above the judicious use of money in perfecting his schemes, and Governor Pierpont urged him to use up to $10,000, if necessary, to assure the passage of the first consolidation act in 1867.[34] Enemies of the completed consolidation were critical of Mahone's unprecedented annual salary of $25,000 and inferred that Mahone was treating the line as a family or personal possession.[35] Mahone had more serious difficulties with his northern rivals, the Pennsylvania and the B. and O., and later with English investors who in June, 1876, helped maneuver the company into receivership.[36]

Plagued by unpaid interest on debts owed the state by several railroads,[37] and finding its extensive stockholdings not profitable, the state government of Virginia soon decided upon a policy of retrenchment which included the liquidation of most of its railroad securities. As early as October, 1868, Richard T. Wilson, representing B. and O. interests, had attempted, without success, to buy up the state's interest in the Virginia and Tennessee Railroad.[38] The act of June, 1870, which provided for Mahone's consolidation, also provided that the new Atlantic, Mississippi and

33. *Commercial and Financial Chronicle*, June 24, 1871, p. 784. The new line stretched 408 miles across Virginia from Norfolk to Bristol.

34. Blake, *op. cit.*, pp. 81-85. Being a good conservative, Mahone was also interested in "controlling" the votes of certain citizens, especially Negroes. On election days he sent the hundreds of Negroes in his employ to repair the track at points so distant that their return late at night made impossible their participation in the election. *Ibid.*, pp. 144-145.

35. *Ibid.*, pp. 88-89. The salary was high, being equal to that of President Grant. A. S. Buford of the Richmond and Danville was getting only $5,000 in 1871. General Beauregard as the president of two railroads in 1870 claimed a combined salary of only $11,000. Some critics of Mahone interpreted the A. M. and O. to mean "All Mine and Otelia's." The maiden name of Mrs. Mahone was Otelia Butler.

36. The reorganized company became the Norfolk and Western.

37. *Commercial and Financial Chronicle*, July 11, 1868, p. 56; July 10, 1869, p. 40; September 25, 1869, p. 401. In mid-1868 seven railroads owed the state a total of $3,146,744. Unpaid interest on the debt stood at $843,855 in July, 1869.

38. Robert Selph Henry, *The Story of Reconstruction* (Indianapolis, 1938), p. 350 (hereafter cited as *Reconstruction*). General Stoneman disapproved the plan, and, of course, William Mahone was incensed at any proposal destined to block his anticipated rail consolidation.

RAILROADS OF THE SOUTH

Ohio Railroad might buy from the state all the state-held stock in the four predecessor companies.[39] The next month, July, 1870, another special act directed the Board of Public Works to sell the state-owned stock in the Richmond and Danville, holdings that soon wound up in the hands of Tom Scott of the Pennsylvania.[40] General legislation approved March 28, 1871, permitted the sale of all remaining railroad stock held by Virginia. Many of the securities were sold at public auction February 5, 1872, but some still remained unsold early in 1873.[41] Thus by the early 1870's the state of Virginia had liquidated practically all of her once extensive rail holdings.

Likewise in North Carolina, the postwar years saw a dissipation of the earlier dreams of Carolinians to have a state-controlled rail system patterned to their local needs. In rail mileage in 1870 North Carolina had her proportionate share, on a basis of both population and area.[42] It was also an average state in new postwar rail construction, adding 38 per cent to her system by 1875 while the region as a whole added 46 per cent.[43] In the field of railroad manipulation, speculation, and government extravagance, North Carolina was well beyond the average. In the two short years of 1868 and 1869 the legislature authorized the issuance of $27,850,000 of state bonds to thirteen different railroads in the state.[44] Of the $17,640,000 of bonds actually issued to the railroads very little was spent for honest construction. In fact, the railroads of North Carolina expanded their mileage more slowly from 1868 to 1871 than during the rest of the first postwar decade.[45] Instead, the receipts from the sales of the state bonds

---

39. The A. M. and O. gave the state $4,000,000 second mortgage bonds for the state-owned stock.

40. Fairfax Harrison, *A History of the Legal Development of the Railroad System of the Southern Railway* (Washington, D. C., 1901), pp. 93-94, 475.

41. *Commercial and Financial Chronicle*, December 16, 1871, p. 806; February 1, 1873, p. 154.

42. In 1870 North Carolina's 1,178 miles of railroad constituted 10½ per cent of the total for the ten states. Both her population and her area accounted for 11 per cent of the totals for the region.

43. Poor, *Manual of the Railroads of the United States for 1877-1878*, p. ix.

44. Reginald C. McGrane, *Foreign Bondholders and American State Debts* (New York, 1935), pp. 335-336.

45. Only ninety-three miles were built during the three years, 1869, 1870, and 1871. The increase for the decade ending in 1875 was 372 miles.

went into the pockets of the railroad ring, where it was spent for such things as bribery in North Carolina, bankrupt railroads in Florida, and gambling junkets in New York City.[46]

During Reconstruction in North Carolina Negroes were not prominent in the new government, except as voters, nor were carpetbaggers especially numerous in office. The railroad ring that dominated the legislature in 1868 and 1869 was composed of both migrants from the North and local Republicans. The governor who cooperated with the ring was a native of the state, the personally honest, but generally incompetent W. W. Holden. General Milton S. Littlefield of New York was the active leader of the ring. His chief aides were George W. Swepson, a native Tarheel who had already served an apprenticeship in railroad plundering,[47] and John T. De Weese, a colonel from Indiana who had stayed in the South for purely financial reasons.

During the legislative session of 1868 General Littlefield installed a bar in the west wing of the state house, supplying free wine, liquor, and cigars to the members, and cashing without discount their per diem checks.[48] Charmed by the genial manners and good fellowship of their host, many good conservatives enjoyed this "third house" without giving up their right to condemn Littlefield in public.[49] George Swepson, paymaster of the ring, was more specific with his gratuities, paying over $133,000 in direct bribes to a dozen or more officials and legislators.[50] In

46. Cecil Kenneth Brown, *A State Movement in Railroad Development: The Story of North Carolina's First Effort to Establish an East and West Trunk Line Railroad* (Chapel Hill, 1928), pp. 198-199; Charles Nordhoff, *Cotton States in the Spring and Summer of 1875* (New York, 1876), p. 95; McGrane, *loc. cit.*; Hilary A. Herbert and others, *Why the Solid South* (Baltimore, 1890), p. 80.
47. Near the war's end Swepson had exchanged nearly worthless new state bonds for $58,000 in prewar state bonds held by the North Carolina Railroad. Many of the bonds were exchanged after the directors of the railroad had specifically ordered the operation to be stopped. J. G. de Roulhac Hamilton, *Reconstruction in North Carolina* (New York, 1914), pp. 203-204.
48. The expenses of the bar were met by Littlefield's note, an obligation which he later refused to honor.
49. Hamilton, *op. cit.*, pp. 353, 363, 430. The conservatives were not so fortunate in August, 1868, when the railroads of the state, following the lead of President W. A. Smith of the North Carolina Railroad, refused to grant them special passenger rates to their state convention. Rates for delegates attending the Republican Convention were reduced over one-half.
50. *Ibid.*, p. 431; McGrane, *loc. cit.* An acquaintance of an aged Negro legislator found the Negro one evening happily counting money in his hotel

return for all these favors, the ring at will pushed through the pliable legislature its favored railroad measures. It would even permit the passage of projects not its own, for a mere 10 per cent cut of the bond issues authorized.[51]

Wishing to avoid public offense as much as possible, the Littlefield gang kept many of its favored projects quiet until after the election in November, 1868. Even during the special session of 1868, however, it ignored the provision of the state constitution which prohibited the legislature from contracting any new debt (unless the same bill levied a tax to pay the bond interest) until the state bonds were selling at par.[52] By December, 1868, acts had been passed providing for the exchange of new state bonds for the securities of the Chatham Railroad, the Williamston and Tarboro Railroad, and the Western North Carolina Railroad. The generosity increased the next year and when in the late summer of 1869 over $10,000,000 in new bonds had been issued to aid various railroads, at least one financial journal in the North urged caution upon the bond-buying public.[53] While most of the bond issues granted carried with them the special tax levies upon the railroads benefited, these taxes were insufficient, and by 1869 the state was unable to meet the total interest due on its bonds.[54] The state, which in 1867 had had a fair credit standing with a total debt of $14,000,000, had nearly doubled its debt in two years with railroad bond issues of $13,313,000.[55]

Over half of the state aid given by North Carolina in 1868 and 1869 went to a single road, the Western North Carolina.[56]

---

room. The old Negro said: "Well, boss, I's been sold in my life 'leven times and 'fo 'de Lord, dis is de first time I eber got de money!" Herbert and others, *op. cit.*, p. 80.

51. Hamilton, *op. cit.*, pp. 430-434. The leaders of the ring also received special favors. Swepson speculated profitably in state bonds because he knew the plans of the state treasurer. Swepson, Littlefield and Andrew Jackson Jones were all recipients of rail bonds given them by railroad companies at prices well below the market.

52. *Ibid.*, p. 429. The bonds were selling at about seventy-five cents on the dollar earlier in 1868.

53. *Commercial and Financial Chronicle*, September 11, 1869, p. 331.

54. Henry, *Reconstruction*, pp. 368-369.

55. Poor, *Manual of the Railroads of the United States for 1869-1870* (New York, 1869), p. 458; Hamilton, *op. cit.*, pp. 448-449.

56. The state authorized bond issues totalling $27,850,000, but only $17,640,-000 were actually issued. Of those issued, several of the recipient railroads re-

CARPETBAGGERS LEND A HAND

The state had generously subscribed to this line which was chartered in 1855 as it was slowly built from Salisbury westward toward the mountain town of Asheville. The early postwar aid continued to be substantial and the road was honestly built and administered until mid-1868 when it had reached a point one hundred miles west of Salisbury.[57] In the summer of 1868 the Littlefield ring saw real possibilities in the road and decided to move in. Legislation of August 19, 1868, divided the road into two divisions, one east of Asheville and the other west, each to be capitalized at a new higher figure of $6,000,000. Littlefield and Swepson marked the unbuilt western division as their own and a pliable legislature soon increased that division's capital stock to $10,000,000, the state government to subscribe to two-thirds of this amount, payable in state bonds.[58]

Aided by a former president of the line, Samuel Mc D. Tate of Morganton, Swepson and Littlefield next quickly organized the new division, freezing out bona fide would-be stock subscribers and electing Swepson president. Through fraudulent stock subscriptions they convinced Governor Holden that all prerequisites had been met and the state treasurer issued the ring $6,367,000 in crisp new state bonds. Soutter and Company, the state's fiscal agents in New York City, sold the bonds for Swepson and Littlefield at an average of about fifty-three cents on the dollar. Very little of the three million dollars was used to give Asheville a rail connection with the outside world.[59] During the next two years much of the money was spent by Littlefield and Swepson in rail adventures further south in Florida.[60] After the collapse of the Holden regime in 1870, Littlefield fled the state, and during the next few years the new officers of the ravaged railroad tried with

---

turned bonds to the value of $4,345,000, leaving only $13,313,000 finally outstanding. The bonds issued (none being returned) to the Western North Carolina amounted to $6,980,000.

57. Brown, *A State Movement in Railroad Development*, pp. 191-192; *Commercial and Financial Chronicle*, March 14, 1868, p. 344.
58. Hamilton, *op. cit.*, pp. 436-438; Brown, *loc. cit.*
59. Edward King, *The Great South* (Hartford, 1875), pp. 505-506.
60. Brown, *op. cit.*, pp. 198-199. The Eastern Division of the road, under more sober and honest management, used most of the proceeds from its $613,000 of state bonds for legitimate construction purposes.

only slight success to make a profitable settlement with the members of the ring.[61]

The North Carolina legislature was also generous in the aid it gave the Wilmington, Charlotte, and Rutherford Railroad. During 1868 and 1869 this 125-mile line running from Wilmington to Rockingham, N. C., received $3,000,000 in state bonds to pay for new stock subscriptions. As long as R. H. Cowan of Wilmington was president, the railroad honestly used the proceeds from the sale of the bonds. However, Dr. William Sloan, who succeeded Cowan in July, 1869, misused nearly all of the state aid received during his term of office. The third president, Andrew Jackson Jones, a favored member of the Littlefield-Swepson Ring, was most profligate in his use of the state assistance. Jones never accounted to his company for the 1,320 bonds issued to him and he cashed many of them in order to help finance a pool with Swepson and Littlefield that was attempting to bolster the price of state bonds generally. He used at least sixty of them directly as chips in a single evening of gambling in New York City. New York gossip claimed that some bonds were circulating among the demimonde of the city, specifically in the hands of Josie Mansfield, the buxom and unfaithful mistress of Jim Fisk.[62]

Like Virginia, North Carolina disposed of much of its state-owned railroad stock during the Reconstruction. Robert Rufus Bridgers, ex-Confederate Congressman and a highly respected citizen of Wilmington, was the prime mover in the sale of the state's stock in the Wilmington and Weldon Railroad. Bridgers became president of the road at the end of the war in 1865 and immediately turned to the problem of restoration. Finding he needed more financial aid than was available in the South, he appealed to a Confederate sympathizer in Baltimore, William Thompson Walters. As a condition of his assistance, Walters

61. *Ibid.*, p. 205. The troubles of the Western North Carolina were not over, for the 1870's brought endless litigation and numerous efforts at reorganization. The East Tennessee, Virginia, and Georgia, the Richmond and Danville, and the Southern Security Company were all interested in the road. Eventually the line was controlled by the Richmond and Danville. *Commercial and Financial Chronicle*, August 24, 1872, p. 252; December 14, 1872, p. 797; Harrison, *Legal Development of the Southern Railway*, pp. 269-270.

62. Hamilton, *op. cit.*, pp. 439-440, 442-445.

CARPETBAGGERS LEND A HAND

insisted that Bridgers buy up control of the railroad for Baltimore interests. In addition to buying private holdings, Bridgers persuaded the state to sell its Wilmington and Weldon stock. On March 31, 1869, the State Board of Education sold 4,000 shares of Wilmington and Weldon stock for $148,000 ($37 per share) and 2,000 shares of Wilmington and Manchester stock for $10,000 ($5 per share), all to W. T. Walters of Baltimore.[63] Never prosperous in the early postwar years, the Wilmington and Manchester was in receivership by 1868, and in 1870 was reorganized by the Baltimore interests as the Wilmington, Columbia and Augusta.[64] The two roads, the Wilmington and Weldon, and the Wilmington, Columbia, and Augusta, were closely associated throughout the 1870's and retained Bridgers as their president until the year of his death, 1888.[65]

The reign of railroad graft and corruption in North Carolina ended with the impeachment of Governor Holden. Finding bribery, blackmail, and organized stealing no longer profitable or healthy the members of the Littlefield gang fled or went into hiding. Littlefield settled in Florida and all the efforts of North Carolina to force his return were unavailing.[66] De Weese found Cleveland to his liking and invested his "savings" in real estate there. Both Jones and Swepson were arrested in North Carolina but the former died while appealing his sentence, and the latter was never punished. North Carolina was left a heritage of unbuilt railroads, depleted holdings of rather worthless rail securities, a huge debt, and ruined state credit.[67]

In both length and severity the general Reconstruction picture

---

63. Herbert and others, *Why the Solid South*, p. 79; Brown, *op. cit.*, pp. 43-44. The actual authority for the sale was given by the Holden administration two weeks later in an act of April 12, 1869.

64. Poor, *Manual of the Railroads of the United States for 1869-1870*, pp. 43-44; *The Railroad Gazette*, October 22, 1870, p. 80.

65. Walters' associate, the able Baltimore banker, Benjamin Franklin Newcomer, stood at Bridger's elbow as vice president for the roads, *The Railroad Gazette*, December 10, 1870, p. 249.

66. Hamilton, *op. cit.*, p. 450. Littlefield managed to escape every effort to capture him for the $5,000 reward offered by North Carolina. On one occasion, to escape return he surrendered himself to a Florida sheriff and faced local bribery charges.

67. *Commercial and Financial Chronicle*, December 13, 1873, p. 803; December 31, 1881, p. 744.

RAILROADS OF THE SOUTH

in South Carolina exceeded that of North Carolina. In the field of railroad corruption this was not true. While the operations of South Carolina's railroad ring were of a different sort from those of the state to the north, they were in general no worse. Corrupt railroad practice in North Carolina affected nearly all the roads to some degree since such a large proportion of them either received aid or had it offered to them. In South Carolina the railroad spoilsmen directed nearly all their attention to only two lines. Both lines were companies in which the state was financially interested prior to the war.[68] Since the war had so thoroughly destroyed much of the state's rail system, new construction after the war was slow to get under way. Carpetbag railroad activity had little effect on the new construction once it was started, and from 1868 through 1875, 328 miles of new line were added to the civil war system.[69]

Carpetbaggers and Negroes were very prominent in the South Carolina railroad ring. Most of their activity was during the administration (1868-1872) of the pliable Governor Robert K. Scott. To make the work of the ring easier, many of its members were also state officials. Scott, the colonel of an Ohio volunteer regiment, had entered the state as a prisoner of war, but at the war's end had moved into Republican politics via an assistant commissionership in the Freedman's Bureau. While possibly not corrupt at heart, the governor was weak and especially vulnerable to feminine and alcoholic allurements. On one occasion the gang gave a burlesque star a percentage in order to gain his signature to a bond issue.[70] "Honest John" Patterson, the leader of the ring, had been a legislator, newspaperman, and henchman to Simon Cameron in Pennsylvania before he entered South Carolina in 1869.[71] Miles G. Parker, state treasurer, had come to the state as an officer in a Negro regiment and after the war had become a

---

68. Herbert and others, *op. cit.*, pp. 96-97.
69. Poor, *Manual of the Railroads of the United States for 1877-1878*, p. ix. The increase was 32 per cent for the decade, since the state possessed 1,007 miles in 1865.
70. Francis Butler Simkins and Robert Hilliard Woody, *South Carolina During Reconstruction* (Chapel Hill, 1932), pp. 113-114.
71. Patterson claimed that he was honest since he was honest enough to "stay bought." He himself "bought" a seat as U. S. Senator in 1872 for a reported $40,000.

hotel keeper in Charleston. The comptroller general, John L. Neagle, was a native of the state who had served in the Confederate army as an assistant surgeon. Although his earlier training for the ministry had ended disastrously with his expulsion from college for stealing, he was still more honest than Parker, and, therefore, often got no cut in the graft.[72] Most interesting of the group was Daniel Henry Chamberlain, a native of Massachusetts who had been educated at Phillips Academy, Yale, and Harvard. Coming to South Carolina in 1867 to be a planter, the short and prematurely bald Chamberlain soon won a place for himself in Radical ranks. Although he was attorney general under Scott, and later a Radical governor himself, the cold, temperate, little man never looked the part of a carpetbagger.[73]

Negroes were also much in evidence, both as recipients of bribes and in management. Every Negro legislator was anxious for committee appointments, especially those that paid the best.[74] Of the twelve members in the board of directors of the gang-controlled Greenville and Columbia Railroad in 1870, two were Negroes, A. J. Ransier and F. L. Cardozo, mulatto secretary of state.[75]

South Carolina came out of the Civil War with a manageable state debt only slightly over $5,000,000. As late as 1870 it stood at only $6,100,000[76]—a figure small in comparison to the debts of the two states to the north, North Carolina and Virginia. In the early postwar years South Carolina still held as assets stock in varying amounts in nearly all of the railroads of the state.[77] Nearly half of all the state-held railroad stock was in a single

72. Simkins and Woody, *loc. cit.*
73. *Ibid.* Chamberlain's classmate at Yale, H. H. Kimpton, became financial agent for the state in New York City. Although he had but two years of banking experience, he understood perfectly the plans and needs of his friends in South Carolina.
74. James S. Pike, *The Prostrate State, South Carolina Under Negro Government* (New York, 1874), p. 109 (hereafter cited as *The Prostrate State*). The House, in its eagerness to spread the loot, increased the Railroad Committee to eighteen members.
75. *The Railroad Gazette*, May 28, 1870, p. 201; Simkins and Woody, *op. cit.*, pp. 200-208; Pike, *op. cit.*, pp. 172-174.
76. *Commercial and Financial Chronicle*, January 1, 1870, p. 11.
77. *Ibid.*, March 6, 1869, p. 295. The holdings as of 1868 stood at $2,754,660 (par value) in eleven different companies.

company, the Blue Ridge, the amount at par being $1,310,000. Greenville and Columbia Railroad stock was the second largest holding of the state. While some of these assets were nearly worthless, the state's credit was still in satisfactory shape on the eve of the Scott administration.

Of the two roads raided by carpetbaggers in South Carolina, the Greenville and Columbia was both the older and the more important. The road was a 142-mile serpentine line running from the capital westward to Greenville. Incorporated in 1845 and finished by 1853, the road was so poorly built that South Carolinians expected the rickety line to be swept away by some spring freshet.[78] The state had aided in the construction of the road with both stock subscriptions and bond endorsements and in 1869 the state stock had a par value of $433,960 and the endorsed bonds amounted to nearly a million more.[79] In the winter of 1869-1870 John Patterson organized a ring composed of seven state officials, two legislators, and George W. Waterman, Governor Scott's brother-in-law.[80]

Early in January, 1870, Chamberlain enthusiastically explained, in a letter to Kimpton, the plans of the ring: to buy up control of the company through private purchases and purchase of the state stock, then to purchase short adjacent lines, and finally to mortgage the whole system of 269 miles at a rate of $20,000 per mile.[81] The ring commissioned Scott's predecessor, former Governor James L. Orr, and J. P. Reed, both directors of the Greenville and Columbia, to buy up quietly throughout the state up to $350,000 (par value) of private stock holdings, paying from $1.75 to

---

78. Simkins and Woody, *op. cit.*, pp. 200-201.
79. *Commercial and Financial Chronicle*, March 6, 1869, p. 295. The stock held by the state was a little less than a third of the total issue.
80. In addition to Patterson and Waterman the group consisted of Parker (State Treasurer), Neagle (Comptroller General), Chamberlain (Attorney General), F. L. Cardozo (Secretary of State), H. H. Kimpton (Financial Agent for the state), Reuben Tomlinson (State Auditor), C. P. Leslie (Land Commissioner), Joseph Crews (Chairman of House Railroad Committee), and Timothy Hurley (state representative).
81. Daniel Chamberlain to H. H. Kimpton, January 5, 1870, Simkins and Woody, *op. cit.*, pp. 203-204. The plan was to buy at foreclosure sale the thirty-one-mile Laurens Railroad, and also to buy the seventy-mile Spartanburg and Union, both tributary lines to the Greenville and Columbia. Of the entire scheme Chamberlain wrote: "There is a mint of money in this or I am a fool."

$2.00 per share. For their trouble the ring paid the two men $20,000. The Patterson group next easily persuaded the legislature to pass a law March 1, 1870, establishing a Sinking Fund Commission whose function was to sell damaged state property, specifically the damaged granite and marble on the Statehouse grounds. Members of the railroad ring controlled a majority of the five-man Commission and on March 2, 1870, the Commission sold to the ring the state's holdings of Greenville and Columbia stock, 21,698 shares at $2.75 a share for $59,969.50. Money obtained through Kimpton's illegal sale of state bonds in New York City financed the entire purchase operation (both private and state purchases), amounting to around $100,000.[82]

A few weeks later the railroad ring, now also directors of the recently reorganized railroad, pushed through the legislature a bill relegating the state-held lien on the road to the status of a second mortgage. This permitted the new directors to put on the market their new first mortgage bonds, securities which Kimpton was soon busily peddling in New York at fifty-five cents on the dollar. Even though the ring had thimblerigged the state out of both its stock and its mortgage in the Greenville and Columbia, the new managers could not make the road profitable. By 1871 its financial condition was desperate and in 1872 it was sold under foreclosure to the South Carolina Railroad.[83]

Few southern railroads had more checkered or complicated histories than the Blue Ridge line, the second South Carolina railroad marked for special attention by the Patterson ring. Chartered in 1852, the road was projected as a transmontane line to connect Anderson, South Carolina, with Knoxville.[84] By 1861, $2,500,000 furnished primarily by the state and the city of Charleston had been spent, but the line had been constructed only thirty-three

---

82. *Ibid.*, pp. 200-208; Herbert and others, *Why the Solid South*, pp. 96-97; Pike, *The Prostrate State*, pp. 172-174.
83. Harrison, *Legal Development of the Southern Railway*, p. 321.
84. Poor, *Manual of the Railroads of the United States for 1869-1870*, pp. 134-135; Somers, *The Southern States*, p. 58. The need for the line is illustrated by Somers' comment in 1870 that produce from Kentucky destined for the interior of South Carolina was often forced to be carried 1,000 miles when the destination was no more than 200 miles from the starting point.

miles west of Anderson to Walhalla, South Carolina.[85] Hoping to renew the stalled construction, the legislature on September 15, 1868, authorized the issuance of $4,000,000 in bonds for the company, provided that they could be sold at par, a provision that rendered the whole plan useless.[86]

Shortly after gaining control of the Greenville and Columbia, John Patterson turned his attention to the Blue Ridge. In March, 1871, the legislature passed an act permitting the consolidation of the Greenville and Columbia, and the Blue Ridge, and also withdrawing the par sale requirement for the $4,000,000 bond issue.[87] In conjunction with several associates Patterson next bought the state's 13,100 shares (an original investment of $1,310,000) of Blue Ridge stock for $1 a share in July, 1871.[88] Having acquired control of the line for only $13,100, Patterson reorganized the company with himself as president and with Governor Scott's brother-in-law included in the new Board of Directors. Although the new company made optimistic statements to the press,[89] the $4,000,000 of new bonds still had no real value, owing to the poor credit of the state. Early in 1872 Patterson went to the legislature again and in February, 1872, an act was passed permitting the Blue Ridge to exchange the $4,000,000 of state bonds for a new $1,800,000 issue of Revenue Bond Scrip.[90] To get the act passed over Governor Scott's veto, Patterson and Kimpton had to pay the legislators $42,859 in bribes.[91] Patterson hardly got his money's worth for the scrip was soon valueless because of court injunctions and a repeal of the taxing feature. By April,

---

85. Anderson was located near the western end of the Greenville and Columbia Railroad.
86. Herbert and others, *loc. cit.* Neither the credit of the railroad or the state could justify par value for the bonds.
87. Simkins and Woody, *op. cit.*, pp. 208-222.
88. *Ibid.* The state held a majority of all the stock and Patterson could ignore the $1,000,000 of stock still held by the city of Charleston.
89. *Commercial and Financial Chronicle*, July 15, 1871, p. 83.
90. The new issue was to be paid for in four years through special state taxes.
91. Simkins and Woody, *loc. cit.* Some of the purchased members during the railroad operations were quite clever in their rationalizations. Senator Beverly Nash in justifying his acceptance of a large bribe said: " . . . I merely took the money because I thought I might as well have it and invest it here as for them to carry it off out of the state." Henry, *Reconstruction*, p. 446.

1873, the Blue Ridge was declared bankrupt in court action. The line was never extended past Walhalla.

Railroad corruption in South Carolina generally ended with the termination of Governor Scott's second term. After having plundered the state, the chief members of the railroad ring went on to other things. "Honest John" Patterson went on to a seat in the United States Senate, having bought the post for $40,000 in the winter of 1872. Chamberlain remained in the state to be the last Reconstruction governor and then retired to a successful law practice in New York City. Governor Scott returned to Ohio and real estate. The carpetbaggers were gone. South Carolina with her unbuilt and pillaged railroads remained.[92]

At the time of the war Georgia possessed the most extensive rail network of any southern state. Georgia continued to expand her rail system at well above the average rate in the years after 1865. Between the war and 1873 established companies and new promoters added 840 miles of new line, more construction than took place in all three of the coastal states just to the north.[93] Georgia railroads were generally prosperous in the postwar years. No fewer than five major lines in the state were paying annual dividends of from 6½ per cent to 10 per cent by 1868.[94]

The railroad fever in Georgia expressed itself also in a general system of state aid instituted by the legislature in 1868.[95] Practically all of the railroad aid bills were passed during the corrupt administration of Rufus B. Bullock, 1868-1871, and most of them in the two-year period, 1869-1870. While carpetbaggers and native Republicans practiced considerable railroad chicanery during these years, they were also years of real railroad growth. Georgia added over half of her early postwar (1865-1875) rail construction in the three years 1869 through 1871.[96] Established and prosperous lines like the Georgia Central, Georgia Railroad, and At-

---

92. Simkins and Woody, *op. cit.*, pp. 136, 542-546.
93. Georgia built 840 miles in the 8 years. Virginia, North Carolina, and South Carolina together added only 740 miles. Poor, *Manual of the Railroads of the United States for 1877-1878*, p. ix.
94. *Commercial and Financial Chronicle*, September 12, 1868, p. 327.
95. C. Mildred Thompson, *Reconstruction in Georgia, Economic, Social, Political, 1865-1872* (New York, 1915), p. 231; *Commercial and Financial Chronicle*, October 8, 1870, p. 466.
96. Poor, *Manual of the Railroads of the United States for 1877-1878*, p. ix.

lanta and West Point suffered materially from the new competition and bitterly fought the general aid program with expensive lobbying activity.[97] John Pendleton King, Augusta conservative, one-time U. S. Senator, and long-time president of railroads in Georgia, protested the aid program most vehemently. In 1869 King, then president of both the Georgia Railroad and the Atlanta and West Point, stated that the uncertainty of all railroad investments was much increased by the expanding state aid program. In his annual report to the Atlanta and West Point, King stated: "No policy could be more unjust and oppressive than the policy of 'state aid.' It is a distinguishing feature in this policy that the citizen who has built his own enterprise with his own means, is taxed to build up rival enterprises, by which his own may be ruined."[98] King and his colleagues who ran other old, established companies did not have to worry too long, however, for most of the new companies had their competitive positions rapidly undermined by mismanagement and corruption.

In Georgia's reconstruction carpetbaggers and Negroes were not as conspicuous as in South Carolina. The governor of the radical regime in the state was Rufus B. Bullock, a short-time resident of the state, who had come from New York to Augusta in 1859 where he was connected with the Southern Express Company. Foster Blodgett of Augusta, as a close crony of Bullock, was always sure of some lucrative appointive position. There were also carpetbaggers in the Bullock entourage. A. L. "Fatty" Harris moved his three hundred pounds plus from Vermont down to Georgia where he lived well at the government trough. An early favorite of the governor was Colonel Ed Hurlburt, another visitor from the North.[99]

Hannibal I. Kimball from New England was the prime mover in railroad activities during Bullock's administration. Born in Maine in 1832, Kimball had moved as a youth to Connecticut where he soon built up a successful carriage business in the 1850's. Soon after the War, in 1866, he expanded his interests by com-

97. Thompson, *op. cit.*, p. 317.
98. *Commercial and Financial Chronicle*, September 18, 1869, p. 364.
99. Thompson, *op. cit.*, pp. 221-225. Hurlburt quarreled with Bullock before the end of the Governor's term.

bining with George M. Pullman and associates in establishing a new company to provide and operate sleeping cars throughout the South. Although a good Methodist, he saw nothing wrong in selling the cars without bothering to complete delivery.[100] On his first visit to Atlanta, Kimball was attracted by the auction sale of a corner lot on Peachtree street.[101] He bought the lot for $6,000 and from that day forward his career became intertwined with the booming real estate, railroad, and political interests of the thriving new state capital.

Kimball never sought political office. Nevertheless, from July, 1868, until October, 1871, he was the close friend, political adviser, and financial agent of the governor of the state, the amiable and ample Rufus Bullock. Several times during the relationship Kimball made large cash deposits to a bank account opened freely to the governor.[102] The tall handsome promoter was munificently openhanded with all who could help him and thus became a great favorite with the Republican office holders.[103] Kimball's persuasive powers were so great that his fellow citizens claimed the only way to resist him was to refuse to see him.[104] The recipients of his favors were glad to pass legislation authorizing $400,000 for the purchase of a new state capitol. They paid Kimball the money for a remodeled opera house which he had bought shortly before for only $30,000.[105] Many Georgians also thought that he had used state bonds, intended for railroad purposes, in paying for Kimball House, a magnificent hotel he erected in Atlanta.[106]

The years 1869 and 1870 were big years in Georgia for railroad aid. The legislature offered to endorse the bonds (at $12,000

---

100. McGrane, *Foreign Bondholders and American State Debts*, p. 305; Edward King, *The Great South*, pp. 352-354.
101. Henry, *Reconstruction*, pp. 175-176.
102. Thompson, *op. cit.*, pp. 217-222.
103. The extravagant manner of dispensing state funds led to a popular Negro song: "H. I. Kimball's on de floor, It ain't gwine ter rain no more."
104. Raymond B. Nixon, *Henry W. Grady* (New York, 1943), pp. 108-109.
105. McGrane, *loc. cit.* The opera house was not finished when Kimball purchased it. However, his gain on the total transaction was obviously immense.
106. King, *loc. cit.*; Somers, *The Southern States*, p. 97. Costing $600,000, the hotel was one of the largest and most elaborately appointed in the South. Equipped with steam elevators, a vast lobby, and a French cook who was paid $250 a month, the Kimball House could accommodate a thousand guests.

to $15,000 per mile of completed road) of practically any new proposed line. By the fall of 1870 potential aid amounting to nearly $30,000,000 had been authorized in the name of internal improvements.[107] By the end of the Bullock regime the state had offered aid to thirty-seven different companies, nearly all of which had only a paper existence.[108] Most of the dream railroads never materialized, however, and by 1872 only seven railroads had actually received and used endorsed bonds from the state.[109] Two additional roads, the Macon and Augusta, and the Atlanta and Richmond Air-Line, returned their state-endorsed bonds when they discovered that they could make better financial arrangements independent of the state.

Kimball was president of four of the seven lines that received state assistance, the Brunswick and Albany, the Bainbridge, Cuthbert and Columbus, the Cartersville and Van Wert, and the Cherokee.[110] The Brunswick and Albany was Kimball's favorite and consequently received the bulk of the state aid.[111] This road had been started before the War under the name of the Brunswick and Florida, but the sixty miles of completed track had been seized by the Confederacy in 1863 for use on more essential lines.[112] Reorganized in 1869 as the Brunswick and Albany, the new company was soon applying for state aid. Kimball obtained $1,880,000 in state-endorsed bonds for the 235 miles of contemplated line although no more than 172 miles were in operation when the company went into receivership in 1872.[113] The state also en-

107. *Commercial and Financial Chronicle*, October 8, 1870, p. 466. If all the contemplated lines had actually been built, over 1,700 miles of new lines would have been added to the state's total.
108. Thompson, *op. cit.*, pp. 236-238.
109. *Ibid.* From most of these lines the state received a first lien on the railroad. *Commercial and Financial Chronicle*, December 10, 1870, p. 754.
110. Two of these four were actually the same since the Cartersville and Van Wert became the Cherokee. Both lines received state aid, however, in their own name. The remaining three roads to get endorsed bonds were the South Georgia and Florida, the Alabama and Chattanooga, and the Macon and Brunswick.
111. King, *op. cit.*, p. 352.
112. Poor, *Manual of the Railroads of the United States for 1869-1870*, p. 371.
113. *Commercial and Financial Chronicle*, December 10, 1870, p. 754; Frederick A. Cleveland and Fred Wilbur Powell, *Railroad Promotion and Capitalization in the United States* (New York, 1909), pp. 222-223; Poor, *Manual of the Railroads of the United States for 1877-1878*, pp. 747-748.

dorsed first mortgage bonds for the company amounting to $3,330,-000.[114] Kimball built the first miles of the road quite honestly, but soon was satisfied with anything that could show two fairly parallel bars of iron.[115] Opponents in the state were positive that Kimball had used bribery to obtain his extraordinary state assistance.[116]

The state aid granted the other Kimball lines was just as irregular. The Cartersville and Van Wert, a proposed forty-five mile feeder line to the state-owned Western and Atlantic, was financed entirely with state-endorsed bonds, as the capital stock brought in no cash at all. State aid of $12,500 per mile was to be granted as each five-mile section was completed. However, the state gave Kimball $100,000 in endorsed bonds when only one and one-half miles were completed and Bullock endorsed $175,000 more when only three miles of track had been laid.[117] The state endorsed an additional $300,000 in bonds after the line was reorganized as the Cherokee Railroad. Comparable legal limitations accompanied the aid planned for the Bainbridge, Cuthbert, and Columbus Railroad, but before a single mile had been completed, Governor Bullock endorsed 240 bonds for the road in Kimball's New York City office. The total endorsements for the road ran to $600,000.[118]

The state-owned Western and Atlantic was another railroad where corruption prevailed during the Bullock regime. After the war-torn road was returned to the state, the efficient superintendent, Major Campbell Wallace, used the fairly heavy earnings of the road to return it to first class condition.[119] From 1865 to 1868 the operating ratio stayed below 72 per cent and the road was easily earning an annual net revenue for the state of from $300,000 to $400,000.[120]

114. Cleveland and Powell, *loc. cit.*; Thompson, *op. cit.*, pp. 320-322.
115. King, *op. cit.*, pp. 352-354.
116. Thompson, *op. cit.*, p. 237. Kimball probably used some of the $2,548,-000 authorized common stock as legislative gifts. None of the capital stock was ever paid in cash.
117. McGrane, *op. cit.*, p. 307; Thompson, *op. cit.*, pp. 231-232, 322-323.
118. Thompson, *op. cit.*, pp. 231, 236-238.
119. Herbert and others, *Why the Solid South*, pp. 136-137; Henry, *Reconstruction*, p. 175.
120. Herbert and others, *loc. cit.*; Thompson, *op. cit.*, p. 244.

The corruption in the road under the Bullock administration was one of management, not construction, since the line had long since been completed and was fully in operation by 1868. Also the graft was different from that of the Kimball-sponsored roads, as there was enough loot for every deserving Republican to obtain a share. In July, 1868, Governor Bullock removed all the old officials of the line and replaced them with his own crew, consisting of Colonel Ed Hurlburt as superintendent, "Fatty" Harris as supervisor, and Foster Blodgett as treasurer. Hurlburt was a spoilsman in the management of the line and staffed the road with many extra employees of the correct political faith. Nevertheless, he maintained a certain semblance of railroad efficiency, kept the operating ratio within reason, and even returned $25,000 per month into the state treasury.[121]

Hurlburt broke with Bullock late in 1869 and on January 1, 1870, the governor elevated to the superintendency Foster Blodgett, a henchman who neither had nor claimed any experience in railroading.[122] The mismanagement soon became colossal. Hurlburt had spent $985,633 in operating the road for twelve months, but Blodgett spent $2,043,293 for the same period.[123] Old employees were dismissed wholesale and their places taken by political "patriots." Most of the well-paying (by the sale of tickets enroute for cash) conductor jobs were reserved for the sons of legislators. Fraud in the purchasing and supply departments was especially flagrant. Blodgett furnished Kimball's Cartersville and Van Wert line with crossties, machinery, several cars, and a locomotive, all without compensation.[124] N. P. Hotchkiss, company auditor, explained to a subsequent investigating committee that he had saved $30,000 in a year or two out of a $2,000

---

121. Thompson, *loc. cit.;* Herbert and others, *loc. cit.* In August, 1869, Hurlburt played host to forty newspapermen of the state with a special excursion over the road. The train was fully equipped with many baskets of food, liquor, and champagne. The representative of the Atlanta *Constitution*, the young, then unknown Henry Grady was suspicious concerning the presence of Bullock on the avowedly non-political trip. Nixon, *Henry W. Grady*, pp. 69-70.

122. Blodgett later said he had been appointed to the post to run the road's "public and political policy."

123. Herbert and others, *loc. cit.*

124. Thompson, *op. cit.*, pp. 238-245. Kimball's sleeping car company sold several cars to Blodgett's road for $30,000, but neglected ever to deliver the order.

CARPETBAGGERS LEND A HAND

salary only by practicing the "most rigid economy."[125] Passes were freely given and soon half of the passengers were riding free.[126] Both roadbed and rolling stock suffered serious dilapidation from faulty maintenance and by the summer of 1870 connecting roads both to the north and to the south were complaining of the line's unsafe operating conditions, as well as the uncertainty of financial settlements.[127]

By the autumn of 1870 public clamor against graft in the Western and Atlantic was so loud and insistent that the idea of leasing the road received support from both major parties. Bullock, Kimball, and the Republicans were willing to consider such a prospect only because it seemed evident that the Democrats would win the next election. If the gold mine could be leased at once to the "right people" it might not prove a complete loss.[128] On October 24, 1870, the legislature passed a law to lease the road for a minimum of $25,000 per month, the lessees to be financially responsible with a majority of the leasing group to be bona fide citizens of the state.[129] In the two months before Christmas, 1870, three rival groups prepared and presented bids to Governor Bullock. The strongest of the three groups appeared when Joseph E. Brown resigned as Chief Justice of the Georgia Supreme Court to join with Kimball, John P. King of the Georgia Railroad, and other interested parties in forming a company which offered to lease the road for $25,000 per month.[130] The rival railroads of Macon, the Central, the Macon and Western, and the Southwestern, sought to get a share in the Brown-Kimball-King group but without success. Deciding they lacked political prestige, the Macon group appealed to friends in Washington, D. C., and soon enlisted in their cause Senator Simon B. Cameron of Pennsylvania, Tom Scott, vice-president of

125. U. B. Phillips, *A History of Transportation in the Eastern Cotton Belt to 1860* (New York, 1913), p. 332.
126. This was especially true when the railroad was used to transport loyal African voters to some dubious election district. At such times the voter's instruction sheet served as a railroad ticket.
127. Henry, *op. cit.*, pp. 426-427.
128. Thompson, *op. cit.*, pp. 245-255.
129. *Ibid.*; *The Railroad Gazette*, November 12, 1870, p. 152.
130. *The Railroad Gazette*, December 31, 1870, p. 320; *Commercial and Financial Chronicle*, December 31, 1870, p. 853.

the Pennsylvania Railroad, and John S. Delano, the son of the Secretary of the Interior. This turned the trick and just before the bid submission deadline the two groups combined with a final total of twenty-three directors.[131]

On December 27, 1870, Governor Bullock accepted the bid of the reorganized Brown syndicate and leased them the road for twenty years at $25,000 per month. He turned down the bids of two other groups, one of them offering to pay $34,500 per month, on the grounds that they lacked adequate financial backing and were not representative of the entire state.[132] The financial resources of the successful syndicate were more than adequate as they admitted the spending of thousands of dollars in buying favorable press comment and in retaining lawyers all over the state.[133] The money Kimball had advanced to procure the lease was of little avail, for Kimball's and Bullock's scheme to have Kimball replace Brown as president of the campany failed when the Macon group supported Brown.[134] Kimball soon retired from the group, disposing of both his shares and those of his father-in-law, George Cook. Alexander H. Stephens was another man early to leave the group. Stephens retired as soon as he heard that Bullock had not accepted the highest bid.[135] Though subject

[131]. Thompson, *op. cit.*, pp. 245-250. Each subgroup held eleven shares with the twenty-third share going to the supposedly neutral William B. Dinsmore of New York, president of the Southern Express Company. Important in the Brown group in addition to the original trio were: George Cook, father-in-law of Kimball, H. B. Plant, a friend of Bullock, Alexander H. Stephens, and E. W. Cole, representing the Nashville and Chattanooga Railroad. The most important figures in the Macon group were: Cameron, Scott, Delano, William T. Walters of Baltimore who was interested in the railroads serving Wilmington, N. C., William S. Holt, president of the Southwestern, and Benjamin H. Hill of Athens. *Commercial and Financial Chronicle*, December 31, 1870, p. 853.

[132]. James Houston Johnston, *Western and Atlantic Railroad of the State of Georgia* (Atlanta, 1931), pp. 64-70.

[133]. Nixon, *Henry W. Grady*, pp. 118-119. The business manager of the Atlanta *Constitution* admitted that Brown had paid his paper $5,000 for printing communications favoring the lease. Brown said the legal retainers were justified "as retaining fees in the event of litigation."

[134]. Thompson, *op. cit.*, pp. 252-253.

[135]. *The Railroad Gazette*, January 21, 1871, p. 392. Favoring the idea of a lease and believing that Brown, though his political opponent, was no rogue, Stephens had written to Brown in the fall expressing his willingness to pledge $10,000 to the undertaking. The company was glad to accept the modest pledge for the prestige value of the Stephens' name.

to continuing criticism the lease was ratified two years later by both houses of a conservative legislature.[136]

When the newly elected Democratic legislature convened in 1871 Bullock realized that his regime was over. Faced with impeachment threats, Bullock resigned October 23, 1871, and fled the state. The legislature proceeded to investigate the vast issue of state-endorsed railroad bonds.[137] The amount of the total state debt was in dispute but some figures ran as high as $17,000,000.[138] When the legislature began seriously to consider repudiation, Henry Clews, New York financial agent of Bullock, published a plea in an Atlanta paper, admitting fraud, but urging that the state safeguard its credit by refusing to repudiate.[139] The repudiation party prevailed, however, and by the mid-1870's over $10,000,000 of endorsed railroad bonds had been declared void.[140]

Kimball also left the state in the fall of 1871. He claimed that financial losses suffered in the Chicago Fire of October 8, 1871, forced him to return North.[141] Actually, the political debacle suffered by Bullock was much more responsible for his leaving the state, broken both in health and fortune. On February 6, 1874, Kimball voluntarily returned to Atlanta and denounced all the charges made against him. Many Atlantans, including Henry Grady, were inclined to be lenient to the returned New Englander, perhaps because they could see in their city so many tangible benefits of his promoting genius. A Fulton County grand jury indicted Bullock (who had also returned) but not Kimball.[142] The leading citizens at once proffered the promoter a vindication banquet at Kimball House. After Bullock's subsequent acquittal, he also stayed in Atlanta and even became pres-

136. *Commercial and Financial Chronicle*, August 17, 1872, p. 220.
137. *Ibid.*, December 16, 1871, p. 806; May 11, 1872, p. 626; August 3, 1872, p. 155.
138. *Ibid.*, January 20, 1872, p. 84.
139. Thompson, *op. cit.*, pp. 234-235.
140. *Commercial and Financial Chronicle*, September 28, 1872, p. 414; Poor, *Manual of the Railroads of the United States for 1877-1878*, p. 944.
141. Wallace P. Reed, ed., *History of Atlanta, Georgia* (n.p., 1889), Part II, 162; Howard Douglas Dozier, *The History of the Atlantic Coast Line* (New York, 1920), p. 134.
142. Nixon, *op. cit.*, pp. 108-109. Kimball was so thoroughly rehabilitated that he later missed election as mayor of the city by only fifty-four votes.

ident of the local chamber of commerce. Seemingly, the new "northern" city of Atlanta could be more forgiving of its Bullocks and Kimballs than could Raleigh or Columbia.

Georgia's western neighbor, Alabama, also experienced postwar railroad activity that was closely associated with carpetbag rule. Like most southern states its primary concern in the first years of peace was in rail rehabilitation rather than new construction. The rehabilitation was slow for the poverty was intense. The people were so poor in the summer of 1865 that a round trip of an Alabama and Florida train from Mobile to Montgomery netted only $13 in passenger fares.[143] By 1867, however, the railroad spirit was booming and new construction soon started in earnest.[144]

In the first postwar decade Alabama added new trackage to its rail network more rapidly than any other Confederate state east of the Mississippi. The new lines constructed by 1875 totalled 927 miles, an increase of 115 per cent over 1865 figures.[145] Some of this heavy building was directly due to the extensive system of state, county, and municipal aid instituted in 1867 and expanded in the next two years. On February 19, 1867, the state legislature, a home rule, pre-Radical group, passed the first postwar railroad aid bill.[146] Under the act the state agreed to endorse first mortgage railroad bonds to the extent of $12,000 per mile, to be granted in twenty-mile sections.[147] No real effort was made to utilize this law as the conditions were difficult, and as rail promoters contended that the aid offered was insufficient to attract northern or European capital.

The first Reconstruction legislature succumbed to the argu-

143. Fleming, *Civil War and Reconstruction in Alabama*, p. 260.
144. *De Bow's Review*, February, 1867, p. 217. Through 1867, the railroads of the state added only 46 miles of new line. In the next five years 777 additional miles were laid.
145. Poor, *Manual of the Railroads of the United States for 1877-1878*, p. ix.
146. Herbert and others, *Why the Solid South*, pp. 51-53.
147. John Witherspoon Du Bose, *Alabama's Tragic Decade* (Birmingham, 1940), p. 151. The conditions under which the aid was granted were fairly onerous: the endorsed bonds could be sold for no less than 90 per cent of par, the directory of any participating railroad was to include two state-appointed members, the state governor could sell the road if the company defaulted on interest payments, the railroads must purchase rail and track supplies from local producers wherever possible, and all state-aided lines were to carry free of charge all state freight.

ments of the promoters and in the summer of 1868 liberalized the aid program by increasing the endorsement to $16,000 per mile to be granted in five-mile sections after the first twenty miles had been completed.[148] The arguments of the scheming promoters were often direct and financial in character, as many legislators let it be known that their votes for railroad measures could be purchased for $500 to $1,000. Some of the promoters, having far more audacity than cash, relied for bribery money on advances procured from the financial agents who would handle the proposed bonds.[149] Governor William H. Smith made a show of opposition to the state aid program in November, 1869, but the legislature responded the next March with a simple act declaring that all past actions of the government in behalf of railroads were ratified and legal.[150] Earlier legislation of December 31, 1868, permitted railroads to apply to county and city governments for capital stock subscriptions, the subscriptions to be financed through county bond issues.[151] Several railroads, especially two new lines, the East Alabama and Cincinnati, and the Selma, Marion, and Memphis, made numerous aid applications under this act. Several counties, especially those like Dallas which had a large propertyless Negro majority, were nearly ruined financially through such applications. Frequently Democratic promoters were even more conspicuous than the Radicals in this local financial jobbery.[152]

The Alabama and Chattanooga Railroad was both the most important and the most corrupt of the ten lines aided by the state aid program. This ambitious project proposed to connect Chattanooga with Meridian, Mississippi, a distance of 295 miles. An earlier company, the twenty-six-mile North-East and South-West

---

148. Fleming, *op. cit.*, pp. 589-591.
149. Herbert and others, *loc. cit.*; Du Bose, *op. cit.*, p. 239. Negro votes could generally be purchased quite cheaply and one member of the legislature was reported to have said the Negro members "Sold their votes for prices that would have disgraced a Negro in the time of slavery."
150. Fleming, *loc. cit.*
151. *Ibid.*, pp. 604-605. When such an application was made the county was legally forced to hold an election to decide the issue of aid. The bond issues were to be amortized through special property taxes.
152. Nordhoff, *Cotton States in the Spring and Summer of 1875*, pp. 89-90; Fleming, *loc. cit.*

RAILROADS OF THE SOUTH

Alabama Railroad (Meridian to York, Alabama), in attempting to find fresh capital in the North found instead the Stanton brothers of Boston. John C. Stanton and Daniel N. Stanton, both nearly penniless "capitalists," were glad to leave New England for the bright prospects in Alabama. The elder brother John was soon well established among the carpetbag officials in Montgomery and in November, 1868, received legislative permission to combine his recently acquired North-East and South-West line with the equally short Wills Valley Railroad, running out of Chattanooga, into the Alabama and Chattanooga.[153]

John Stanton next started to build the road. He persuaded farmers living along the proposed right of way to quit their crops for the promise of high railroad wages. He also contracted for a thousand Chinese railroad builders from San Francisco. Both the Chinese and the farmers frequently had a long wait for their pay.[154] Ex-Governor Patton, as president of the new company gave an air of respectability to the railroad.[155] Brother Daniel, as president of the contracting company, was little more than a figurehead. All three men, aided by agents of the New York banking houses of Henry Clews and Co. and Soutter and Co., soon started to work on state officials to obtain the vital state-endorsed bond issues.[156] Since none of the capital stock had brought any cash into the company, the early sale of the state bonds was an absolute necessity. Governor Smith endorsed $1,800,000 in bonds as early as November 15, 1869, without bothering to inform himself as to the company's satisfaction of the prerequisite conditions. Even where two rails of iron provided a certain technical legal compliance, the line was a jerry-built structure and was never properly equipped. Before he left office late in 1870, Governor Smith had endorsed $4,720,000 of bonds for the entire 295-mile road plus an extra $580,000, or a total of $5,300,000.[157] Much

---

153. Du Bose, *op. cit.*, pp. 153, 177-179; McGrane, *Foreign Bondholders and American State Debts*, p. 288. Stanton also was instrumental in getting the state aid program raised from $12,000 to $16,000 per mile.

154. Du Bose, *op. cit.*, pp. 179-181.

155. In 1865 when he visited the company's headquarters in Boston the home office officials reproached Patton for allowing the railroad's charter to cost them $200,000, Fleming, *op. cit.*, pp. 591-600.

156. McGrane, *loc. cit.*

157. Fleming, *op. cit.*, p. 604.

of this was fraudulent since the entire road when finished was valued at only $4,018,388, and since in the fall of 1870 no more than 233 miles of the 295-mile line was in operation.[158]

Not content with excessive and fraudulent bond endorsements, John Stanton asked the legislature in February, 1870, for a direct grant of $2,000,000 in 8 per cent, twenty-year state bonds. The bill failed to pass the lower house on February 4, 1870, but extraordinary financial activity in the Stanton suite at the Exchange Hotel caused the bill to be quickly reconsidered and it was easily passed, sixty-two to twenty-seven, the next day.[159] With the bill passed, the bonds were quickly issued and hastily sold in Europe. Stanton used much of the proceeds in expanding his real estate holdings in Chattanooga, building an opera house and a new hotel, the Stanton House.[160] Stanton also used some of the money in a vain effort to reelect Governor Smith in 1870. On election day the elder Stanton marched to the polls at the head of nine hundred of his employees. He registered them, gave them each a Radical ticket and had them vote in a body.[161] Early in 1871 Smith's successor, Robert Lindsay, uncovered vast endorsement irregularities but could prove nothing more on his predecessor than that he had been criminally careless.[162]

With Smith no longer in office and the easy source of state aid dried up, Stanton's railroad soon was in financial difficulties, defaulting on its bond interest due January 1, 1871. On June 8, 1871, the U. S. District Court of Alabama placed the company in receivership with a receiver appointed by Governor Lindsay

---

158. *The Railroad Gazette*, November 12, 1870, p. 153. Twenty of the miles receiving endorsed bonds (at $16,000 per mile) were located outside of the state near Chattanooga, were rented from another corporation, and had already been endorsed to the extent of $8,000 per mile by the state of Georgia.

159. Fleming, *op. cit.*, pp. 592-594. Some members of the legislature were reported to have received $500 for a favorable vote. The president of the Alabama and Chattanooga, ex-Governor Patton, opposed the special aid bill. He was punished by being removed from office and was replaced by Daniel Stanton, who was back in Boston.

160. Du Bose, *loc. cit.* Some of Stanton's critics accused him of trying to imitate Jim Fisk of New York, and H. I. Kimball of Atlanta.

161. Fleming, *op. cit.*, p. 597.

162. *Ibid.*, pp. 594-596; Herbert and others, *Why the Solid South*, pp. 51-53. In a letter of April 3, 1871, Smith wrote: "I admit that if I had attended to the endorsement and issue of these bonds, that all this never would have occurred."

to be put in possession of the road.¹⁶³ The receiver, Colonel John H. Gindrat, discovered as he took over the road in August, 1871, that the southern end of the road was not in operation because unpaid employees at Meridian had taken possession of, and hidden, vital locomotive and machinery parts.¹⁶⁴ The receiver pacified the claimants and put the road in operation as far as possible. During the next few years the legal history of the road was very complicated as the Stantons, the State of Alabama, and rival southern roads struggled for its control.¹⁶⁵ John Stanton and his associates continued to try to repossess the road but were always embarrassed by a financial stringency so acute that on one occasion one of Stanton's attorneys told him he doubted if Stanton could find two other respectable Alabama lawyers who would trust him for $2.50.¹⁶⁶ The road continued to lose money and in the depression after 1873 Edward King reported that no one seemed to care who owned the road or whether it was operated.¹⁶⁷ The line was eventually redeemed in 1877 when Emile Erlanger and Company of London purchased the road and reorganized it as the Alabama Great Southern Railroad.¹⁶⁸

The Alabama and Chattanooga was only one of ten railroads that participated in the Alabama state aid program. As most of the projected lines were short ones, the proposed new construction totalled only 675 miles, but something over $15,000,000 in railroad bonds were endorsed by the state.¹⁶⁹ State officials failed

---

163. Du Bose, *op. cit.*, pp. 179-181, 188; *Commercial and Financial Chronicle*, February 4, 1871, p. 140; June 17, 1871, p. 753. The receiver found on taking over the road that it would probably require over $500,000 to put the road in good shape. Twenty-four miles of the track in operation was formed of old rails ruined during the war by Sherman.

164. *Commercial and Financial Chronicle*, September 2, 1871, p. 305.

165. *Ibid.*, September 2, 1871, p. 305; August 24, 1872, p. 252. The East Tennessee, Virginia and Georgia Railroad, the Mobile and Ohio, and the Southern Securities Company combine were all reported to be interested in operating the line.

166. Du Bose, *op. cit.*, p. 186.

167. Edward King, *The Great South*, p. 312. King discovered he could not buy a ticket at the depot, that the schedule was completely erratic, and that often conductors ran the trains for what they could make out of them.

168. *Commercial and Financial Chronicle*, August 25, 1877, p. 186; Poor, *Manual of Railroads of the United States for 1885*, p. 962.

169. Cleveland and Powell, *Railroad Promotion*, pp. 221-222; *Commercial and Financial Chronicle*, December 23, 1871, p. 839; December 14,1872, p. 802. Governor Lindsay in December, 1871, listed the total as $15,420,000, but other estimates ran as high as $16,751,000.

CARPETBAGGERS LEND A HAND

to keep complete and exact records of the endorsements for six of the ten companies. In every case the endorsements were carelessly given without thorough inspection of the newly built track, and five of the railroads never finished the mileage for which they received endorsed bonds.[170] With the exception of the Alabama and Chattanooga, the South and North Alabama Railroad had the longest projected line and also received the greatest state aid. Hoping to help the road achieve its objective of joining by rail the northern and southern agricultural regions of the state, the legislature gave the road special aid in December, 1868, and later on March 3, 1870, raised its rate of endorsement from $16,000 to $22,000 per mile.[171] In another special act a week earlier, February 25, 1870, the legislature aided the already constructed Mobile and Montgomery by endorsing $2,500,000 of its bonds. The East Alabama and Cincinnati was a much smaller company with equally big plans. John Stanton, Governor Smith, and two carpetbag state senators, J. J. Hinds and J. L. Pennington, organized the company, built twenty-five miles of road with substandard rails and flimsy trestles, and collected $400,000 in endorsed bonds.[172] The Selma, Marion, and Memphis was another line where the promoters received full endorsement from the state but never completed their road. Their president, the honest and God-fearing General Nathan Bedford Forrest, impoverished himself to help pay the company's debts when the railroad failed.

Alabama granted little additional aid to its railroads after 1870. While Governor Lindsay early in 1871 was extremely critical of his predecessor's railroad activities, the next year he

170. Fleming, *Civil War and Reconstruction in Alabama*, p. 604. The ten roads receiving endorsements were: Alabama and Chattanooga (295 miles, faulty records), East Alabama and Cincinnati (25 miles, never completed), Mobile and Alabama Grand Trunk (50 miles, faulty records), Montgomery and Eufaula (60 miles), Mobile and Montgomery (previously built, faulty records), Savannah and Memphis (40 miles, never completed), Selma and Gulf (40 miles, faulty records, never completed), Selma, Marion, and Memphis (45 miles, faulty records, never completed), New Orleans and Selma (20 miles, never completed), South and North Alabama (100 miles, faulty records).

171. *Ibid.*, pp. 600-601; Du Bose, *op. cit.*, pp. 156-158. In 1871 the road to the north, the Louisville and Nashville, obtained control of the South and North Alabama.

172. Du Bose, *op. cit.*, pp. 165-166; Poor, *Manual of the Railroads of the United States for 1877-1878*, p. 392.

was claiming that the state's rail investments and liens were basically sound and secure.[173] All of this changed with the Panic of 1873 for nearly all of the state's railroads tumbled into the pit of bankruptcy.[174] The state endeavored to exchange straight state bonds for the endorsed railroad bonds at a ratio of one to four, but few railroads took advantage of the offer.[175] The indebtedness of the state was so high, $30,000,000 for all classes of debt, that its credit became seriously impaired.[176] At the same time the appraised value of all railroads in the state declined from $25,943,052 in 1871 to $12,033,763 in 1875.[177] Alabama had built some additional railroads, but the cost had been terrific.

The bulk of the carpetbagger railroad activity occurred in the five states of Virginia, North Carolina, South Carolina, Georgia, and Alabama. The relative absence of railroad carpetbag activity in the five states of Florida, Mississippi, Louisiana, Tennessee, and Kentucky can be explained by one or more of the following: lack of railroads and railroad interest, constitutional limits on the use of state credit, political moderation, or just the absence of carpetbaggers and Reconstruction. With the exception of Kentucky, which naturally never suffered Reconstruction (and partly because of this built new railroads at a record-breaking rate), the four other states built new railroads in the first postwar decade very slowly. Their total new construction was only 726 miles, little more than a sixth of the decade's construction for the ten states.[178]

Of the ten southern states, Florida had the fewest, the weakest, and the poorest railroads in the decade after the Civil War. Limited geographically to the northern third of the state, the railroads in 1865 were bankrupt and minus both equipment and traffic.[179] However, the roads still managed to run trains on a

173. *Commercial and Financial Chronicle*, December 14, 1872, p. 802.
174. James F. Doster, *Alabama's First Railroad Commission* (Tuscaloosa, Alabama, 1949), pp. 8-9.
175. *Commercial and Financial Chronicle*, May 17, 1873, p. 659; December 13, 1873, p. 803.
176. King, *The Great South*, p. 333; Poor, *Manual of the Railroads of the United States for 1877-1878*, p. 940-941.
177. From the State Auditor's Report, Fleming, *op. cit.*, p. 603.
178. Poor, *Manual of the Railroads of the United States for 1877-1878*, p. ix.
179. McGrane, *Foreign Bondholders and American State Debts*, pp. 299-300; C. Wickliffe Yulee, *Senator Yulee of Florida* (n. p., 1917), pp. 33-34.

CARPETBAGGERS LEND A HAND

triweekly-to-weekly schedule.[180] George W. Swepson and Milton S. Littlefield, already past masters of railroad embezzlement in North Carolina, appeared on this scene in the spring of 1869. Using funds obtained from their North Carolina activities, and also a worthless check for $412,400, Swepson bought at auction two bankrupt roads, the Pensacola and Georgia and the Tallahassee.[181] The two lines were combined into the Jacksonville, Pensacola and Mobile Railroad in June, 1869, and the next month a pliant state legislature passed aid bills which eventually netted Swepson and Littlefield $4,000,000 in state bonds.[182] As usual very few of the proceeds were used for legitimate railroad purposes.[183]

In the first postwar decade the railroads of Mississippi built only 120 miles of new line, the slowest proportional increase of any of the southern states.[184] The slow rate of construction was caused partly by the state constitutional provision which prohibited any use of the state credit, thereby precluding any general state railroad aid program. As a result Mississippi suffered no great railroad swindles during the period.[185]

Louisiana was also relatively free of railroad scandal. All early postwar railroad construction occurred in the years 1869 through 1871, the same years that the state legislature passed several railroad aid bills.[186] Aid was voted in the form of state bonds to three railroads, the North Louisiana and Texas, the New Orleans, Mobile, and Chattanooga, and the New Orleans, Mobile, and Texas. As of 1875 only a small portion of the total

---

180. *Commercial and Financial Chronicle*, December 23, 1865, p. 825. On some of the shorter lines horse-drawn cars were used and frequently the driver had to force sleeping alligators or bear cubs off the strap iron track. King, *op. cit.*, pp. 387-388.

181. Brown, *A State Movement in Railroad Development*, pp. 198-199; Herbert and others, *Why the Solid South*, p. 148.

182. *Commercial and Financial Chronicle*, July 10, 1869, p. 47; Cleveland and Powell, *Railroad Promotion*, p. 223.

183. King, *op. cit.*, p. 418.

184. The rate of increase was only 13 per cent against a regional average of 46 per cent. Of the 120 miles of new construction, 92 were built in a single year, 1869.

185. Nordhoff, *Cotton States in the Spring and Summer of 1875*, p. 75; James Wilford Garner, *Reconstruction in Mississippi* (New York, 1901), p. 314.

186. Poor, *Manual of the Railroads of the United States for 1877-1878*, pp. ix, 947.

state debt of $21,872,320 was attributable to postwar railroad assistance.[187]

Tennessee, both before and after the war, had a most generous railroad aid program. In the prewar years it was very successful and only Georgia and Virginia possessed more trackage in 1860.[188] The postwar aid, though expensive, produced fewer results and $13,000,000 of state bonds produced only 334 miles of new track by 1875.[189] One reason the aid built so few roads was the poor credit of the state. The state debt already was so large (in 1869 of the southern states only Virginia had a larger debt) that the railroads were forced to dispose of their new bonds at discounts of from 50 per cent to 70 per cent. Even so, bribery was rampant in the promotion of new bond issues. Wine, women, and new suits of clothes were all used as legislative inducements.[190] Even the good governor, "Parson" William G. Brownlow, was involved in the receipt of a questionable railroad gift of five $1,000 bills.[191] Neither Negroes nor carpetbaggers were conspicuous in the corruption of the railroad aid program.[192] The railroad aid bills all provided that the state could seize any road defaulting on its interest payments and by the fall of 1867 "Parson" Brownlow was threatening seizure of at least a dozen different roads.[193] Many roads were seized and sold by the state, but some roads managed to pay their debts by buying up state bonds at a large discount.[194] The state debt which had stood at $43,000,000 in 1871 had dropped to $23,000,000 by 1876.[195] By the end of the decade the credit of Tennessee had been redeemed.

187. *Ibid.*, p. 947.
188. In 1865 Tennessee had 1,296 miles, Virginia, 1,407, and Georgia, 1,420.
189. *Commercial and Financial Chronicle*, February 8, 1868, p. 168; October 23, 1869, p. 523; Poor, *Manual of the Railroads of the United States for 1877-1878*, p. ix
190. E. Merton Coulter, *William G. Brownlow* (Chapel Hill, 1937), p. 379.
191. *Ibid.*, p. 380.
192. James Welch Patton, *Unionism and Reconstruction in Tennessee, 1860-1869* (Chapel Hill, 1934), p. vii.
193. *De Bow's Review*, November, 1867, p. 466; *Commercial and Financial Chronicle*, October 26, 1867, p. 534.
194. *Commercial and Financial Chronicle*, September 24, 1870, p. 401; September 16, 1871, p. 369; September 30, 1871, p. 429; April 20, 1872, p. 521.
195. *Ibid.*, August 15, 1874, p. 167; Poor, *Manual of the Railroads of the United States for 1877-1878*, p. 957.

CARPETBAGGERS LEND A HAND

That widespread railroad corruption prevailed to a greater or lesser degree in every southern state in the postwar years should not have been unexpected. The whole country, North and South alike, was in the grip of a boom psychology. The standards of both commercial conduct and political morality were low. In addition, the universal railroad fever and the existence of Radical Reconstruction governments in southern states made the result nearly inevitable. Northern businessmen, promoters, and politicians were carrying on activities comparable to those of Littlefield, Kimball, and Stanton. In the border state of Kentucky in 1872 General John C. Breckinridge was involved in the promotion of a railroad contracting company whose business was both highly confidential and, it was hoped, highly profitable.[196]

The typical southern railroad marked for exploitation by the carpetbagger was a new company, more often projected than in operation, poorly built when it was constructed, and even more poorly financed. As compared to the railroads of other states in 1875, the average southern railroad cost the least to build, had the lightest traffic, and paid the lowest dividends.[197] Railroads which were owned and managed by carpetbaggers helped to create these low averages. The typical carpetbag railroad was also poorly financed. The capital structure was normally nearly all borrowed money for the capital stock was generally so full of water it was useful for little else than gifts or bribes. As a result of the high fixed charges due to bond interest, such railroads were the first to feel a decline in traffic or a business depression.

Carpetbaggers achieved permanent control over very few of the railroads they promoted, built, or stole. In nearly every case the return of conservative rule in the Statehouse, the threat of exposure, or exposure itself resulted in the loss of control by the carpetbag group. In the Carolinas, Littlefield and Swepson could not keep their Western North Carolina, nor did John Patterson and his ring long retain control over the Greenville and Columbia. In Georgia, Kimball soon lost his chain of roads, and in Alabama

---

196. John Echols to John C. Breckinridge, December 2, 1872; Breckinridge Papers, Manuscripts Division, Library of Congress.

197. *Commercial and Financial Chronicle*, July 3, 1875, p. 2.

RAILROADS OF THE SOUTH

the Stanton brothers had their Alabama and Chattanooga seized by the state.

During the depression years that followed the Panic of 1873 many of the carpetbag roads succumbed to a more permanent northern control as the bondholders stepped in to maintain their interests. The carpetbag period also resulted in aggravating the disastrous effects of the depression on nearly all southern lines. By the early 1870's practically all of the political railroad spoilsmen had left the South. They left behind a heritage of poorly constructed, financially weak railroads which were not prepared for the financial problems of the future.

CHAPTER 6

SOUTHERN AMBITIONS OF THE PENNSYLVANIA RAILROAD

By 1871 the worst of the railroad carpetbaggism had run its course. In North Carolina, Georgia, and Alabama investigation and exposure were replacing the previous fraud and corruption. But in the same year a northern corporation, the Pennsylvania Railroad, embarked upon a railroad plan so bold and ambitious as to dwarf the schemes of the earlier Stantons, Kimballs, and Littlefields. The earlier operators and promoters had planned and built short roads, none of which served more than a single state. The new combine, put together by the Pennsylvania-dominated Southern Railway Security Company, had fingers of control in a dozen different railways operating two thousand miles of roads in seven southern states.[1] Such a combination was possible because it was supported by the solid financial backing of a successful corporation rather than by the promises and dreams of penniless promoters. The northern financiers that controlled the Southern Railway Security Company were not interested in the fraudulent construction of short, state-aided lines, but rather in the gaining of legitimate profits through expanding the services and revenues of railroads already in operation. The corporate effort, however, like the individual efforts before, failed to achieve any permanent continuous control over any substantial southern

[1]. *Southern Railway Valuation Docket No. 556*, Report of Accounting Section (Richmond and Danville), II, 225, Record Group 134, National Archives; *Commercial and Financial Chronicle*, March 23, 1872, p. 386; Fairfax Harrison, *A History of the Legal Development of the Railroad System of the Southern Railway Company* (Washington, 1901), p. 20.

RAILROADS OF THE SOUTH

rail mileage. The Panic of 1873 proved to be the strongest enemy of combination.

Prime mover behind the combination, the Pennsylvania Railroad had been chartered in April, 1846, as a line to connect Harrisburg and Pittsburgh, a distance of 248 miles. John Edgar Thomson, first as chief engineer, and later as president, pushed the road through and over the mountains to complete the original line by early 1854.[2] Throughout the 1850's the company's mileage continued to expand and in 1861 the road was in excellent shape to share in the huge volume of business created by the war. The volume of traffic increased every year and in 1865 the gross earnings were more than double those of 1861. Profits were high and the company declared annual cash dividends of from 8 per cent to 10 per cent.[3]

In the early postwar years the company continued to expand and to pay good dividends. From 1865 to 1872 the average cash dividends were 9 per cent, and in addition several stock dividends were declared.[4] When the road started seriously to invade the South in 1871-1872, the company was a giant as compared to the railroads of the southern states. The capital structure (capital stock plus funded debt) of the Pennsylvania Railroad stood at over $86,000,000 in 1872, a sum one-quarter as large as the capitalization for all the roads in the ten southern states. The colossus of the North had a valuation larger than that of all twenty-four major roads in the three states of Georgia, South Carolina, and North Carolina.[5] The contrast was even more marked in revenue and business. The gross earnings of the Pennsylvania for 1872 were $22,000,000, or half as much as the total for the seventy principal lines in the southern states. John Edgar Thomson's line had both the size and the financial stature

---

2. Henry V. Poor, *Manual of the Railroads of the United States for 1885* (New York, 1885), p. 267.

3. Henry V. Poor, *Manual of the Railroads of the United States for 1869-1870* (New York, 1869), pp. 242-246.

4. Henry V. Poor, *Manual of the Railroads of the United States for 1873-1874* (New York, 1873), p. 563.

5. *Ibid.*, pp. 566, xlii-xliv. The contrast in motive power and rolling stock was even greater. In 1872 the Pennsylvania possessed 593 locomotives and 18,470 freight cars. The ten southern states could claim only 1,600 locomotives and 20,000 freight cars.

adequate for an adventure in southern railroad empire building.

Without exception, the men who chartered and managed the Southern Railway Security Company were men of substance, well known in northern political and financial circles. Naturally, several of them were high in the administration of the Pennsylvania Railroad, especially John Edgar Thomson and Thomas A. Scott. Thomson began railroad work as a young man in the late 1820's; he was soon a surveyor and later became chief engineer for the Georgia Railroad.[6] He worked in the South for fifteen years before becoming chief engineer of the Pennsylvania Railroad in 1847. His attachment for, and interest in, the South continued and he deeply regretted the disruption of political ties between the two sections of the country in 1861.[7] As the judicious and rather cautious president of the Pennsylvania he laid the foundations of the expanding and prosperous system in his twenty-two-year administration (1852-1874). Thomson was an early and avid advocate of the economies and operational advantages possible through railroad combination.[8]

Thomson secured the election of Thomas A. Scott to the vice presidency of the road in 1860 and the two men made a perfect combination for more than a dozen years. Thomson could be bold but was inclined toward caution; Scott was something of a plunger who needed an occasional hand of restraint. Thomson, a rather reticent man, was not an able negotiator and was not at ease in any public appearance; the younger Scott had a natural charm and fondness for people which qualified him for those chores disliked by his superior.[9] Scott succeeded to the presidency upon Thomson's death in 1874, but was forced to retire because of poor health in 1880. By a quirk of fate the

6. Mary G. Cumming, *Georgia Railroad and Banking Company* (Augusta, Georgia, 1945), pp. 66-67. Thomson is reported to have coined the word Atlanta as the name for the western terminus of the Georgia Railroad.

7. Samuel R. Kamm, *The Civil War Career of Thomas A. Scott* (Philadelphia, 1940), p. 23.

8. Nelson M. Blake, *William Mahone of Virginia, Soldier and Political Insurgent* (Richmond, 1935), p. 76 (hereafter cited as *William Mahone*).

9. Kamm, *op. cit.*, p. 8; George H. Burgess and Miles C. Kennedy, *Centennial History of the Pennsylvania Railroad Company, 1846-1946* (Philadelphia, 1949), p. 347 (hereafter cited as *Pennsylvania Railroad*).

man of enterprising and expansive temperament was president during the belt-tightening years following the Panic of 1873.

Other members of the Southern Security group, such as James Donald Cameron and George Washington Cass, were also in the Pennsylvania family. James Cameron early followed in the grimy economic and political footsteps of his father Simon and in 1863 became president of the Northern Central Railway, a Pennsylvania-controlled line running down to Baltimore.[10] Tom Scott and the two Camerons pretty well dominated Republican politics in the state after the elder Cameron was returned to the senate in 1867.[11] George Washington Cass, nephew of Lewis Cass and a good Pittsburgh Democrat, was also in the Pennsylvania circle since he was president of the Pittsburgh, Fort Wayne and Chicago Railway from 1856 to 1881, long after its 999-year lease to the Pennsylvania Company in 1869. Cass was also a director of the Pennsylvania Railroad during the 1860's.

Other directors of the holding company were not so closely connected with the parent line. Of the two representatives from Baltimore, William Thompson Walters and Benjamin Franklin Newcomer, only the latter was directly interested in the Pennsylvania and was for several years a director, under Cameron, of the Northern Central. Both Walters and Newcomer had large interests in two railroads of North Carolina, the Wilmington and Weldon, and the Wilmington, Columbia, and Augusta. James Roosevelt, of Hyde Park, New York, was one of the original organizers of the Southern Railway Security Company in 1871. Roosevelt served as president of the company in 1872-1873.[12] Henry Bradley Plant was one of the few members of the group who knew something of the South prior to the organization of the holding company.[13] In 1854 the Adams Express Company made

---

10. Cameron left the road's presidency in the middle 1870's as he became more involved in politics.

11. Kamm, *op. cit.*, p. 191.

12. *The Railroad Gazette*, December 14, 1872, p. 535; *Commercial and Financial Chronicle*, June 14, 1873, p. 794. James Roosevelt was the father of an American president who was no friend of monopoly in the 1930's.

13. In 1853 Mrs. Plant's ill health forced the family to move to Florida. The lady's health was greatly improved by a season in the vicinity of Jacksonville. H. B. Plant's interest in the South dates from this early trip. G. H. Smyth, *Life of Henry Bradley Plant* (New York, 1898), p. 46.

him general superintendent for the area south of the Ohio and Potomac rivers. He was still in the South in 1861 and spent the war years in the Confederacy as guardian of the interests and property of the express company.[14] Richard T. Wilson was the only native southerner in the group. A merchant in Loudon, Tennessee, before the war, Wilson served the Confederacy in the Commissary Department, but at the end of the war was the fiscal agent in London for Davis' government. After the war he moved to New York City where he established a banking firm. He continued to be interested in the South, especially in railroad affairs.[15] The managers of the Southern Railway Security Company were all men of prestige, property, and experience.

The Pennsylvania Railroad, in the person of Tom Scott, became interested in extensions southward soon after the Civil War. Obviously the first step was an extension to Washington from Baltimore, since the latter city already could be reached by the Northern Central Railway. The Baltimore and Ohio was the only road connecting the two cities and wishing to maintain its monopoly, it refused to accommodate the Pennsylvania by selling through tickets, checking baggage, or permitting through trains.[16] Scott's answer was to obtain control of the Baltimore and Potomac Railroad, a line chartered by Maryland May 6, 1853, to run from Baltimore to Pope's Creek, a town forty miles south of Washington.[17] The State of Maryland granted the Baltimore and Potomac permission to construct branches not exceeding twenty miles in length. After securing authority from Congress, February 5, 1867, to construct the branch into the Dis-

---

14. *Commercial and Financial Chronicle*, September 12, 1874, p. 270. Plant reorganized that portion of the company under his control in May, 1861, as the Southern Express Company. Plant appointed Rufus B. Bullock (later governor of Georgia) as superintendent of the Eastern Division of the new company. A. L. Stimson, *History of the Express Business* (New York, 1881), p. 160.

15. Blake, *op. cit.*, p. 101.

16. Howard W. Schotter, *The Growth and Development of the Pennsylvania Railroad Company* (Philadelphia, 1927), p. 86 (hereafter cited as *Pennsylvania Railroad*).

17. Henry V. Poor, *Manual of the Railroads of the United States for 1877-1878* (New York, 1877), p. 414.

trict of Columbia, the Pennsylvania started construction in 1868.[18] The nineteen-mile "branch" to the Capitol was completed July 2, 1872, and the "main line" to Pope's Creek January 1, 1873.[19] A tunnel under Baltimore to connect the new Washington line with the Northern Central was completed the same year.[20]

Even before the Baltimore and Potomac reached Washington and the new depot facing "The Mall" just north of the capitol building, Tom Scott had a fresh scheme afoot. With Simon Cameron back in the Senate it was not difficult for Scott to obtain Congressional permission, June 21, 1870, to extend the new line over the Long Bridge to a connection with existing or future railroads in Virginia.[21] John W. Garrett of the B. and O. had tried to gain the same privilege for his road a decade earlier, but without success.[22]

Before venturing further south the Pennsylvania Railroad decided to establish a holding company to secure control of such southern railroads as might be essential to the formation of a through line between principal northern coastal cities and major cities in the South. Early in the year 1871 the Southern Railway Security Company, one of America's earliest holding companies, was organized with George Washington Cass as president.[23] Earlier the same winter several of the Southern Security group, such as Scott, Simon Cameron, H. B. Plant, and William T. Walters, had participated in the lease of the Western and Atlantic from the state of Georgia.[24] Reports were already

18. Schotter, *op. cit.*, pp. 86-87.
19. Poor, *Manual of the Railroads of the United States for 1885*, p. 362.
20. *Ibid.* President John W. Garrett of the rival B. and O. stated that the Pennsylvania-built tunnel under Baltimore was an effort to divert trade "in the interests of rival cities." Burgess and Kennedy, *Pennsylvania Railroad*, pp. 273-274.
21. Schotter, *loc. cit.*
22. Festus P. Summers, *The Baltimore and Ohio in the Civil War* (New York, 1939), p. 40. In 1860 the opposition of Senator Cameron (and the Pennsylvania Railroad) had kept Garrett's proposal from being approved.
23. Burgess and Kennedy, *op. cit.*, pp. 279-281; Harrison, *Legal Development of the Southern Railway*, pp. 93-94.
24. *The Railroad Gazette*, December 31, 1870, p. 320; January 21, 1871, p. 391. At least six of the total twenty-three shares in the lessee company were held by men friendly to the Pennsylvania Railroad.

THE PENNSYLVANIA RAILROAD

current in the South that the Pennsylvania Railroad had big plans for southern railroads.[25]

During the same early months of 1871, Tom Scott and his agents were busy down in Richmond trying to obtain a charter for a road to connect Washington directly with Richmond. Opposition to the charter was intense but by March, 1871, the Governor of Virginia had signed a bill chartering the Washington and Richmond Railroad.[26] Instead of building the newly chartered road, the Pennsylvania shifted to an older line, the Alexandria and Fredericksburg. By the late fall of 1871 they were in control of the latter road and on July 2, 1872, completed the line from Long Bridge to Quantico, Virginia, where it connected with the Richmond, Fredericksburg, and Potomac Railroad.[27] Late in 1871 the Pennsylvania was reported to have gained control of the Richmond, Fredericksburg, and Potomac, but if any efforts were made they were not then successful.[28]

South of Richmond, Tom Scott and his associates in the Southern Railway Security Company gained a controlling interest in two lines during 1871, the Richmond and Petersburg Railroad and the Richmond and Danville Railroad. As of January, 1870, the state of Virginia owned $385,600 of common stock in the Richmond and Petersburg and 24,000 shares (three-fifths of the total issue) of the stock of the Richmond and Danville.[29] The legislature in acts passed in June and July, 1870, and March, 1871, provided for the sale of all the state-owned railroad stock. Even before the final approval of the March legislation permitting the sale of the Richmond and Petersburg stock, it was rumored in the North that the Pennsylvania Rail-

---

25. *Ibid.*, January 21, 1871, p. 391; February 25, 1871, p. 513.
26. *Ibid.*, February 25, 1871, p. 512; March 4, 1871, p. 535; March 18, 1871, p. 583.
27. Henry V. Poor, *Manual of the Railroads of the United States for 1872-1873* (New York, 1872), p. 593; Poor, *Manual of the Railroads of the United States for 1877-1878*, p. 349; *Commercial and Financial Chronicle*, August 24, 1872, p. 252.
28. *Commercial and Financial Chronicle*, December 23, 1871, p. 840; Burgess and Kennedy, *op. cit.*, pp. 273-274; Poor, *Manual of the Railroads of the United States for 1873-1874*, p. 31.
29. *Commercial and Financial Chronicle*, April 13, 1867, p. 456; March 12, 1870, p. 332; Harrison, *loc. cit.*

RAILROADS OF THE SOUTH

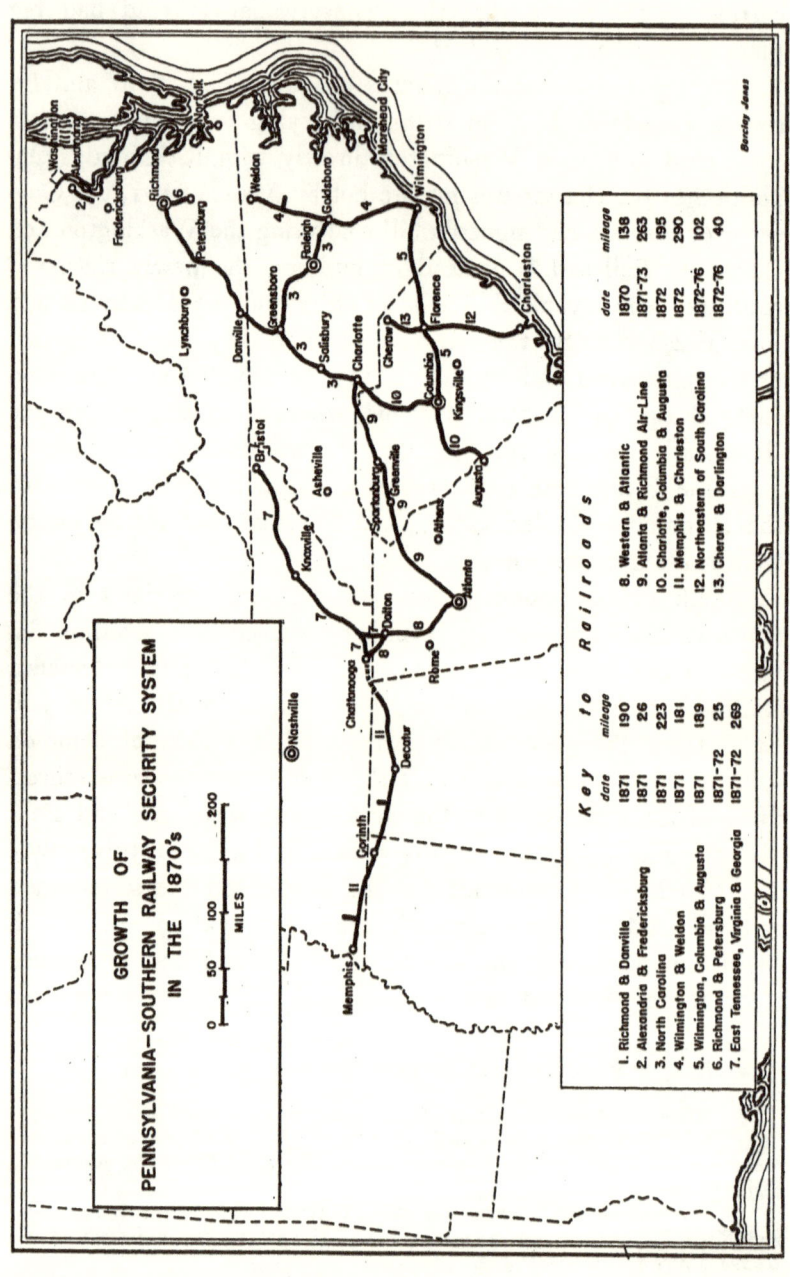

road had purchased the state stock, now valued at $500,000.[30]

The sale was completed and the portfolio of the Southern Railway Security Company soon included 6,871 shares, a controlling majority of the stock issue.[31] The value of the Richmond and Petersburg to the syndicate lay in the fact that the road connected with the Mahone lines at Petersburg, and also was one of the connecting lines running toward Weldon, North Carolina. Through the Walters and Newcomer interests in the Wilmington and Weldon (181 miles) and the Wilmington, Columbia, and Augusta (207 miles), the Southern Railway Security Company already possessed a firm hold on the transportation facilities in the coastal regions in both Carolinas.[32]

But the second road obtained from Virginia, the 190-mile Richmond and Danville Railroad, was the major interest of Tom Scott and his friends in the spring and summer of 1871. Chartered March 9, 1847, opened from Richmond to Danville by May, 1856, and extended forty-eight miles to Greensboro, North Carolina, during the war, the Richmond and Danville was already one of the major lines in the upper South. During the early 1870's it became the very cornerstone of the rail empire built by the Southern Railway Security Company, and was destined to be the parent line of the new direct rail route from Richmond to Atlanta.

The second of the legislative acts authorizing the sale of state-owned railroad stock (the act approved July 11, 1870) permitted the R. and D. to buy the 24,000 state-held shares for $1,200,000 in company bonds, payable in twelve semiannual installments of $100,000 each.[33] The Richmond and Danville officials accepted the opportunity offered and made a first pay-

30. *The Railroad Gazette*, March 25, 1871, p. 609; *Commercial and Financial Chronicle*, April 1, 1871, p. 397. H. H. Ellison, of Richmond, was the representative buying the stock for the Pennsylvania.
31. *Commercial and Financial Chronicle*, March 23, 1872, p. 386.
32. Walters, Newcomer, J. D. Cameron, and D. Willis James, all members of the holding company, served as directors for the two Wilmington roads in the 1870's.
33. Harrison, *Legal Development of the Southern Railway*, pp. 93-94. The state-held stock amounted to three-fifths of the total share capital. *Commercial and Financial Chronicle*, April 13, 1867, p. 456.

ment of $100,000, receiving 2,000 shares from the state.[34] In the spring of 1871 reports were current that the Pennsylvania had obtained control of the R. and D. and some stories said that a scheme concocted in the Governor's mansion resulted in the Pennsylvania's obtaining the road. Tom Scott was alleged to have given the Governor's brother, James Walker, 2,000 shares of stock for his services.[35] Formal action was taken May 5, 1871, when the Richmond and Danville entered into a contract with Tom Scott, as trustee for the Southern Railway Security Company. Scott agreed to furnish the necessary state bonds to purchase Virginia's entire holding, and the R. and D. agreed that the stock thus redeemed should be issued to Scott. The eleven remaining payments were anticipated and Scott effected a final settlement August 31, 1871, receiving for his group the 24,000 shares of stock.[36]

A fairly intense opposition tried to stem this growing Pennsylvania encroachment upon the transportation system of Virginia. Some of the opposition was by private individuals, but most of it came from rival corporations, especially the Baltimore and Ohio, and William Mahone's Atlantic, Mississippi, and Ohio. The Pennsylvania-Baltimore and Ohio rivalry was of longer standing for the two roads had been bitter competitors since before the Civil War. Seeking a north-south line to connect his B. and O. in Washington with the southern rail network, President Garrett started in March, 1866, to buy up stock in the Orange, Alexandria, and Manassas Railroad.[37] In September, 1871, Garrett persuaded the officials of the 270-mile Orange, Alexandria, and Manassas to let the B. and O. advance funds necessary for the purchase of the state-held stock and the next year he was able to announce that the B. and O. controlled the

---

34. Harrison, *loc. cit.*
35. *The Railroad Gazette*, March 18, 1871, p. 583; Blake, *William Mahone*, p. 120.
36. Harrison, *loc. cit.*; *Southern Railway Valuation Docket No. 556*, Report of Accounting Section (Richmond and Danville), II, 225, Record Group 134, National Archives; Stuart Daggett, *Railroad Reorganization* (Cambridge, Mass., 1908), pp. 146-147.
37. Edward Hungerford, *The Story of the Baltimore and Ohio Railroad, 1827-1927* (New York, 1928), II, 112-113.

Virginia road.[38] Garrett's control of a road to Lynchburg and Harrisonburg, Virginia, was of small value, however, for he still lacked connections with roads further south in the Carolinas. Before he could complete these connections, the lines further south had been gobbled up by Tom Scott.

William Mahone's opposition to Tom Scott was somewhat more effective, and certainly more appealing, since he was a Virginian fighting the good fight for a local railroad, the Atlantic, Mississippi, and Ohio. Scott's two roads running south from Richmond, the Richmond and Danville and the Richmond and Petersburg, both intersected Mahone's line (at Burkeville and Petersburg) and tended to divert traffic from the Mahone road to northern cities. The threat of such a diversion of traffic aroused the people of Norfolk, who held mass meetings to protest the loss of trade for their terminal and port.[39]

During the spring of 1871, when the Pennsylvania was negotiating for the purchase of two roads and gaining a charter for a third, the opposition of Mahone was so bitter that on one occasion he came to blows in the streets of Richmond with John M. Lyon, attorney for the interests favoring the Pennsylvania.[40] Convinced that the Pennsylvania combine presented a greater threat to Virginia railroads than either Garrett's B. and O. or C. P. Huntington's Chesapeake and Ohio, Mahone took his fight into politics and endeavored to defeat any candidate who favored the "Bucktails" as the Pennsylvania interests were labelled. In line with this policy he circulated throughout the state hundreds of copies of the *Bucktail Swindle*, an exposé of the frauds connected with the sale of the Richmond and Danville stock.[41] The Pennsylvania retaliated with a threat to build a competing $10,-000,000 line west from Norfolk, the Norfolk and Great Western.[42] Despite Mahone's insistence that a steadfast Virginia had

38. *Ibid.*; Harrison, *op. cit.*, pp. 475-476; Blake, *William Mahone*, p. 120; Poor, *Manual of the Railroads of the United States for 1869-1870*, p. 299.
39. *The Railroad Gazette*, February 25, 1871, p. 513. Norfolk was the eastern terminal for the Mahone line.
40. *Ibid.*, April 1, 1871, p. 10. During the course of this quarrel General Mahone's pistol was discharged, without any reported damage, however.
41. Blake, *op. cit.*, pp. 123, 139.
42. *Ibid.*, pp. 122-123. On a later occasion, however, there were reports that the Pennsylvania had agreed to endorse an issue of Atlantic, Mississippi,

RAILROADS OF THE SOUTH

little to fear from Scott's "infernal designs," the total effect of his opposition was no more availing than that of the Baltimore and Ohio.[43]

East of the mountains the chief objective of the Southern Railway Security Company was to forge together a through line from Richmond to Atlanta. Having gained control of the Richmond and Danville by the end of August, 1871, the next step was to have the R. and D. obtain a working control of the North Carolina, specifically that portion running from Greensboro to Charlotte. This road was chartered early in 1849. The state of North Carolina subscribed to three-fourths of the $4,000,000 capital stock and pushed the 223-mile road to completion by 1852.[44] It was part of the state's east-west system of railroads and ran in a flat horseshoe curve from Goldsboro via Raleigh, Greensboro, and Salisbury to Charlotte. Its normal east-west flow of traffic had been disturbed during the Civil War when the transportation requirements of Virginia and Richmond necessitated the building of the Piedmont Railroad from Danville to Greensboro. The Richmond and Danville secured control of the Piedmont even before its completion in 1864.[45]

Despite relative prosperity in the early years after the war, the political management of the North Carolina Railroad (the Governor appointed eight of the twelve directors) made the future of the company unstable. In 1869 the directors rejected the offer of the Raleigh and Gaston to lease the North Carolina for $240,000 annually. A little later the stockholders rebuffed President William A. Smith's suggestion that the North Carolina

---

and Ohio Railroad bonds, perhaps looking towards better combined service between Mahone's line and the Pennsylvania-controlled East Tennessee, Virginia, and Georgia. The two roads connected at Bristol. *Commercial and Financial Chronicle*, January 6, 1872, p. 20.

43. William Mahone to N. B. Meade, March 18, 1872, in Blake, *op. cit.*, p. 123. Mahone's own road was soon in financial difficulties when it failed to pay interest falling due January 1, 1874. Henry V. Poor, *Manual of the Railroads of the United States for 1875-1876* (New York, 1875), p. 321.

44. Henry V. Poor, *Manual of the Railroads of the United States for 1877-1878* (New York, 1877), p. 358. *Commercial and Financial Chronicle*, December 13, 1873, p. 803.

45. Cecil Kenneth Brown, *A State Movement in Railroad Development: The Story of North Carolina's First Effort to Establish an East and West Trunk Line* (Chapel Hill, N. C., 1928), p. 165.

THE PENNSYLVANIA RAILROAD

should try to buy the road to the south, the Charlotte, Columbia, and Augusta.[46] Even before the Pennsylvania acquired control of the Richmond and Danville, the latter road was looking with envious eyes upon that portion of the North Carolina running from Greensboro to Charlotte. The directors of the North Carolina were well aware that if they did not deal with the R. and D., the latter road might steal their traffic by connecting Greensboro and Charlotte with a parallel road.[47]

The issue was joined in the summer of 1871. Control over the North Carolina was complicated in July by the existence of two rival groups of state-selected directors. Both Republican Governor Todd R. Caldwell and the Democratic legislature had selected eight men to take office at the annual stockholders meeting scheduled for July 13, 1871, at Greensboro.[48] Both new groups of appointees were cautious to act, fearing court injunctions. Since the suggestion to have no annual meeting appealed to some large stockholders, the meeting adjourned for lack of a quorum. During the next two months neither group tried to take office and the old board continued to manage the road. The Richmond and Danville employed former Governor Thomas Bragg to press their case with the old board during the interval. In a secret night meeting at Company Shops (a few miles east of Greensboro), September 11, 1871, nine of the old board met and unanimously agreed to lease the entire road to the Richmond and Danville for thirty years for an annual rental of $260,000.[49] This coup occurred only twelve days after the Pennsylvania had formally taken over the Richmond and Danville. At Charlotte the newly controlled line not only connected with the Atlanta and Richmond Air-Line (then being built), but also with the Charlotte,

---

46. Henry V. Poor, *Manual of the Railroads of the United States for 1872-1873* (New York, 1872), p. 183; Brown, *op. cit.*, pp. 72-80, 170-173.

47. Brown, *op. cit.*, p. 168. The Atlantic, Tennessee, and Ohio and the Dan River and Coalfield when completed would serve as a new line between the two cities.

48. *Ibid.*, pp. 174-177. It was generally understood that Caldwell's Republicans favored a lease to the R. and D., while the Democrats opposed it.

49. *Commercial and Financial Chronicle*, September 23, 1871, p. 402; Poor, *Manual of the Railroads of the United States for 1872-1873*, p. 182; Brown, *op. cit.*, pp. 174-181. The rental of $260,000 was sufficient to pay bond interest, sinking fund charges, and an annual dividend of 6 per cent on the capital stock.

Columbia and Augusta.⁵⁰ At the eastern terminal of Goldsboro it connected with the Wilmington and Weldon, already controlled by the Southern Railway Security Company.

Shortly after gaining the lease, the Richmond and Danville officials announced their intention of broadening the gauge of the North Carolina Railroad from the 4 feet 8½ inches typical of many North Carolina roads to the five-foot gauge used on the R. and D. and most other southern lines. This change was provided for in the lease, but court injunctions and a hostile legislature delayed the change until 1875 when the North Carolina Supreme Court upheld the lessee company.⁵¹ During several years in the middle 1870's the traffic on the leased line was insufficient to meet the annual rental, but the R. and D. never seriously contemplated giving up the lease.⁵²

South of Charlotte (the southern terminal of the North Carolina Railroad) the Southern Railway Security Company was interested in two railroads. Running southward, the recently reorganized Charlotte, Columbia and Augusta Railroad connected with the Wilmington, Columbia and Augusta. The second road, the projected Atlanta and Richmond Air-Line Railroad, was the more important.

At the end of the Civil War, rail service between Charlotte and Atlanta, even when the roads had been thoroughly repaired, was something less than adequate. Nearly all the railroads in the region ran toward the coast, having been built to serve Wilmington, Charleston, or Savannah. Even before the appearance of the Southern Security Company in the South, the Richmond and Danville was planning, as an extension southward, the air line route between the two cities.⁵³ By 1869 the Carolinas and

---

50. Poor, *Manual of the Railroads of the United States for 1872-1873*, pp. 427, 574.

51. Brown, *loc. cit.* The final action of those opposing the change in gauge was the passage of a state law forbidding the change under penalty of a $50 per mile per day fine. The court held the law impaired the obligation of the original contract. *Commercial and Financial Chronicle*, March 13, 1875, p. 267.

52. Poor, *Manual of the Railroads of the United States for 1877-1878*, p. 358; *The Railroad Gazette*, August 16, 1873, p. 335. The Southern Railway, successor to the Richmond and Danville, renewed the lease for ninety-nine years at a slightly higher rental in 1896.

53. *The Railroad Gazette*, July 23, 1870, p. 391.

Georgia had granted the necessary charters and A. S. Buford, also president of the Richmond and Danville, had been elected as the first president.[54] The officials of the company started construction at once and the first fifty-three miles out of Atlanta were in operation in 1871. However, the bulk of the 265-mile line was not finished and ready for traffic until the spring and summer of 1873.[55]

The Richmond and Danville supplied most of the financing of the construction of the new line, but the Southern Railway Security Company was indirectly responsible as well.[56] Financially embarrassed by the Panic of 1873, the holding company was soon disposing of its interest in the Air-Line to the Pennsylvania.[57] The Air-Line itself was also in financial difficulty, facing as it had to a major business depression within the first year after its completion. The road was placed in the hands of a receiver in November, 1874, and the bondholders purchased it at a foreclosure sale December 5, 1876.[58] Earlier the Pennsylvania Railroad had relieved the Richmond and Danville of the bulk of its liabilities incurred on account of the Air-Line.[59] Financially, the early history of the new road was an unhappy story for all concerned. Its construction, however, completed a portion of one of the major trunk lines in the South.

The Charlotte, Columbia, and Augusta Railroad also started from Charlotte, running via the capital of South Carolina to Augusta, Georgia. The road was the result of a consolidation July 8, 1869, of the Charlotte and South Carolina with the

---

54. Poor, *Manual of the Railroads of the United States for 1869-1870*, p. 264.

55. *Commercial and Financial Chronicle*, September 13, 1873, p. 355; Henry V. Poor, *Manual of the Railroads of the United States for 1874-1875* (New York, 1874), p. 37. The new Piedmont Air-Line route was scheduled to send passengers from New York to New Orleans in sixty-six hours without any change of cars.

56. The state of Georgia had endorsed $240,000 of bonds for the new road but these were returned to the state when the Atlanta and Richmond Air-Line discovered it could negotiate its own securities to better advantage.

57. *Commercial and Financial Chronicle*, January 3, 1874, p. 14. The reported amount exchanging hands was $1,825,000.

58. Poor, *Manual of the Railroads of the United States for 1885*, p. 394. The company was reorganized as the Atlanta and Charlotte Air-Line Railway in February, 1877.

59. *The Railroad Gazette*, January 9, 1875, p. 10; *Commercial and Financial Chronicle*, June 12, 1875, p. 568; February 19, 1876, p. 180.

Columbia and Augusta.[60] The Southern Railway Security Company started to buy up control of the road at the same time that they were building the Atlanta and Richmond Air-Line. By early 1872 they held 13,024 shares, a majority of the share capital in the company and had both W. T. Walters and B. F. Newcomer on the Board of Directors.[61] The road remained fairly prosperous during the 1870's and, unlike so many southern lines, escaped receivership. Nevertheless, the Southern Railway Security Company decided upon a general policy of retrenchment and offered all 13,024 shares for sale (along with many other securities) late in the year 1876.[62] The resulting shift in control, however, was not great since the Richmond and Danville obtained control in the fall of 1878.[63]

West of the mountains, the East Tennessee, Virginia, and Georgia Railroad was the major interest of the Pennsylvania group. Organized November 26, 1869, as a consolidation of two earlier roads, this line from Chattanooga to Bristol, Tennessee, had been for a dozen years Tennessee's only direct route to Virginia and other states to the north.[64] Running northeastward out of Knoxville, the East Tennessee and Virginia had been chartered in 1849 and was opened to Bristol in June, 1855. A year later the officials of the East Tennessee and Georgia opened their line from Knoxville to Dalton, Georgia.[65] Shortly after the war the roads began to operate as a unit and by the fall of 1868 they had the same president, Colonel Thomas H. Callaway, resident of Knoxville and one of the early promoters of the roads.[66]

60. *Commercial and Financial Chronicle*, July 24, 1869, p. 112; Poor, *Manual of the Railroads of the United States for 1872-1873*, p. 423. Even before the consolidation the two roads had had the same president, William Johnston of Charlotte.
61. *Commercial and Financial Chronicle*, March 23, 1872, p. 386; Poor, *Manual of the Railroads of the United States for 1872-1873*, p. 424.
62. *The Railroad Gazette*, December 8, 1876, p. 540; *Commercial and Financial Chronicle*, December 9, 1876, p. 576.
63. *Commercial and Financial Chronicle*, September 14, 1878, p. 280; October 19, 1878, p. 409; March 13, 1880, p. 271.
64. Poor, *Manual of the Railroads of the United States for 1877-1878*, p. 227.
65. The twenty-nine mile extension from Cleveland, Tennessee, to Chattanooga was also completed and added to the system prior to the Civil War.
66. *Commercial and Financial Chronicle*, September 10, 1870, p. 338. Poor, *Manual of the Railroads of the United States for 1869-1870*, pp. 40, 249.

THE PENNSYLVANIA RAILROAD

A little earlier, Richard T. Wilson and Charles M. McGhee had begun to buy up stock in both companies. Their task was made easier when the Tennessee Legislature in May, 1866, provided for the distribution among various turnpike companies of the state's 4,225 shares of East Tennessee and Georgia stock. Wilson and McGhee proceeded at once to buy up nearly all of this state stock.[67] The stockholders of the East Tennessee and Virginia, at about the same time, decided to change the provision in their original charter prohibiting any single stockholder from casting more than five hundred votes at any meeting. With this change large holdings became more profitable and McGhee and Wilson expanded in the second company also.[68] Both men were on the new board of directors of the consolidated company, but Thomas Callaway remained as president until his death August 29, 1870.[69] Wilson succeeded him as president and was reelected throughout the 1870's.[70]

At the same time that Wilson was learning the duties of a railroad president, Tom Scott, Simon Cameron, and W. T. Walters were becoming interested in the lease of the Georgia-owned Western and Atlantic. Since both roads connected at Chattanooga, the Pennsylvania people naturally thought of expanding their interests to the East Tennessee road and were reported as negotiating in that direction in January, 1871.[71] The Pennsylvania held 10,000 shares (a majority control) of the East Tennessee, Virginia, and Georgia Railroad by November, 1871, and transferred the bulk of their holdings to the Southern Railway Security Company during the next few months.[72] Wilson remained as president under the Pennsylvania control and soon became a director of the Southern Railroad Security Company.[73]

William Mahone, president of the connecting road to the east,

---

67. Harrison, *Legal Development of the Southern Railway*, pp. 664-665. The 4,225 shares constituted about a third of the total stock issue.
68. *Ibid.*
69. *Commercial and Financial Chronicle*, December 18, 1869, p. 792; September 10, 1870, p. 338.
70. *Ibid.*, September 24, 1870, p. 401.
71. *The Railroad Gazette*, January 21, 1871, p. 391.
72. *Commercial and Financial Chronicle*, November 4, 1871, p. 604; March 23, 1872, p. 386.
73. *The Railroad Gazette*, June 14, 1873, p. 244.

and other opponents of Wilson claimed that Wilson, McGhee, and Joseph Jaques (vice president of the company) had made extensive personal profits by selling the 10,000 shares of stock to the Pennsylvania for par, after buying them up at only thirty to sixty cents on the dollar.[74] Mahone carried his fight to the annual stockholders meeting in Knoxville early in November, 1872, but his efforts to unseat the trio were decisively defeated by a share vote of 15,346 to 599.[75] Wilson continued to control the company throughout the 1870's, but the interest of the Pennsylvania in the East Tennessee, Virginia and Georgia lagged after the Panic of 1873 and especially after the critical report of the Stockholders Investigation Committee in 1874.[76]

Since the Memphis and Charleston Railroad was one of the most important roads connecting with the East Tennessee line at Chattanooga, Tom Scott also became interested in this line.[77] The Pennsylvania officials started to negotiate with the Memphis and Charleston in the winter of 1871-1872 and by March 5, 1872, had reached an agreement to have the Southern Railway Security Company lease the road for ninety-nine years.[78] The holding company took possession of the road July 1, 1872, and guaranteed the company to pay all bond interest plus dividends of 3 per cent for the first five years and 6 per cent thereafter.[79] Joseph Jaques, already vice president and superintendent of the East Tennessee road, became general manager of the Memphis and Charleston. The lease was never a profitable one and the lessee company had difficulty in making the required 3 per cent dividend even before

---

74. *Commercial and Financial Chronicle*, November 4, 1871, p. 604; *The Railroad Gazette*, November 23, 1872, p. 506.

75. *The Railroad Gazette*, November 23, 1872, p. 506; *Commercial and Financial Chronicle*, November 16, 1872, p. 659; November 23, 1872, p. 692. Mahone was hoping, had he succeeded in defeating the Wilson group, to manage the road himself in the interests of his own Atlantic, Mississippi, and Ohio Railroad.

76. Daggett, *Railroad Reorganization*, pp. 147-148; Burgess and Kennedy, *Pennsylvania Railroad*, pp. 296-297; *The Railroad Gazette*, September 26, 1874, p. 376.

77. The Memphis and Charleston road ran 270 miles from Memphis to Stevenson, Alabama. From Stevenson to Chattanooga it had running rights over the tracks of the Nashville and Chattanooga.

78. *Commercial and Financial Chronicle*, December 16, 1871, p. 808; September 14, 1872, p. 353.

79. Poor, *Manual of the Railroads of the United States for 1873-1874*, p. 134.

the Panic of 1873. In line with its policy of retrenchment in 1874, the Southern Security Company was glad to cancel the lease April 30, 1874, when the company was returned to its owners.[80] The management of the company remained sympathetic to the Pennsylvania group, however, as R. T. Wilson was elected president of the road in October, 1874.

In addition to the eleven roads reviewed above which the Pennsylvania and its holding company controlled, there were also several minor roads either within the rail empire, or at least candidates for inclusion. Two of the smaller roads which it controlled, the Northeastern of South Carolina and the Cheraw and Darlington, together formed a 142-mile route from Charleston north to Cheraw.[81] From 1872 to 1876 the Southern Security Company held large blocks of stock in each company and elected several of their own group to directorships of the two short lines.[82] During the early 1870's the holding company also dabbled in the affairs of several other railroads. In 1871 and 1872 it was reported to be interested in helping John Stanton salvage his bankrupt Alabama and Chattanooga.[83] At the same time two vehicles of the Southern Railway Security Company, the Richmond and Danville and the East Tennessee, Virginia, and Georgia, were both interested in helping to revitalize the Western North Carolina Railroad, the road that Littlefield and Swepson had so thoroughly pillaged.[84] The Pennsylvania Railroad also was interested in the Mississippi Central Railroad, having invested $1,300,000 in the bonds of that company.[85] This investment did not bring with it control of the road.

80. *Commercial and Financial Chronicle*, September 20, 1873, p. 380; March 21, 1874, p. 297; April 11, 1874, p. 376; May 2, 1874, p. 448; Harrison, *Legal Development of the Southern Railway*, p. 751; Poor, *Manual of the Railroads of the United States for 1877-1878*, p. 236.

81. The roads met at Florence, South Carolina, where they both connected with the Walters and Newcomer road, the Wilmington, Columbia, and Augusta.

82. *Commercial and Financial Chronicle*, March 23, 1872, p. 386; *The Railroad Gazette*, December 8, 1876, p. 540; Poor, *Manual of the Railroads of the United States for 1874-1875*, pp. 118, 132.

83. *Commercial and Financial Chronicle*, September 2, 1871, p. 305; August 24, 1872, p. 252; *The Railroad Gazette*, September 2, 1872, p. 398.

84. Brown, *A State Movement in Railroad Development*, pp. 210-213; Harrison, *op. cit.*, pp. 269-270; *Commercial and Financial Chronicle*, August 24, 1872, p. 252.

85. Schotter, *Pennsylvania Railroad*, p. 152.

RAILROADS OF THE SOUTH

The thirteen roads controlled by the Pennsylvania-Southern Security group totalled over 2,100 miles in total length and formed a network serving the South with three trunk lines: (1) a coastal route from Washington to Wilmington and Charleston, (2) a Piedmont route from Richmond to Atlanta and Augusta, and (3) a western route from Bristol to Atlanta and Memphis. The thirteen roads as of 1872 had the following mileage:

Alexandria and Fredericksburg	26 miles
Richmond and Petersburg	25 miles
Richmond and Danville	190 miles
Wilmington and Weldon	181 miles
Wilmington, Columbia, and Augusta	189 miles
Cheraw and Darlington	40 miles
Northeastern of South Carolina	102 miles
North Carolina	223 miles
Charlotte, Columbia, and Augusta	195 miles
Atlanta and Richmond Air-Line	263 miles
Western and Atlantic	138 miles
East Tennessee, Virginia and Georgia	269 miles
Memphis and Charleston	290 miles
Total	2,131 miles

With such a vast transportation network, Tom Scott was soon accused of creating a monopoly and in Tennessee the courts referred to the corporation simply as "Tom Scott."[86] But southerners also noted a new economy in Scott's railroad management and had to admit that the roads were probably run more efficiently under the combination.[87] In spite of efficient and eco-

86. *Commercial and Financial Chronicle*, September 23, 1871, p. 402; Harrison, *op. cit.*, p. 751.

87. *Commercial and Financial Chronicle*, August 24, 1872, p. 252. Tom Scott was also interested in a railroad empire in the Southwest during the 1870's. After a brief connection with the Union Pacific, Scott became president of the Texas and Pacific in February, 1872. This newly organized line hoped to complete a road from northeastern Texas via El Paso to San Diego. Projected branches were also intended to reach the Mississippi River cities of Memphis, Vicksburg and New Orleans. With the aid of his associate, General Grenville M. Dodge, Scott hoped to persuade Congress to grant a generous subsidy to his company. During the winter months of 1876-1877 Scott and Dodge worked vigorously with Republican leaders in Washington to work out a political compromise which would place Rutherford B. Hayes in the White House, win support for Hayes from among southern conservative elements, and assure Con-

THE PENNSYLVANIA RAILROAD

nomical management the roads were not prosperous. The Richmond and Danville paid no dividends, the Wilmington roads paid nothing, and the North Carolina and Memphis and Charleston roads earned barely enough to meet the guaranteed rentals.[88] After the Panic of 1873 rail business and gross earnings dropped at a dangerous rate, especially for some of the larger roads in the combination.[89]

Failing to see any profit in the combination, the Pennsylvania Railroad Stockholders Investigating Committee in 1874 was quite critical of the whole southward expansion program.[90] The Southern Railway Security Company held a special meeting in New York City, November 21, 1873, in order to consider a general policy of retrenchment.[91] Feeling the pressure, James Roosevelt resigned as president of the company the same month, to be replaced by the relatively unknown William Hugbart.[92] In 1874 the holding company surrendered its lease of the Memphis and Charleston and by late 1876 it was putting up for sale the bulk of its securities except for the Richmond and Danville.[93] Earlier the Pennsylvania Railroad in its annual report for 1873 had charged off its entire investment in the southern expansion to

---

gressional passage of the Texas and Pacific subsidy bill. Hayes gained the White House, enjoying for a short time the benefits of a coalition between southern conservatives and northern Republicans, but Scott failed to obtain Congressional approval for his subsidy program. He finally gave up in 1880, selling his holdings in the Texas and Pacific to Jay Gould. See C. Vann Woodward, *Reunion and Reaction* (Boston, 1951).

88. Daggett, *Railroad Reorganization*, pp. 147-148.

89. For the five roads, the Richmond and Danville, the Wilmington and Weldon, the Wilmington, Columbia and Augusta, the East Tennessee, Virginia and Georgia, and the Memphis and Charleston, the aggregate gross earnings declined from $5,336,000 in 1872-1873 to $4,164,000 in 1875-1876, a drop of 22 per cent. Poor, *Manual of the Railroads of the United States for 1877-1878*, pp. 227, 231, 233, 236, 354.

90. *The Railroad Gazette*, September 26, 1874, p. 376; Burgess and Kennedy, *Pennsylvania Railroad*, pp. 296-297.

91. *The Railroad Gazette*, November 22, 1873, p. 475. The directors of the holding company at this time were: James Roosevelt, Thomas Scott, M. K. Jesup, H. B. Plant, R. T. Wilson, G. W. Cass, D. Willis James, B. F. Newcomer, W. T. Walters, and J. D. Cameron. *Commercial and Financial Chronicle*, June 14, 1873, p. 794.

92. *The Railroad Gazette*, November 22, 1873, p. 474.

93. Daggett, *loc. cit.*; *The Railroad Gazette*, December 8, 1876, p. 540; *Commercial and Financial Chronicle*, December 9, 1876, p. 576.

profit and loss.[94] The Pennsylvania officials felt that all investments in the South were making a poor showing because of the financial exhaustion and slow recuperation in that region. The Pennsylvania retained its control of the Richmond and Danville (the Southern Security Company having given it up) until 1880 when the shares were sold to the Clyde Syndicate.[95] Several of the members of the new Clyde Syndicate, such as Walters, Newcomer, Plant, and Wilson, had also been in the Southern Railway Security Company.

Several factors were responsible for the collapse of the Southern Railway Security Company and for the decision of the Pennsylvania Railroad to write off or dispose of its southern rail investments. The profits anticipated for the combination never materialized, even in the relatively prosperous early 1870's. The Panic of 1873 for many lines changed the problem of absent profits into very real financial losses. Finally the Pennsylvania came to realize that it already possessed an adequate stage for a successful rail expansion program in the trunk-line territory north of the Potomac and Ohio rivers. The Pennsylvania officials, however, did not consider their southern adventure a complete loss. The board of directors may well have thought their money well spent for it did result in blocking the ambitions of the rival Baltimore and Ohio.[96]

The southern expansion of the Pennsylvania Railroad also had other significant results. While the original combination efforts of this northern corporation were not destined to succeed, later efforts by other groups were successful. Getting the urge from its own experience in the combination, the East Tennessee, Virginia, and Georgia Railroad started to expand on its own in the early 1880's. It brought half a dozen small lines within its orbit and by 1884 had a system embracing over 1,100 miles.[97] The Richmond and Danville had started a junior-sized rail em-

---

94. *The Railroad Gazette*, March 14, 1874, p. 91. The company compared the action taken to that taken with earlier investments after the Panic of 1857.

95. Harrison, *Legal Development of the Southern Railway*, p. 246; *Commercial and Financial Chronicle*, June 19, 1880, p. 651.

96. Burgess and Kennedy, *op. cit.*, pp. 279-281.

97. Harrison, *op. cit.*, pp. ix-x; Poor, *Manual of the Railroads of the United States for 1885*, pp. 479-481.

THE PENNSYLVANIA RAILROAD

pire even while under the control of the Southern Railway Security Company. After 1880 under the guidance of the Clyde Syndicate and later using the Richmond and West Point Terminal Railway and Warehouse Company, the R. and D. expanded with almost explosive speed. By 1885 its total controlled system amounted to over 2,600 miles.[98] The two North Carolina railroads, the Wilmington and Weldon and the Wilmington, Columbia, and Augusta, also were soon to furnish the nucleus of the Atlantic Coast Line. Thus, while one of America's first holding companies had failed, it had given a real impetus to several later extensions and combinations. The future of southern railroads lay in the direction of consolidation.

98. Poor, *Manual of the Railroads of the United States for 1885*, pp. 390-391.

CHAPTER 7

A STORY OF RECEIVERSHIP

THE DECADE of the 1870's was a period of rapid but uneven railroad construction and expansion for the nation. New construction early in the decade was so fast that the new mileage added to the nation's system in the three years 1870, 1871, and 1872 more than equalled the total network of the nation fifteen years before.[1] The record year for the decade was 1871, when the railroads added 7,670 new miles of iron, an increase of nearly 15 per cent for a single year.[2] The rate of growth and new construction had been phenomenal ever since the Civil War. In the years from 1865 to 1873 the nation's rail system had doubled, increasing from 35,085 miles to 70,784 miles. After 1873 the new construction lagged and during the rest of the decade only a single year, 1879, produced much over a third of 1871's record construction. The total new construction from 1873 to January 1, 1880, was only 16,195 miles, an increase of less than 25 per cent.[3]

The Panic of 1873 was the prime factor responsible for this marked drop in railroad construction. Financial trouble came quickly to many American railroads following the failure of Jay Cooke and Company in September, 1873. Some thirty-four railroads had defaulted on their bond interest even before the Panic was well started and by November, fifty-five railroads represent-

---

[1] Henry V. Poor, *Manual of the Railroads of the United States for 1877-1878* (New York, 1877), p. viii. The new mileage in 1870 was 5,690 miles; 1871, 7,670 miles; and 1872, 6,167 miles, a total of 19,527. The entire country possessed but 18,374 miles in 1855.

[2] *Ibid.* This record for new construction was surpassed only four times in succeeding years, 1881, 1882, 1886, and 1887.

[3] Henry V. Poor, *Manual of the Railroads of the United States for 1885* (New York, 1885), p. xv.

A STORY OF RECEIVERSHIP

ing an eighth of the entire railroad debt were in default.[4] When the Panic was only a year old, 108 companies were in default on their bond interest with the $497,000,000 of bonds affected representing a quarter of the entire railroad debt.[5] The list of defaulting roads grew each year and by 1876, 216 railroads were in default on their bond interest.[6] During the same years total gross earnings fell off even though the rail network was still slowly expanding. While some railroads managed to continue their normal dividend payments, the bulk of the lines were unable to do so and the dividend rate per operated mile of road declined by over a quarter between 1871 and 1876.[7] Under such conditions a marked curtailment of new railroad construction was but natural.

The railroads of the ten southern states at the beginning of the Panic were not in a financially strong position. In the southern states the funded or bonded debt represented about three-fifths of the total capital structure, whereas in the rest of the nation the ratio was nearly half and half. While the ten states possessed nearly a fifth of the nation's total mileage, in 1874-1875 they had only a tenth of the nation's total gross earnings. Their average operating ratio (operating expenses to gross earnings) was 66.9 per cent which was several points higher than the national average. The net earnings for the region were only 9 per cent of the national total and the ratio of earnings to total valuation was below the national average. Railroads in the ten states in 1874 paid total dividends of only $1,068,455, or less than 2 per cent of the total for the United States. Of the two hundred

4. *Commercial and Financial Chronicle*, November 15, 1873, pp. 647-648; October 10, 1874, pp. 363-366.

5. *The Railroad Gazette*, October 24, 1874, p. 410; *Commercial and Financial Chronicle*, October 10, 1874, pp. 363-366. Very few of these defaulting railroads were immediately threatened with foreclosure as their officials managed in most cases to arrange for a delay in paying the coupons due. *The Railroad Gazette*, May 2, 1874, p. 162.

6. Poor, *Manual of the Railroads of the United States for 1877-1878*, pp. x-xxix.

7. *Ibid.*, p. i. The average dividend rate per mile of operated line is given below:
1871, $1,278; 1872, $1,130; 1873, $1,017; 1874, $972; 1875, $1,046; 1876, $932.

dividend paying roads, only fourteen were in the South. Clearly the southern lines were not prepared for a depression.[8]

As a result, railroads in the southern states suffered correspondingly more in the Panic of 1873 than did the roads of the North. By November, 1873, a dozen southern lines with 2,000 miles of road had failed to pay bond interest when due.[9] Within another year an additional 10 lines were in default and by 1876 over 4,000 miles of road were in the possession of the courts due to foreclosure proceedings.[10] In the same year, 55 railroads, or 43 per cent of the 127 southern lines, were in default on their bond coupons. In five southern states, Virginia, Florida, Alabama, Louisiana, and Kentucky, half or more of the roads were behind in their interest payments.[11] In the rest of the nation in 1876, less than a quarter of the lines were in default.[12]

In the South both the large and the small lines were in financial difficulty. Of the 127 railroads in the 10 states in 1876, 45 were over 100 miles in length and 82 were under that length.[13] Of the longer lines, 17 were in default in 1876. This was less than 40 per cent of the individual companies, but since many of the defaulting roads were among the longest in the South the total mileage in default was 4,648 or 44 per cent. Nearly half of the shorter lines, 38 out of 82, failed to pay their bond interest in the same year.[14] Default in interest payments normally led to receivership. Short and long roads suffered alike. Of the longer roads in the South, 25 different lines were in receivership some-

8. *Commercial and Financial Chronicle,* July 3, 1875, p. 2.
9. *Ibid.,* November 15, 1873, pp. 647-648.
10. *Ibid.,* October 10, 1874, pp. 363-366; *The Railroad Gazette,* June 16, 1876, p. 270.
11. Poor, *Manual of the Railroads of the United States for 1877-1878,* pp. xxxii-xxxvi. In the rest of the nation only Arkansas and Dakota had half or more of their lines in financial trouble.
12. *Ibid.,* pp. x-xxxix. In the non-southern states only 161 out of 683 companies were behind in their bond interest. In New England and the Middle Atlantic states only 16 per cent of the companies were in default. Further west in the five states of the Old Northwest, 34 per cent of the companies were in difficulty. No other region in the country came even close to the rate of default found in the South.
13. The 45 longer roads totalled 10,452 miles or an average of 232 miles each. The shorter roads had an aggregate mileage of 3,295, or an average of only 40 miles per road.
14. Poor, *Manual of the Railroads of the United States for 1877-1878,* pp. xxxii-xxxvi.

A STORY OF RECEIVERSHIP

time during the decade of the 1870's.[15] The total mileage affected, 6,056 miles, was nearly three-fifths of the total mileage for the long roads.

As a result of this extensive default and receivership, the lag in new railroad construction after 1873 was especially noticeable in the South. Southern railroad expansion had been lagging behind the national average ever since the Civil War. In 1861 the Confederacy possessed nearly a third of the total rail network of the nation. At the end of the war her portion was little more than a quarter of the total, and before 1873 it had dropped to a fifth. In 1880 the 14,811 miles in the southern states constituted less than 16 per cent of the national total.[16] The lag in new construction was greatest in the middle and late 1870's. In the years from 1873 to 1879 the southern lines built only 1,356 miles of new road. During these years the South was constructing only 8 per cent of the total new construction for the entire nation. The low year was 1875 when only fifty miles of new track was completed. In that year six of the ten states laid down not a single mile of new iron.[17] The lag in new construction, especially in the South, can be seen in the following table:

Year	U. S. Construction During Year	U. S. Total at End of Year	Southern Construction During Year	Southern Total at End of Year	Southern % of Total
1870	6,070	52,914	733	11,229	21.2%
1871	7,379	60,293	1,094	12,323	20.4%
1872	5,878	66,171	261	12,584	18.9%
1873	4,097	70,268	393	12,977	18.2%
1874	2,117	72,385	260	13,237	18.2%
1875	1,711	74,096	50	13,287	17.8%
1876	2,712	76,808	344	13,631	17.7%
1877	2,280	79,088	180	13,811	17.4%
1878	2,629	81,717	128	13,939	17.0%
1879	4,746	86,463	394	14,333	16.5%
1880	6,876	93,349	478	14,811	15.8%

15. Based upon an examination of the annual issues of Henry V. Poor, *Manual of the Railroads of the United States* for the 1870's.
16. Poor, *Manual of the Railroads of the United States for 1877-1878*, p. ix; Poor, *Manual of the Railroads of the United States for 1885*, p. xiv.
17. Poor, *Manual of the Railroads of the United States for 1885*, p. xiv; Poor, *Manual of the Railroads of the United States for 1877-1878*, p. ix.

RAILROADS OF THE SOUTH

No critic could accuse the South of building superfluous mileage in the late 1870's.

Prior to the Panic of 1873 very few railroads in the South had succumbed to northern financial influence or control. With the exception of the several roads temporarily held by the carpetbaggers and the system of lines built by the Southern Railway Security Company from 1870 to 1872, only four major roads were northern controlled before 1873. These roads were the Chesapeake and Ohio, the Macon and Brunswick, the Selma, Rome and Dalton, and Morgan's Louisiana and Texas.

Of the four lines the Chesapeake and Ohio was by far the most important and was soon trying to compete as a trunk line with the Baltimore and Ohio and other more northern roads. This company was the result of a consolidation completed August 31, 1868, of the Virginia Central and the Covington and Ohio Railroads.[18] The state of Virginia had earlier given extensive aid to the Virginia Central and also to the short and incomplete Blue Ridge Railroad (which was included in the new system), but was not inclined in the postwar years to give any further direct financial assistance.[19] The first president of the newly combined road, General William C. Wickham, an ex-Confederate cavalry officer from Richmond, realized he had inadequate financial backing to complete the road, as projected, from Covington, Virginia, to the Ohio River.[20] He directed his first efforts to find new financial support towards Europe, but these resulted in indifferent success.[21]

General Wickham next turned to New York City and was soon negotiating with a group headed by the Connecticut Yankee

18. Henry V. Poor, *Manual of the Railroads of the United States for 1869-1870* (New York, 1869), p. 407.
19. *Commercial and Financial Chronicle*, March 12, 1870, p. 332; Frederick A. Cleveland and Fred Wilbur Powell, *Railroad Promotion and Capitalization in the United States* (New York, 1909), pp. 108, 213-214. Both Virginia and West Virginia did, however, exempt the new C. and O. from state taxation until the road was declaring 10 per cent dividends. *Commercial and Financial Chronicle*, December 19, 1868, p. 783.
20. The plan was to furnish Cincinnati with a shorter route to the sea than that provided by the B. and O. or other more northern routes. *Commercial and Financial Chronicle*, June 2, 1866, p. 697.
21. *Ibid*, October 3, 1868, p. 441; February 6, 1869, p. 172; November 27, 1869, p. 683.

A STORY OF RECEIVERSHIP

from California, Collis P. Huntington, and backed by the New York banking firm of Fisk and Hatch.[22] Fresh from his laurels of completing the Central Pacific, Huntington proposed to build and equip the two-hundred-mile extension for $15,000,000, although he admitted seeing construction difficulties in the mountains of West Virginia as great as those the Central Pacific had faced in crossing the great mountains of the West.[23] Huntington replaced Wickham as president of the company November 27, 1869, and soon northern directors were outnumbering those from Virginia seven to four.[24] Southerners never again controlled the Chesapeake and Ohio.

The capitalists built the road. Using money borrowed through Fisk and Hatch, Huntington employed up to seven thousand men at a time in pushing the road across and through the mountains towards the new Ohio River town of Huntington, West Virginia.[25] On the way coal deposits were discovered, deposits so vast that mining engineers estimated that a single mountain county could supply world needs for hundreds of years.[26] Officials drove the final spike January 29, 1873, completing the 428-mile through line from Richmond to Huntington.[27] The two hundred miles of new construction doubled the length of the road and provided another transmontane trunk line to the Ohio. The cost, however, had been high. In doubling the length of the road the capital structure had increased fivefold, standing at $38,000,000 in 1873.[28] Even before the Panic of 1873 net earnings per year

---

22. *Ibid.*, June 26, 1869, p. 816; November 27, 1869, p. 683.

23. James Poyntz Nelson, *The Chesapeake and Ohio Railway* (Richmond, Virginia, 1927), p. 26; *Commercial and Financial Chronicle*, December 11, 1869, p. 743.

24. Nelson, *op. cit.*, pp. 78-79; Henry V. Poor, *Manual of the Railroads of the United States for 1872-1873* (New York, 1872), p. 570. Wickham was relegated to the post of vice president, remaining in that position until his death in 1888. Other new members included on the board of directors in addition to Huntington were William H. Aspinwall, William B. Hatch, and Pliny Fisk.

25. *Commercial and Financial Chronicle*, April 2, 1870, p. 429.

26. *Ibid.*, September 30, 1871, p. 429; September 21, 1872, p. 388. The *Chronicle* reported the *Greenbrier Independent* as claiming "There is coal enough in Fayette County alone to last the world a thousand years."

27. Henry V. Poor, *Manual of the Railroads of the United States for 1874-1875* (New York, 1874), p. 111; *Commercial and Financial Chronicle*, February 1, 1873, p. 149.

28. Poor, *Manual of the Railroads of the United States for 1869-1870*, pp.

were averaging only about 1 per cent of the total investment. The road was in financial trouble by November, 1873.[29]

The story was much the same for the three shorter roads further south. The 187-mile Macon and Brunswick was partially in operation by 1867 with nearly 50 miles completed west of Brunswick, Georgia.[30] The management, which was entirely local and southern, found it impossible, however, to finish the road without financial assistance. The aid came from two sources, $2,550,000 of bonds endorsed by Georgia and new capital from New York City.[31] The road was completed to Macon early in 1870. The New York money also brought outside control for by 1871 over half of the directors were northern men.[32] The state of Georgia had its turn at control in July, 1873, when it seized the road for its failure to pay the interest due on the state-endorsed bonds.[33] The interlude in northern financial influence was but temporary, however, as R. T. Wilson began negotiating to buy the line in 1880, and did buy it for the East Tennessee, Virginia, and Georgia Railroad in July, 1881.[34]

Northerners were also in early control of the Selma, Rome and Dalton Railroad. Shortly after the road was reorganized out of the older Alabama and Tennessee River Railroad, northern influence became dominant. By 1869 seven of the eleven directors as well as the president, F. H. Delano of New York, were from the North.[35] The history of the line in the 1870's generally paralleled that of the Macon and Brunswick. The road was early in

---

407-408; Poor, *Manual of the Railroads of the United States for 1874-1875*, pp. 111-112. Over 60 per cent of the capital structure consisted of funded debt.

29. *Commercial and Financial Chronicle*, November 1, 1873, p. 587; November 15, 1873, p. 649. Huntington was reported to have offered $100,000 to help meet the November bond interest that was due. However, no other directors offered to help with the remainder due.

30. C. Mildred Thompson, *Reconstruction in Georgia, Economic, Social, Political, 1865-1872* (New York, 1915), pp. 319-320.

31. *Ibid.*; Cleveland and Powell, *Railroad Promotion*, pp. 222-223.

32. Poor, *Manual of the Railroads in the United States for 1872-1873*, p. 512. The northerners did keep George H. Hazlehurst of Macon in as president of the company.

33. *Commercial and Financial Chronicle*, July 12, 1873, p. 53.

34. *Ibid.*, February 14, 1880, p. 169; February 21, 1880, p. 192; March 6, 1880, p. 248; July 23, 1881, p. 100. Poor, *Manual of the Railroads of the United States for 1885*, p. 480.

35. Poor, *Manual of the Railroads of the United States for 1869-1870*, p. 432.

receivership and suffered from fraud at the hands of the receiver, T. A. Walker, and a former president, John Tucker of New York City.[36] On June 14, 1880, R. T. Wilson purchased at foreclosure sale the portion of the line in Alabama (171 miles) for $1,700,000. Wilson later transferred the property to the East Tennessee, Virginia and Georgia Railroad at an advance of nearly half a million dollars.[37]

The fourth line, Morgan's Louisiana and Texas Railroad, was located in Louisiana, running from Algiers to Brashear. Its predecessor, the New Orleans, Opelousas and Great Western, was placed on the block for foreclosure sale May 25, 1869. Several interests attended the sale, including representatives for the Illinois Central Railroad and for the aggressive Charles Morgan of New York City, owner of a line of steamers serving the Texas and Louisiana Gulf Coast. The Morgan agent, C. A. Whitney, obtained the road with a bid of $2,050,000.[38] Morgan retained sole ownership of the line until its sale to the Southern Pacific Company in 1884.[39]

With the exception of the above four roads and the lines under the control of the Southern Railway Security Company, northerners were far from prominent in the management of southern railroads prior to the Panic of 1873. Of the forty-five major roads (over 100 miles in length) in 1870-1871, forty-three companies furnished lists of active boards of directors. These lists totalled over four hundred directors. Of those giving addresses only eighty-one directors, or 19 per cent of the total group, came from the North. Over 80 per cent, or 345, came from the South. A few companies had a majority of directors with northern addresses, but a majority of the companies were completely free of any northerners in their official boards. Of the eighty-one northern men, forty-nine, or nearly two-thirds of the group, came from

---

36. *Commercial and Financial Chronicle*, June 16, 1877, p. 566. Walker and Tucker worked a scheme to issue Receiver's Certificates for the purchase of rolling stock already on the road.

37. *Ibid.*, June 19, 1880, p. 651; April 29, 1882, p. 479. Fairfax Harrison, *A History of the Legal Development of the Railroad System of the Southern Railway* (Washington, 1901), p. 811.

38. *Commercial and Financial Chronicle*, April 10, 1869, p. 459; May 29, 1869, p. 684.

39. Poor, *Manual of the Railroads of the United States for 1885*, p. 474.

New York City. Baltimore was second with eight and Boston furnished five. Of the forty-three companies furnishing director lists only seven, or less than a sixth, had northern presidents.[40]

Of the forty-five longer major southern railroads, twenty-five companies suffered receivership some time during the 1870's.[41] A few companies, such as the Alabama and Chattanooga and the Brunswick and Albany, were in default before the panic, but most of the interest defaulting occurred in 1873 and 1874.[42] Since normally a defaulting company managed to forestall actual receivership for several months, most of the formal receivership proceedings came in 1874, 1875, or 1876. The bulk of the foreclosure sales came after 1876 with 1880 being a top year for the major lines.

A comparison study of the twenty-five roads suffering receivership with the twenty roads that escaped receivership in the decade shows some interesting and significant differences. Several of the contrasts go far in explaining why one company succeeded while a competitor was facing receivership.

The lines that faced default, receivership, and foreclosure in the decade as a group were somewhat longer, cost more to build, and had inferior capital structures, as compared to the twenty companies that were free of receivership. The average receiver-

---

40. The above figures came from lists of directors found in Henry V. Poor, *Manual of the Railroads of the United States for 1871-1872* (New York, 1871) and Poor, *Manual of the Railroads of the United States for 1872-1873*.

41. The twenty-five defaulting companies by states were as follows:
   Virginia (3), Atlantic, Mississippi and Ohio; Chesapeake and Ohio; Washington City, Virginia Midland and Great Southern.
   North Carolina (2), Carolina Central; Western North Carolina.
   South Carolina (5), Greenville and Columbia; Port Royal; Savannah and Charleston; South Carolina; Wilmington, Columbia and Augusta.
   Georgia (4), Atlanta and Richmond Air-Line; Atlantic and Gulf; Brunswick and Albany; Macon and Brunswick.
   Florida (1), Jacksonville, Pensacola and Mobile.
   Alabama (4), Alabama and Chattanooga; Mobile and Montgomery; Selma, Rome and Dalton; Western of Alabama.
   Mississippi (1), Mobile and Ohio.
   Louisiana (2), New Orleans and Mobile; New Orleans, St. Louis and Chicago.
   Kentucky (3), Louisville, Cincinnati and Lexington; Louisville, Paducah and Southwestern (Elizabethtown and Paducah); St. Louis and Southeastern.

42. For some companies default came quite late. Both the South Carolina Railroad and the Wilmington, Columbia and Augusta defaulted in 1878.

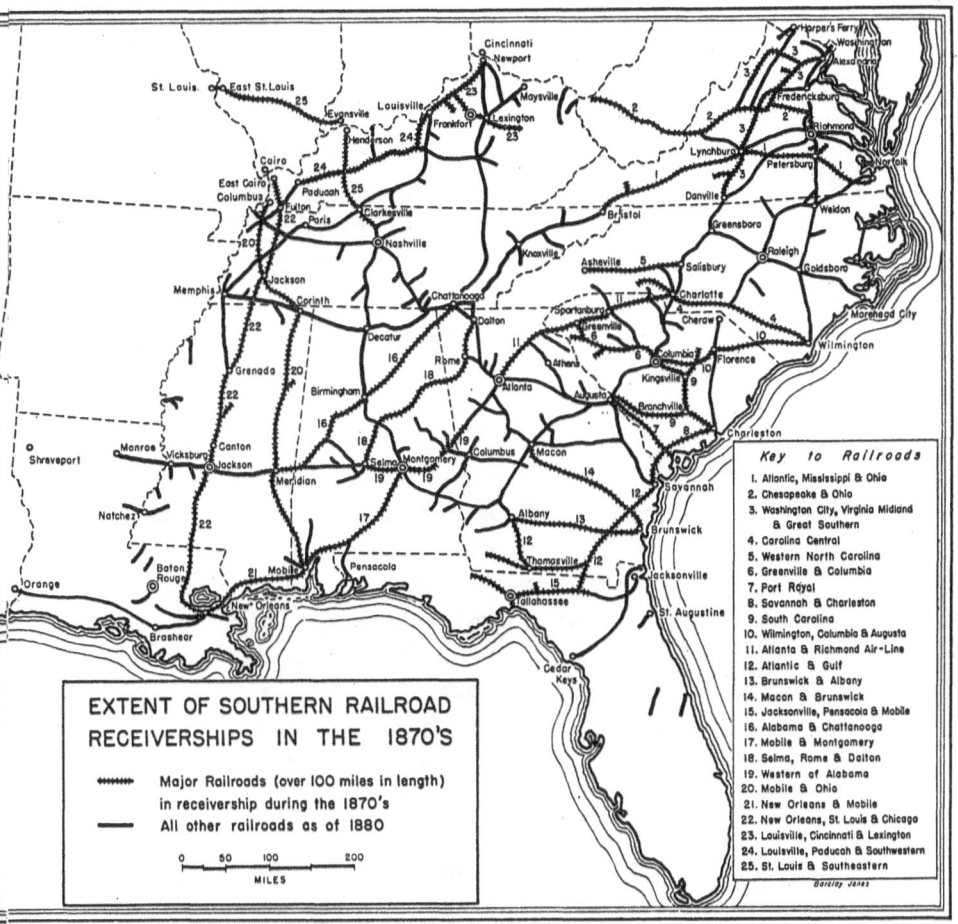

ship road was 230 miles in length as compared to an average 190-mile line for the more prosperous roads. The difference in cost per mile was much more significant. The receivership lines on the average had cost $39,000 per mile to build, while the shorter, more prosperous roads had cost only $27,000 per mile to build.[43] A third of the receivership lines were capitalized at figures of over $40,000 per mile with Huntington's Chesapeake and Ohio

[43]. The average for the entire South in 1873 was $36,000 per mile of road. Henry V. Poor, *Manual of the Railroads of the United States for 1873-1874* (New York, 1873), p. xlviii.

topping the list at $88,000 per mile.[44] By contrast, over a third of the more prosperous lines were capitalized at not over $20,000 per mile of road. In a region where traffic and railroad business was relatively light, even in prosperous times, heavily capitalized roads were sure to face financial difficulties in depression years. This was especially true for the twenty-five receivership lines since so large a part of their capital was borrowed. The defaulting roads had 57 per cent of their capital structure in funded debt and only 43 per cent in capital stock. The ratio was almost reversed for the non-receivership lines where 55 per cent was in stock and only 45 per cent in bonds or funded debt. The defaulting companies on the average had to pay interest on $23,000 of bonds per mile. The prosperous companies had an average funded debt of just over $12,000 per mile of line. This marked difference between the two groups of roads in fixed charges explains the presence of defaults in one group and the absence in the other.[45]

The lines that suffered receivership were also less efficient than the major companies that escaped receivership. In the years just before the Panic of 1873, the roads destined for receivership had an average operating ratio (operating expenses to gross receipts) of 71½ per cent while the lines that were to escape receivership had a much better and lower ratio of only 63½ per cent. Net earnings for prosperous roads were also somewhat larger on the average because their traffic density was usually greater. For example, in 1870-1871 the Louisville and Nashville (392 miles in length), a line which did not suffer receivership in the 1870's, had gross earnings of $3,153,000, while William Mahone's Atlantic, Mississippi and Ohio (428 miles in length), a line that did go into receivership, had gross earnings of but $1,925,000.[46] In the years before the Panic of 1873 the prosperous roads had

44. Other high cost lines were: New Orleans and Mobile, $83,000 per mile; Western North Carolina, $56,000 per mile; and Selma, Rome and Dalton, $54,000 per mile.

45. Figures on mileage of roads, capitalization per mile, and bond-stock ratios are based on company reports found in Poor, *Manual of the Railroads of the United States for 1872-1873* and Poor, *Manual of the Railroads of the United States for 1873-1874*.

46. Poor, *Manual of the Railroads of the United States for 1872-1873*, pp. 163-165, 478. Mahone's road had a funded debt of $9,493,000 while that of the L. and N. stood at $8,752,000.

A STORY OF RECEIVERSHIP

average net earnings that were equivalent to 14 per cent of their funded debt. The roads headed for default had net earnings equal to only 5 per cent of their funded debt. After taxes and other deductions had been made the remainder was generally not adequate to pay the bond interest coupons due. The result was default and eventual receivership.

There were also marked and significant differences in the management of the two groups of roads. The roads that failed in the 1870's had a much greater degree of northern financial influence in the early 1870's than the companies that were to escape receivership. Seven-eighths of all northern directors on southern roads (furnishing lists of directors in 1870-1871) were associated with the railroads headed for receivership. These 25 companies in 1870-1871 had a total of 252 directors of whom 181 were local southerners and 71 (or 28 per cent) were from the North. The 18 railroads that escaped receivership had only 10 directors (or 6 per cent) from the North out of a total list of 174 men.[47] Prior to the Panic of 1873 seven of the forty-three lines had northern presidents. Six of these companies suffered default and receivership during the panic. Too frequently in the early 1870's northern management of southern railroads was associated with uneconomical construction, unwise financing, or even outright fraud, illustrations of which were C. P. Huntington's Chesapeake and Ohio, Colonel H. S. McComb's New Orleans, St. Louis and Chicago, and John Stanton's Alabama and Chattanooga.[48]

The few southern railroads that were paying regular dividends in the early 1870's present the greatest contrast to the receivership roads. Five of the major southern lines were paying fairly regular dividends before the Panic of 1873: the North Carolina Railroad, the Central of Georgia, the Southwestern of Georgia,

---

47. The two major lines out of the forty-five that furnished no lists of directors in 1870-1871 were the Southwestern Railroad of Georgia, leased and operated by the Central of Georgia, and Morgan's Louisiana and Texas, a line owned solely by Charles Morgan. Neither road was in receivership during the 1870's.

48. Figures and conclusions concerning operating ratios, earnings, and management are based on company reports found in Poor, *Manual of the Railroads of the United States for 1871-1872;* Poor, *Manual of the Railroads of the United States for 1872-1873;* and Poor, *Manual of the Railroads of the United States for 1873-1874.*

the Georgia Railroad, and the Louisville and Nashville.[49] These five companies had a total capital structure composed of 71 per cent capital stock and only 29 per cent funded debt. They had cost on the average only $26,000 per mile to build. Their aggregate net earnings of over $3,000,000 in 1871-1872 were equivalent to 29 per cent of the total funded debt. They were operated with great efficiency for the average operating ratio for the group was a low 59 per cent.[50] Everyone of the roads was managed by southerners and not a single man of the forty-four directors came from the North.

The comparisons made in the above paragraphs between receivership and non-receivership roads are summarized below:[51]

	25 Receivership Roads	20 Non-receivership Roads	5 Dividend-Paying Roads
Average cost per mile of road	$39,000	$27,000	$26,000
Percentage of capital structure composed of funded debt	57%	45%	29%
Funded debt per mile of road	$23,000	$12,000	$8,600
Operating ratio	71½%	63½%	59%
Net earnings to total funded debt	5%	14%	29%
Percentage of northern directors of 1870-1871	28%	6%	0%

Despite the fact that there was a relatively heavy northern influence in the management of the twenty-five receivership roads, the bulk of them prior to default were southern controlled. With but few exceptions this local control was lost as the roads experienced receivership and foreclosure sale. At the end of the decade, southerners could claim control, at the very most, of but

49. The dividends paid in 1871-1872 were: North Carolina, 6 per cent; Central, 10 per cent; Southwestern, 8 per cent; Georgia, 8 per cent; and L. and N., 7 per cent.
50. Poor, *Manual of the Railroads of the United States for 1872-1873*, pp. xlii-xlv.
51. The five dividend-paying roads are also included in the twenty non-receivership roads.

A STORY OF RECEIVERSHIP

six of the roads that had experienced receivership. At the end of the receivership decade not a single road of the twenty-five could boast of both continued local financial control and also an independent existence outside of a larger rail system. The post-receiver ship destinies of the twenty-five roads fall into three rather distinct patterns: (1) those roads already largely northern controlled before receivership and naturally still northern controlled after receivership; (2) those roads largely southern controlled before receivership which after receivership remained independent lines, but under northern management; and (3) those lines largely southern controlled before receivership which after receivership were included in new rail combinations, most of which were northern dominated.

Five railroads are included in the first category of being northern controlled both before and after receivership: The Chesapeake and Ohio, the Wilmington, Columbia and Augusta, the Alabama and Chattanooga, the Macon and Brunswick, and the Selma, Rome and Dalton. The Chesapeake and Ohio had defaulted on bond coupons late in 1873 and in 1875 was placed in receivership by the United States Circuit Court.[52] Judge Bond of the same court appointed Vice President William C. Wickham as receiver early in 1876, making easier the realization of the reorganization plans of a bondholder's committee headed by A. S. Hatch and C. P. Huntington. At the foreclosure sale April 2, 1878, at Richmond, A. S. Hatch, chairman of the reorganization committee, purchased the road for $2,750,000. In the reorganization during the early summer of 1878, Huntington remained as president, Hatch became first vice president, and Wickham second vice president.[53] The Wilmington, Columbia and Augusta experienced no greater changes in management as a result of its receivership and reorganization. Default came to the line early

---

52. *Commercial and Financial Chronicle*, October 16, 1875, p. 371.
53. *Ibid.*, January 8, 1876, p. 42; April 6, 1878, p. 342; July 20, 1878, p. 67. S. F. Van Oss, *American Railroads as Investments* (New York, 1893), pp. 764-765. The new organization was a Railway Company rather than a Roadroad Company. In other ways many of the old problems remained. The line still lacked adequate connections in the West and a deep water port in the East. Both gross and net earnings remained low relative to the total capital structure of the company.

in 1878 due to financial difficulties associated with its lease of the sister road to the north, the Wilmington and Weldon. Throughout 1878 and early 1879 the first mortgage bondholders worked for foreclosure of the road.[54] Their efforts were finally successful and early in October, 1879, the bondholders committee (which included both W. T. Walters and B. F. Newcomer of Baltimore) purchased the road at a foreclosure sale for $860,500.[55] The officers elected at the reorganization meeting in January, 1880, were largely the same old group. R. R. Bridgers of Wilmington was retained as president and seven of the ten directors were from the old board.[56] Six of the ten were from Baltimore.

For the other three roads of the group, receivership and foreclosure brought more drastic management changes, even though the control remained out of southern hands. Longest of the three, the Alabama and Chattanooga had early been in financial difficulties due to the management of those consumate carpetbaggers, John C. Stanton and his brother, Daniel. The company on January 1, 1871, made default on its bond interest and a state-appointed receiver seized the road the following summer.[57] A long receivership followed, complicated by suits and cross suits which prevented the bondholders from getting possession of their property.[58] From 1872 through 1876 the press was filled with accounts of intended sales, reported sales, and protested sales of the property, but on January 22, 1877, the road was finally sold. John Swann purchased the road at the foreclosure sale for the account of Emile Erlanger and Company of London. The new English management renamed the road the Alabama Great Southern and soon added it to other roads controlled by their English corporation, the Alabama, New Orleans, Texas, and Pacific Junc-

---

54. Four-fifths of the bonds were held in Baltimore. *Commercial and Financial Chronicle*, November 9, 1878, p. 488.

55. *Ibid.*, October 4, 1879, p. 350.

56. *Ibid.*, January 24, 1880, p. 84; Poor, *Manual of the Railroads of the United States for 1877-1878*, pp. 234-236.

57. Poor, *Manual of the Railroads of the United States for 1873-1874*, p. 583; Walter L. Fleming, *Civil War and Reconstruction in Alabama* (Cleveland, 1911), pp. 597-598. Default was easy since the road was built entirely with bonds.

58. *Commercial and Financial Chronicle*, July 27, 1878, p. 85.

A STORY OF RECEIVERSHIP

tion Railways Company.[59] The decade of the 1870's found most of the railroads of Alabama in receivership and by 1880 many of them were being incorporated in other out-of-state systems.[60] The other two roads which suffered receivership while northern controlled, the Macon and Brunswick and the Selma, Rome and Dalton, also had a change in management due to foreclosure. Both roads were sold to R. T. Wilson by 1881 and soon were included in the East Tennessee, Virginia and Georgia system.

The second category of roads, those largely southern controlled before receivership which remained independent but under a new northern management after receivership, included eight railroads. The eight were the Atlantic, Mississippi and Ohio, the Carolina Central, the South Carolina Railroad, the Brunswick and Albany, the Jacksonville, Pensacola and Mobile, the Mobile and Ohio, the New Orleans, St. Louis and Chicago, and the Elizabethtown and Paducah.

The experience of William Mahone's Virginia road, the Atlantic, Mississippi and Ohio, was typical of the group. Shortly after his consolidation coup in 1870 had been completed, Mahone decided to refinance much of the company's debt through the issuance of new first mortgage bonds to the amount of $15,000,000. In the summer of 1871 he contracted with John Collinson of London, England, to offer $6,000,000 of the new 7 per cent bonds in the London market.[61] The financial panic of 1873 came as a severe blow to the Atlantic, Mississippi and Ohio. Even before the failure of Jay Cooke and Company, John Collinson from England was warning that the money market in London was at

---

59. *Ibid.*, May 4, 1872, p. 593; February 8, 1873, p. 180; June 7, 1873, p. 763; February 7, 1874, p. 143; May 15, 1875, p. 476; October 7, 1876, p. 352; November 4, 1876, p. 450; July 27, 1878, p. 85. Harrison, *Legal Devlopment of the Southern Railway*, pp. 976-977. Henry V. Poor, *Manual of the Railroads of the United States for 1882* (New York, 1882), pp. 465-466. The parent holding company by 1882 also controlled the Vicksburg and Meridian, the New Orleans and Northwestern, and the Cincinnati Southern.

60. James F. Doster, *Alabama's First Railroad Commission, 1881-1885* (University, Alabama, 1949), pp. 8-9, 24-28.

61. Poor, *Manual of the Railroads of the United States for 1872-1873*, p. 480; Nelson M. Blake, *William Mahone of Virginia, Soldier and Political Insurgent* (Richmond, 1935), pp. 121-122; *Commercial and Financial Chronicle*, November 18, 1871, p. 667. Mahone also agreed to purchase English iron for renewing portions of his main line.

very low ebb.⁶² The A. M. and O. had a hard fall and winter with net earnings dropping nearly 20 per cent. The company was late in paying its October coupons and defaulted on its payments in January, 1874. Mahone pulled his gray slouch hat lower over his blue eyes and started in earnest a policy of retrenchment. Some employees were laid off with a promise of reemployment when business justified it. Those remaining had their wages cut 10 per cent. The road's officials faced a 20 per cent salary reduction.⁶³ Throughout 1874 and 1875 Mahone succeeded in placating the English bondholders and he was satisfied after a winter trip to London late in 1875 that he had convinced them that a policy of forebearance was best.⁶⁴

Receivership came to Mahone's line in 1876. In a surprise move early in March, 1876, John Collinson notified Mahone he could no longer approve the latter's reorganization plans. On March 14, 1876, New York and English brokers filed a bill of complaint against the A. M. and O. in the United States Circuit Court of Virginia demanding foreclosure of the road and the appointment of a receiver.⁶⁵ On June 6, 1876, Judge Bond of the Circuit Court appointed Charles L. Perkins of New York and Major Henry Fink, general superintendent of the line, as receivers of the road.⁶⁶ The receivership, lasting nearly five years, was plagued chiefly by a long dispute between rival bondholder groups from England and Holland.⁶⁷ During the receivership period the poker-playing Mahone exerted himself to his utmost to retain control of the road.⁶⁸ Until he discovered that the

---

62. Blake, *op. cit.*, pp. 126-127.
63. *Ibid.*, pp. 127-128. Mahone postponed indefinitely the construction of the line from Bristol to Cumberland gap.
64. *Commercial and Financial Chronicle*, December 11, 1875, p. 569; Blake, *op. cit.*, pp. 128-130.
65. Blake, *op. cit.*, pp. 128-134; *Commercial and Financial Chronicle*, March 18, 1876, p. 280. Northern railroad interests were glad to align themselves against a man who had so frequently opposed them in the past. Mahone had always felt a pride in keeping his line as Virginian as possible. As early as 1867 he had opposed a northern concern, the Adams Express Company, by doing his own express business.
66. *Commercial and Financial Chronicle*, June 10, 1876, p. 567.
67. *Ibid.*, October 19, 1878, p. 407; May 10, 1879, p. 476; July 10, 1880, p. 43.
68. Poker was one of Mahone's favorite recreations. He had learned to play as a boy in his father's tavern. During his railroad days he liked to play

A STORY OF RECEIVERSHIP

English bondholders opposed the idea, he seriously sought appointment as receiver of the road. Failing in this, he turned to politics, hoping that as governor of the state he might save his line. Here, too, he met defeat, in 1877. He did, however, retain the presidency of the line and also helped arrange the terms of the foreclosure sale in 1881.[69]

The road was sold February 10, 1881. Three groups were actively interested in the bidding: Edward King, president of the Union Trust Company, represented the foreign bondholders, General Thomas M. Logan represented the Clyde Syndicate and the Richmond and Danville, and Clarence H. Clark represented several Philadelphia and New York capitalists. After a lively bidding, including some seventy bids, Clarence H. Clark purchased the road for $8,605,000.[70] Later in the spring, Clark and his associates organized their new property as the Norfolk and Western Railroad. The Norfolk and Western was definitely a northern road. Of the thirteen new directors five came from New York, five from Philadelphia, and only three from Virginia. In Mahone's day the entire board had been from Virginia.[71]

The story was much the same for the other seven roads. The Carolina Central suffered receivership twice during the decade. Originally chartered as the Wilmington, Charlotte and Rutherfordtown, the locally controlled road had financial difficulty in repairing and extending its line in the late 1860's.[72] The road passed into receivership July 1, 1872, was sold in 1873, and shortly re-

---

with the cattle raisers and shippers of southwestern Virginia. Later in Washington as a U. S. Senator, he and his senatorial cronies frequently held a session at the Chamberlain Hotel. Throughout his railroad difficulties Mahone always retained a sense of humor. When an inspection trip on his line ended in a minor head-on collision he rebuked the engineers with the statement: "You men won't be satisfied, of course, until you can pass each other on a single track." Blake, *op. cit.*, pp. 273-274.

69. *Ibid.*, pp. 130-134, 147. After the line was sold and reorganized Mahone claimed $125,000 from the new road for earlier services as president. *Commercial and Financial Chronicle*, November 26, 1881, p. 587.

70. *Commercial and Financial Chronicle*, February 12, 1881, p. 182. General Logan was Clark's closest competitor, making his final bid at $8,601,000.

71. Poor, *Manual of the Railroads of the United States for 1882*, pp. 374-376; Poor, *Manual of the Railroads of the United States for 1873-1874*, pp. 402-404.

72. Robert Somers, *The Southern States Since the War, 1870-1871* (New York, 1871), pp. 34-35.

organized as the Carolina Central Railway. With the reorganization, control shifted to the North for both the President, Dr. Charles H. Roberts, and the chief stockholder, Edward Matthews, came from New York.[73] The road was in receivership again in April, 1876, and sold in foreclosure May 31, 1880. The new company, the Carolina Central Railroad, was also a northern-controlled concern. During 1883 the Seaboard and Roanoke acquired a controlling interest in the line.[74]

Further south, South Carolina's oldest railroad, the South Carolina Railroad, had a rather similar experience. After the war a purely local group, headed by a prominent conservative, William J. Magrath, ran the road and faced the problems of expensive rehabilitation, lowered freight rates, and increasing competition.[75] The company escaped default in 1873 but the middle 1870's were years of declining revenue and a marked depreciation in the market value of the capital stock.[76] A heavy floating debt finally forced receivership upon the line in October, 1878.[77] The road was sold at public auction in Charleston, July 28, 1881. Two bidders were present, W. H. Brawley, representing a New York City group, and Samuel Lord, representing local financial interests. The road was sold to the New York group for $1,275,000. Thus one of the oldest roads in the South passed out of the hands of Charleston men who had financed and directed the line for more than half a century.[78]

The Brunswick and Albany in Georgia and the Jacksonville, Pensacola and Mobile also moved from a tenuous local control prior to receivership to a complete foreign or northern control

---

73. *Commercial and Financial Chronicle*, April 18, 1874, p. 398; January 2, 1875, p. 15.

74. *Ibid.*, June 5, 1880, p. 600; November 19, 1881, p. 559. Poor, *Manual of the Railroads of the United States for 1885*, p. 409.

75. Francis Butler Simkins and Robert Hilliard Wood, *South Carolina During Reconstruction* (Chapel Hill, 1932), pp. 195-200; Samuel M. Derrick, *Centennial History of the South Carolina Railroad* (Columbia, S. C., 1930), pp. 244-249.

76. Derrick, *op. cit.*, pp. 244-249, 251-253. Northern capitalists such as Samuel Sloan (1,700 shares) and J. Pierpont Morgan (133 shares) were becoming interested in the road by 1878. Sloan was a director of the company.

77. Poor, *Manual of the Railroads of the United States for 1882*, p. 423; Harrison, *Legal Development of the Southern Railway*, pp. 1197-1198.

78. *Commercial and Financial Chronicle*, July 30, 1881, p. 125; Derrick, *op. cit.*, pp. 254-257.

A STORY OF RECEIVERSHIP

after foreclosure. Hannibal I. Kimball maintained a pretense of local management over his Brunswick and Alabama while he was extending it with state-endorsed bonds in 1870 and 1871.[79] After Kimball retired from the state, the creditors started seizing rolling stock for debts due them and soon the road was in receivership.[80] On October 16, 1873, the German bondholders bought the road at foreclosure sale for $530,000.[81] It was operated for their account throughout the remainder of the decade, producing gross earnings barely sufficient to meet operating expenses.[82] In Florida, another carpetbagger, Milton S. Littlefield of New York (and North Carolina), controlled the Jacksonville, Pensacola and Mobile Railroad in the early 1870's.[83] Littlefield's management of the road was short for it was sold in foreclosure May 7, 1873, to D. P. Holland of Tallahassee. Receivership again engulfed the line and it was at the center of endless litigation throughout the 1870's.[84] The line was sold a second time September 25, 1879, to the bondholders for $50,000, subject to a prior lien of about $800,000.[85] The bondholders soon combined their line with the Florida Central into the Florida Central and Western. This latter company was itself included in a consolidation, February 28, 1884, which created the Florida Railway and Navigation Company. The Florida Railway and Navigation Company, including 529 miles of consolidated lines, was northern controlled with B. S. Henning of New York City as president.[86]

---

79. Thompson, *Reconstruction in Georgia, Economic, Social, Political, 1865-1872*, pp. 320-322.
80. *Commercial and Financial Chronicle*, November 4, 1871, p. 605. Poor, *Manual of the Railroads of the United States for 1872-1873*, pp. 555-556.
81. *Commercial and Financial Chronicle*, October 18, 1873, p. 523.
82. *Ibid.*, January 5, 1878, p. 18; November 20, 1880, p. 535.
83. Reginald C. McGrane, *Foreign Bondholders and Amercian State Debts* (New York, 1935), pp. 299-300; Poor, *Manual of the Railroads of the United States for 1872-1873*, p. 576.
84. Poor, *Manual of the Railroads of the United States for 1874-1875*, p. 241; Henry V. Poor, *Manual of the Railroads of the United States for 1875-1876*, (New York, 1875), p. 693; Edward King, *The Great South* (Hartford, Connecticut, 1875), p. 418; *Commercial and Financial Chronicle*, October 28, 1876, p. 247; September 1, 1877, p. 212.
85. *Commercial and Financial Chronicle*, September 27, 1879, p. 329.
86. Poor, *Manual of the Railroads of the United States for 1882*, pp. 447, 448, 449; Poor, *Manual of the Railroads of the United States for 1885*, p. 450. The new Florida Railway and Navigation Company in 1885 dominated the rail network of Florida, having nearly half of the total mileage in the state.

The last three roads in the group were located west of the mountains: the Mobile and Ohio, the Elizabethtown and Paducah, and the New Orleans, St. Louis and Chicago. In the early 1870's the Mobile and Ohio was the most important of the three lines. The Mobile and Ohio suffered severely in the Civil War, estimates of the loss running to 65 per cent of the original cost.[87] The line was restored and by the winter of 1870-1871 had so much business that Robert Somers reported the road's rolling stock inadequate for the traffic.[88] Much of the trade territory of the road was, however, "not over promising country" as General Superintendent Alfred L. Rives candidly admitted to his brother in 1873.[89] The road was locally controlled following the war and in the early 1870's only a single northerner, William Butler Duncan of New York, was included in the board of directors. Abraham Murdock of Columbus, Mississippi, was president until 1873.[90]

In 1873 and 1874, both the gross and net earnings of the road substantially fell at the same time that the floating debt increased. In December, 1873, Rives told his brother that he was not too happy with his position or the road's prospects.[91] In May, 1874, the company defaulted on its coupons and was subsequently placed in receivership.[92] William Butler Duncan, already president of the line, was made one of the two receivers for the road. He remained in the dual position until the end of the receivership in 1883.[93] When Duncan became president he brought more

87. Harrison, *op. cit.*, pp. 1471-1472.
88. Somers, *The Southern States*, p. 150. Much of this heavy traffic was seasonal. Somers admitted that the road was, like most Southern lines, unproductive to the stockholders.
89. Alfred L. Rives to William Rives, May 3, 1873, William Rives Papers, Manuscripts Division, Library of Congress, Washington, D. C.
90. Poor, *Manual of the Railroads of the United States for 1872-1873*, pp. 206-208; Poor, *Manual of the Railroads of the United States for 1873-1874*, pp. 369-371.
91. Alfred L. Rives to William C. Rives, December 26, 1873, William Rives Papers, Manuscripts Division, Library of Congress, Washington, D. C. Rives wanted to return to Virginia, hoping for a job on the B. and O. He remained with the Mobile and Ohio throughout the decade, however, and in the early 1880's was elevated to vice president and included in the board of directors.
92. Poor, *Manual of the Railroads of the United States for 1877-1878*, pp. 214-217.
93. *Commercial and Financial Chronicle*, January 27, 1883, p. 108.

A STORY OF RECEIVERSHIP

northerners into the board of directors and by 1876 they clearly dominated the group.[94] In 1874 Abraham Murdock was relegated to the position of Commissioner of Lands and Immigration. The Duncan group managed to reorganize the company without a foreclosure sale.[95]

The Elizabethtown and Paducah Railroad was a post-Civil War line opened in September, 1872, between the two cities named in its title. It also included a forty-five-mile branch line northward to Louisville, completed in 1874. The road was Kentucky controlled with Louisville interests being dominant.[96] On September 1, 1874, shortly after having completed the Cecilia extension to Louisville, the company defaulted on its first mortgage coupons.[97] The line was placed in receivership and sold in foreclosure in Louisville, August 24, 1876. Trustees of the European bondholders purchased the main line for $700,000. Northern stockholders purchased the Louisville branch at the same time and subsequently sold it to the Louisville and Nashville Railroad.[98] The European bondholders reorganized their main line as the Paducah and Elizabeth Railroad. The Paducah and Elizabeth was consolidated with the Memphis, Paducah and Northern in 1882 to form a new road, the Chesapeake, Ohio and Southwestern, a line controlled by Collis P. Huntington and associates from New York City.[99] Thus one more line was acquired by northern interests.[100]

Twelve southern railroads belonged in the third group of

94. Poor, *Manual of the Railroads of the United States for 1877-1878*, pp. 214-217.

95. *Commercial and Financial Chronicle*, November 4, 1876, p. 451; Henry V. Poor, *Manual of the Railroads of the United States for 1882* (New York, 1882), p. 458.

96. Poor, *Manual of the Railroads of the United States for 1873-1874*, p. 684; *Commercial and Financial Chronicle*, September 5, 1874, p. 248.

97. Poor, *Manual of the Railroads of the United States for 1877-1878*, p. 538.

98. *Ibid.*; *Commercial and Financial Chronicle*, August 26, 1876, p. 208; February 3, 1877, p. 111.

99. Poor, *Manual of the Railroads of the United States for 1885*, pp. 496-497. *Commercial and Financial Chronicle*, August 31, 1881, p. 176.

100. The eighth and last railroad in the group, the New Orleans, St. Louis, and Chicago, defaulted in 1876, entered receivership in the same year, and was sold in foreclosure the following year. The complete story of the line will be reviewed in Chapter 8, "The Illinois Central Goes South."

RAILROADS OF THE SOUTH

the receivership lines: those roads largely southern controlled before receivership which after receivership were included or combined into larger rail combinations. The twelve lines at the conclusion of their respective receiverships came under the control of four different rail combinations: (1) the Richmond and Danville—Richmond and West Point Terminal Railway and Warehouse Company System, (2) a new combination created at the end of the decade by Henry Bradley Plant, (3) the Louisville and Nashville, and (4) the Georgia group of still independent lines.

The Richmond and Danville system acquired four of the twelve lines in the late 1870's or early 1880's. The four lines were situated in the area between the Potomac and Atlanta. The Washington City, Virginia Midland and Great Southern Railroad had the closest physical connection with the Richmond and Danville, since the two roads had been connected at Danville in 1874. In November, 1872, when the company had been formed out of two earlier roads, the Orange, Alexandria and Manassas and the Lynchburg and Danville, the board of directors was completely dominated by men from Virginia.[101] However, the Baltimore and Ohio had earlier acquired a practical control of the line through gradually buying up the capital stock.[102] The road went into receivership in July, 1876, and was sold at auction December 20, 1880, in Alexandria. Robert Garrett of the B. and O. and others from Baltimore bought the road for $5,600,000.[103] Garrett reorganized his new property as the Virginia Midland Railway in February, 1881, and shortly thereafter sold his controlling interest in the company to John S. Barbour who was associated with parties interested in the Richmond and Danville.[104] By early 1883 the Virginia Midland was completely controlled by the Richmond and West Point Terminal Railway and Ware-

---

101. Poor, *Manual of the Railroads of the United States for 1873-1874*, p. 613; Poor, *Manual of the Railroads of the United States for 1877-1878*, p. 620.
102. Edward Hungerford, *The Story of the Baltimore and Ohio Railroad, 1827-1927* (New York, 1928), II, 112-113.
103. *Commercial and Financial Chronicle*, December 25, 1880, p. 673; Poor, *Manual of the Railroads of the United States for 1882*, p. 397.
104. *Commercial and Financial Chronicle*, September 3, 1881, p. 256.

A STORY OF RECEIVERSHIP

house Company, a holding company controlled by the Richmond and Danville.[105] A second line, the Western North Carolina Railroad, was acquired by the Richmond Terminal Company a little earlier. The Western North Carolina, after its costly experience with Messrs. Littlefield and Swepson, was plagued with receivership and endless litigation throughout the 1870's. The state operated the road in the last years of the decade and employed several hundred convicts to grade and extend the road toward the Tennessee line.[106] Growing tired of state operation, North Carolina sold the road April 27, 1880, to William J. Best of New York. Best almost immediately assigned his interest over to a Richmond Terminal group composed of A. S. Buford, W. P. Clyde and Thomas M. Logan.[107]

The Richmond and Danville also acquired two other lines further south. The Greenville and Columbia, like the Western North Carolina, had been pillaged by carpetbaggers. The company defaulted January 1, 1872, and after a long delay was placed in receivership November 28, 1878. W. P. Clyde, William A. Courtney, Joseph Bryan, and Thomas M. Logan purchased the road in the interest of the Richmond Terminal Company at a foreclosure sale in Charleston, April 15, 1880.[108] The second road was the Atlanta and Richmond Air-Line Railway. Shortly after the line's completion in September, 1873, the company defaulted on its bond interest and passed into the hands of a receiver November 25, 1874.[109] The bondholders purchased the road for $1,600,000 at public auction in Atlanta, December 5, 1876, and reorganized the road as the Atlanta and Charlotte Air-

105. *Ibid.*, February 3, 1883, p. 141; March 24, 1883, p. 332.
106. *Ibid.*, December 14, 1872, p. 797; May 2, 1874, p. 456; December 2, 1876, p. 550. Cecil Kenneth Brown, *A State Movement in Railroad Development: The Story of North Carolina's First Effort to Establish an East and West Trunk Line Railroad* (Chapel Hill, 1928), p. 213.
107. Brown, *op. cit.*, pp. 226-230; *Commercial and Financial Chronicle*, March 6, 1880, p. 249.
108. *Commercial and Financial Chronicle*, April 17, 1880, p. 408; Harrison, *Legal Development of the Southern Railway*, p. 325. The Clyde Committee found it difficult to comply with the terms of the sale, but the sale was finally ratified by the courts by October, 1880.
109. *Commercial and Financial Chronicle*, August 15, 1874, p. 167; Poor, *Manual of the Railroads of the United States for 1877-1878*, p. 580.

RAILROADS OF THE SOUTH

Line Railway early the following year.[110] The directors of the new company, all of whom were either from New York City or Baltimore, leased their road March 26, 1881, to the Richmond and Danville.[111]

The hard-working and temperate Henry Bradley Plant, already president of the Southern Express Company, acquired two of the receivership roads at the end of the decade. The two roads acquired, the Atlantic and Gulf and the Savannah and Charleston, formed the nucleus of the Plant System, a network that at the end of the century included over two thousand miles of road in South Carolina, Georgia, Florida, and Alabama. The Atlantic and Gulf had a 237-mile main line from Savannah across the southern edge of Georgia to Bainbridge. President John Screven hoped that his road would become a through line to Mobile but the route lay through poor country, the anticipated traffic never developed, and the destination was never reached. Receivership came to the road in 1877 after a default on bond interest due January 1, 1877.[112] Henry Bradley Plant purchased the road at a foreclosure sale in Savannah, November 4, 1879. He bought the line for $300,000, subject to mortgages amounting to $2,710,000. The new property was organized as the Savannah, Florida and Western in the winter of 1879-1880.[113] Plant became the new president and John Screven left railroading to return to his rice plantation. The second road acquired, the Savannah and Charleston, had been completely destroyed by the war and was very slow to recover. Even in 1873-1874 Edward King remarked that the only good thing about a trip on the road was the scenery.[114] The line was never prosperous and faced an early default in September, 1873. After a lengthy receivership the

---

110. *Commercial and Financial Chronicle*, December 9, 1876, p. 575; April 21, 1877, p. 369.

111. The lease gave the R. and D. complete control of a through line from Richmond to Atlanta. The annual rental was $462,500, an amount equal to bond interest plus 5 per cent dividends on the capital stock.

112. Poor, *Manual of the Railroads of the United States for 1877-1878*, p. 366; *Commercial and Financial Chronicle*, March 3, 1877, p. 203.

113. *Commercial and Financial Chronicle*, November 8, 1879, p. 488; December 6, 1879, p. 608. Howard Douglas Dozier, *History of the Atlantic Coast Line* (New York, 1920), pp. 132-137.

114. King, *The Great South*, p. 364.

A STORY OF RECEIVERSHIP

line was put on the auction block in Charleston, June 7, 1880. Again Plant was the successful bidder, getting the road for $300,200. Plant renamed his property the Charleston and Savannah Railway, made himself president, and selected a new board of directors dominated by New York and Baltimore men.[115]

The expanding Louisville and Nashville was the third system to claim several southern railroads as they came out of receivership. The growing Kentucky road acquired four roads, two at the southern end of the line and two others near the northern terminal. The Mobile and Montgomery was the first of the southern roads obtained. Charles T. Pollard of Montgomery, a prominent railroad contractor in Alabama, was president of this 179-mile line. Pollard's road was in financial difficulty as early as 1872 and was in receivership by 1873.[116] The bondholders, chiefly from the North and from England, purchased the road at foreclosure sale November 16, 1874.[117] The new management, almost entirely composed of New York men, was reported to have sold out to the L. and N. as early as 1876, but the transfer in control was certainly complete by late 1879.[118] Having acquired the bulk of the stock, the L. and N. made its domination doubly sure by leasing the line for twenty years from January 12, 1881. A similar fate befell the New Orleans and Mobile Railroad. As part of the earlier New Orleans, Mobile and Texas, the line in the early 1870's already was under considerable northern influence.[119] The road soon fell into financial difficulties and the several portions, projected and in operation, were separately organized. The New Orleans and Mobile defaulted on its bond interest July 1, 1874, and was put in the hands of the mortgage trustees. The

---

115. *Commercial and Financial Chronicle*, June 12, 1880, p. 625. W. T. Walters and B. F. Newcomer of Baltimore, important in the two roads out of Wilmington, were on the board of directors. H. B. Plant was also a director of the two Wilmington roads.

116. *Ibid.*, August 16, 1873, p. 218; Poor, *Manual of the Railroads of the United States for 1875-1876*, p. 477.

117. *Commercial and Financial Chronicle*, November 21, 1874, p. 518; February 24, 1877, p. 180.

118. *Ibid.*, November 25, 1876, p. 525; December 6, 1879, p. 608; March 6, 1880, p. 247.

119. *Ibid.*, May 27, 1871, p. 657. Leading stockholders at the time included Oakes Ames of Massachusetts, E. D. Morgan of New York, and several New York City banking firms.

bond holders purchased the road at a foreclosure sale April 24, 1880, and two weeks later, May 8, 1880, leased the road for fifty years to the Louisville and Nashville. The L. and N. had previously been interested in outright purchase of the road and by 1882 did possess over 99 per cent of its capital stock.[120]

Two other receivership roads at the northern end of the system came under L. and N. domination at about the same time. A Kentucky line, the Louisville, Cincinnati and Lexington Railroad, defaulted in 1873 and went into receivership in September, 1874. A syndicate of Louisville and Lexington men purchased the road October 1, 1877, for $731,500.[121] They reorganized their property but changed the name only to the extent of substituting Railway for Railroad. Two years later, in 1879, a local Louisville syndicate held about 60 per cent of the total stock issue and proposed to sell only when their stock had reached par. The Chesapeake and Ohio, the Pennsylvania, and the L. and N. were all reported to be interested in the property.[122] The Louisville and Nashville was the successful bidder and bought the property July 8, 1881.[123] A little earlier, in 1879, the L. and N. had acquired portions of another line in receivership when it purchased the Kentucky and Tennessee Divisions of the St. Louis and Southeastern Railway.[124]

The acquisition of the above four roads came at a time (1879-1882) when the Louisville and Nashville was experiencing growing pains. In the late 1870's the L. and N. was still a locally controlled railroad with Louisville men dominating its board of directors. In 1879 Horatio Victor Newcomb, thirty-five-year-old son of H. D. Newcomb, Louisville commission merchant and friend of James Guthrie, was elected president of the road. But the same year three New York men came in as new directors. One

---

120. Poor, *Manual of the Railroads of the United States for 1882*, p. 476; *Commercial and Financial Chronicle*, February 14, 1880, p. 169; May 1, 1880, p. 466; May 15, 1880, p. 519.
121. *Commercial and Financial Chronicle*, October 6, 1877, p. 335.
122. *Ibid.*, June 14, 1879, p. 599; January 24, 1880, p. 91. The *New York World* reported that Tom Scott of the Pennsylvania was interested in joining with the L. and N. to lease or buy the Louisville, Cincinnati and Lexington.
123. Poor, *Manual of the Railroads of the United States for 1882*, p. 499.
124. *Ibid.*, p. 501; *Commercial and Financial Chronicle*, April 12, 1879, p. 378; July 26, 1879, p. 96.

A STORY OF RECEIVERSHIP

of the three, E. H. Green, replaced Newcomb as president in 1880.[125] At the same annual meeting a 100 per cent stock dividend was approved.[126] A majority of the directors selected in 1880 were from the North, from either New York City, or Philadelphia.[127] The reign of James Guthrie and his Louisville friends had ended.[128]

Not one of the twenty-three receivership lines escaped significant northern financial influence or control for any appreciable time after reorganization or foreclosure sale. The two remaining lines, the Western Railroad of Alabama and the Port Royal Railroad, ended their receivership years by coming under the control of the two independent and locally controlled Georgia roads, the Central of Georgia and the Georgia Railroad. The Western of Alabama went into receivership after failing to pay bond interest due January 1, 1873. In April, 1875, William M. Wadley, president of the Central Railroad of Georgia, and J. S. Davies, vice president of the Georgia Railroad, made a joint bid for the road which resulted in its purchase for $3,129,166.01.[129] The purchasers took possession June 1, 1875. The second line was the Port Royal Railroad, running from Port Royal, South Carolina, to Augusta, Georgia. Both northern capital and financial aid from the Georgia Railroad helped push the road through to completion by March 1, 1873.[130] This financial backing, however, was not sufficient to keep the road from defaulting November 1, 1873, and being placed in receivership in May, 1875. The road

---

125. *Commercial and Financial Chronicle*, October 4, 1879, p. 358; October 16, 1880, p. 403.

126. *Ibid.*, October 9, 1880, p. 382. The company managed to pay a 6 per cent cash dividend on the doubled stock issue in the year 1881. In succeeding years it was unable to do so. Poor, *Manual of the Railroads of the United States for 1885*, p. 505.

127. Henry V. Poor, *Manual of the Railroads of the United States for 1881* (New York, 1881), p. 475.

128. The northern control was further increased early in 1882 when the Mayor of Louisville, Charles D. Jacob, sold to E. H. Green 10,000 shares of L. and N. stock which had long been held by the city. Reports had been current since 1879 that Louisville was considering liquidating her L. and N. holdings. In 1879 it held nearly a fifth of all outstanding shares. *Commercial and Financial Chronicle*, July 12, 1879, p. 41; March 4, 1882, p. 264.

129. *Ibid.*, April 24, 1875, p. 398.

130. *The Railroad Gazette*, October 8, 1870, p. 33; Poor, *Manual of the Railroads of the United States for 1874-1875*, p. 746.

was sold under foreclosure, June 6, 1878, to the Union Trust Company of New York City. The new owners renamed the line the Port Royal and Augusta Railway and selected a board of directors consisting of one from Port Royal and eight from New York City.[131] This dominant northern influence was not permanent, however, as the Central Railroad of Georgia purchased a controlling interest in the line in June, 1881. Formal control shifted December 1, 1881, after the Central of Georgia had selected its own southern board of directors at the November annual meeting.[132]

Undoubtedly the railroads of the South would have suffered even more severely from default and receivership during the 1870's had they not at the same time been successfully experimenting with one of the nation's first successful railroad-pooling arrangements.[133] Uncontrollable and ruinous railroad rate competition was typical of all sections of the nation after the Civil War, but in the South it was especially bad due to the generally weak financial structure of the region's railroads.[134] Colonel Albert Fink estimated that southern rate wars reduced the gross rail earnings about 42 per cent below what regular rates would have yielded.[135]

Some efforts at southern railroad cooperation and rationalization of rates appeared in the late 1860's. By 1871 many southern railroads were participating in annual conventions of general ticket agents.[136] In January, 1868, the Green Line Transportation Company, a fast freight line, was organized.[137] Not a for-

131. *Commercial and Financial Chronicle*, June 8, 1878, p. 575; June 29, 1878, p. 654.
132. *Ibid.*, November 26, 1881, p. 589.
133. George H. Burgess and Miles C. Kennedy, *Centennial History of the Pennsylvania Railroad* (Philadelphia, 1949), p. 360.
134. Charles Francis Adams, Jr., *Railroads, Their Origin and Problems* (New York, 1880), p. 170.
135. Henry Hudson, "The Southern Railway and Steamship Association" in William Z. Ripley, *Railway Problems* (New York, 1913), p. 129.
136. *The Railroad Gazette*, April 8, 1871, p. 20.
137. William H. Joubert, *Southern Freight Rates in Transition* (Gainesville, Florida, 1949), pp. 31-32. The Green Line expanded rapidly and by 1873 twenty-one railroads were included. The Green Line was much larger than any of the other southern fast freight lines (i. e. the White Line, the Union Line, and the Crescent Line) and correspondingly wielded a much greater influence in rate stabilization.

A STORY OF RECEIVERSHIP

mal corporation, and with a very simple administrative structure, the Green Line was created with two purposes in mind: (1) to control certain commodity freight rates of the member roads, and (2) to facilitate the movement of through freight between the West and the South by a system of car exchanges. The line was a success from the start and resulted in faster schedules, an elimination of destructive competition, and the creation of a relatively stable rate structure.[138]

But the organization of the Southern Railway and Steamship Association on October 13, 1875, was a far more important step toward rate stabilization. Membership in the new pooling organization was open to any southern railroad south of the Ohio and Potomac Rivers and east of the Mississippi. By 1877, twenty-seven corporations were members and the pool was sufficiently successful to be attracting favorable comment from railroad men throughout the nation.[139] The principal executive officer of the new organization was the general commissioner. Colonel Albert Fink, for several years the vice president and general superintendent of the Louisville and Nashville, was selected as the first commissioner. Fink held the position for less than a year, but he so ably administered the new pool that northern railroads were eager to call him to New York on behalf of new pooling arrangements covering the Trunk Lines.[140] At the outset the pool controlled only the through freight business with Eastern cities.[141] A permanent division of this business was agreed upon, based principally upon the traffic records of the past, and each line was expected to carry the appointed amount, so far as possible. From time to time, as new roads were completed and joined the pool, or as older lines proved that they deserved a larger share of the business, the division of business was readjusted.[142] Freight rates were maintained in an orderly fashion, but at the same time there was a steady downward trend from 1875 to 1887. Freight rates

---

138. *Ibid.*, pp. 32-40.   139. *Ibid.*, p. 48; Adams, *op. cit.*, pp. 172-173.
140. Hudson, "The Southern Railway and Steamship Association," *loc. cit.*, p. 130; Burgess and Kennedy, *Pennsylvania Railroad*, p. 360.
141. Freight business with the West was included only in 1886. Another association, the Southern Passenger Association, at a later time was organized to cover passenger traffic.
142. Hudson, *op. cit.*, pp. 140, 151-152.

RAILROADS OF THE SOUTH

from New York, Boston, or Baltimore to Atlanta, for example, were reduced roughly one-third between 1876 and 1884.[143] Other beneficial results were: (1) the reduction in number and severity of rate wars, (2) the creation of an effective method to settle rate and traffic disputes, (3) the elimination of much personal rate discrimination, and (4) the establishment of the first uniform freight rate classification in the South.[144]

The rationalization of the freight rate structure plus the mere passage of time brought a degree of prosperity to the southern railroads. Not a single new interest default occurred among the major railroads after 1878. New railroad construction picked up a bit in 1879 and 1880, preliminary to the rapid construction of the next decade.[145] Southern rail securities which had slumped badly in 1874 and 1875 to reach record lows by 1876 and 1877 began to turn upward the next two years. Many southern roads that had escaped receivership saw their common stock reach prices in 1880 which were fairly comparable with the highs of 1873. This can be seen in the market prices of the five companies listed below.[146]

	Jan. 1873	Jan. 1874	Jan. 1875	Jan. 1876	Jan. 1877	Jan. 1878	Jan. 1879	Jan. 1880
Central of Georgia	95	67	53	46	37	40	69	70
Charlotte, Columbia, and Augusta	30	35	35	5	—	—	—	20
East Tenn., Va., and Georgia	53	60	50	40	35	35	35	50
Georgia Railroad	97	85	70	70	73	70	70	82
Memphis and Charleston	24	14	13	5	4	6	5	38

Much of the rail security appreciation came early in the year 1879, but northern editors began to see marked improvement in southern railroad efficiency as early as 1877.[147] Clearly the southern lines were well on their way to recovery by 1880.

---

143. *Ibid.*, p. 151.
144. Joubert, *op. cit.*, p. 62.
145. *Ibid.*, p. 70; Poor, *Manual of the Railroads of the United States for 1885*, p. xiv.
146. The quotations were taken from the first issues of the *Commercial and Financial Chronicle* for the several years.
147. *Commercial and Financial Chronicle*, April 7, 1877, p. 309; May 24, 1879, p. 513.

A STORY OF RECEIVERSHIP

In the process of receivership, foreclosure, and reorganization in the 1870's many southern railroads shifted from southern to northern management. In fact, nearly all of the twenty-five major roads suffering receivership succumbed to new northern financial influence. This can be seen in an examination of the lists of boards of directors of the major roads. Of the forty-five major lines (over 100 miles in length as of 1870-1871) in 1880-1881, thirty-four companies furnished lists of their boards of directors.[148] These lists totalled 335 directors. Of this group, 125 men, or 37 per cent, came from the North and only 210, or well less than two-thirds, came from the South. Ten of the roads had boards of directors clearly dominated by men with northern addresses. While in 1870 a majority of the companies were completely free of northern men in their management, by 1880 no more than half a dozen lines had official boards which were purely local and southern. Of the northern directors about two-thirds came from New York City, a fifth from Baltimore, and the remainder from Philadelphia and other northern cities. Several of the railroads, such as the North Carolina Railroad and the Western North Carolina, had official boards almost entirely local, even though their destinies were clearly controlled by parent corporations dominated by northerners. Probably the presidencies of the several lines would be a more accurate gauge of the degree and extent of northern control. In 1870 less than a sixth of the major southern railroads possessed northern presidents. By 1880-1881 nearly half of the lines had presidents from the north, and only eighteen out of the thirty-four companies could still claim southerners in positions of top management.[149]

The decade of the 1870's was a hard period for southern railroads. Barely recovered from the destruction of the Civil War and the rehabilitation problems that followed that conflict, most roads faced the new problems of the Panic of 1873 without the

---

148. Most of the other eleven companies were without boards of directors due to their consolidation with other larger companies, such as the Louisville and Nashville, the Richmond and Danville, or the East Tennessee, Virginia and Georgia.

149. The above figures came from lists of directors found in Poor, *Manual of the Railroads of the United States for 1881*, and Poor, *Manual of the Railroads of the United States for 1882*.

benefit of any good years of prosperity and dividends behind them. Ill-prepared to cope with new problems, the southern lines suffered much more in the resulting depression years than did the northern roads. Over half of the southern railroads experienced the trying sequence of default, receivership, foreclosure and reorganization in the years from 1872 through 1880. By the end of the decade a measure of prosperity and optimism had returned, but in the total experience many southern lines had come under direct or indirect northern domination. The new optimism expressed itself in consolidation and expansion, twin movements of a future decade.

CHAPTER 8

THE ILLINOIS CENTRAL GOES SOUTH

IN MANY ways the experience of the New Orleans, St. Louis and Chicago Railroad in the mid-1870's was a typical southern railway sequence of default, receivership, and foreclosure. But at the same time the results of that receivership were not typical. Most of the major southern lines having financial difficultes in the 1870's found themselves at the end of the decade either northern controlled or in new southern rail combinations which were largely dominated by northern influences. The New Orleans, St. Louis and Chicago road was the only major line that fell to northern control through the process of being annexed to a railroad company that was physically located in the North. In acquiring the New Orleans-to-Cairo road the Illinois Central in 1877 took the first step in a series of southern extensions which were to entitle that company to be called the "Main Line of Mid-America."

The real beginnings of a north-south trunk line from the Gulf to the Great Lakes came in 1850 when Senators Stephen A. Douglas of Illinois and William R. King of Alabama maneuvered through Congress the first land-grant act aiding the building of a railroad. On September 20, 1850, President Fillmore signed the bill which granted six alternate sections of land per mile of railroad to the Mobile and Ohio in Alabama and Mississippi, and to the Illinois Central in Illinois.[1] Chartered February 10, 1851, and dominated from the outset by eastern capitalists, the Illinois Central finished its charter lines from Cairo to Dunleith, with a

---

1. *Mobile and Ohio Valuation Docket no. 149*, Accounting Report, I, 13, Record Group 134, National Archives. Henry V. Poor, *Manual of the Railroads of the United States for 1869-1870* (New York, 1869), pp. 322-323.

branch to Chicago, by September, 1856.² The new road thus served the entire length of the state. Once recovered from the Panic of 1857, the line became prosperous and renewed dividend payments in 1859, maintaining thereafter an unbroken dividend record for seventy-two years.³

Further south the other half of the great new trunk line, the Mobile and Ohio, had started its construction in October, 1849, almost a year before the passage of the land-grant act.⁴ But even additional financial assistance from Alabama, Mississippi, and Tennessee could not materially speed construction on the new southern line. It took over a decade to complete the road to Columbus, Kentucky, where a twenty-mile steamer connection was made with the Illinois Central at Cairo.⁵

Even the slow progress of the Mobile and Ohio was of concern to Mobile's neighbor to the west, the Crescent City. New Orleans opened her arms to the railroad idea in a series of railroad conventions early in the decade.⁶ In the spring of 1852 the New Orleans, Jackson and Great Northern Railroad was organized in Louisiana and Mississippi. James Robb, New Orleans banker and art collector, was the first president of the road. He and his successors completed the road in six years, providing through service from New Orleans to Canton, Mississippi, in the spring of 1858.

Simultaneously in northern Mississippi other railroad promoters were organizing and starting to build the Mississippi Central Railroad. Judge Harvey W. Walter and Walter Goodman, both of Holly Springs, Mississippi, organized the new line early in 1852 and proposed to build a railroad from Canton north to the

2. Carlton J. Corliss, *Main Line of Mid-America, The Story of the Illinois Central* (New York, 1950), pp. 20-29, 62-63 (hereafter cited as *Main Line of Mid-America*.)
3. *Ibid.*, p. 97.
4. Henry V. Poor, *Manual of the Railroads of the United States for 1877-1878* (New York, 1877), pp. 214-215.
5. *Ibid.*, p. 215; *Commercial and Financial Chronicle*, January 26, 1867, pp. 105-106. The last rails were laid on the line in April, 1861.
6. Corliss, *op. cit.*, pp. 175-177; Thomas D. Clark, *A Pioneer Southern Railroad* (Chapel Hill, 1936), pp. 60-61; Robert S. Cotterill, "Southern Railroads, 1850-1860," *Mississippi Valley Historical Review*, 10 (March, 1924), 396-405.

Tennessee state line.[7] President Goodman obtained some cash stock subscriptions and many subscriptions payable only in slave labor. With slave labor and English rails he slowly built the northern portions of the road but there still remained in 1858 the unfinished "Big Gap" of eighty-six miles south of Water Valley, Mississippi.[8] At a standstill for lack of funds, Goodman appealed for aid to President William H. Osborn of the Illinois Central. Osborn's line was having its own financial difficulties but the northern president gave Goodman his full moral support and sent Vice President George B. McClellan south to inspect the new road. McClellan's favorable report was instrumental in gaining for Goodman's road financial support from George Peabody of London. English money soon made possible the completion of the eighty-six-mile gap and the Mississippi portion of the road was completed by January, 1860.[9] The Tennessee portion of the Mississippi Central, the forty-eight-mile line between Grand Junction and Jackson, Tennessee, had earlier been built as the Mississippi Central and Tennessee Railroad. The two roads were consolidated in 1859 under the title of the older line, the Mississippi Central. From 1860 when the "Big Gap" was completed, the two roads, the Mississippi Central and the New Orleans, Jackson and Great Northern, operated as a single trunk line. Using that portion of the Mobile and Ohio from Jackson, Tennessee, to Columbus, Kentucky, the new trunk line furnished New Orleans with direct rail communication nearly to the mouth of the Ohio River.[10] However, the Civil War quickly snuffed out the growing rail traffic between the Illinois Central at Cairo and the Gulf cities to the south.

The Civil War treated very differently the still disjointed portions of the new Lakes-to-Gulf rail route. North of Cairo the Illinois Central experienced a boom of new war business. Trainloads of recruits, horses, forage, ordnance, and wounded and returning veterans moved up and down the line. By 1863 the system was so swamped with traffic that even newly built and purchased rolling stock and locomotives proved inadequate. Much

---

7. Corliss, *op. cit.*, pp. 184-186.
8. *Ibid.*, pp. 187-189; Clark, *op. cit.*, p. 91.
9. Corliss, *op. cit.*, pp. 187-190.   10. *Ibid.*, pp. 190-196.

equipment had to be borrowed or rented from neighboring lines.[11] Even though the Illinois Central, by the terms of the 1850 land-grant act, carried this huge government business at greatly reduced rates it still made highly satisfactory profits. It paid dividends throughout the war, paying 8 per cent in 1863 and 1864, and 10 per cent in 1865.[12]

The war was not so generous to the lines south of Cairo. The 472-mile line from Columbus to Mobile, the Mobile and Ohio, suffered grievously from general neglect, its inability to obtain replacement parts, and especially from raids by Sherman.[13] The Mississippi Central also suffered heavily throughout the entire extent of its line. Situated in a region fought over by both sides, the Mississippi Central lost bridges, rolling stock, and buildings to the raiding parties of both armies. Losses on the New Orleans, Jackson and Great Northern were as heavy. By the end of the war the New Orleans road had seen over 90 per cent of its rolling stock and motive power lost or destroyed. Seventy-eight bridges were out, and whole divisions of the road partly destroyed three years before were rusting and crumbling away after years of decay and neglect.[14] The Gulf-to-Cairo route was but a shell of its former self in the spring of 1865.

The New Orleans, Jackson and Great Northern was one of the first lines to start the difficult task of rebuilding and reconstruction. On June 24, 1865, the Federal Army returned the shattered road to its owners. On July 3, the management of the company directed the new president, Judge C. C. Shackleford of Canton, Mississippi, to proceed to Washington where he was to negotiate with the government for rolling stock and mail contracts.[15] Shackleford was successful in his trip and returned south

---

11. *Ibid.*, pp. 124-127.
12. Poor, *Manual of the Railroads of the United States for 1869-1870*, pp. 321-322. A 10 per cent stock dividend was also declared in 1865.
13. *Commercial and Financial Chronicle*, January 26, 1867, pp. 105-106. The Mobile and Ohio also lost heavily due to a large debt owed the road by the Confederate Government. Fairfax Harrison, *A History of the Legal Development of the Railroad System of the Southern Railway Company* (Washington, D. C., 1901), pp. 1433-1434.
14. Henry M. Flint, *Railroads of the United States, Their History and Statistics* (Philadelphia, 1868), pp. 352-354.
15. *Ibid.*, pp. 352-355; Corliss, *op. cit.*, p. 201.

with a promise that his road could soon purchase government-owned cars and engines. Turning to the rehabilitation of the road itself, he selected returned Confederate General P. G. T. Beauregard to be his chief engineer and general superintendent.[16]

Beauregard gladly accepted the $3,500 job and started at once to rebuild track and replace bridges.[17] In the next two years he built or repaired 90 bridges, replaced 50,000 ties, and rebuilt numerous depots and other right of way structures. Long before all these projects were fully completed, however, through service of a sort at least had been resumed in October, 1865, between New Orleans and Canton, Mississippi.[18] The road soon showed a gratifying increase in business, with receipts in November, 1865, being four times those of the preceding July. As a result of the growing traffic much of the rehabilitation expense was met out of current revenue.[19] Beauregard gained an early reward for his diligence. In November, 1865, the directors voted to raise his salary to $5,000 per year and the following April they elected him president of the company to succeed Judge Shackleford, who had just resigned.[20]

As president, Beauregard next turned to problems of railroad finance. He made a trip to London to reassure the large bondholders there, and to arrange for a possible funding of the accrued interest due. He succeeded in converting the huge interest arrearage into a second mortgage and returned home after considering a new position as commander of the Rumanian army.[21] Back home in New Orleans he found time, in addition to his rail-

16. Corliss, *loc. cit.*
17. Minutes of the Board of Directors Meeting, *New Orleans, Jackson and Great Northern Railroad, Minute Book*, Volume III, June 5, 1865, Illinois Central Archives, Newberry Library, Chicago (hereafter cited as I. C. Archives). The salary of $3,500 was a reduction from the prewar pay schedule when the general superintendent received $5,000.
18. Flint, *op. cit.*, pp. 354-356; Robert Selph Henry, *The Story of Reconstruction* (Indianapolis, 1938), p. 124; James Wilford Garner, *Reconstruction in Mississippi* (New York, 1901), pp. 143-144. The best schedule in the first months of operation was 13 hours for the 206-mile trip.
19. Flint, *op. cit.*, pp. 354-355; *De Bow's Review;* March, 1866, p. 319.
20. Minutes of the Board of Directors Meeting, *New Orleans, Jackson and Great Northern Railroad, Minute Book*, Volume III, November 2, 1865; April 17, 1866; Illinois Central Archives, Newberry Library, Chicago.
21. Corliss, *op. cit.*, p. 202; *Commercial and Financial Chronicle*, October 27, 1866, p. 522; Henry, *Reconstruction*, p. 178.

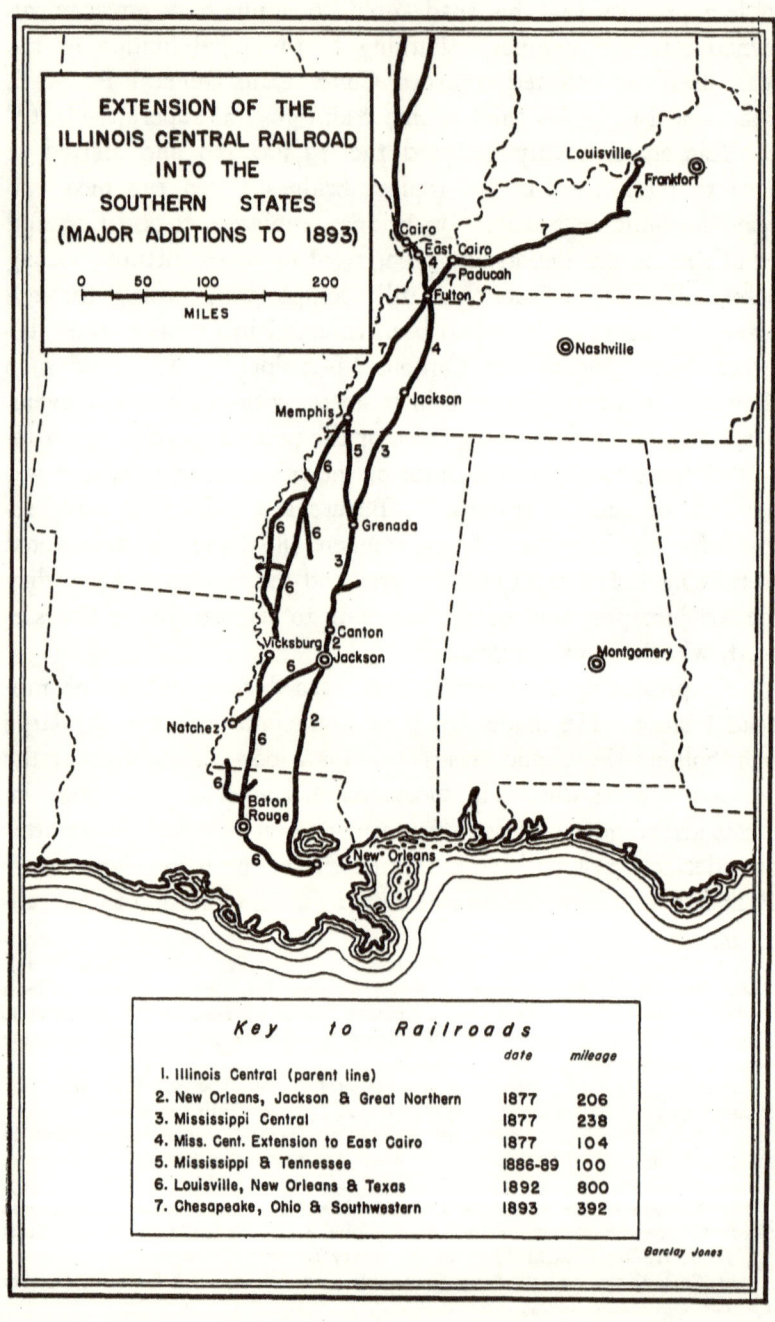

road duties, to become interested in the production and marketing of a new electric railroad brake.[22] He also became financially interested in the short, six-mile New Orleans and Carrollton Railroad. He was lessee of the road in 1867 and later its president.[23]

But Beauregard's pleasant days as a railroad executive were not to last. Towards the end of 1869 Beauregard became fully aware that the carpetbag interests, which had for some months managed the Mississippi Central, sister road to the north, were looking enviously in his direction. He expressed his fears and appealed for financial assistance in a letter to Baron d'Erlanger of Paris, shortly after Christmas, 1869.[24] Henry S. McComb, a smooth-shaven, round-faced colonel from Wilmington, Delaware, was the carpetbagger who was looking with eager eyes upon Beauregard's rail domain.

Colonel McComb had made his start in southern railroading in September, 1865, when he offered his services to the Mississippi Central. The rehabilitation of the Mississippi Central, a problem every bit as great as that facing Beauregard down in New Orleans, was in the hands of General Absolom M. West, who had succeeded Walter Goodman as president of the road in October, 1864.[25] General West convinced his board of directors that they should appoint McComb as their agent to represent them in Washington, D. C.[26] A month later the board authorized McComb to purchase for them fifty-nine new box cars.[27]

22. G. T. Beauregard to Colonel Duncan, June 14, 1867, P. G. T. Beauregard Papers, Letter Book No. 40, Manuscripts Division, Library of Congress. Beauregard hoped to be able to interest such men as William Wadley of the Central of Georgia, and Generals William Mahone and Joseph Johnston in the project.
23. G. T. Beauregard to T. P. May, May 4, 1867, P. G. T. Beauregard Papers, Letter Book No. 40, Manuscripts Division, Library of Congress. Poor, *Manual of the Railroads of the United States for 1869-1870*, p. 312. The short Carrollton line was principally a horse and mule-car road.
24. G. T. Beauregard to Baron Emile d'Erlanger, December 27, 1869, P. G. T. Beauregard Papers, Letter Book No. 41, Manuscripts Division, Library of Congress. Beauregard proposed to d'Erlanger that the Frenchman head up a group of European capitalists in order to purchase the stock of the New Orleans, Jackson and Great Northern. Beauregard confidently predicted that his road could soon be paying dividends of as much as 8 per cent.
25. Corliss, *op. cit.*, pp. 199-201.
26. Minutes, Board of Directors Meeting, September 4, 1865, *Record Book, Mississippi Central Railroad, 1863-1870*, I. C. Archives.
27. Minutes, Board of Directors Meeting, October 3, 1865, *Record Book,*

RAILROADS OF THE SOUTH

By 1867 the rehabilitation of the Mississippi Central had proceeded sufficiently for the directors to be seriously considering an extension of their road north from Jackson, Tennessee, to Milan where they would gain a direct connection with the Louisville and Nashville Railroad to Louisville. When the L. and N. failed to cooperate as anticipated, the Mississippi Central turned to McComb. Colonel McComb proposed instead that he and his associates, incorporated as the Southern Railroad Association, should lease the Mississippi Central and as lessees build the extension to Milan.[28] West and his board agreed with McComb, and on May 12, 1868, they approved a sixteen-year lease of their line to the Southern Railroad Association.[29] McComb's Southern Railroad Association continued to operate the Mississippi Central until the latter road and the New Orleans, Jackson and Great Northern were consolidated under the title of the New Orleans, St. Louis and Chicago.[30]

Beauregard's position in control of his road was vulnerable because so large a portion of the common stock of the company was held by state or city governments. Late in 1869 private individ-

---

Mississippi Central Railroad, 1863-1870, I. C. Archives. About the same time McComb was making comparable contracts with the Mississippi and Tennessee Railroad, a 100-mile line which ran from Memphis to connect with the Mississippi Central at Grenada, Mississippi. In 1865 and 1866 many Memphis merchants made financial contributions to the reconstruction of this road. Their assistance was rewarded and recognized when the company placed in their coaches placards advertising the stores that had aided the railroad's reconstruction.

28. Minutes, Board of Directors Meetings, July 16, 1867; March 20, 1868; May 4, 1868; *Record Book, Mississippi Central Railroad, 1863-1870*, I. C. Archives. McComb was also a figure of importance in northern railroads. He was at this time a director of the Union Pacific and also a member of the Credit Mobilier. Poor, *Manual of the Railroads of the United States for 1869-1870*, p. 405; Henry Kirke White, "The Building and Cost of the Union Pacific," in William Z. Ripley, *Railway Problems* (New York, 1913), pp. 111, 121.

29. Minutes, Board of Directors Meeting, May 12, 1868, *Record Book, Mississippi Central Railroad, 1863-1870*, I. C. Archives; *Commercial and Financial Chronicle*, May 9, 1868, p. 600; Poor, *Manual of the Railroads of the United States for 1869-1870*, pp. 17-18. The Board of Directors at this time was composed entirely of gentlemen from Tennessee and Mississippi.

30. *Commercial and Financial Chronicle*, August 1, 1874, p. 119. During the same years, McComb's influence was growing in the management of the Mississippi and Tennessee Railroad. He was soon a director and in 1873 he became the road's president. Henry V. Poor, *Manual of the Railroads of the United States for 1874-1875* (New York, 1874), pp. 118-120.

THE ILLINOIS CENTRAL

uals, chiefly from Louisiana and Mississippi, held 35,000 shares, or only a sixth of the 200,000 shares outstanding. The city of New Orleans owned 80,000 shares, Louisiana 64,000, and Mississippi 20,000.[31] In the late winter of 1870 McComb and his friends started to negotiate for the purchase of this government-held stock. Beauregard hoped to do the same thing himself but he never found the necessary financial backing.[32] In early March he claimed that Governor Henry Clay Warmoth was working hard to get legislation passed which would permit the sale of the public-owned stock to the McComb Ring. Beauregard had heard that McComb planned to pay but $3.00 a share when the market value was over $5.00 per share.[33]

McComb's plans to purchase the stock held by state and city succeeded and early in April, 1870, both the Mayor of New Orleans and Governor Warmoth came to General Beauregard's office to apply for a transfer of the stock held by their respective governments.[34] Using money obtained from the sale of Mississippi Central Income and Equipment Bonds, McComb soon had purchased nearly three-fourths of the stock of Beauregard's road.[35] McComb was still not sure of himself, however, and obtained a court injunction against the holding of the annual meeting and election of directors.[36]

On the designated day, Monday, April 25, 1870, the McComb

31. G. T. Beauregard to Baron Emile d'Erlanger, December 27, 1869, P. G. T. Beauregard Papers, Letter Book No. 41, Manuscripts Division, Library of Congress. The stock with a par value of $25.00 brought only $4.50 to $5.00 in the open market. Public officials and the company management had long been in dispute as to whether the city and state governments could vote their shares as did individual holders. Beauregard maintained they had no legal right to do so. G. T. Beauregard to General Wirt Adams, May 23, 1870, Letter Book No. 41.

32. G. T. Beauregard to General Sam Jones, February 3, 1870; G. T. Beauregard to W. Isaac Sherman, February 14, 1870; G. T. Beauregard to General Dan Adams, March 25, 1870; P. G. T. Beauregard Papers, Letter Book No. 41, Manuscripts Division, Library of Congress.

33. G. T. Beauregard to Editors, *New Orleans Bee*, March 11, 1870, P. G. T. Beauregard Papers, Letter Book No. 41.

34. Board of Directors Meeting Minutes, April 9, 1870, *Minute Book of New Orleans, Jackson and Great Northern Railroad*, Volume III, I. C. Archives.

35. *Miscellaneous Legal Records Book, Mississippi Central Railroad*, p. 251, I. C. Archives.

36. G. T. Beauregard to General Dan Adams, April 23, 1870, P. G. T. Beauregard Papers, Letter Book No. 41.

forces appeared, bringing with them the sheriff who handed to Beauregard a notice of the dissolution of the earlier injunction. Both before and after receiving the notice, Beauregard attempted to disperse the crowd of stockholders, calling them trespassers. McComb and his lieutenants stood fast in spite of the old General, organized a meeting, and proceeded to the election of a full board of directors.[37] Beauregard refused to recognize McComb's action as legal, kept his old board of directors largely intact, and met with them four times in the next six weeks.[38] Several of the men who were on both boards of directors continued to meet with Beauregard's group. Eight of the eighteen in Beauregard's board attempted in mid-May to work out a compromise with the opposition which would result in relegating Beauregard to a position of Travelling Financial Agent. Beauregard expressed deep surprise at the disloyalty of the group and told them that he would never quit under fire.[39] McComb appealed to the courts for possession of the road.[40] On June 17, 1870, the Federal Court decided in favor of McComb and he and his directors took legal possession of the railroad.[41] General Beauregard continued a losing legal battle for some months but never had sufficient financial backing to achieve success. By the fall of 1870 he was looking for new employment and was complaining of a hand-to-mouth existence.[42]

37. Stockholders Meeting Minutes, April 25, 1870, *Minute Book of New Orleans, Jackson and Great Northern Railroad*, Volume III, I. C. Archives. McComb's board of nineteen men included five from Beauregard's incumbent board: Williamson Smith, E. J. Forstall, L. E. Houston, W. A. Gordon, and A. Schreiber.
38. *Ibid.*, III, 364-375.
39. Memorandum of G. T. Beauregard, May 20, 1870, P. G. T. Beauregard Papers, Letter Book No. 41.
40. McComb's board met twice while waiting the court's decision. On April 26, ten of the nineteen directors were present. Only five appeared for a second meeting a week later.
41. *The Railroad Gazette*, June 18, 1870, pp. 274-275. During the course of the directors meeting June 17, McComb gave the holdover directors one last chance to come into the new group. Most of them appeared during the hour.
42. G. T. Beauregard to General Wirt Adams, November 2, 1870; G. T. Beauregard to Henry Schroder, July 17, 1871, Letter Book No. 41, G. T. Beauregard to General I. D. Freeman, August 27, 1872, Letter Book No. 42, P. G. T. Beauregard Papers. Both Beauregard and McComb continued to complain about each other. Beauregard was always eager to pass on any bad news about McComb's management of his old road.

McComb was now clearly in control of the 442-mile route from New Orleans north to Jackson, Tennessee. Upon taking over the New Orleans and Jackson line he complained bitterly about the general run-down condition of the company, i. e., the empty treasury, unpaid bills, back wages due employees, irregular bookkeeping, and improper bonding of company agents.[43] One of his first executive steps was to establish through service without change of cars from the Crescent City to Jackson, Tennessee.[44] The speed achieved was nothing sensational, however, as McComb ordered Colonel E. D. Frost, superintendent of the Mississippi Central, to place an absolute maximum of 25 m.p.h. on passenger train operation and 12 m.p.h. on freight operation.[45] Even though his management was that of an absentee, since he remained in Wilmington, Delaware, or New York City much of the time, Colonel McComb's direction of the two roads showed a detailed knowledge of railroad problems and also a marked interest in operational economy.[46] In spite of the stress upon economy the two roads were not prospering. By 1872 the New Orleans, Jackson and Great Northern had a floating debt of $1,582,000 while that of the Mississippi Central stood at $503,000.[47] In 1872 Colonel McComb and his southern railroads were not many steps ahead of the sheriff.

McComb was saved financial disaster in 1872 when the Illinois Central expressed a real interest in establishing a through line from Chicago to New Orleans. In the years immediately following the Civil War the Illinois Central had experienced a slow

---

43. "Annual Report to Stockholders of New Orleans, Jackson and Great Northern Railroad, April 10, 1871," *Minute Book of New Orleans, Jackson and Great Northern Railroad*, I. C. Archives.

44. *The Railroad Gazette*, September 17, 1870, p. 584; Corliss, *Main Line of Mid-America*, p. 203.

45. H. S. McComb to E. D. Frost, November 26, 1870, H. S. McComb Papers and Letters, 1870, I. C. Archives.

46. H. S. McComb to E. D. Frost, November 1, 1870; November 7, 1870; November 8, 1870; November 16, 1870; November 28, 1870; November 29, 1870; H. S. McComb Papers and Letters, 1870, I. C. Archives. Colonel Frost was later made general superintendent of the New Orleans and Jackson line as well as the Mississippi Central.

47. Henry V. Poor, *Manual of the Railroads of the United States for 1873-1874* (New York, 1873), pp. 602-604. McComb's Southern Railroad Association had an additional claim of $3,283,000 against the Mississippi Central.

but steady increase in its traffic with the South. The growth of this new traffic was definitely slowed by the delay and expense of the twenty-mile water transshipment of merchandise from Cairo to Columbus.[48] Southern hopes that the Illinois Central would take postive steps to improve north-south rail traffic were seemingly rewarded when President John M. Douglas of the Illinois Central in 1870 entered into direct negotiations with the Mobile and Ohio.[49] But the Mobile and Ohio was not interested in building the twenty-four mile connecting link and nothing positive came out of the negotiations. By 1872 the officials of the Illinois Central were ready to consider a different southern connection.

In the winter of 1871-1872 one of these officials, the director and former president, William H. Osborn, accompanied by his wife, visited Cuba for several weeks. On their return they stopped in New Orleans where Mr. Osborn made an extensive survey of the port facilities and the railroad that ran north from that point.[50] In March, 1872, Osborn strongly urged the Illinois Central board of directors, meeting in New York City, to extend financial assistance to McComb's two roads, with the object of modernizing both roads and extending the northern line, the Mississippi Central, from Jackson, Tennessee, northward to East Cairo. The directors agreed to a plan whereby each southern company was to make a new $8,000,000 consolidated mortgage. In each case $5,000,000 was to be used to refund previous issues. The New Orleans, Jackson and Great Northern was to use its remaining $3,000,000 for general improvements. The Mississippi Central was to use its $3,000,000 in building the 104-mile Cairo extension. The Illinois Central for its part agreed to purchase yearly $100,000 of the new bonds of each company. On April 11, 1872, the three roads entered into a formal agreement to the same effect.[51] The three roads naturally also agreed to

48. William K. Ackerman, *Historical Sketch of the Illinois Central Railroad* (Chicago, 1890), p. 112.
49. *De Bow's Review*, April, 1868, pp. 445-447; Minutes of Annual Shareholders Meeting, May 25, 1870, Minutes of Board of Directors, July 6, 1870, *Illinois Central Minute Book*, Volume II, I. C. Archives.
50. Corliss, *op. cit.*, pp. 171-173.
51. *Ibid.*, pp. 204-205; Minutes of Board of Directors, March 30, 1872; Minutes of Stockholders Meeeting, May 9, 1872, *Illinois Central Minute Book*, Volume II, I. C. Archives.

route traffic over each others' lines and to apportion on a mileage basis through-traffic revenue.

McComb started at once to build the extension to East Cairo. It was hoped that the extension itself could be completed in seven months and that a bridge could be built across the Ohio in two years.[52] The new road pushed northward slowly, however, and was not opened for traffic until late in December, 1873.[53] On December 24, 1873, the first through passenger train between New Orleans and Chicago was ferried across the Ohio on the new car ferry, the steamer "H. S. McComb."[54] Further south on his New Orleans, Jackson and Great Northern, McComb was also busy. Two-thirds of the $3,000,000 of new bonds issued by the Jackson road were expressly earmarked in the tripartite agreement for such projects as filling, bridging, rail renewal, and new depot construction along the main line of the road.[55] McComb also found available money for an expensive project in the pine woods of southern Mississippi, 105 miles up the line from New Orleans. Here at the newly platted town site of McComb City, Colonel McComb located extensive machine shops and terminal facilities. The management claimed many advantages for the extensive change: escape from the epidemics of New Orleans, reduced labor costs due to absence of high city prices, and better locomotive and equipment utilization.[56] Later the Illinois Central was to be very critical of certain expenditures connected with the project.

52. *Commercial and Financial Chronicle*, May 18, 1872, p. 659. The estimate on the bridge was extremely optimistic for a boat transfer was used almost until the end of the next decade. The Illinois Central bridge at Cairo was opened for rail traffic late in 1889.
53. *Ibid.*, December 13, 1873, p. 797; Corliss, *op. cit.*, p. 205.
54. Corliss, *op. cit.*, pp. 205-206. The new steamer could carry in a single trip six passenger or twelve freight cars. A second steamer, the slightly smaller "W. H. Osborn," was added in 1875. At Cairo the trucks of the cars were exchanged from the five-foot gauge of the South to the four-foot-eight-and-one-half-inch gauge of the North. The regular passenger schedule in 1875 for the 912-mile run from Chicago to New Orleans was 49 hours 40 minutes. The present-day schedule is about sixteen hours.
55. Stockholders Meeting Minutes, April 27, 1872, *Minute Book, New Orleans, Jackson and Great Northern Railroad*, Volume II, I. C. Archives.
56. Report of General Superintendent, New Orleans, Jackson and Great Northern Railroad, January 1, 1873, I. C. Archives; Corliss, *op. cit.*, p. 203.

But in the spring of 1874 the management of the Illinois Central was well pleased with the expanding business due to its new southern connection.[57] Colonel McComb was also happy with the new arrangements and determined to join his portions of the new through route into a single company. In June and July, 1874, he arranged for the consolidation of the Mississippi Central and the New Orleans, Jackson and Great Northern into the New Orleans, St. Louis and Chicago Railroad. McComb issued new stock for the new company and most of it was held by the Southern Railroad Association. Naturally, McComb was the new president. The new board of directors was composed largely of northern men. Twelve of the twenty-one directors lived in the North, most of them in New York City or Philadelphia.[58] Friends of the new combination claimed that it ranked just behind the Pennsylvania, the New York Central, the B. and O., and the Erie as a great trunk line.[59]

Nevertheless, the new consolidated company did not prosper. The depression following the Panic of 1873 reduced all railroad business. The line's gross earnings in its first fiscal year (1874-1875) were no larger than the separate total gross earnings of the two predecessor companies in 1872, a year when the Cairo extension had not been completed. The net earnings for 1874-1875 were barely sufficient to meet the interest due on the much enlarged funded debt.[60]

Plagued by a declining traffic in its own area and suffering under what seemed the unfair competition of rate-cutting competitors who were in receivership, the Illinois Central by 1875 was growing somewhat irritable at the rather poor showing of its

---

57. Minutes of Stockholders Meeting, May 27, 1874, *Illinois Central Minute Book*, Volume II, I. C. Archives. The following August the board of directors decided to engage a mineral expert to investigate possible iron ore deposits accessible to its southern connections.

58. Henry V. Poor, *Manual of the Railroads of the United States for 1875-1876* (New York, 1875), p. 616.

59. *Commercial and Financial Chronicle*, July 4, 1874, p. 17; July 18, 1874, p. 62. Poor, *Manual of the Railroads of the United States for 1877-1878*, p. 812.

60. Poor, *Manual of the Railroads of the United States for 1877-1878*, p. 813. The funded debt in 1875 stood at $21,391,000. Taxes and other payments met put the company in the red by $151,000 for 1874-1875. Even then many bills remained unpaid.

southern connection.⁶¹ As a result, charges and countercharges flew back and forth between the central offices of the two companies. In January, 1875, James C. Clarke, general manager of the Illinois Central, suggested to the southern road that a reduction in passenger fare (from $33 to perhaps $28) for the Chicago to New Orleans run would undoubtedly bring a marked increase in business.⁶² Colonel E. D. Frost, general manager of the New Orleans, St. Louis and Chicago, was not receptive to the idea. From April through June, 1875, both Frost and McComb complained that their northern connection was discriminating against them in the routing of through traffic. Clarke replied that it was unthinkable that his road would follow such a policy, since the Illinois Central had so much at stake in the success of McComb's road.⁶³ The southern complaints were probably made in an effort to blame some one else for the line's poor showing. Actually the Illinois Central continued to fulfill all its contractual obligations to the southern line. In the fall of 1875 it started to provide McComb's line with an additional lot of five hundred new freight cars.⁶⁴

During the same year, however, the Illinois Central was wooing the Mobile and Ohio, principal competitor of the New Orleans, St. Louis and Chicago. In April, 1875, Clarke was suggesting to Frost that it might be well to make arrangements with the Mobile and Ohio concerning the designation of routes for unconsigned freight south of Cairo.⁶⁵ Naturally, Frost's line was not too happy about sharing any of the south-bound freight going over its Cairo extension. But Clarke continued to argue that Illinois Central traffic could be augmented by better relations with Wil-

61. *Illinois Central Minute Book*, II, 321; J. C. Clarke to W. K. Ackerman, June 14, 1875, *J. C. Clarke, Out Letters, 1875*, I. C. Archives.
62. J. C. Clarke to E. D. Frost, January 19, 1875, *J. C. Clark, Out Letters, 1875*, I. C. Archives. Clarke was of the rough and ready school of railroading. Tall and forthright in manner, he had come up from the ranks. He was famous for his ability to get along with laboring groups. He was vice president of the Illinois Central by 1877 and president by 1883.
63. J. C. Clarke to E. D. Frost, April 13, 1875; J. C. Clarke to John M. Douglas, June 20, 1875, *J. C. Clarke, Out Letters, 1875*, I. C. Archives.
64. Directors Board Meeting Minutes, November 17, 1875, *Illinois Central Minute Book*, Volume II, I. C. Archives.
65. J. C. Clarke to E. D. Frost, April, 1875, *J. C. Clarke, Out Letters, 1875*, I. C. Archives.

liam Butler Duncan's Mobile and Ohio.[66] In July he was even considering the possibility of sharing the expense necessary to renew boat connections between Cairo and the Mobile and Ohio terminal twenty miles down river at Columbus.[67]

By the spring and summer of 1875, McComb's railroad was ill-prepared to cope with any real or imagined disloyalty on the part of its northern partner road. In April, 1875, the auditor of the Illinois Central, William K. Ackerman, was down in New Orleans looking over the route's southern terminal. He reported to President John M. Douglas that McComb seemed about to give up the financial struggle. Ackerman found most of the southern company officials quite reticent, but one of the directors admitted that their large floating debt was troubling them and that many of the employees had been unpaid for three months.[68] McComb had considerable difficulty in meeting his bond interest May 1, and his efforts to start catching up on back wages were not successful. By late May many merchants were refusing further credit both to the workers and to their company, the New Orleans, St. Louis and Chicago Railroad.[69] Hard pressed for cash, Colonel McComb started to liquidate certain assets of the company. On June 24, 1875, he sold his road's half interest in the steamer "H. S. McComb" to the Illinois Central. The boat retained its name and the legal transfer of title affected in no way the interchange of business at Cairo.[70]

The Illinois Central was acquiring other financial interests in

---

66. J. C. Clarke to W. Butler Duncan, May 15, 1875, *J. C. Clarke, Out Letters, 1875*, I. C. Archives.

67. J. C. Clarke to A. L. Rives, General Manager, Mobile and Ohio, July 16, 1875, *J. C. Clarke, Out Letters, 1875*, I. C. Archives. Such an arrangement would have cut out the N. O., St. L. and C. completely. Nothing came of the proposal, however.

68. W. K. Ackerman to President Douglas, April 21, 1875, *In Letters to President Douglas, 1875*, I. C. Archives. The director, A. Schreiber, had been in the road's management for some time; he was one of the five directors of Beauregard's regime that was retained by Colonel McComb in April, 1870.

69. James Johnson to President Douglas, May 3, 1875; Lewis V. F. Randolph to President Douglas, May 10, 1875; James Johnson to James C. Clarke, May 22, 1875; *In Letters to President Douglas, 1875*, I. C. Archives.

70. J. C. Clarke, to W. K. Ackerman, July 3, 1875; J. C. Clarke to E. D. Frost; *J. C. Clarke, Out Letters, 1875*, I. C. Archives. At the same time McComb also disposed of all his interests in other interchange equipment at Cairo, such as tracks, buildings and car hoists.

the line to the south. Every since the tripartite agreement of April, 1872, the Illinois Central had been gradually increasing its holdings of the bonds of the southern lines. In January, 1874, the directors agreed to sponsor a plan of bond exchange whereby the Illinois Central would exchange its own 5 per cent sterling bonds for the Consolidated Gold bonds of the Mississippi Central or the New Orleans, Jackson and Great Northern. The stockholders approved the plan in May, 1874, and subsequently the Illinois Central exchanged $5,000,000 of its bonds for the same amount of 7 per cent bonds of the southern roads.[71] In September, 1874, the board of directors was sufficiently concerned about their growing southern investment to request the counsel of their company to define their legal rights in the event of any default.[72] A year later, in September, 1875, after having heard all spring and summer of McComb's financial embarrassment, the board of directors requested that their company auditor and chief engineer be permitted to inspect the southern road.[73]

The reports sent back were not encouraging. Leverett H. Clarke, chief engineer of the Illinois Central, found the road bed in bad shape with embankments narrow and ditches filled in. He reported that some recently laid iron was wearing out because of faulty maintenance.[74] Auditor Ackerman discovered that the line's employees were owed some $301,000 in back wages as of October. The floating debt was also large.[75]

Early in the fall of 1875, Colonel McComb appealed to the Illinois Central for additional financial aid. In a letter dated September 25 to the president and directors he admitted that he

71. *Illinois Central Minute Book*, Volume II, 289, 335, I. C. Archives. Ackerman, *Historical Sketch of the Illinois Central Railroad*, pp. 112-113.

72. *Illinois Central Minute Book*, II, 365. The following spring their concern was deepened when it was discovered that the consolidated mortgage of the Mississippi Central had not been properly recorded in the counties through which ran the northern end of the line. W. H. Osborn to President Douglas, June 23, 1875, *In Letters to President Douglas, 1875*, I. C. Archives.

73. Board of Directors Meeting, September 6, 1875, *Illinois Central Minute Book*, II, 394-395, I. C. Archives.

74. L. H. Clarke to Mr. Ott, October 2, 1875, *In Letters to President Douglas, 1875*, I. C. Archives. The poor track maintenance was due to a small labor force under indifferent supervision and direction.

75. Affidavit of W. K. Ackerman, *Miscellaneous Legal Records Book, Mississippi Central Railroad*, p. 187, I. C. Archives.

already owed the Illinois Central $300,000 in back bond interest. He now wished additional forbearance equal to the interest due on the next four coupons of the bonds held by the Illinois Central. McComb claimed that this additional credit, to run for two years, would permit his company to get on its feet.[76] President Douglas and the board seriously considered McComb's appeal for several weeks. After extended conferences, the board, October 20, 1875, found all the proposals impracticable and voted to refuse the New Orleans, St. Louis and Chicago any further credit.[77] In October, 1875, the directors of the Illinois Central considered it improbable that the southern road would be able to meet the twin requirements of: (1) keeping its road in a reasonable working order and (2) meeting its obligations to its creditors.[78]

Late in 1875, one other possible solution to the problem was briefly considered. As early as July, 1875, it had been suggested that the Illinois Central would gain strategically, and the southern road would gain financially, if the former road purchased the 104-mile Cairo extension from the lattter company.[79] In September, Treasurer Lewis V. F. Randolph pointed out to President Douglas the complicated financial negotiations that would probably be encountered in such a proposal.[80] Nevertheless, President Douglas and William H. Osborn started to negotiate with Colonel

76. Colonel McComb to President and Directors, Illinois Central Railroad, September 25, 1875, *Supporting Papers, Board Minutes, Illinois Central, 1875*, I. C. Archives. McComb needed the advance, in part, to pay a debt owed Tom Scott and the Pennsylvania Railroad. The Pennsylvania had given McComb some financial backing for his southern railroads as early as 1870. McComb was trying in 1875 to free himself from these entanglements.

77. *Illinois Central Minute Book*, II, 397, 399, 401, I. C. Archives.

78. Down in New Orleans General Beauregard was gleeful at the turn of events. He wrote: "What I have been long expecting is now about to take place, i.e. the breaking up of the Jackson R. R. swindle. . . . The . . . hopes of our people are that the Illinois Central will get possession of it for all [they] want is that it should be made a first class road." Beauregard was also hopeful that in any reorganization of the line he might again obtain employment, perhaps as general superintendent. G. T. Beauregard to Colonel Ayer, October 26, 1875, *In Letters to President Douglas, 1875*, I. C. Archives.

79. William H. Green to President of Illinois Central, July 4, 1875, *In Letters to President Douglas, 1875*, I. C. Archives. Green was a Cairo attorney in the employ of the Illinois Central.

80. L. V. F. Randolph to President Douglas, September 16, 1875, *In Letters to President Douglas, 1875*, I. C. Archives.

McComb.[81] Douglas considered McComb's price of $3,800,000 too high, especially since Chief Engineer Leverett H. Clarke thought the road had cost but $2,250,000 to build. Douglas also opposed the purchase because he feared an unencumbered title would be difficult to obtain. By late November the purchase negotiation had ended. At the same time President Douglas privately urged foreclosure of McComb's road.[82]

At the end of the year the financial picture seemed a little brighter for the New Orleans, St. Louis and Chicago Railroad. During the last week in 1875 McComb's paymaster paid up the employees through October and started to meet the November payrolls as well. McComb discharged some men and cut the unskilled labor wage from $1.25 to $1.00 a day.[83] But McComb failed to meet the interest payments due January 1, 1876. President Douglas at once urged his board of directors to press for a receivership. They delayed their decision a few weeks but on February 26, 1876, they started legal action to bring about the appointment of a receiver.[84] The next two weeks were hectic ones as the Illinois Central representatives in New Orleans, headed by Judge John A. Campbell, tried to outmaneuver the minions of McComb. William H. Osborn in New York and President Douglas in Chicago were in almost daily communication with each other and with their agents in New Orleans. Since so many of their messages passed over the telegraph line controlled by McComb's road they soon inaugurated a cipher code. Colonel McComb was given the appropriate code name of "subtle." The entire list of code names used by the Illinois Central officials for their New Orleans messages follows:[85]

[81]. Colonel H. S. McComb to President and Directors of Illinois Central Railroad, October 29, 1875, *Supporting Papers, Board Minutes, Illinois Central, 1875*, I. C. Archives.

[82]. J. M. Douglas to Board of Directors, November 23, 1875, *Supporting Papers, Board Minutes, Illinois Central, 1875*, I. C. Archives.

[83]. *Commercial and Financial Chronicle*, February 12, 1876, p. 157; W. H. Osborn to President Douglas, December 31, 1875, *In Letters to President Douglas, 1875*, I. C. Archives.

[84]. J. M. Douglas to L. V. F. Randolph, January 15, 1876, *Supporting Papers, Board Minutes, 1876; Illinois Central Minute Book*, II, 413, 423, I. C. Archives.

[85]. *Miscellaneous Legal Records Book, Mississippi Central Railroad*, p. 169, I C. Archives.

Code Name	Meaning
party	Illinois Central
James	Mr. A. Schreiber
porter	a receiver
Marshall	the Circuit Judge
Captain	the District Judge
subtle	Col. McComb
Jones	General Edward Walthall
fast	President Douglas
slow	William H. Osborn
William	Junius B. Alexander
north	Mississippi Central
south	New Orleans, Jackson and Great Northern

"Subtle" McComb gave Judge Campbell and the latter's superiors in the North something to worry about. Late in February, McComb was attempting to push his own receivership proceedings which would probably result in a receiver of his own choice.[86] Early in March, McComb's men, both in New York and New Orleans, started to destroy vital company records necessary to any orderly receivership.[87] Throughout the two weeks McComb privately collected the bulk of his road's February traffic revenue, estimated at $100,000, and removed it from normal company channels.[88]

But McComb could not prevent the receivership. On March 10, 1876, Judge Woods of the U. S. Circuit Court for the District of Louisiana appointed Junius B. Alexander of New York to be receiver for the New Orleans, Jackson and Great Northern. Judge Woods was reported to be an intimate friend of McComb, but the connection was of no avail in this instance, since the Alexander appointment was exactly what the Illinois Central group desired.[89]

[86]. Charles E. Whitehead to John M. Douglas, March 1, 1876, *In Letters to President Douglas*, I. C. Archives.

[87]. Telegram, W. H. Osborn to Charles E. Whitehead, March 3, 1876, *Miscellaneous Legal Records Book, Mississippi Central Railroad*, 207, I. C. Archives

[88]. W. H. Osborn to President Douglas, March 2, 1876, *In Letters to President Douglas*, I. C. Archives.

[89]. *Commercial and Financial Chronicle*, March 18, 1876, p. 281; Letter from Board of Directors of Illinois Central to J. B. Alexander, March 14, 1876, *Supporting Papers, Board Minutes, 1876*, I. C. Archives.

THE ILLINOIS CENTRAL

About the same time the governor of Tennessee took possession of the portions of the Mississippi Central within his state and appointed General Rufus Polk Neely, long associated with the line, as receiver for the road.[90] Both Neely and Alexander cooperated with the Illinois Central.

Obviously the receivers did not find the property in good shape. The employees, still two to three months behind in their pay, were so demoralized that safe operation of the road was difficult. The maintenance and repair problem was desperate. Less than fifty tons of spare rails were to be found on the entire road, no supplies were on hand in the machine shops, and the fuel supply was exhausted. The remnants of locomotive boilers, long since exploded, were still listed as engines on the company books. Receiver Alexander did find one item in good supply. The road was overstocked with lawyers and lobbyists. Alexander estimated that McComb had spent in his last year over $100,000 in legal fees to procrastinate just debts.[91] James C. Clarke, general manager of the Illinois Central, spent several weeks in the spring and summer of 1876 thoroughly inspecting the receivership road. In the fall of 1876 in his report back to his home office he maintained that the only policy that would ever bring the northern line any real profit from its southern connection was one of aggressive expansion and improvement. He argued that the roadbed and transfer facilities should be so improved as to permit a doubling of the speed of through passenger service. He maintained that a vast potential traffic in fruits, fish, oysters, butter, cheese, and poultry was possible if the Illinois Central would only invest heavily in an improvement and modernization program.[92]

The Illinois Central board of directors seemingly agreed in

90. James C. Clarke to John M. Douglas, April 24, 1876, *In Letters to President Douglas*, I. C. Archives.

91. William K. Ackerman, *Historical Sketch of the Illinois Central Railroad*, p. 117; J. C. Clarke to President Douglas, April 24, 1876, *In Letters to President Douglas*; Junius B. Alexander to President and Directors of the Illinois Central Railroad, June 7, 1876, *Supporting Papers, Board Minutes, 1876*, I. C. Archives.

92. J. C. Clarke to Colonel Frost, November 30, 1876; J. C. Clarke to W. K. Ackerman, November 3, 1876; *J. C. Clarke, Out Letters*, I. C. Archives.

general with the Clarke point of view for in mid-December, 1876, they requested him to proceed south and cooperate with the receivers of the Mississippi Central and the New Orleans, Jackson and Great Northern.[93] They elected Clarke to be second vice president and hoped that the two receivers would, in effect, make him general manager of the entire line from Cairo to New Orleans.[94] Receivers Neely and Alexander did not disappoint them and soon the direct management of the two lines was in the capable hands of General Manager Clarke, with offices in New Orleans.[95] A little earlier, in the summer of 1876, another change took place in the management of the northern line when John M. Douglas resigned as president of the Illinois Central. The directors filled the vacancy by elevating William K. Ackerman to the position of first vice president and acting president.[96]

One of Acting President Ackerman's first problems was continuing difficulties with Colonel McComb. The board of directors had earlier decided to ignore the affair of the $100,000 in cash receipts which Colonel McComb had appropriated in the last days before receivership.[97] Even after the appointment of the receivers McComb continued in his efforts to delay and postpone the legal proceedings necessary to the receivership. Wil-

93. During the receivership both the courts and the Illinois Central ignored the 1874 combination of the two roads into the New Orleans, St. Louis and Chicago. In both receivership and foreclosure sale the earlier organization prevailed.
94. *Illinois Central Minute Book*, II, 478-479, I. C. Archives.
95. Poor, *Manual of the Railroads of the United States for 1877-1878*, p. 814.
96. Ackerman, *op. cit.*, pp. 108, 131-132. Retiring and diffident in disposition, Douglas was frequently misunderstood. His resignation came shortly after the southern line's receivership, and certain portions of the Illinois press connected the two events. The *Springfield State Journal* in July, 1876, claimed that the Illinois Central had lost $6,000,000 to $8,000,000 in its southern venture and inferred that as a result Douglas was being forced out. Ackerman, his successor, still stoutly defended Douglas and denied that any ill feeling existed between Douglas and the board of directors. The criticism of the Springfield paper may well have been due to an old feud between the paper's editor, D. L. Phillips, and Osborn, one time president of the road and still a stalwart director. *Newspaper Clipping Scrapbook, Illinois Central*, Volume I, I. C. Archives.
97. W. H. Osborn to President Douglas, March 2, 1876, *In Letters to President Douglas; Illinois Central Minute Book*, II, 430, 432, I. C. Archives. The board of directors made a halfhearted effort in April to investigate McComb's misapplication of funds but no progress was made and the project was allowed to drop.

lim H. Osborn, who was actively engaged during the receivership in protecting and furthering the interests of the Illinois Central, maintained that McComb's tactics of delay would boomerang against him. By September, 1876, creditors of the southern lines were collecting evidence from accessible company documents which would saddle the Colonel with personal embarrassment and financial obligations.[98]

In the fall months of 1876, Osborn himself dug into the company records and came up with some sensational charges against McComb. Osborn discovered fraud or the misapplication of funds of at least three types: (1) the building of McComb City, Mississippi, (2) the construction of the Cairo extension, and (3) construction of the Kosciusko branch. Osborn was quite certain that a minimum of $600,000 had been misappropriated.[99] The McComb City expenditures were typical. McComb spent at least $412,000 in the building and development of the project, a sum nearly three times the estimated value of $150,000 which Osborn placed upon the land and buildings. It was seemingly intended as a "company town" as McComb spent $45,000 for a hotel and also erected such structures as a slaughter house, bakery and fire engine house.[100] Successful criticism of McComb as a builder of cities was difficult since the crafty Colonel had been careful to get full approval for all his actions from his board of directors.[101]

McComb was also protected on some of the other counts. The books of the Mississippi Central listed the cost of the Cairo extension at $9,691,000, when McComb himself had valued it at but $3,800,000 (in 1875) and the Illinois Central engineering experts in 1876 thought its cost should have been no more than

98. W. H. Osborn to J. B. Alexander, September 20, 1876, *Supporting Papers, Board Minutes, 1876*, I. C. Archives.

99. W. H. Osborn to the Directors of the Illinois Central, *Supporting Papers, Board Minutes, 1876*, I. C. Archives.

100. *Illinois Central Minute Book*, II, 480-484; *Supporting Papers, Board Minutes, 1876*, I. C. Archives. McComb purchased the original land for the shops and city, some 300 acres, at about $110 an acre. Later he purchased from Tom A. Scott (Pennsylvania Railroad) and Thomas K. Porter an additional 152 acres at the very high figure of over $700 an acre.

101. Minutes of Board of Directors, April 13, 1874, *Minute Book, New Orleans, Jackson and Great Northern Railroad*, Volume III, I. C. Archives.

$2,271,000. And the eighteen-mile Kosciusko branch had cost McComb $49,000 per mile to build, while Chief Engineer Clarke estimated it at but $22,000 per mile and Osborn estimated it at even less.[102] As Mr. Osborn pointed out, any misuse or misappropriation of the 1872 tripartite agreement bond proceeds was due in great measure to the carelessness of the three trustees appointed to check the use of the bond proceeds. The three trustees were John Newell, then president of the Illinois Central (April, 1871, to September, 1874), Junius B. Alexander, later receiver of the New Orleans, Jackson and Great Northern, and E. J. Forstall, at the time a director of the New Orleans, Jackson and Great Northern.[103] The man the trustees appointed to check and supervise the actual construction of the Cairo extension was Chief Engineer Clarke of the Illinois Central. Thus any official criticism by the Illinois Central of McComb's actions would inevitably reflect upon a past president, the incumbent chief engineer, and the man the company had selected to be the receiver of the southern lines.[104]

Nor was McComb on the defensive. Early in December, 1876, his representative appeared before the Illinois Central director's meeting in New York with a proposition for a cash settlement. McComb held $41,650.50 of Mississippi Central bonds which he was willing to hold pending the sale and reorganization of the company. He also held unpaid interest coupons for both southern lines amounting to $228,115.41. For these coupons

---

102. *Supporting Papers, Board Minutes, 1876* (for Directors Meeting of December 20, 1876), I. C. Archives.

103. Osborn's thoughts on the situation indicate that he considered Forstall to have been the most careful and diligent of the three trustees. By November, 1876, Alexander seemed very anxious to resign the receivership.

104. W. H. Osborn to Directors of Illinois Central, November 17, 1876; W. H. Osborn to Illinois Central Executive Committee, November 21, 1876; *Supporting Papers, Board Minutes, 1876*, I. C. Archives. Osborn also uncovered other examples of misuse of company funds by McComb. McComb was accustomed to paying bills owed the Louisiana Jockey Club with company funds. On twelve different occasions within nine months (September, 1872, to May, 1873) he advanced to S. H. Edgar of New Orleans a total of some $4,600. The advances were listed under "Sundries" in McComb's books. Edgar, vice president of the New Orleans road, used the money to buy stock. McComb also took care of himself. During the four years, 1870 to 1874, he drew from just one of his roads, the Mississippi Central, $104,920.10 as presidential salary.

THE ILLINOIS CENTRAL

he wished the Illinois Central to pay $150,000 in cash, upon confirmation of the foreclosure sales. This settlement was to close all claims and controversies between Colonel McComb and the Illinois Central.[105] The board of directors followed the reluctant advice of Osborn that the interests of the company would be best served if they forgot the past. Wishing to push ahead with the foreclosure sales the board decided to give up any idea of further litigation against McComb, since at best it would be tedious and slow. On December 20, 1876, they agreed to pay McComb $150,000 for his unpaid coupons.[106] The next week the Illinois Central, in order to speed the foreclosure sale, agreed to relieve the Southern Railway Association of responsibility in the receivership suits in New Orleans. Down in New Orleans Judge John Campbell said he hated to make the concession, but that maybe they should forgive even the "biggest sinner, H. S. McComb," since it was Christmas time.[107]

The Illinois Central was prepared to buy the lines in receivership by the end of 1876. In November, 1876, Vice President Ackerman, William H. Osborn, and Lewis V. F. Randolph were designated as a Purchasing Committee for the New Orleans, Jackson and Great Northern.[108] Everyone expected the Illinois Central to be the new owner since the northern road held a large portion of the defaulting road's bonds and since it had advanced nearly $400,000 to the line during receivership.[109] The line was sold at auction, subject to prior liens, March 17, 1877, for $1,050,000 to the above named Purchasing Committee. The Illinois Central board selected Osborn to manage the reorganization of their new southern possession.[110] Osborn reorganized the line as the New Orleans, Jackson and Northern Railroad, May 12,

105. Board of Directors Meeting, December 14, 1876, *Illinois Central Minute Book*, II, 471-472, I. C. Archives.
106. Board of Directors Meeting, December 20, 1876, *Illinois Central Minute Book*, II, 480-484, I. C. Archives. McComb received his final portion of the $150,000 payment in the summer of 1877.
107. *Supporting Papers, Board Minutes, 1876* (for Directors Meeting of December 26, 1876), I. C. Archives.
108. *Illinois Central Minute Book*, II, 467, I. C. Archives.
109. *Commercial and Financial Chronicle*, December 23, 1876, p. 622; February 10, 1877, p. 134.
110. *Illinois Central Minute Book*, II, 505, 515, I. C. Archives.

1877.[111] He was the new president, Clarke remained as general manager, and the board was composed largely of men already connected with the Illinois Central.[112]

The same general sequence of events occurred in the foreclosure of the Mississippi Central. In the spring of 1877 the sale of the line was postponed until the following August 23.[113] As before, the Illinois Central selected a Purchasing Committee which it sent off to Jackson, Mississippi. The representatives of the Illinois Central bought the road on the appointed day for $425,000, subject to prior mortgages.[114] Again William Osborn was made responsible for the reorganization of the new property. He had reorganized the line under the new name of Central Mississippi Railroad by November 5, 1877.[115]

The Central Mississippi had a brief legal existence, for three days later, November 8, 1877, it was consolidated with the New Orleans, Jackson and Northern to form the Chicago, St. Louis and New Orleans Railroad.[116] William H. Osborn was the president of the consolidated lines and a majority of the board directly represented the interests of the Illinois Central.[117] Throughout the independent existence of the Chicago, St. Louis and New Orleans the Illinois Central held a majority of the common stock.[118] One of Osborn's first tasks was to free the

111. Poor, *Manual of the Railroads of the United States for 1877-1878*, p. 814.
112. Osborn had been well paid for his services in connection with the receivership. He was paid $12,000 for his year's work in 1876. Several months later he was given an additional $10,000 for his services in connection with the foreclosure of the Mississippi Central. Ackerman at this time received only $9,000 a year ($10,000 after becoming president in October, 1877). Clarke, as general manager in New Orleans, was paid $12,000.
113. *Commercial and Financial Chronicle*, April 28, 1877, p. 397.
114. *Ibid.*, September 1, 1877, p. 212; Board of Directors Minutes, September 12, 1877, *Illinois Central Minute Book*, Volume II, I. C. Archives.
115. Board of Directors Minutes, September 19, 1877, *Illinois Central Minute Book*, Volume II, I. C. Archives. Henry V. Poor, *Manual of the Railroads of the United States for 1882* (New York, 1882), p. 473.
116. Poor, *loc. cit.* The Illinois Central board had approved the consolidation of the two roads at the same time they agreed to create the Central Mississippi.
117. *Illinois Central Minute Book*, II, 561-565, I. C. Archives; Corliss, *Main Line of Mid-America*, p. 206. Seven of the twelve directors were Illinois Central men and five lived south of the Ohio River.
118. *Illinois Central Minute Book*, II, 614; III, 14, I. C. Archives. In

THE ILLINOIS CENTRAL

northern half of his road (the old Mississippi Central) from a debt owed to the state of Tennessee. This was accomplished late in 1877 when he turned over to the comptroller of Tennessee, in settlement of the debt, $1,199,000 in state bonds. The Illinois Central had for some months been buying up Tennessee bonds at forty-five to fifty-five cents on the dollar.[119] This fresh obligation of the parent line was cited by some as just another example of the onerous burden the southern lines had become. While the Illinois Central was financially hard pressed in 1877 and 1878 its recovery was rapid, as was that of the southern lines.

The early recovery and prosperity of the Cairo-to-New Orleans road was due as much to the energy and operational skill of its first general manager, James C. Clarke, as it was to the sagacity and foresight of its first president, William H. Osborn.[120] As general manager, Clarke was concerned with efficient train operation and the proper maintenance of his property. One of his first acts as general manager under the two receivers was to insist that the drab depots south of Cairo receive some paint.[121] While his line possessed the advantages of moderate grades, cheap fuel, and low wages,[122] his early months in office were plagued by the twin problems of light traffic and revenue, and the miserable condition of the track and roadbed. He faced the first problem with hard work and a program of economy which included wage and salary reductions of from 5 per cent to 33 per cent in the spring of 1877.[123] The problem of poor track, which was so bad that in a single month, December, 1877, his road suffered

---

October, 1878, the northern company held 57,849 shares out of 81,675 shares outstanding.

119. *Illinois Central Minute Book*, II, 558, 570-571, I. C. Archives.

120. Ackerman, *Historical Sketch of the Illinois Central Railroad*, pp. 113-114.

121. J. C. Clarke to General R. P. Neely, February 27, 1877; J. C. Clarke to Colonel Frost, February 27, 1877, *J. C. Clarke, Out Letters*, I. C. Archives.

122. *Commercial and Financial Chronicle*, May 12, 1877, p. 440.

123. J. C. Clarke to W. K. Ackerman, May 10, 1877; May 14, 1877, *Ackerman Letters, 1876 to 1878*, I. C. Archives. Clarke may have used still another technique in facing his problem for he wrote Ackerman that his motto was the old Methodist doctrine: "Shift our cares off onto Old Master and don't forget to pray."

over one hundred broken rails,[124] he faced in a different way. He filled in three and one-half miles of open trestle work with solid embankments, laid 1,341,500 new ties (equal to 2,080 ties for every mile of road), replaced wooden truss bridges with iron, and replaced every iron rail with steel.[125] In the early fall of 1880 the Illinois Central board requested Clarke to change the gauge of his entire road from the five-foot gauge, still nearly universal in the South, to the narrower 4 feet 8½ inches, the standard gauge of the Illinois Central and the North.[126] Clarke responded, and on July 29, 1881, after many weeks of careful preparation, 3,000 of his men changed the entire 550-mile line between dawn and three o'clock in the afternoon.[127]

But track repair, maintenance, and gauge conversion were not all. Many new structures and depots were built, and new rolling stock was added to the equipment roster. Twelve hundred new cars were built in the company shops, and many more were purchased from the Illinois Central.[128] Better equipment and roadbed led to faster schedules. By 1882 the Chicago-to-New Orleans passenger schedules were comparable with the Chicago-to-New York passenger runs.[129] Gross earnings also improved. From a low of $2,842,000 in 1878 they increased to over $4,000,000 by 1881.[130]

With its southern connection now well constructed, well equipped, and prosperous, the Illinois Central determined to make the relationship between the two roads closer and more permanent. Early in January, 1880, there were rumors of an outright con-

124. J. C. Clarke to Vice President Ackerman, January 13, 1878, *Ackerman Letters, 1876-1878*, I. C. Archives.
125. Ackerman, *op. cit.*, p. 118; *Commercial and Financial Chronicle*, February 16, 1878, p. 164. Clarke stuck to his job so closely that the Illinois Central board of directors had to order him out of the yellow fever district near New Orleans in July, 1878. *Illinois Central Minute Book*, II, 608, I. C. Archives.
126. *Illinois Central Minute Book*, III, 59, I. C. Archives.
127. Corliss, *op. cit.*, pp. 206-207. The accomplishment was without precedent in American railroad history. When the remaining southern roads converted five years later they leaned heavily on Clarke's experience.
128. Ackerman, *loc. cit.; Illinois Central Minute Book*, II, 629, I. C. Archives. In 1878 the two roads entered into a contract with the Pullman Palace Car Company for the use of their sleeping cars.
129. Ackerman, *op. cit.*, pp. 118-119.
130. *Ibid.*, p. 123.

THE ILLINOIS CENTRAL

solidation of the two companies.[131] The rumors were premature, but two years later the northern parent did initiate a proposal of another sort, namely, a long-term lease of the southern line. January 27, 1882, the board of the Illinois Central proposed a four-hundred-year lease with a fixed rental of 4 per cent on the common stock.[132] A few weeks later at the annual meeting of the Chicago, St. Louis and New Orleans, the shareholders unanimously approved the lease.[133] The stockholders of the Illinois Central gave their approval the following May. The formal lease was completed June 13, 1882, and went into effect January 1, 1883.[134] For all practical purposes the track of the Illinois Central extended to New Orleans and the Gulf.

During the next two decades the Illinois Central acquired much additional mileage in the states south of Cairo. The principal additions were the Mississippi and Tennessee Railroad, the Louisville, New Orleans and Texas Railroad, and the Chesapeake, Ohio and Southwestern Railroad. The Mississippi and Tennessee, a one-hundred-mile road running from Grenada, Mississippi, to Memphis, was the first road gained by the Illinois Central. From the time of their original construction the Mississippi Central and the Mississippi and Tennessee, though independent, had worked as a team with a free interchange of traffic.[135] In the postwar years H. S. McComb had gained control over the Mississippi and Tennessee about the same time that he was acquiring the two roads connecting New Orleans and Jackson, Tennessee.[136] Even after the two latter roads went into receivership in 1876 friendly relations continued. Escaping receivership, the Mississippi and Tennessee was still a McComb road at the time that Osborn and Clarke were revitalizing the new Chicago, St. Louis and New Orleans. After the death of Colonel McComb the

---

131. *Commercial and Financial Chronicle*, January 24, 1880, p. 91.

132. *Illinois Central Minute Book*, III, 132, I. C. Archives. The Illinois Central also assumed all bond interest payments.

133. *Commercial and Financial Chronicle*, March 4, 1882, p. 264. At the same meeting William H. Osborn resigned as president and was succeeded by James C. Clarke.

134. Henry V. Poor, *Manual of the Railroads of the United States for 1885* (New York, 1885), pp. 676-677.

135. Corliss, *op. cit.*, p. 241.

136. *Commercial and Financial Chronicle*, December 16, 1871, p. 807.

control of the line changed. It was reported that the Illinois Central was buying up the stock held by the McComb heirs, but R. T. Wilson was the successful bidder. Early in 1884 Wilson paid sixty-seven cents on the dollar for the $450,000 of stock in the McComb estate.[137] Wilson was interested with C. P. Huntington in the newly completed Louisville, New Orleans and Texas, a competitor of the Illinois Central, running from Memphis to New Orleans. When Huntington and Wilson in October, 1884, severed traffic exchange relations with the Illinois Central at Grenada, James C. Clarke replied with plans to build a rival road from his line to Memphis.[138] The Huntington-Wilson interests soon changed their tune and sought an agreement with the Illinois Central. This resulted in the purchase of a controlling interest of the line by Edward H. Harriman, a director of the Illinois Central since 1883.[139] Harriman became president of the Mississippi and Tennessee in May, 1886, and three years later his line was leased for four hundred years to the Illinois Central.[140] The other two major Illinois Central acquisitions were also purchased from C. P. Huntington and associates. By 1891, the Louisville, New Orleans and Texas Railroad had grown, through several purchases and combinations of its own, to a system of over eight hundred miles. Huntington's road was not prospering, however, not because of financial mismanagement, but because of the lack of traffic in a region as yet largely undeveloped. Early in 1892, as he saw his road nearing bankruptcy, Huntington opened negotiations with the Illinois Central. President Stuyvesant Fish urged his share holders to approve the proposed purchase since he saw it as a valuable second line down the Mississippi Valley. The stockholders favored the proposal and on October 24, 1892, Fish purchased the road, which represented a $43,000,000 investment, for $5,000,000 in cash and $20,000,000

137. *Ibid.*, August 11, 1883, p. 151; April 12, 1884, p. 455. McComb owned a clear majority of the stock since only $825,000 was outstanding.

138. Corliss, *loc. cit.*

139. *Illinois Central Minute Book*, III, 417-419, I. C. Archives; *Commercial and Financial Chronicle*, May 15, 1886, p. 604.

140. *Commercial and Financial Chronicle*, May 15, 1886, p. 604; April 6, 1889, p. 462.

THE ILLINOIS CENTRAL

in bonds backed by the Illinois Central.[141] Huntington continued his policy of liquidation the following year when he disposed of his Chesapeake, Ohio and Southwestern Railroad, extending 392 miles from Louisville to Memphis. The acquisition of this line by the Illinois Central was important because it would strengthen the mid-section of its system southward from Cairo to Memphis. President Fish and Edward H. Harriman negotiated with Huntington through the summer and fall of 1893 and the sale was announced in December of that year. Huntington sold three-quarters of the capital stock and most of the junior securities.[142]

With the acquisition of the Huntington roads the main outline of the Illinois Central system south of the Ohio was complete. In 1893 the total system encompassed over four thousand miles of road, and nearly half of that mileage was in the South. Paralleling the greater portion of the length of the Mississippi, the Illinois Central had a variety of traffic matched by few other American railroads. In the 1890's it was one of the leading carriers of cotton (600,000 bales a year), lumber (575,000 tons a year), coal (1,750,000 tons a year), and corn (600,000 tons a year).[143] By 1900 the Illinois Central was the "Main Line of Mid-America." The road of Stephen A. Douglas and William H. Osborn, of William K. Ackerman and James C. Clarke, of Stuyvesant Fish and Edward H. Harriman was in the South to stay.

141. *Ibid.,* June 11, 1892, p. 964; October 22, 1892, p. 679; Corliss, *op. cit.,* pp. 242-243.
142. Corliss, *op. cit.,* pp. 261-262; *Commercial and Financial Chronicle,* December 23, 1893, p. 1,083.
143. S. F. Van Oss, *American Railroads as Investments* (New York, 1893), p. 724. A large portion of these goods were exchanged with the 52 railroads which crossed the 912-mile line between Chicago and New Orleans.

CHAPTER 9

PROSPERITY, EXPANSION, AND CONSOLIDATION

WHILE THE 1870's had been years of receivership and failure, the next decade, that of the 1880's, was a period of record-breaking railroad prosperity and expansion. Relatively few receiverships or foreclosure sales occurred in either the North or South during the decade. Railroad building was extremely rapid through the 1880's and consolidation and merger became the general rule. With the difficulties of political reconstruction finally a thing of the past, the early years of Henry W. Grady's "New South" were years of railroad prosperity, expansion, and consolidation. An expanding northern influence and control over southern railroads accompanied these prosperous years of construction and merger.

Of the last three decades in the nineteenth century, the ten years from 1880 to 1890 were the most prosperous. This was true of the South as well as the rest of the nation. As early as April, 1877, the northern press was noting the first indications of an economic recovery in the South, especially as those states gained their final restoration of local self government.[1] But, in 1878 a general caution still remained concerning the safety of rail securities.[2] Railroad stock moved upward about 20 per cent in value during 1879 and stocks continued to advance in the

1. *Commercial and Financial Chronicle*, April 7, 1877, p. 309.
2. George Campbell, *White and Black, the Outcome of a Visit to the United States* (New York, 1879), p. 380. In 1878 financial authorities on American railway securities who were friends of Campbell told the Englishman that no railroad shares were safe—that if the railroad's shares were listed above par you might with "tolerable prudence" buy the line's first bonds.

186

EXPANSION AND CONSOLIDATION

early 1880's.[3] Southern railroads soon gained a degree of prosperity, especially as compared to their earlier performance. This was generally maintained throughout 1883 and 1884 in spite of rather poor crops in the region and a declining stock market in 1884.[4]

In 1885 and 1886 the country rather quickly recovered from the Depression of 1884. This recovery was particularly marked in the South and especially among southern railroads. Expansion and economic growth came most definitely to those cities, such as Atlanta and Memphis, which were served by the newly built railroads.[5] Relative southern prosperity continued throughout the rest of the decade.[6]

The general prosperity in the 1880's is well indicated by the level of common stock prices during the decade. The index of common stock prices stood, on the average, at a higher level in the decade of the eighties than during either the preceding or the following decade. The average index for the 1870's was 34, for the 1880's, 42½, and for the 1890's, 40.[7] The low yearly average for the decade, 36.3 for 1885, was higher than any of the years in the preceding decade from 1874 through 1879, and also higher than any of the middle years in the 1890's, 1894 through 1897.[8] Railroad stocks followed the same general pattern, and stood at a

3. *Historical Statistics of the United States, 1789-1945* (Washington, D. C., 1949), p. 281; *Commercial and Financial Chronicle*, May 24, 1879, p. 513.
4. *The Railroad Gazette*, December 7, 1883, p. 809; June 6, 1884, p. 429. *Commercial and Financial Chronicle*, January 5, 1884, pp. 7-9.
5. *Commercial and Financial Chronicle*, January 9, 1886, pp. 37-39; September 11, 1886, p. 285; William D. Kelley, *The Old South and the New* (New York, 1888), p. 122; *Eleventh Census of the United States, 1890*, "Population," Part 1, lxvii; Gerald M. Capers, Jr., *The Biography of a River Town, Memphis: Its Heroic Age* (Chapel Hill, N. C., 1939), pp. 218-219. Memphis, gaining seven new railroads in the dozen years after 1880, increased its population from 33,592 to 64,495 in the decade of the 1880's, an increase of 92 per cent. The increase in Atlanta from 37,409 to 65,533 was almost as rapid. By contrast New Orleans had but a 12 per cent population increase (216,090 to 242,039) and Richmond gained only 28 per cent (63,600 to 81,388).
6. *Commercial and Financial Chronicle*, February 15, 1890, p. 223.
7. *Historical Statistics of the United States, 1789-1945*, p. 281. The average five-year index for all common stocks (1926=100) was as follows:

1871-1875, 37   1881-1885, 43   1891-1895, 38½
1876-1880, 31   1886-1890, 42   1896-1900, 41½

8. *Ibid.*

RAILROADS OF THE SOUTH

higher level in 1881 (59.4) than during any other year in the last three decades of the century.[9]

Southern railroad stocks were also buoyant during the decade. After a rapid recovery in 1879 they moved to highs for the decade in 1881 and 1882, slumped to a low for the decade in 1885, and then returned to a relatively high and stable plateau by 1887. Several southern railroad stocks were considerably more bullish and buoyant in the recovery of 1885 and 1886 than the nation's railroads as a whole. The following table would indicate this to be true for several southern lines.[10]

Year	U. S. Railroad Stock Index	Average for Eight Southern Roads
1880	49.3	63
1881	59.4	85
1882	55.7	94
1883	53.5	61
1884	45.0	58
1885	43.4	43
1886	50.8	55
1887	52.4	72
1888	48.4	69
1889	48.1	70
1890	48.4	79

The prosperity of the 1880's was not reflected to any great degree in dividends paid on the railroad stock. Railroad dividends did materially increase in volume and regularity from 1878 ($53,000,000 in dividends) to 1882 ($102,000,000 in dividends) but the increase was not maintained during the rest of the decade. In 1880 the nation's railroads paid total dividends of $77,000,000 on capital stock of $2,708,000,000 or an average return of 2.84 per cent. By 1885 the total dividends paid were

9. The average five-year index for railroad stocks (1926=100) was as follows:
1871-1875, 43   1881-1885, 51½   1891-1895, 44
1876-1880, 37   1886-1890, 49½   1896-1900, 47

10. The national railroad stock indices are found in *Historical Statistics of the United States for 1789-1945*, p. 281. The eight southern lines include the Central of Georgia, the Charlotte, Columbia and Augusta, the Chesapeake and Ohio, the East Tennessee, Virginia and Georgia, the Georgia Railroad, the Louisville and Nashville, the Memphis and Charleston, and the Nashville, Chattanooga and St. Louis. Average stock quotations for the eight southern roads were listed in the January issues of the *Commercial and Financial Chronicle* from 1880 to 1890.

EXPANSION AND CONSOLIDATION

no larger; stock that totalled $3,817,000,000 yielded an average dividend of but 2.02 per cent. By 1890 the yield had dropped to an average of 1.83 per cent.[11] This drop in the rate of dividends was due to several factors: (1) a relatively higher funded debt with interest payments increasing from $107,000,000 to $226,000,000 per year within the decade, (2) while the gross traffic earnings nearly doubled in the decade, the operating ratio increased from 58 per cent to 64 per cent, and (3) a general decline in rates during the decade to less than one cent per ton mile for freight and 2.14 cents per mile for passenger traffic.[12] As in the period prior to 1880, southern railroad dividends in the decade lagged well behind the national average. The average dividend rate for southern railroads approached only a bare 1 per cent even in the good years, 1882, 1889, and 1890.[13] Throughout most of the decade the financial editors of the North were nearly unanimous in their belief that southern railroads were poor dividend payers.[14] From 1887 through 1890, however, many southern railroads joined the ranks of dividend-paying roads and northern financial comment soon noted a growing rail prosperity south of the Ohio and the Potomac.[15]

Regardless of an indifferent dividend record, railroad mileage expanded throughout the decade at a record-breaking rate. Increasing the total rail network from 93,296 miles in 1880 to 166,817 miles in 1890, American railroads added more mileage in this decade than in any comparable period in American history. The rate of new construction was almost unbelievable. With the exception of two years, 1884 and 1885, a minimum of 5,000 new

11. Henry V. Poor, *Manual of the Railroads of the United States for 1893* (New York, 1893), p. xiii.
12. *Ibid.*, pp. vi-xiii.
13. *Ibid.*, pp. xi-xii.
14. *Commercial and Financial Chronicle*, July 23, 1881, p. 101; December 23, 1882, p. 721; December 22, 1883, p. 681; December 27, 1884, p. 724; July 11, 1885, p. 37; June 26, 1886, p. 770.
15. *Ibid.*, December 31, 1887, p. 875; December 29, 1888, p. 791; July 6, 1889, p. 7; December 28, 1889, p. 842; July 12, 1890, p. 36. Among the more regular southern railroads that paid dividends were: the Central of Georgia, the East Tennessee, Virginia and Georgia (first preferred), the L. and N., the Nashville, Chattanooga and St. Louis, the Norfolk and Western (preferred), the Wilmington, Columbia and Augusta, and the Wilmington and Weldon.

RAILROADS OF THE SOUTH

miles of line was built each year in the decade. One peak of construction was reached in 1882 when 11,568 miles of new line were completed. Five years later, in 1887, an all time record of 12,982 miles was made. The decade included the four biggest construction years in the entire history of American railroading, 1881, 1882, 1886, and 1887.[16]

New construction was every bit as rapid in the South as in the nation as a whole. In fact, for the decade southern construction was slightly more rapid than for the nation. The national increase was less than 79 per cent while the southern increase from 14,778 to 29,263 miles was a gain of 98 per cent. From 1880 to 1886 new southern construction was a rapid as for the rest of the nation. In the last three years of the decade, new southern rail construction proceeded at an unusually rapid rate. Between 1887 and 1890 one-third of all new construction occurred in the South. The relation of southern mileage to total national mileage is shown in the following table:[17]

Dec. 31 of	Mileage of U. S.	Mileage in ten southern states	Per cent in the South
1880	93,296	14,778	15.8%
1881	103,143	16,125	15.6
1882	114,712	17,605	15.4
1883	121,455	18,847	15.5
1884	125,378	19,894	15.8
1885	128,987	20,809	16.1
1886	137,986	22,142	16.0
1887	149,913	23,478	15.7
1888	156,173	25,499	16.2
1889	161,319	27,444	17.0
1890	166,817	29,263	17.6

During these last years of the decade the South was frequently building new lines faster than any other section in the nation.[18]

During the entire decade the South constructed new mileage more rapidly than most of the other sections of the country. While

16. Henry V. Poor, *Manual of the Railroads of the United States for 1888* (New York, 1888), p. xxv; Poor, *Manual of the Railroads of the United States for 1893*, p. xiv. The construction in 1881 was 9,874 miles, and in 1886, 8,018 miles.
17. In 1865 the South had possessed a quarter of the nation's rail network.
18. *Commercial and Financial Chronicle*, April 14, 1888, p. 461; July 14, 1888, p. 33; July 13, 1889, p. 33; December 28, 1889, p. 839; May 17, 1890, p. 679; October 11, 1890, p. 473.

EXPANSION AND CONSOLIDATION

the South was nearly doubling its rail network in the decade the New England states built less than 1,000 miles for an 1890 total of but 6,841 miles. The South added more new lines every single year of the decade than New England built in the entire period. In 1880 the five Middle Atlantic states (New York, Pennsylvania, New Jersey, Maryland, and Delaware) had a few hundred more miles of line than the South, but by 1890 the southern states had nearly 50 per cent more mileage than the region just to the north. In the last three years of the decade alone the South built more new line than did the Middle Atlantic states in a decade. Both proportionately and in actual new mileage built, the South was also well ahead of the five states of the Old Northwest. Only the two-thirds of the nation west of the Mississippi built more rapidly than the ten southern states. The increases for the various regions are as follows:[19]

Area	Mileage in 1880	Mileage in 1890	Increase	Per cent of increase
New England	5,977	6,841	864	14%
Middle Atlantic states	15,181	20,115	4,934	32%
South	14,778	29,263	14,485	98%
Old Northwest	25,109	36,945	11,836	47%
West of the Mississippi	31,560	72,200	40,640	129%

The ten southern states as a group nearly doubled their rail network within the decade, but individual state performance varied widely. Proportionately, Georgia added new lines not quite as rapidly as her sister states, but she still laid down more new road, 2,134 miles, than any other state in the South and was clearly in the lead in total mileage in 1890 with 4,593 miles of track. Construction in Florida was extremely rapid since it more than quadrupled its rail lines in the decade. Louisiana, Mississippi, and North Carolina also built new railroads at well above the average rate. Two states, Kentucky and Alabama, each nearly doubled their total trackage in the decade, and built new road at about an average speed. The remaining three states, Virginia, South Carolina, and especially Tennessee, were much slower in adding new mileage. Even so, each of the three states built more

19. Poor, *Manual of the Railroads of the United States for 1888*, p. xxv; Henry V. Poor, *Manual of the Railroads of the United States for 1891* (New York, 1891), p. xviii.

RAILROADS OF THE SOUTH

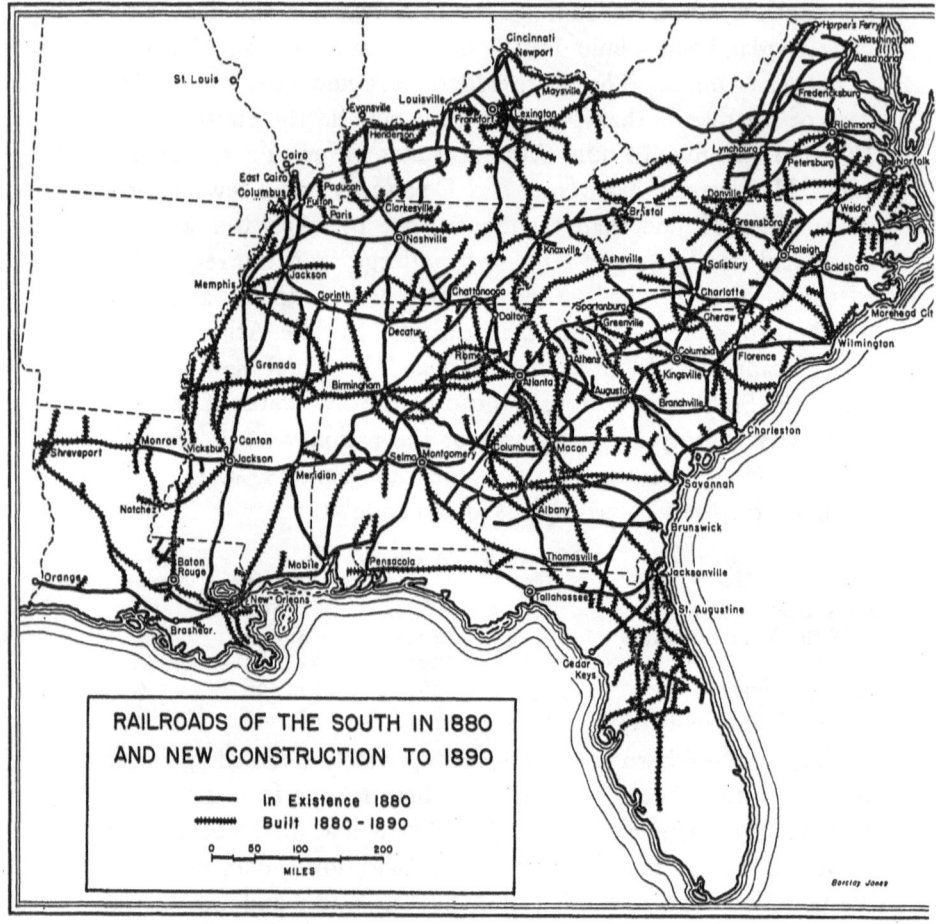

new line in the decade than all of New England. A résumé of the southern construction for the decade follows:[20]

In the 1880's the South also experienced a relative boom in other industrial areas. In both textile and iron production the region made real strides forward. In the 1870's the South possessed no more than 6 per cent of the nation's cotton textile spindles and looms, and processed no more than a tenth of the cotton manufactured in the nation.[21] In the fall of 1881 Atlanta

20. Poor, *Manual of the Railroads of the United States for 1888*, p. xxv; Poor, *Manual of the Railroads of the United States for 1891*, p. xviii.
21. *Commercial and Financial Chronicle*, November 21, 1874, p. 515; September 13, 1879, p. 268.

EXPANSION AND CONSOLIDATION

State	Mileage Dec. 31, 1880	Relative rank	Mileage Dec. 31, 1890	Relative rank	Increase in decade	Per cent increase
Va.	1,893	2	3,368	3	1,475	78%
N. C.	1,486	6	3,128	4	1,642	110
S. C.	1,427	7	2,297	9	870	61
Ga.	2,459	1	4,593	1	2,134	87
Fla.	518	10	2,489	7	1,971	380
Ala.	1,843	3(tie)	3,422	2	1,579	86
Miss.	1,127	8	2,471	8	1,344	119
La.	652	9	1,750	10	1,098	168
Tenn.	1,843	3(tie)	2,799	6	956	52
Ky.	1,530	5	2,946	5	1,416	93
10 states	14,778	—	29,263	—	14,485	98

gave southern textile manufacturing a boost with its International Cotton Exposition. The reformed carpetbagger Hannibal I. Kimball was the Director General and Henry Grady helped manage the publicity.[22] By 1882 enough new southern cotton mills were built, or were in the planning stage, to nearly double the area's spindles. Georgia and the two Carolinas remained the leading states in southern textile production.[23] By 1890 an eighth of the nation's spindles were in southern mills and southern manufacturing establishments were consuming nearly a third as much cotton as were the mills of the North.[24]

The south also made comparable gains in iron production. At the beginning of the decade the ten southern states produced but 264,000 tons of pig iron out of a national total of 4,295,000 tons.[25] Even by 1880, Alabama, with its new iron center of Birmingham, was out in front of Virginia and Tennessee in iron production. Birmingham was the result of (1) a railroad junction (the connection of the South and North Alabama Railroad with the Alabama and Chattanooga near Elyton), (2) some fancy realty schemes by John Stanton and John T. Milner, and (3) the rich iron ore deposits of Jefferson county.[26] Alabama's production continued to

---

22. *Ibid.*, September 3, 1881, p. 237; January 7, 1882, pp. 2-3; Raymond B. Nixon, *Henry W. Grady* (New York, 1943), pp. 184-185.
23. *Commercial and Financial Chronicle*, April 22, 1882, p. 466.
24. *Ibid.*, September 13, 1890, p. 329; December 7, 1895, p. 992.
25. *Ibid.*, February 5, 1887, p. 164.
26. Henry V. Poor, *Manual of the Railroads of the United States for 1872-1873* (New York, 1872), p. 511; A. K. McClure, *The South, Its Industrial, Financial and Political Condition* (Philadelphia, 1886), pp. 97-98; George R.

pace the other southern states and by 1889 only Pennsylvania and Ohio were ahead of it in the entire country. In 1890 Alabama was producing nearly a tenth of the nation's pig iron and the South was accounting for nearly a fifth of the 10,307,000 tons produced in the country.[27]

Southern railroads expressed their new maturity and development in another way during the decade when they changed their tracks to standard gauge in 1886. At the beginning of the decade well over 80 per cent of southern mileage was still the five-foot gauge. North of the Ohio and west of the Mississippi the great bulk of the lines were of the English standard gauge of 4 feet 8½ inches. Actually there were fourteen different broad gauges in operation as well as seven different narrow gauges.[28] The broad gauges were:

6 feet	259 miles	4 feet 9¼ inches	260 miles
5 feet 6 inches	128 miles	4 feet 9 inches	12,335 miles
5 feet ½ inch	20 miles	4 feet 8¾ inches	1,935 miles
5 feet	12,281 miles	4 feet 8½ inches	71,403 miles
4 feet 10½ inches	20 miles	4 feet 8 inches	6 miles
4 feet 10 inches	53 miles	4 feet 3 inches	8 miles
4 feet 9⅜ inches	175 miles	4 feet 1 inch	4 miles

Some of the 12,281 miles of southern five-foot gauge were changed early in the decade. The Chesapeake and Ohio, the Mobile and Ohio, and the Chicago, St. Louis, and New Orleans were among the roads to make the early change-over. By 1885-1886 the remainder of the southern lines were convinced of the desirability of the change, seeing the advantages of closer ties to the North, easier junction transfers, and speedier transportation.[29] Prelimi-

---

Leighton, *Five Cities, the Story of Their Youth and Old Age* (New York, 1939), pp. 100-101, 110-111. The new town was early a city of perpetual promise. Abram S. Hewitt, thinking of the mineral wealth of the new city, declared in 1872: "The fact is plain, Alabama is to be the manufacturing center of the habitable globe."

27. *Commercial and Financial Chronicle*, January 31, 1891, p. 186.

28. Census Office, *Report of the Agencies of Transportation in the United States* (Washington, D. C., 1883), p. 294. The Erie Railroad had shifted from the broad six-foot gauge in 1878 and the Atlantic and Great Western in 1880. *Commercial and Financial Chronicle*, May 29, 1886, p. 649. For all practical purposes all six of the gauges between 4 feet 8 inches and 4 feet 9⅜ inches were considered standard since rolling stock was interchanged with little difficulty.

29. *Commercial and Financial Chronicle*, May 29, 1886, p. 649.

EXPANSION AND CONSOLIDATION

nary planning and preparations kept superintendents and engineers busy during the late winter and early spring months of 1886. Most of the actual narrowing of gauge occurred on Monday and Tuesday, May 31, and June 1, 1886. The change in most cases was only three inches, making the gauge four feet, nine inches, the same as that of the Pennsylvania Railroad.[30] The project was a fairly expensive one, and often involved additional expenditures for new rolling stock and motive power.[31] The southern railroads had also cooperated in an earlier railroad advance in November, 1883, when all the nation's railways shifted to standard time.[32]

Railroad consolidation was another characteristic of the 1880's. The extensive merger and combination of railroads in the South came somewhat later than for the country as a whole. Much railroad consolidation occurred in the North in the first dozen years after the Civil War.[33] For the South the extensive physical destruction of the Civil War plus the depth of the financial panic after 1873 caused a delay in consolidation until the decade of the 1880's.[34] Once started, however, the process of consolidation proceeded quite rapidly.[35]

Several factors were instrumental in creating the drive towards rail consolidation. Closer relations with the North and the increase in through traffic soon showed up the waste prevalent at every change of cars or gauge. The growing shipment of garden truck north in the 1880's and the general experience with fast freight lines also illustrated the advantages of cooperation and combination. The same arguments were seen in the benefits accruing to those companies that had participated in that early pool-

30. *Ibid.;* U. B. Phillips, "Railway Transportation in the South," *South in the Building of the Nation* (Richmond, 1909), VI, 311; Samuel M. Derrick, *Centennial History of the South Carolina Railroad* (Columbia, South Carolina, 1930), pp. 263-264.
31. *Commercial and Financial Chronicle*, December 20, 1884, p. 706; May 29, 1886, p. 649.
32. *Ibid.*, November 17, 1883, p. 523.
33. Charles Francis Adams, Jr., *Railroads, Their Origins and Problems* (New York, 1880), pp. 116-117.
34. *The Railroad Gazette*, October 21, 1881, pp. 586-587; S. F. Van Oss, *American Railroads as Investments* (New York, 1893), pp. 788-789; Howard Douglas Dozier, *The History of the Atlantic Coast Line* (New York, 1920), p. 139.
35. *The Railroad Gazette*, October 21, 1881, pp. 586-587.

RAILROADS OF THE SOUTH

ing arrangement, the Southern Railway and Steamship Association. Also, consolidation was made easier in 1880 and 1881 when so many lines moved from receivership through foreclosure sale to a general company reorganization. Just slightly later the new spirit of optimism and business revival created an atmosphere favorable to new consolidations and areas of concentrated financial control.[36]

Some of the new rail expansion in the decade was due to the construction of completely new roads. For example, in 1890 of the fifty-eight southern railroads which operated at least one hundred miles of line, eighteen were lines which had been chartered and constructed since 1880. Only two of the eighteen roads, however, the Georgia Pacific (518 miles) and the Louisville, New Orleans and Texas (795 miles), were roads of any real size.[37] The eleven larger companies of 1880 (those with more than 400 miles of road) were responsible for much of the rail expansion in the decade and also for most of the consolidation. These eleven companies with a total of 7,006 miles in 1880 consolidated into but nine systems in 1890 with an aggregate of 16,051 miles. Their growth is shown on the following page.[38] The nine systems in 1890 had an average length nearly treble that of the longer lines at the beginning of the decade. Their aggregate length of 16,051 miles also accounted for 55 per cent of the total southern rail mileage in 1890.

The three largest southern railroad systems in 1890, the Louisville and Nashville, the Richmond and Danville, and the East Tennessee, Virginia and Georgia had a total mileage just under 10,000 miles and alone constituted over a third of all southern mileage.[39]

The East Tennessee, Virginia and Georgia Railroad expanded almost as rapidly during the decade as the two larger roads. Its

---

36. *Ibid.*; Dozier, *op. cit.*, pp. 124-126, 138-139; *Commercial and Financial Chronicle* (Investors Supplement) March 13, 1880, p. 1.

37. The mileage figures for these eighteen roads are found in Henry V. Poor, *Manual of the Railroads of the United States for 1891*. The 18 lines had an aggregate length of but 4,243 miles or an average of 236 miles each.

38. Henry V. Poor, *Manual of the Railroads of the United States for 1881* (New York, 1881); Poor, *Manual of the Railroads of the United States for 1891*.

39. For a review of the expansion of the two largest lines see Chapter 10, "The Louisville and Nashville," and Chapter 11, "The Richmond and Danville."

EXPANSION AND CONSOLIDATION

Company	1880 Mileage	1890 Mileage
Chesapeake and Ohio	436	953
Norfolk and Western	428	1,099
Richmond and Danville	563	3,123
Virginia Midland	405 (into the R. and D.)	
Central of Georgia	713	1,312
Savannah, Florida and Western	422 (the Plant System)	1,284
Mobile and Ohio	528	687
Chicago, St. Louis and New Orleans	571 (part of the Ill. Cen.)	893
East Tennessee, Virginia and Georgia	592	2,594
Louisville and Nashville	1,840	4,106
Nashville, Chattanooga and St. Louis	508 (into the L. and N.)	
	7,006 miles total or an average of 637 miles per road.	16,051 miles total or an average of 1,783 miles per road.

1890 mileage of nearly 2,600 miles was practically five times its length as of 1880. In 1880 the road was a line of but modest size with a financial and fiscal record of which its largely southern management could be quite proud. With its acquisition in 1880 of the Selma, Rome and Dalton, the road's main line stretched 478 miles from Bristol, Tennessee, to Selma, Alabama.[40] Several branches along the Tennessee portion of the main line gave it a total length of 592 miles. Before starting its extensive program of expansion in the 1880's the East Tennessee, Virginia and Georgia had been quite modestly capitalized at no more than $34,000 per mile.[41] It also paid dividends every year (except for 1877) during the depression of the 1870's.[42] The road had a favorable operating ratio during the same years, ranging from 60 per cent to 68 per cent.[43] In 1880 Colonel Edwin W. Cole of Tennessee

---

40. Poor, *Manual of the Railroads of the United States for 1881*, p. 446; *Commercial and Financial Chronicle*, June 19, 1880, p. 651.

41. Henry V. Poor, *Manual of the Railroads of the United States for 1877-1878* (New York, 1877), p. 229; Stuart Daggett, *Railroad Reorganization* (Cambridge, Mass., 1908), p. 151. The ratio of stock to funded debt was unfavorable, however, since capital stock represented little more than a fifth of the cost of the road.

42. Poor, *Manual of the Railroads of the United States for 1877-1878*, p. 229; Poor, *Manual of the Railroads of the United States for 1881*, p. 447.

43. Poor, *Manual of the Railroads of the United States for 1881*, p. 447.

RAILROADS OF THE SOUTH

was president of the line and only four of the fifteen directors were from the North.[44] Northern control was thus something less than complete.

All this was to change in the decade of the 1880's. Colonel Cole in the fall of 1880 convinced the stockholders of his company of the desirability of some expansion and consolidation.[45] But the following spring the purchase and construction plans expanded as a New York syndicate, headed by General Samuel Thomas, George I. Seney, and Calvin S. Brice, took over the road. The Syndicate claimed assets of $16,000,000 and had huge plans for its new line.[46] By November, 1881, the tall and affable Samuel Thomas, who had risen from the ranks during four years in the Union Army to be a Brigadier General at the age of twenty-five, was the new president of the East Tennessee, Virginia and Georgia. George I. Seney, native New Yorker and, since the late 1870's, president of the Metropolitan Bank of New York, Calvin S. Brice and several other New Yorkers were included in the new board of directors.[47] With Thomas as president and a majority of the board from the North the road was definitely no longer locally controlled.

The new management added much new mileage in 1881 and 1882. In mid-July, 1881, Colonel Cole, George Seney and their associates purchased the 197-mile Macon and Brunswick.[48] The new acquisition connected Macon, a rail hub only second in importance to Atlanta in the state's rail system, with the seaport of Brunswick. However, the new road did not physically connect with the parent line, there being a gap of some 160 miles between Macon and Rome, Georgia, which was served by the earlier acquired Selma, Rome and Dalton Railroad. Colonel Cole and his backers proposed to build immediately a new line via Atlanta to

44. *Ibid.*, p. 449; *Commercial and Financial Chronicle*, May 29, 1880, p. 567.
45. *Commercial and Financial Chronicle*, October 23, 1880, p. 429.
46. *Ibid.*, May 21, 1881, p. 552.
47. Henry V. Poor, *Manual of the Railroads of the United States for 1882* (New York, 1882), p. 481.
48. *Ibid.*, p. 480; *Commercial and Financial Chronicle*, July 23, 1881, p. 100. This road had been purchased a few months earlier at a foreclosure sale by R. T. Wilson.

EXPANSION AND CONSOLIDATION

fill the gap, the new line being organized as the Cincinnati and Georgia Railroad.[49] The road was built in slightly more than a year and was completed in October, 1882.[50]

An extension was made at the Alabama end of the Y-shaped line about the same time. During 1881 and 1882 the management of the parent line acquired all the bonds and majority of the capital stock of the ninety-five-mile Alabama Central Railroad. This road connected at Selma with the Selma, Rome and Dalton and ran westward to Lauderdale, Mississippi.[51] Trackage rights on the Mobile and Ohio allowed it to enter Meridian, Mississippi. About the same time the president of the East Tennessee road and the president of the Norfolk and Western made a new working agreement for the interchange of through traffic from Norfolk to western points such as Atlanta, Chattanooga and Memphis.[52]

The 292-mile Memphis and Charleston (from Memphis to Chattanooga) formed a third southern and western arm to the main original trunk line of the East Tennessee road.[53] The East Tennessee road during the last days of the Southern Railway Security Company had acquired a major interest in the Memphis and Charleston. In the early summer of 1877 it leased the Memphis and Charleston for twenty years from July 1, 1877, the lease to be terminable by either party on six-months notice.[54] During 1878 and 1879 the yellow fever epidemic greatly reduced the earnings of the Memphis and Charleston. In return for promised

49. *Commercial and Financial Chronicle*, July 23, 1881, p. 100; September 3, 1881, p. 254; Poor, *Manual of the Railroads of the United States for 1882*, p. 480.

50. *Commercial and Financial Chronicle*, October 14, 1882, p. 430; November 18, 1882, p. 574. Once incorporated in the East Tennessee, Virginia and Georgia, the 158-mile line became known as the Atlanta Division.

51. Poor, *Manual of the Railroads of the United States for 1882*, pp. 452, 480.

52. *Commercial and Financial Chronicle*, October 1, 1881, p. 357, November 18, 1882, p. 574. In 1882 General Thomas' road was also adding much new rolling stock and motive power. Thomas claimed that business was so good that they needed still more equipment.

53. For the last thirty-eight miles of the route, from Stevenson, Alabama, to Chattanooga, the Memphis and Charleston used the tracks of the Nashville, Chattanooga and St. Louis Railway.

54. Fairfax Harrison, *A History of the Legal Development of the Railroad System of the Southern Railway Company* (Washington, D. C., 1901), p. 675; Poor, *Manual of the Railroads of the United States for 1882*, pp. 482-483.

financial assistance by the East Tennessee line the Memphis and Charleston officials signed a modification of the original lease by which they waived their right to terminate the lease before its terminal date of July 1, 1897.[55]

In the early 1880's both the stockholders and the directors of the Memphis and Charleston started to agitate for a cancellation of the lease, alleging that they were not bound by the lease modification since the East Tennessee had failed to give them any significant financial assistance.[56] In the fall of 1882 President Vernon K. Stevenson of the Memphis and Charleston finally obtained a commitment from General Thomas to the effect that his East Tennessee road would agree to a cancellation of the lease upon the payment of $400,000.[57] However, the Memphis and Charleston officials failed to obtain the necessary cash by November 1, 1882, the date agreed upon, and when they did offer payment the next January they found both President Samuel Thomas and Director Calvin S. Brice busy with previous engagements. Calvin Brice was quite busy during the fall of 1882, for that was the period when he and Seney were busy north of the Ohio River with another line, the Nickel Plate, a tottering line near receivership which they sold on profitable terms to W. H. Vanderbilt. The East Tennessee officials also intimated that an additional bonus payment might be required.[58] Before the Memphis and Charleston could successfully appeal to the courts for justice, a syndicate operating in the interests of the East Tennessee line had quietly purchased by September, 1883, a controlling interest in the stock of the lessor company.[59] There was no serious doubt concerning the control of the road during the rest of the decade. By 1884 the Memphis and Charleston had executive officers and a

55. Harrison, *op. cit.*, p. 759; *Commercial and Financial Chronicle*, December 14, 1878, p. 626; December 13, 1879, p. 631.
56. *Commercial and Financial Chronicle*, November 19, 1881, p. 560; March 4, 1882, p. 265; January 10, 1885, p. 61.
57. *Ibid.*, August 19, 1882, p. 212; August 26, 1882, p. 236; October 14, 1882, p. 435.
58. *Ibid.*, January 20, 1883, p. 81; January 27, 1883, p. 108.
59. *Ibid.*, February 17, 1883, p. 196; September 1, 1883, p. 234; January 10, 1885, p. 61. *The Manual of Statistics, Railroad, Grain and Produce, Cotton, Petroleum, Mining Dividends and Production* (n. p., 1885), p. 99.

EXPANSION AND CONSOLIDATION

board of directors noticeably similar in personnel to that of the East Tennessee line.[60]

By 1882 the East Tennessee, Virginia and Georgia Railroad had nearly trebled its length as of 1880, expanding from 592 miles of line to 1,453.[61] But the quality of the financing by the new northern management did not equal the speed of the general expansion. The new managers, especially the banker and philanthropist George I. Seney, were very generous with water in issuing the new stock and bond issues necessary for their expanding lines.[62] By 1883 each mile of the East Tennessee system was saddled with $79,927 of stock or bonds, as contrasted to a total capitalization of but $22,937 per mile back in 1875.[63] In 1884 the total capital structure stood at nearly $88,000,000.[64]

Throughout 1883 and 1884 the floating debt increased and the net earnings were barely sufficient to meet the interest due on the funded debt.[65] Nevertheless, the management continued to think in terms of further expansion, even after the failure in May, 1884, of George Seney's Metropolitan Bank in New York City.[66] Several of the directors made personal loans to help meet the bond interest due July 1, 1884, but by the following January a general default was inevitable. Receivership followed immediately and by the end of January, 1885, Henry Fink, previously general manager of the road, had been appointed receiver for the entire system.[67] The receivership of the road was fairly short since the old management contrived to establish a plan of reorganization that satisfied most of the security holders.[68] In March, 1886, the

60. Henry V. Poor, *Manual of the Railroads of the United States for 1885* (New York, 1885), pp. 482, 485; Harrison, *op. cit.*, p. 763.
61. Poor, *Manual of the Railroads of the United States for 1882*, p. 480.
62. Henry Clews claimed that Seney was especially reckless in his stock watering, seemingly never having learned that respectable financial practice called for a gradual and discreet watering technique. Henry Clews, *Fifty Years in Wall Street* (New York, 1915), pp. 162-165.
63. Daggett, *Railroad Reorganization*, p. 151.
64. Poor, *Manual of the Railroads of the United States for 1885*, p. 481.
65. Daggett, *loc. cit.*; *Commercial and Financial Chronicle*, June 14, 1884, p. 706; November 8, 1884, p. 520.
66. *Commercial and Financial Chronicle*, March 15, 1884, p. 332; May 17, 1884, p. 581; May 24, 1884, p. 619.
67. *Ibid.*, January 3, 1885, p. 4; January 10, 1885, p. 60; January 31, 1885, p. 151.
68. *Ibid.*, May 8, 1886, p. 575.

RAILROADS OF THE SOUTH

United States Circuit Court in Knoxville, Tennessee, ordered the sale of the company and the old management group purchased the road at foreclosure sale the following May 25.[69] The owners on July 1, 1886, reorganized the line as the East Tennessee, Virginia and Georgia Railroad. The old Thomas-Brice group dominated the new board of directors as Thomas was elected president and Fink vice president.[70]

Shortly after the reorganization of the East Tennessee road it came under the control of the Richmond and Danville system. As early as September, 1883, Richmond and Danville personnel, such as George S. Scott, were included in the board of directors of the Tennessee road. Later in the same year the East Tennessee Company gave up its traffic arrangements with the Norfolk and Western for a new traffic agreement with the R. and D. and its tributary road, the Western North Carolina.[71] Rumors of Richmond and West Point Terminal Company (completely controlled by northern men) influence in the East Tennessee line were current in 1886, and by early February, 1887, the rumor became a fact when Richmond and West Point Terminal men took over the management of the Tennessee road.[72] Under the new management the East Tennessee, Virginia and Georgia continued to expand through consolidation, especially between 1887 and 1890. Its principal additions consisted of the Mobile and Birmingham (150 miles) in 1887, the Alabama Great Southern (295 miles) in 1890, the Cincinnati, New Orleans and Texas Pacific (336 miles) in 1890, and the Louisville Southern (124 miles) also in

---

69. *Ibid.*, March 20, 1886, p. 364; May 29, 1886, p. 652. Poor, *Manual of the Railroads of the United States for 1891*, p. 194.

70. *Commercial and Financial Chronicle*, June 12, 1886, p. 728; July 3, 1886, p. 22. Thomas and Brice had earlier purchased the interest in the company held by George Seney. The new company had a capital structure of $77,000,000 as compared to $88,000,000 for the old company. The common stockholders lost about 60 per cent in exchanging for new common stock. Daggett, *op. cit.*, p. 157.

71. *Commercial and Financial Chronicle*, September 22, 1883, p. 321; December 29, 1883, p. 719.

72. *Ibid.*, January 9, 1886, p. 60; February 5, 1887, p. 184. Poor, *Manual of the Railroads of the United States for 1891*, p. 472. The Richmond and West Point Terminal Company had controlled the Richmond and Danville system since November, 1886.

EXPANSION AND CONSOLIDATION

1890.[73] By 1890 the East Tennessee system consisted of 2,954 miles.

Of the remaining six large systems as of 1890, five roads, the Chesapeake and Ohio, the Norfolk and Western, the Plant System, the Mobile and Ohio, and the Chicago, St. Louis and New Orleans, were all northern controlled by 1880 or very shortly thereafter.[74] All these major lines expanded during the 1880's, either through new construction or consolidation, but in no case was the expansion accompanied by a significant regional shift in financial control toward the South.

The Chesapeake and Ohio more than doubled in length during the decade, increasing from 436 to 953 miles by 1890. The first extension was seventy-five miles of new construction from Richmond east to Newport News, Virginia. At the same time this was completed, in 1882, C. P. Huntington made arrangements with the Old Dominion Steamship Company for a daily line of first-class steamers between his Virginia port and New York City.[75] Even with the new port facilities, Huntington's road was not prosperous. The road was financially embarrassed by 1885 and finally in 1887 President Huntington himself applied for the appointment of a receiver.[76] Drexel, Morgan and Company successfully worked out a plan of reorganization and the road escaped a foreclosure sale. Melville E. Ingalls replaced Huntington as president, but the latter remained on the board of directors.[77] Ingalls, originally from Maine, had already made a good record for himself in railroading as president of the Big Four

---

73. Harrison, *Legal Development of the Southern Railway*, pp. ix-x, 977; *Commercial and Financial Chronicle*, March 29, 1890, p. 437; April 19, 1890, p. 560; Poor, *Manual of the Railroads of the United States for 1891*, p. 194.

74. The last of the five, the Chicago, St. Louis and New Orleans, was under the northern control of the Illinois Central even before 1880, as was explained in the preceding chapter.

75. *Commercial and Financial Chronicle*, November 13, 1880, p. 511; October 29, 1881, p. 467; January 21, 1882, p. 85. Poor, *Manual of the Railroads of the United States for 1885*, p. 380.

76. *Commercial and Financial Chronicle*, May 2, 1885, p. 541; October 29, 1887, p. 572.

77. *Ibid.*, October 6, 1888, p. 410; Poor, *Manual of the Railroads of the United States for 1891*, pp. 104-108; Van Oss, *American Railroads as Investments*, pp. 764-765; Carl Snyder, *American Railways as Investments* (New York, 1907), p. 156.

RAILROADS OF THE SOUTH

road north of Cincinnati. Expansion continued under the new management. In 1889 the Chesapeake and Ohio obtained, through foreclosure sale, the Richmond and Alleghany Railroad, a line running 230 miles from Richmond via Lynchburg to Clifton Forge, Virginia.[78] In the same year Ingalls completed construction of an auxiliary road, the Maysville and Big Sandy (143 miles), which gave the Chesapeake and Ohio a direct connection with Cincinnati.[79] Huntington's old road at last had a useful connection in the West.

The Norfolk and Western Railroad experienced a comparable expansion in the decade, from 428 to 1,099 miles, but without the embarrassment of a second receivership. Its first major expansion was made in 1883 when it acquired a controlling interest in the stock of the Shenandoah Valley Railroad, a 238-mile line running from Roanoke to Hagerstown, Maryland.[80] From 1886 to 1888 the Norfolk and Western negotiated without success for the entire East Tennessee system, both during the latter's reorganization and after control had passed to the Richmond and West Point Terminal Company.[81] Also during the decade the road expanded into the mountains of Virginia and West Virginia. Early in the 1880's Vice President (later President) Frederick J. Kimball pushed construction of several branch lines towards the coal deposits in the rugged mountains of the region. In March, 1883, the Norfolk and Western shipped out the first of many subsequent loads from the new coal area. In 1890 the Norfolk and Western left the South and acquired the Scioto Valley and New England Railroad, a line extending 129 miles from Ironton, Ohio, to Columbus, Ohio.[82] Throughout the period the Norfolk and Western was one of the better managed

---

78. *Commercial and Financial Chronicle*, April 20, 1889, p. 527.
79. Poor, *Manual of the Railroads of the United States for 1891*, pp. 104-108.
80. *Commercial and Financial Chronicle*, January 13, 1883, p. 56; February 17, 1883, p. 193.
81. *Ibid.*, April 16, 1887, p. 496; July 21, 1888, p. 63.
82. *Ibid.*, June 21, 1890, p. 875; Poor, *Manual of the Railroads of the United States for 1891*, p. 806. This addition required the construction of the 195-mile Ohio Extension from the main part of the system in Virginia down the Big Sandy River to Ironton on the Ohio River.

EXPANSION AND CONSOLIDATION

southern roads. From 1888 to 1890 it paid dividends on its preferred stock.[83]

Further south Henry Bradley Plant was also expanding his rail holdings during the decade. The keystone of the Plant system was the Savannah, Florida and Western which he had reorganized at the beginning of the decade out of the Atlantic and Gulf, a road earlier purchased at a foreclosure sale. A little later he purchased a second road in the same way, the Charleston and Savannah Railway.[84] In 1882 Plant organized, with the assistance of such northern capitalists as Henry Morrison Flagler, Morris K. Jessup, and W. T. Walters, the Plant Investment Company. The new company quickly expanded its rail holdings. In 1884 it purchased the South Florida Railroad, a new road that was building from Sanford, Florida, to Tampa.[85] At about the same time the Plant Investment Company acquired from the German owners a controlling interest in the Brunswick and Western, a line that served the same general portion of Georgia as Plant's first line, the Savannah, Florida and Western.[86] At the end of the decade, Plant and his associates obtained a fifth line when they acquired the Alabama Midland Railway in 1890. The Alabama Midland was a recently constructed, 208-mile line running from Bainbridge, Georgia, the western terminal of the Savannah, Florida and Western, to Montgomery, Alabama.[87] Plant was also associated with W. T. Walters and B. F. Newcomer of Baltimore in their control of the Wilmington and Weldon, the Wilmington, Columbia and Augusta, and the Northeastern Railroad of South Carolina. Plant's system plus the Wilmington roads made a total of over two thousand miles.[88]

Unlike the other major systems of the period, the Central of Georgia was locally controlled at the beginning of the decade.

---

83. Poor, *Manual of the Railroads of the United States for 1891*, p. 808.
84. Poor, *Manual of the Railroads of the United States for 1885*, pp. 419, 446.
85. Poor, *Manual of the Railroads of the United States for 1891*, p. 529.
86. *Commercial and Financial Chronicle*, August 30, 1884, p. 233; October 10, 1885, p. 419. Dozier, *The History of the Atlantic Coast Line*, pp. 132-137.
87. *Commercial and Financial Chronicle*, November 3, 1888, p. 532; July 12, 1890, p. 50.
88. Eventually, in the early twentieth century, the Plant System, as well as the Wilmington, roads were all included in the Atlantic Coast Line.

RAILROADS OF THE SOUTH

Everyone of the eleven directors in 1882 was from Georgia.[89] It was a prosperous road and paid regular dividends of from 4 per cent to 8 per cent throughout the 1880's.[90] During the decade the Central also expanded its system, increasing it from 713 to 1,312 miles. In 1880 President William M. Wadley added the Montgomery and Eufaula Railway to the Central system.[91] This eighty-mile road connected the western terminal of the Southwestern Railroad (leased by the Central since 1869) with Montgomery, Alabama. Later in the decade, in 1886, the Central leased the eighty-four-mile Mobile and Girard, a second road that connected its Georgia system with Alabama.[92] At about the same time it was acquiring a group of smaller lines connecting central Georgia with Birmingham, Alabama. These short lines were consolidated in July, 1888, into the Savannah and Western Railway, a 428-mile road whose main stem ran from Americus, Georgia, to Birmingham.[93] The expanding and prosperous Central of Georgia soon attracted the interest of that rail octopus of Virginia, the Richmond and West Point Terminal Company. This holding company acquired control of the Central of Georgia in 1888 and with the shift in control one of the last prosperous southern managed roads was lost to the North.[94]

The extensive railway consolidation in the decade caused a general shifting of financial influence and control from the South to the North. What had been but a trend toward northern control at the beginning of the decade had by 1890 become an accomplished fact. In 1880 of the forty-five major lines, 37 per cent of the directors came from the North and 63 per cent from the South. By 1890 nearly half of the railroad directors of southern railroads were northern men.

In 1890 there were fifty-eight major roads (over 100 miles in length) in the South that furnished lists of directors. These

---

89. Poor, *Manual of the Railroads of the United States for 1882*, p. 433.
90. Poor, *Manual of the Railroads of the United States for 1891*, p. 92.
91. *Commercial and Financial Chronicle*, October 16, 1880, p. 404.
92. *Ibid.*, October 2, 1886, p. 398.
93. *Ibid.*, August 25, 1888, p. 218; Poor, *Manual of the Railroads of the United States for 1891*, p. 97.
94. Poor, *Manual of the Railroads of the United States for 1891*, p. 91; *Commercial and Financial Chronicle*, October 27, 1888, p. 486; Snyder, *American Railways as Investments*, p. 140.

EXPANSION AND CONSOLIDATION

roads constituted the bulk of the southern mileage for they had an aggregate of 21,560 miles, or 74 per cent of the total rail network for the region. Twelve of the 58 lines were really large systems consisting of 500 miles or more. These 12 lines averaged nearly 1,000 miles per road and totalled 11,845 miles. The remaining 46 shorter roads averaged only slightly over 200 miles per road for a total of 9,715 miles. Forty of the companies were older lines with corporate histories preceding 1880, while the remaining eighteen companies were all chartered and built in the decade of the 1880's. The 58 lines had a total of 571 directors in 1890, or an average of nearly 10 directors per road. Of the total group 269, or 47 per cent, were from the North and 302, or 53 per cent, were from the South. The degree of northern or southern financial influence definitely varied with the age or size of the company as indicated below:

	Southern Directors	%	Northern Directors	%
16 newer and shorter roads (built since 1880 and 100-500 miles)	92	63%	54	37%
30 older and shorter roads (started before 1880 and 100-500 miles)	164	58%	120	42%
10 older and longer roads (started before 1880 and over 500 miles)	42	34%	81	66%
2 newer and longer roads (built since 1880 and over 500 miles)	4	22%	14	78%
	302		269	

Quite clearly the shorter lines were more inclined to local control, while the larger systems were more apt to be dominated by the North. Of the 269 northern directors, nearly two-thirds, or 173, lived in New York City, not quite a tenth (25) came from Baltimore, and smaller numbers gave Boston (14) or Philadelphia (13) as their residence. About a sixth of the group, or forty-four, came from other cities or states north of the Ohio and Potomac rivers.[95]

The degree of northern financial influence present in 1890 increases when one looks beyond the bare directorship figures at the companies themselves, their presidents, and the actual mile-

---

95. All the figures and statistics on directorships and road mileage are based on the several company reports in Poor, *Manual of the Railroads of the United States for 1891.*

age controlled. Northern men dominated the boards of directors of a slight majority of the railroad companies, thirty out of fifty-eight to be exact, northern men were presidents of thirty-six of the fifty-eight roads, including nine of the twelve longer lines and two-thirds of the older companies.[96] Since northern directors and presidents predominated in the longer lines, northern control of southern railroads was still greater when viewed upon the basis of mileage controlled. The 30 companies managed by northern men accounted for 14,638 miles of road or 68 per cent of the aggregate mileage of the 58 lines. This can be clearly seen in the table below:

	Southern controlled		Northern controlled	
	Company	Mileage	Company	Mileage
16 newer and shorter roads	10	1,453	6	1,477
30 older and shorter roads	16	3,505	14	3,280
10 older and longer roads	2	1,964	8	8,568
2 newer and longer roads			2	1,313
	28	6,922	30	14,638
Average length per line	247 miles		488 miles	

The above figures indicate that in 1890 twenty-eight southern roads of the fifty-eight major lines were still southern controlled. On a basis of directors this would seem to be true. But, a closer examination of the corporate and financial structure of the "locally controlled" roads reveals that many of them were largely northern managed. Actually thirteen of the twenty-eight lines, because of leases, stock ownership, or other financial ties, were clearly northern dominated. These thirteen lines are described (name, age, length, and actual control) on the following page. With these subtractions from the list of locally controlled roads, only fifteen major southern railroads (over 100 miles in length) remained under real southern management in 1890.[97] These 15 lines had a total length of only 2,550 miles or less than 12 per

96. Of all the longer roads, those over five hundred miles in length, northern men held all the presidencies except in the case of the Central of Georgia, the Georgia Pacific, and the Nashville, Chattanooga and St. Louis.

97. The fifteen roads were: the Atlanta and Florida (105 miles), the Cape Fear and Yadkin (338 miles), the Chattanooga, Rome and Columbus (157 miles), the Covington and Macon (107 miles), the Georgia Railroad (306 miles), the Georgia, Southern and Florida (285 miles), the Louisville, St. Louis and Texas (185 miles), the Marietta and North Georgia (118 miles), the Orange

EXPANSION AND CONSOLIDATION

Name	Age	Length	Actual control
Elizabethtown, Lexington and Big Sandy	old	140	Leased in 1886 to Newport News and Miss. Valley Co., a Huntington holding company.
Port Royal and Augusta	old	112	Majority of stock controlled by the Central of Georgia.
Port Royal and Western Carolina	old	228	Majority of stock owned by the Central of Georgia.
Western Railway of Alabama	old	132	Majority of stock controlled by the Central of Georgia.
Charlotte, Columbia and Augusta	old	372	Leased to Richmond and Danville.
Columbia and Greenville	old	163	Leased to Richmond and Danville.
Virginia Midland	old	412	Leased to Richmond and Danville.
Wilmington and Weldon	old	450	Controlled since 1870's by capitalists from Baltimore.
Charleston and Savannah	old	120	Controlled by H. B. Plant and northern associates.
Central of Georgia	old	1,312	Controlled since 1888 by northern holding company, the Richmond and West Point Terminal Company.
Nashville, Chattanooga and St. Louis	old	652	Majority of stock owned by Louisville and Nashville.
Pensacola and Atlantic Railroad	new	160	Majority of stock owned by Louisville and Nashville.
East and West Railroad of Alabama	new	119	In receivership but under strong northern influence.

cent of the total mileage of the 58 major southern roads. Clearly the decade of the 1880's brought the South not only rail prosperity, expansion, and consolidation, but also a vast expansion of northern financial domination.

Belt (152 miles), the Raleigh and Augusta (129 miles), the Raleigh and Gaston (107 miles), the Savannah, Americus and Montgomery (173 miles), the Tennessee Midland (135 miles), the Western and Atlantic (138 miles), and the Lynchburg and Durham (115 miles).

CHAPTER 10

THE LOUISVILLE AND NASHVILLE

IN THE last third of the nineteenth century the Louisville and Nashville Railroad was one of the few southern lines that managed to expand quite rapidly and still remain fairly prosperous. Even though in its conception it was intended as a trade artery for the Ohio River city of Louisville, the road was essentially a southern line. The first traffic over the new route, when it was opened in 1859, was the movement of supplies destined for drought-ridden southern states.[1] The financial control of the road remained in local and southern hands until after 1880, and as the road expanded in the post-Civil War years nearly every extension carried the line further south.

From the beginning fortune smiled upon the Louisville and Nashville. Instead of destruction and ruin, the Civil War brought the line a flood of new business and early prosperity. While other southern roads were worrying about the problems of rehabilitation the L. and N. was declaring record-breaking dividends. The 1870's brought the road not receivership, but continued expansion. The climax of expansion and consolidation came in the decade of the 1880's and was accompanied by a shift in control to the North.[2] The new northern management at times proved embarrassing but the road again escaped receivership and at the turn of the century consisted of a five-thousand-mile system that was once more paying

---

1. Thomas D. Clark, *The Beginning of the L. and N.* (Louisville, Kentucky, 1933), pp. 8-9.
2. The expansion and addition of new mileage by decades was as follows: 1870's, 1,448 miles added; 1880's, 2,256 miles added; and 1890's, 933 miles added.

dividends.³ In growing up the Louisville and Nashville had experienced few serious growing pains.

The prosperity of the Civil War years was due to the location of the line and also to the careful and crafty management of the road's president, the eccentric and sometimes arrogant James Guthrie. At the outbreak of war the L. and N. was the only line, running through neutral Kentucky as it did, offering direct communication between the railway systems of the South and the North. Anticipating scarcities for the future, the Confederates feverishly bought supplies in the North and shipped them south over the L. and N.⁴ This lucrative traffic continued until September, 1861, when President Guthrie rather reluctantly decided to be a Union man.⁵ He obtained higher than normal rates for his Federal business, a traffic growing so rapidly that he was required to rent extra locomotives from the United States Government.⁶ Guthrie in general cooperated with the government and received his reward in larger and larger profits.⁷ The road's gross earnings increased five-fold during the war, the operating ratio constantly remained below 50 per cent, and dividends of as high as 16 per cent (in 1864) were declared.⁸

This prosperity continued after the war. The road continued to pay good dividends, even one of 40 per cent in 1868.⁹ Net earnings which had been but $75,000 in 1858 were up to $1,142,000 by 1870.¹⁰ While other southern railroads were con-

3. H. V. and H. W. Poor, *Manual of the Railroads of the United States for 1900* (New York, 1901), pp. 418-421.
4. Samuel Richey Kamm, *The Civil War Career of Thomas A. Scott* (Philadelphia, 1940), pp. 93-94; Georgia R. Leighton, *Five Cities, the Story of Their Youth and Old Age* (New York, 1939), p. 62.
5. Leighton, *op. cit.*, pp. 63-65.
6. *Ibid.*; Guthrie claimed the higher rates on the grounds that his road was so near the seat of conflict. For the first year of the war portions of his line did suffer some damage. John H. Kennaway, *On Sherman's Track, or the South After the War* (London, 1867), p. 28; Kamm, *op. cit.*, p. 172.
7. *Memoirs of General W. T. Sherman* (New York, 1891), II, 11-12.
8. Henry V. Poor, *Manual of the Railroads of the United States for 1869-1870* (New York, 1869), p. 57; Ellis Merton Coulter, *The Cincinnati Southern Railroad and the Struggle for Southern Commerce, 1865-1872* (Chicago, 1922), p. 11; *Louisville and Nashville Valuation Docket no. 456*, Accounting Report, II, 57, Record Group 134, National Archives.
9. *Louisville and Nashville Valuation Docket no. 456*, Accounting Report, II, 57, Record Group 134, National Archives.
10. Coulter, *loc. cit.*

cerned with the exorbitant costs of northern money and the general problems of physical reconstruction, James Guthrie was preparing his prosperous road for a general expansion southward. In 1868, the same year that he resigned his seat in the Senate due to failing health, Guthrie gave up the presidency of the L. and N., handing the road over to his good grocer friend, H. D. Newcomb.[11] One of Newcomb's first problems as president was to meet the growing threat of Louisville's up-river rival, the city of Cincinnati.

At the end of the Civil War Cincinnati was at a serious disadvantage in its commercial competition with Louisville for the trade of the South. In 1865 the Queen City was at the upper end of a great "railroad desert," an area stretching from Harpers Ferry to Nashville and untouched by a single rail line.[12] To reach some of their southern patrons, Cincinnati merchants shipped goods via Baltimore and thence by water and rail to the Carolinas or Georgia. The other alternative, a route via Louisville, subjected the merchants of Cincinnati to rate and transfer discrimination at the hands of the L. and N.[13] As business and marketing methods changed in the postwar South, Louisville also gained. The destruction of the plantation system plus the appearance of the freedman as a new direct consumer resulted in the appearance of general merchandise stores at every crossroad. These new southern merchants much preferred the rapid service and cheaper transportation costs available at Louisville to any original cost savings possible 150 miles upstream at Cincinnati.[14] Louisville was rapidly threatening to displace Cincinnati as the chief distributing point of northern merchandise to southern consumers. Louisville merchants and wholesalers contributed further to the

---

11. Leighton, *op. cit.*, p. 66; Poor, *Manual of the Railroads of the United States for 1869-1870*, p. 58.

12. Coulter, *op. cit.*, pp. 27-28; Charles G. Hall, *The Cincinnati Southern Railway, A History* (Cincinnati, 1902), p. 50.

13. Coulter, *op. cit.*, pp. 12-13, 26-27. On one occasion a merchant in Chattanooga ordered goods from Boston and from Cincinnati on the same day. The Boston shipment arrived in ten days; that from Cincinnati, via Louisville, appeared after two months.

14. *Ibid.*, p. 64; J. H. Hollander, *The Cincinnati Southern Railway, A Study in Municipal Activity* (Baltimore, 1894), p. 18; Leighton, *Five Cities*, p. 65; E. A. Ferguson, *Founding of the Cincinnati Southern Railway* (Cincinnati, 1905), p. 13.

diversion of trade by sending hundreds of traveling salesmen into the South, often as far as Texas.

Long dependent upon the Ohio River as the chief artery of their trade, the city fathers of Cincinnati realized after 1865 that the future of their southern business depended upon gaining a direct rail connection with the South. Early in 1866 the Chamber of Commerce proposed offering a $1,000,000 bonus to any association of capitalists who would build a first-class line between Cincinnati and Knoxville, Tennessee.[15] Such a proposition was of questionable legality, for the Ohio state constitution of 1850 specifically prohibited any state, county, or municipal aid to any private enterprise or internal improvement.[16] A careful study of the constitutional limitation led E. A. Ferguson, a Cincinnati attorney, to believe that while Cincinnati could lend no money to a privately built railroad, the city itself could legally build a railroad of its own.[17] Accordingly, a bill permitting Ohio cities of over 150,000 in population to build railroads was introduced at Columbus and by May 4, 1869, both houses of the state legislature had approved the measure by large majorities. Later, at a special election in the summer of 1869, the citizens of Cincinnati approved the project and the city voted $50,000 to five new trustees for purposes of preliminary surveys and planning.[18]

The first project of the trustees was to obtain the approval of the Kentucky and Tennessee legislatures for a right of way through the two states to the intended southern terminus of Chattanooga. The trustees had little difficulty in Tennessee for there the state legislature by January 20, 1870, passed legislation granting the desired right of way.[19] The promoters had more difficulty in Kentucky, however, for the L. and N. was a potent political force

---

15. *Commercial and Financial Chronicle*, March 10, 1866, p. 312; *De Bow's Review*, July, 1866, pp. 106-107; February, 1867, p. 214.

16. Hollander, *loc. cit.*; Ferguson, *op. cit.*, p. 8.

17. Ferguson, *op. cit.*, p. 15; Hall, *op. cit.*, pp. 45-47.

18. Ferguson, *op. cit.*, pp. 15-21. Cincinnati was the only city in Ohio having a population of over 150,000 in 1869.

19. *Ibid.*, pp. 21-27. About the same time certain interests back in Cincinnati were attempting to stop the road, alleging that the whole project was unconstitutional. However, on January 4, 1871, Judge Alphonso Taft of the Ohio Superior Court handed down a decision upholding the constitutionality of the Ferguson Bill.

at the state capital. The trustees employed General John C. Breckinridge, recently returned from exile, as company counsel to help ease the bill through the General Assembly at Frankfort.[20] But neither gentle persuasion nor the $6,000 of entertainment given the Kentucky lawmakers by the city of Cincinnati succeeded.[21] The Frankfort politicians turned down the proposal in March, 1870. Later, however, in February, 1872, the legislature relented and passed the desire legislation.[22]

With the necessary legislation finally approved, the trustees pushed the construction of their line, the Cincinnati Southern Railroad. The financing of the road was difficult, especially during the depression after 1873, since the Cincinnati city bond issues were, by law, to be sold only at par. Nevertheless, the road was finally completed by the end of 1879 and Cincinnati celebrated the formal opening the following March, when 1,100 representative southern merchants were brought to the Queen City in special trains and royally entertained for four days.[23] The 336-mile Cincinnati to Chattanooga line cost the city of Cincinnati $18,000,-000.[24] For its money the city at once gained a much broader trade territory, and freight rates to southern cities declined materially.[25] But Cincinnati did not itself desire to stay in the railroad business, and for that reason leased the entire line on October 12, 1881, to the Cincinnati, New Orleans and Texas Pacific

20. *Ibid.*, pp. 54-55; E. A. Ferguson to General J. C. Breckinridge, December 9, 1872, Breckinridge Papers, Manuscripts Division, Library of Congress. Breckinridge received $3,000 for his services and was in the service of the trustees from 1870 to 1872.
21. Coulter, *op. cit.*, pp. 45-46. Louisville accused Cincinnati of open bribery, but earlier in February, 1870, Louisville had spent $4,370 in entertaining the legislature at the opening of the new railroad bridge across the Ohio.
22. Ferguson, *op. cit.*, pp. 28-29. The L. and N. opposition to the new road was less effective by 1872, for more and more shippers in Kentucky and even Louisville were becoming increasingly critical of the L. and N.'s high and often discriminatory rate structure. Coulter, *op. cit.*, pp. 12-13.
23. *Commercial and Financial Chronicle*, December 13, 1879, p. 631; Hollander, *op. cit.*, p. 49.
24. *Commercial and Financial Chronicle*, April 13, 1878, p. 367; December 13, 1879, p. 631; Hall, *op. cit.*, p. 213.
25. Hollander, *op. cit.*, pp. 81-82. The Louisville and Nashville still managed to discriminate against both the railroad and the merchants of Cincinnati. This was especially true at points where the two roads connected, such as at Chattanooga. James F. Doster, *Alabama's First Railroad Commission, 1881-1885* (University, Alabama, 1949), p. 27.

THE LOUISVILLE AND NASHVILLE

Railway, a company owned partially by Cincinnati men but controlled by interests in England.[26]

President Newcomb's road was also busy expanding while Cincinnati was projecting, financing, and building a line to the south. At the end of the Civil War the Louisville and Nashville owned and operated about 300 miles of road. In addition to the 185-mile main line from Louisville to Nashville, the road had three branches; two of them were quite short serving Bardstown and Lebanon, Kentucky, and the third one was a 46-mile line aimed toward Memphis but ending at the Tennessee state line.[27] Both Guthrie and Newcomb were eager to manage and control directly the two roads which connected their Memphis branch with Memphis: (1) the 82-mile Memphis, Clarksville and Louisville from the state line to Paris, Tennessee, and (2) the 130-mile Memphis and Ohio Railroad from Paris to Memphis.[28] Since Louisville men had always dominated the management of the L. and N., Nashville's natural opposition to the plan was a futile gesture.[29] In the summer of 1867, Governor Brownlow took possession of the Memphis and Ohio because of the road's failure to meet its obligations to the state of Tennessee. A few weeks later, on September 1, 1867, the Louisville and Nashville leased the Memphis and Ohio for ten years.[30] Five years later, June 30, 1872, the L. and N. purchased the road outright. Also, on February 7, 1868, the Louisville line leased the connecting road, the Memphis, Clarksville and Louisville.[31] With the acquisition of the two Tennessee roads the entire 259-mile line

---

26. *Commercial and Financial Chronicle*, August 14, 1880, p. 179; August 27, 1881, p. 225; October 15, 1881, p. 412. Henry V. Poor, *Manual of the Railroads of the United States for 1882* (New York, 1882), pp. 491-492. Hall, *op. cit.*, pp. 58-59.

27. Poor, *Manual of the Railroads of the United States for 1869-1870*, pp. 56-57.

28. *Ibid.*, pp. 115, 151.

29. *Ibid.*, p. 58; *De Bow's Review*, February, 1867, p. 213. Nashville felt that its trade would suffer if the Louisville and Nashville emphasized the Louisville to Memphis route.

30. *Commercial and Financial Chronicle*, August 24, 1867, p. 247; Henry V. Poor, *Manual of the Railroads of the United States for 1877-1878* (New York, 1877), p. 374.

31. Poor, *Manual of the Railroads of the United States for 1877-1878*, p. 374. Later, in October, 1871, the L. and N. purchased the eighty-two-mile road.

RAILROADS OF THE SOUTH

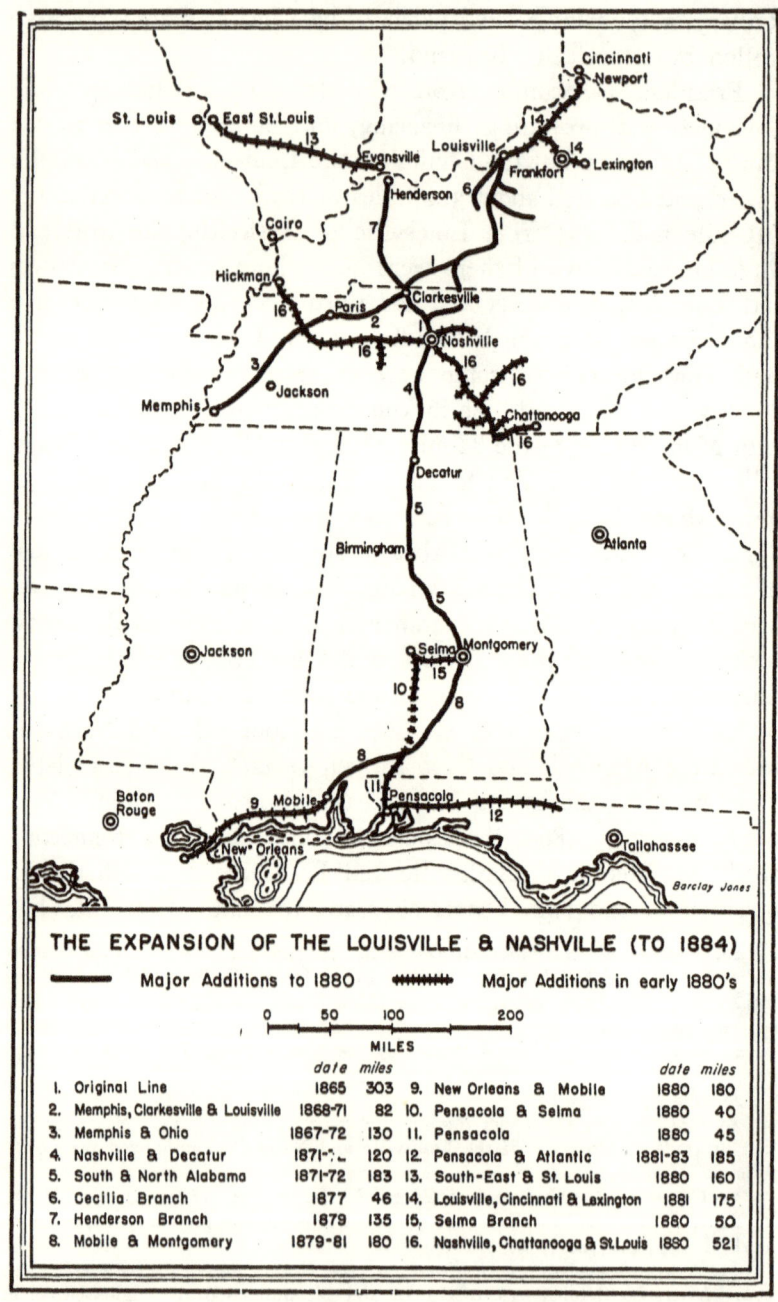

from Memphis to the main line became known as the Memphis Branch.

Newcomb's next major expansion was south of Nashville. Two lines, the Nashville and Decatur Railroad and the South and North Alabama Railroad, connected Nashville with southern Alabama. The Nashville and Decatur, running 120 miles from Nashville south to the Tennessee River at Decatur Junction, was the result of the consolidation, January 1, 1868, of three short lines, the Tennessee and Alabama, the Central Southern, and the Tennessee and Alabama Central.[32] James Withers Sloss, prosperous merchant and plantation owner of Athens, Alabama, was the president of the new consolidation. Sloss's road was not prosperous during its early corporate existence; its financial success really depended upon the completion of the road to the south, the South and North Alabama.[33]

The South and North Alabama was a projected, partially completed, 183-mile road between Decatur and Montgomery, and represented the desire of Alabama to connect by rail the northern and southern parts of the state. The Alabama legislature had generously (after the proper persuasion) endorsed the road's bonds in 1870, but construction still lagged, leaving unfinished a sixty-seven mile gap north of Elyton (later the approximate site of Birmingham).[34]

After efforts to complete the gap had failed, the principal holders of the first mortgage bonds, V. K. Stevenson and Russell Sage, both of New York, came to Montgomery in April, 1871, called the officials of the road to their room in the Exchange Hotel, and demanded an immediate financial settlement. President Francis M. Gilmer, a native southerner and an early promoter of the road, advised his board of directors to give up their line to the bondholders. Knowing that the bankers did not in-

---

32. Henry V. Poor, *Manual of the Railroads of the United States for 1885* (New York, 1885), p. 509.

33. Poor, *Manual of the Railroads of the United States for 1869-1870*, pp. 265-266.

34. *Ibid.*, pp. 314-315; Walter L. Fleming, *Civil War and Reconstruction in Alabama* (Cleveland, 1911), p. 594; Robert Selph Henry, *The Story of Reconstruction* (Indianapolis, 1938), p. 423; John W. Du Bose, *Alabama's Tragic Decade* (Birmingham, 1940), pp. 156-158.

tend to finish the road north of its Elyton connection with John C. Stanton's line to Chattanooga, the directors refused to capitulate. In some fashion, Colonel Sloss, whose Nashville and Decatur road would be rendered nearly useless without the completion of the South and North Alabama Railroad to Decatur, heard of the stormy session. He persuaded Albert Fink, vice president and general superintendent of the Louisville and Nashville, to go to Montgomery with proposals from the L. and N. Albert Fink invited representatives of the South and North Alabama line to Louisville to confer with the directors of the Louisville and Nashville. At these lengthy conferences in the Blue Parlor of the Galt House in Louisville, Colonel Sloss suggested that the L. and N. lease both of the lines south of Nashville and, after completing the Alabama road, operate the entire line as part of the L. and N. system.[35]

In the spring of 1871 President Newcomb and his directors approved the suggestion and both roads were leased. The Nashville and Decatur lease was for thirty years, effective July 1, 1872. By October, 1872, the L. and N. completed the South and North Alabama to Decatur, and eventually acquired a controlling interest of the line's common stock.[36] Newcomb's road thus extended its main line southward three hundred miles to Montgomery, Alabama. The L. and N. was soon very active in promoting the mineral district around the new town of Birmingham.[37]

In 1872, the year its trains first entered Montgomery, the Louisville and Nashville consisted of a system of over nine hundred miles.[38] Much of the newly acquired mileage was not as

35. Du Bose, *op. cit.*, pp. 167-169; Leighton, *Five Cities*, pp. 66, 111; Doster, *Alabama's First Railroad Commission*, pp. 133-134; Clark, *The Beginning of the L. and N.*, pp. 8-9. Some reports indicated that the Galt House conferences all but ended in a brawl, stopped only by the timely arrival of glasses of good Kentucky whisky.

36. Poor, *Manual of the Railroads of the United States for 1885*, pp. 509-510.

37. Doster, *loc. cit.* The L. and N. along with many of its officials and associates, such as Colonel Sloss, invested in the new iron mills of Birmingham. Milton H. Smith, later president of the L. and N., but in the early 1870's the general freight agent of the line, made the first sliding scale freight rate for southern pig iron. In spite of such aid the development of the new iron center was slow, especially after the panic of 1873.

38. Poor, *Manual of the Railroads of the United States for 1877-1878*, p. 376.

productive of traffic as the original main line. Also, the enlarged system was in complete operation less than a year before the depression of 1873 severely reduced all rail business. The L. and N.'s gross revenue in 1874-1875 on 920 miles of road was only 2 per cent larger than the gross revenue on a 615-mile system in 1871-1872.[39] In 1874 the dividend policy, which had seen 7 per cent to 8 per cent dividends paid every year since the war, was drastically changed and for three and a half years no dividends were paid.[40] Between 1873 and 1879, as a result of the reduced prosperity, the Louisville and Nashville had a cautious expansion policy. In the middle 1870's no expansion at all occurred except incidental additional construction on some of the short branches to the original main line. In 1877 a second line out of Louisville was acquired when the L. and N. purchased the forty-six-mile Cecilia branch to Elizabethtown from the Louisville, Paducah and Southwestern Railroad.[41] Two years later, in 1879, Nashville acquired another line to the north when the L. and N. purchased from the St. Louis and Southeastern Railway the 135-mile line running from Nashville to Henderson, Kentucky.[42]

Throughout its expansion in the 1870's the Louisville and Nashville remained a locally controlled road with nearly all its management composed of southern men. As long as James Guthrie or H. D. Newcomb controlled the line, Louisville interests dominated the board of directors. The local southern control was lost at the end of the decade as northern men, chiefly from New York City, became increasingly interested in the road. At the annual meeting in Louisville, October 1, 1879, Horatio Victor Newcomb, son of the Louisville commission merchant who had been an L. and N. president, was selected as the new presi-

---

39. *Ibid.*
40. *Commercial and Financial Chronicle*, October 16, 1875, p. 370; October 6, 1877, pp. 332-333; Henry V. Poor, *Manual of the Railroads of the United States for 1881* (New York, 1881), p. 472. Cash dividends were resumed with 1½ per cent in 1877, 3 per cent in 1878, 4 per cent in 1879, and 8 per cent in 1880.
41. Poor, *Manual of the Railroads of the United States for 1877-1878*, p. 538.
42. *Commercial and Financial Chronicle*, April 12, 1879, p. 378; May 10, 1879, p. 477; July 26, 1879, p. 96; Poor, *Manual of the Railroads of the United States for 1881*, p. 474.

dent of the line. At the same meeting five northern men, four of them from New York, were elected to the twelve-man board of directors. This division of the directorships was equitable since in the summer of 1879 about a third of the share capital was held by New Yorkers.[43] One of the New York men, Edward H. Green, husband of Hetty Green, was chosen first vice president to Newcomb. At the next annual meeting Newcomb resigned as president and was eventually replaced by Christopher Columbus Baldwin of New York City. At this same meeting the directors, now dominated by men from the North, adopted a resolution to increase the capital stock with a 100 per cent stock dividend.[44]

About the same time still greater northern control seemed probable as rumors appeared that the city of Louisville might sell a portion, or all, of its L. and N. stock.[45] In the early 1880's the rumors became a fact for in early March, 1882, Mayor Charles D. Jacob sold 10,000 shares, or over half of the city's holdings, to a New York syndicate headed by Edward H. Green, one of the company directors.[46] Northern influence did increase in 1882 and 1883 and by the latter year only four of the thirteen directors were from Louisville. The control of the speculative interests grew as the names of Thomas Fortune Ryan, Jay Gould, and Russell Sage were added to the directors' list in 1883.[47] The sequence of passed dividends, a growing floating debt, and even rumors of receivership was climaxed in 1884 with the resignation of C. C. Baldwin.[48]

While the new northern control was characterized by reckless and speculative financial policies, it was also marked by one of the

43. Henry V. Poor, *Manual of the Railroads of the United States for 1880* (New York, 1880), p. 469; *Commercial and Financial Chronicle*, July 12, 1879, p. 41; October 4, 1879, p. 358.
44. *Commercial and Financial Chronicle*, October 9, 1880, p. 382; Poor, *Manual of the Railroads of the United States for 1881*, pp. 474-475.
45. *Commercial and Financial Chronicle*, June 7, 1879, p. 579; June 14, 1879, p. 600; July 12, 1879, p. 41.
46. *Ibid.*, March 4, 1882, p. 264.
47. Henry V. Poor, *Manual of the Railroads of the United States for 1884* (New York, 1884), pp. 517-518; *Commercial and Financial Chronicle*, October 6, 1883, p. 373.
48. *Commercial and Financial Chronicle*, February 25, 1882, p. 216; July 22, 1882, p. 88; November 4, 1882, p. 497; Leighton, *Five Cities*, pp. 71-72; Doster, *Alabama's First Railroad Commission*, p. 110.

THE LOUISVILLE AND NASHVILLE

most rapid and expansive consolidation programs in American railroad history. Between 1879 and mid-1881 the L. and N. added over 2,000 miles of new line to its total network, reaching an aggregate of 3,034 miles by June 30, 1881.[49] The expansion continued at a slower pace in the next two years, and the total system included 3,600 miles as the Baldwin administration gave way to that of Milton H. Smith in 1884.[50]

A considerable portion of the Louisville and Nashville expansion in the early 1880's occurred in the Gulf states, especially in the region south of Montgomery. An earlier effort in 1879 to move eastward out of Montgomery had failed when President E. D. Standiford of the L. and N. was outbid by the Central of Georgia at the foreclosure sale of the Montgomery and Eufaula.[51] But later in the year the Louisville and Nashville did purchase a large controlling interest in the 180-mile Mobile and Montgomery. The L. and N. management felt that it had made a good purchase even though it paid nearly par for the stock. A lease for twenty years effective in January, 1881, made their control doubly certain.[52] Also in 1880, the expanding Kentucky railroad acquired a 141-mile line, the New Orleans and Mobile. Again the control was complete since the L. and N. possessed a fifty-year lease as well as practically all of the common stock.[53] Both of the new acquisitions had suffered receivership during the 1870's. Under the new management they became quite profitable and certainly significant portions of a new through route from Louisville to New Orleans.[54]

The Louisville and Nashville also expanded towards and into Florida in these years. During the spring of 1880 the L. and N.

---

49. Poor, *Manual of the Railroads of the United States for 1882*, pp. 500-506.

50. Poor, *Manual of the Railroads of the United States for 1885*, p. 502.

51. Poor, *Manual of the Railroads of the United States for 1881*, p. 427; Doster, *op. cit.*, pp. 24-25.

52. *Commercial and Financial Chronicle*, December 6, 1879, p. 608; February 14, 1880, p. 169; March 13, 1880, p. 273; Poor, *Manual of the Railroads of the United States for 1882*, p. 457.

53. Poor, *Manual of the Railroads of the United States for 1882*, pp. 476-477; *Commercial and Financial Chronicle*, February 14, 1880, p. 169; May 15, 1880, p. 519.

54. Poor, *Manual of the Railroads of the United States for 1885*, p. 505.

negotiated with, and finally purchased from, D. F. Sullivan of Pensacola two short railroads, the forty-mile Pensacola and Selma Railroad (from Selma to Pine Apple, Alabama) and the forty-five-mile Pensacola Railroad (from Pensacola to Pollard, Alabama).[55] The parent line intended to construct at once the sixty-four-mile gap between the two roads (Pine Apple to Pollard) but while construction was started, the short line was not completed until the 1890's.[56] President Baldwin was more diligent in pushing the construction of another line, the Pensacola and Atlantic Railroad, from Pensacola to River Junction, Florida. Owning three-fourths of the capital stock and most of the bonds, the L. and N. rushed the building of this 185-mile new line (chartered March 4, 1881) and the road was completed by February 1, 1883.[57]

The shortest addition at the southern end of the system was destined to create, for a summer at least, the biggest news. In April of 1880, the Louisville and Nashville negotiated with the the Georgia Railroad and the Central of Georgia (joint owners) for a lease of the fifty-mile Selma-to-Montgomery portion of the Western Railroad of Alabama. The lease was to run for five years at a yearly rental of $52,000. It was generally thought that the only purpose of the Louisville and Nashville in making such a lease was to achieve a closer connection with its new lines south of Selma.[58] However, the L. and N. had bigger plans afoot, plans intended to divert an increasing volume of traffic over its new through route from New Orleans to Louisville.

Once securely in possession of the Selma branch, the L. and N. management notified all competing companies that all future business over the fifty-mile road must pay full local rates. This

---

[55] *Commercial and Financial Chronicle*, February 14, 1880, p. 169; September 18, 1880, p. 306.

[56] Poor, *Manual of the Railroads of the United States for 1881*, p. 468; Henry V. Poor, *Manual of the Railroads of the United States for 1893* (New York, 1893), pp. 366-367; H. V. and H. W. Poor, *Manual of the Railroads of the United States for 1900*, pp. 417-419.

[57] *Commercial and Financial Chronicle*, August 20, 1881, p. 201; Poor, *Manual of the Railroads of the United States for 1885*, p. 453.

[58] *Commercial and Financial Chronicle*, April 17, 1880, p. 408; May 1, 1880, p. 447. Poor, *Manual of the Railroads of the United States for 1885*, p. 465.

was aimed at the substantial grain traffic which, after reaching New Orleans via river barges, was distributed to the Gulf states by rail. Of the competing lines, the Illinois Central subsidiary, the Chicago St. Louis and New Orleans, was most drastically affected.[59] The Illinois Central retaliated with special passenger rates from New Orleans to Chicago and soon a full scale rate war was in progress. Every major city in the eastern Mississippi Valley was affected, as well as roads such as the Mobile and Ohio.[60] The Illinois Central was soon selling round-trip passenger tickets from New Orleans to Chicago for $30 and by August one-way tickets could be purchased for the 915-mile trip for only $5.[61] The Louisville and Nashville did not relish a total freight rate war with a rival possessing a more direct route to the North and by late August was ready for a settlement. On August 24, 1880, Vice President E. P. Alexander of the Louisville and Nashville and General Manager James C. Clarke of the New Orleans road met in conference and agreed to end the war with a general restoration of rates to the levels prevailing prior to the conflict. The L. and N. backed down on its notorious local rates at Selma and the agreement was generally recognized as a victory for the Illinois Central.[62]

In the same early years of the decade the Louisville and Nashville also made extensive additions at the northern end of its system. Its first northern extension was the South-East and St. Louis Railway, a 160-mile road from Evansville, Indiana (across the Ohio from Henderson, Ky.) to East St. Louis. One of the L. and N.'s competitors, the Nashville, Chattanooga and St. Louis Railway, was also trying to acquire the Illinois road in 1879 and 1880.[63] Later, in November, 1880, the L. and N. did acquire

59. *Commercial and Financial Chronicle*, May 1, 1880, p. 447; August 21, 1880, p. 191. The Chicago, St. Louis and New Orleans had previously quoted a through rate for grain from New Orleans to Montgomery of twenty cents. The L. and N. demanded seventeen cents for its short fifty-mile haul, making it impossible for the C., St. L. and N. O. to quote through rates east of Selma.

60. Alfred L. Rives to William C. Rives, June 18, 1880, William Rives Papers, Manuscripts Division, Library of Congress. Alfred L. Rives, as vice president and general manager of the Mobile and Ohio, noted the injurious effect of the rate war upon the securities of his company.

61. *Commercial and Financial Chronicle*, August 21, 1880, p. 191.

62. *Ibid.*, August 21, 1880, p. 191; August 28, 1880, p. 217.

63. *Ibid.*, December 13, 1879, p. 632; January 10, 1880, p. 43.

the St. Louis connection both through a lease and also through acquisition of the share capital of the new line.[64] The following summer, on July 8, 1881, the L. and N. purchased an important road in northern Kentucky, the Louisville, Cincinnati and Lexington Railroad. This acquisition gave the parent line a 109-mile connection with Newport, across the river from Cincinnati, as well as a 66-mile branch to Lexington.[65] The Louisville and Nashville was also ambitious for other northern connections in the direction of Chicago. From 1879 until 1881 the L. and N. was reported to be in the process of acquiring the 290-mile road from Louisville to Michigan City, Indiana, the Louisville, New Albany and Chicago Railway. The L. and N. never gained real control, but by 1882 several L. and N. officials were included in the board of directors of the Indiana line.[66] Efforts at gaining another line to Chicago, the Chicago and Eastern Illinois, were no more successful.[67] The Louisville and Nashville never succeeded in getting its lines any further north than St. Louis and Cincinnati.

The middle portion of the system adjacent to Nashville was strengthened in 1880 by the acquisition of a rival road, the Nashville, Chattanooga and St. Louis Railway. The Nashville, Chattanooga and St. Louis Railway was a 521-mile system serving the central part of Tennessee. Its 321-mile main line ran from Chattanooga, via Nashville, to Hickman, Kentucky, a Mississippi River town, 35 miles downstream from Cairo. In the 1870's the southern-controlled Tennessee road was efficiently managed, and succeeded in paying regular dividends of 2½ per cent to 3 per cent even during the depression.[68]

In 1879 the road's president, Colonel Edwin W. Cole of Nashville, decided upon a policy of expansion which soon brought

64. Poor, *Manual of the Railroads of the United States for 1881*, pp. 468, 475; *Commercial and Financial Chronicle*, November 20, 1880, p. 536.
65. *Commercial and Financial Chronicle*, January 24, 1880, p. 91; July 9, 1881, p. 47; November 19, 1881, p. 560.
66. *Ibid.*, December 20, 1879, p. 657; July 24, 1880, p. 95; July 30, 1881, p. 124; Poor, *Manual of the Railroads of the United States for 1882*, p. 634.
67. *Commercial and Financial Chronicle*, January 21, 1882, p. 86; January 28, 1882, p. 114; February 11, 1882, p. 175.
68. Poor, *Manual of the Railroads of the United States for 1877-1878*, pp. 383-385; Poor, *Manual of the Railroads of the United States for 1881*, pp. 484-486.

THE LOUISVILLE AND NASHVILLE

him into conflict with his larger competitor, the Louisville and Nashville. President Cole planned with three consolidations and extensions to transform his rather modest local line into a trunk road connecting St. Louis and Atlanta. The first step was the purchase, in the spring of 1879, of a controlling interest in the Owensboro and Nashville Railroad, a short, forty-one-mile line which Colonel Cole intended to complete so as to connect Nashville with the Ohio River.[69] The second step was the successful negotiation late in 1879 for the control of the South-East and St. Louis Railway, the road from East St. Louis to Evansville.[70] President Cole, already known to some as "King Cole," next looked toward the railroads of Georgia. He was reported late in 1879 to have acquired the controlling interest in the lease of the state-owned Western and Atlantic and even to have been negotiating for a lease of the Central of Georgia.[71]

The Louisville and Nashville did not view favorably these ambitious expansions of Colonel Cole's road. Early in December, 1879, the L. and N. rejected Cole's proposal that the roads consolidate, each company to receive share and share alike in the new organization. During these consolidation negotiations, President Newcomb of the L. and N. had quietly purchased, chiefly from such large holders in New York City as the Vernon K. Stevenson family and the Thomas W. Evans family, a controlling interest in the stock of Colonel Cole's own road, the Nashville, Chattanooga and St. Louis.[72] Thinking themselves secure, with a majority of the stock, the L. and N. permitted the story of their control to be made public. The news surprised Colonel Cole but did not disturb him greatly, as he knew that his company's

---

69. *Commercial and Financial Chronicle*, May 31, 1879, p. 554; August 30, 1879, p. 224; November 29, 1879, p. 563; Poor, *Manual of the Railroads of the United States for 1882*, pp. 507-508.

70. *Commercial and Financial Chronicle*, December 13, 1879, pp. 631-632; January 10, 1880, p. 43; February 28, 1880, p. 222. This still left unfilled a short Ohio River connection between Evansville, Indiana, and Owensboro, Kentucky.

71. *Ibid.*, November 15, 1879, p. 511; February 7, 1880, p. 144; Raymond B. Nixon, *Henry W. Grady* (New York, 1943), pp. 166-168.

72. Nixon, *loc. cit.*; *Commercial and Financial Chronicle*, January 24, 1880, p. 91. Newcomb was reported to have offered a handsome price for the large stock holdings, at the same time threatening to build a competing line from St. Louis to Atlanta if they refused to sell.

charter required a two-thirds majority for affirmative company action. Hurrying to Chattanooga he wired a pool of seven New York brokers whom he knew had recently purchased 60,000 shares of his company's stock. He briefly explained the situation and asked them to hold their stock, but did not offer to buy it himself. The pool was dismayed when their stock began to fall in price and, still having no offer from Colonel Cole, they went to the L. and N. agents, told their story and offered to sell all 60,000 shares at 95, well above the market. Newcomb's agents quickly confirmed the two-thirds majority requirement, but refused to meet the price asked by the pool. Later, after failing to obtain more than 5,000 additional shares in the market, the L. and N. brokers agreed to the proposition of the pool, bought their entire block of stock and thereby acquired 25,000 shares over the requisite two-thirds. Poor Colonel Cole, not knowing of his defeat, continued to pour telegrams into the office of the pool. His last wire read, "Hold the fort. I am the key to the situation."[73]

Colonel Cole soon acknowledged his defeat and late in February announced his resignation as president.[74] Ex-Governor James D. Porter of Tennessee was selected to succeed Colonel Cole, and L. and N. men soon appeared in the board of directors.[75] The Louisville road also forced the Nashville, Chattanooga and St. Louis to disgorge its recently acquired Southeastern and St. Louis, and also the Owensboro and Nashville, so that the parent line could possess them.[76] The Nashville, Chattanooga and St. Louis

---

73. *Commercial and Financial Chronicle*, January 24, 1880, p. 91; Nixon, *op. cit.*, pp. 166-168, 185-186. Down in Atlanta, Grady, already impressed by Cole's expansions and feeling other news in the offing, took a railroad junket into the north for his paper, the Atlanta *Constitution*. He reached Louisville as the L. and N. officials were congratulating themselves on their victory over Cole. Grady was greatly impressed by the younger Newcomb and described him as "the Napoleon of the railroad world." Newcomb was also interested in the reporter from Atlanta and offered Grady a position as his private secretary at $250 per month. Grady refused since it would mean an end to his newspaper work. He did start to speculate in L. and N. stock. Inside of a year he made nearly enough to pay for his new $16,000 home in Atlanta.

74. *Commercial and Financial Chronicle*, February 28, 1880, p. 222. Cole was soon the president of another growing southern road, the East Tennessee, Virginia and Georgia.

75. *Ibid.*, March 20, 1880, p. 298.

76. *Ibid.*, February 28, 1880, p. 222; March 6, 1880, p. 248; April 3, 1880, p. 357; October 9, 1880, p. 380.

was allowed to continue its own separate corporate existence.[77]

The Louisville and Nashville did not acquire the control over the railroads in Georgia that it anticipated through its acquisition of the Nashville, Chattanooga and St. Louis. Any rights or interests gained by Colonel Cole in the early winter of 1879 were at least not held by his railroad at the time the property was turned over to the L. and N.[78] Lengthy conferences between President Newcomb and the officials of both the Central of Georgia and the Georgia Railroad occurred from February to April, 1880, producing a fine crop of rumors and reports concerning an impending gigantic combination. A climax was reached in May and June, 1880, when a most complicated triple play by Georgia politicians and President Newcomb of the L. and N. was reported in the Georgia press. General John B. Gordon retired from his U. S. Senate seat to accept a $14,000 position with the L. and N. Governor Alfred Colquitt appointed Joseph E. Brown to the vacant seat in the Senate and both Brown and Gordon agreed to support Colquitt for reelection. Some reports claimed that Newcomb was to fall heir to Brown's lease of the Western and Atlantic, but this prophecy was never fulfilled.[79]

The net result was the creation of harmonious understandings between the L. and N. and both the major Georgia roads relative to an easier interchange of traffic made possible by the Louisville and Nashville entry into Chattanooga.[80] A year later, in April, 1881, the larger of the two Georgia lines, the Central of Georgia, leased the smaller Georgia Railroad for ninety-nine years at an annual rental of $600,000. A few weeks later, on May 17, 1881, President William Wadley of the Central of Georgia assigned half of his lease to the L. and N. The Louisville and Nashville

---

77. Poor, *Manual of the Railroads of the United States for 1882*, pp. 484, 500-501. Nashville now felt completely captured by the L. and N. By 1880 all six of the lines running to Nashville, originally built as competing lines, were included in the network of "Newcomb's Octopus," Maxwell Ferguson, *State Regulation of Railroads in the South* (New York, 1916), p. 139.

78. *Commercial and Financial Chronicle*, November 8, 1879, p. 489; February 7, 1880, p. 144; March 20, 1880, p. 289.

79. *Ibid.*, February 14, 1880, p. 169; February 21, 1880, p. 192; April 10, 1880, p. 384; Nixon, *op. cit.*, p. 170.

80. *Commercial and Financial Chronicle*, May 22, 1880, p. 543; October 16, 1880, p. 404.

thus acquired a share in the lease of the Georgia Railroad, a system of about six hundred miles.[81] The joint lease was never profitable in the 1880's since nearly every year the Georgia Railroad's net earnings were less than the fixed rental of $600,000.[82]

The entire expansion program of the early 1880's never brought the prosperity anticipated by the management of the Louisville and Nashville. Much of the expansion had been indiscriminate, many of the new roads being of doubtful value with inadequate traffic. Much of the new mileage was badly constructed and poorly equipped.[83] The L. and N. had paid a dividend of 8 per cent in 1880 and 6 per cent in 1881, but only 3 per cent was paid in 1882 when the semi-annual dividend payable in August was passed.[84] Much of the difficulty was due to the great increase in the funded debt and the resulting increase in fixed charges. While the mileage of the system (actually operated by the L. and N. management) had only doubled, from 972 miles in 1879 to 2,065 miles in 1884, the funded debt had more than trebled, from $17,400,000 to $58,900,000.[85] Rumors of a large floating debt in 1882 were soon a fact, for by 1884 the "bills payable" amounted to $3,599,000.[86] During the same years there were also rumors of impending receivership.

The climax came in the spring of 1884 with the scandal concerning the president of the road, C. C. Baldwin. In May and June of 1884 rumors were current that President Baldwin had been illegally using some of the funds of the company in an attempt to hold up the price of the common stock. Baldwin resigned under fire and his directors admitted that some wrong-

81. *Ibid.*, March 26, 1881, p. 334; April 16, 1881, p. 420; May 14, 1881, p. 526; October 22, 1881, p. 439; Mary G. Cumming, *Georgia Railroad and Banking Company* (Augusta, Georgia, 1945), pp. 89-90; Poor, *Manual of the Railroads of the United States for 1882*, pp. 500-501.
82. Henry V. Poor, *Manual of the Railroads of the United States for 1891* (New York, 1891), p. 220.
83. *Commercial and Financial Chronicle*, July 22, 1882, p. 88; S. F. Van Oss, *American Railroads as Investments* (New York, 1893), pp. 737-738.
84. *Commercial and Financial Chronicle*, October 9, 1880, p. 382; July 22, 1882, p. 88; Poor, *Manual of the Railroads of the United States for 1885*, p. 505.
85. Poor, *Manual of the Railroads of the United States for 1885*, p. 508.
86. *Commercial and Financial Chronicle*, February 25, 1882, p. 216; Poor, *Manual of the Railroads of the United States for 1885*, p. 508.

doing had occurred.[87] The annual report of the company later disclosed that the L. and N. had a claim of about $1,000,000 against its former president. Baldwin was understood to have surrendered the bulk of his estate to liquidate the debt.[88] During the summer of 1884, English investors bought large blocks of L. and N. common stock and were reported to have acquired a controlling interest. Late in July, 1884, C. C. Baldwin, Jay Gould, Russell Sage, Thomas F. Ryan and John F. Green all resigned as directors to be succeeded by men representing the foreign security holders.[89] In October, 1884, Milton H. Smith of Louisville became the president and Eckstein Norton of New York, vice president.[90]

The new management was both prudent and honest, and devoted itself wholeheartedly to the financial rehabilitation of the L. and N.[91] The new board of directors in 1884 had a large minority of men from Louisville, but by the 1890's many of the southern members had again given way to men from New York.[92] The real direction of the line during the rest of the century was chiefly in the hands of two men, Milton H. Smith, president from 1884 to 1886, and 1891 to 1921, and Eckstein Norton of New York, president from 1886 to 1891.[93]

Milton Hannibal Smith was the dominant personality in the

87. *Commercial and Financial Chronicle*, May 24, 1884, pp. 606, 613; June 7, 1884, p. 678; Carl Snyder, *American Railways as Investments* (New York, 1907), pp. 412-413. L. and N. common stock was adversely affected by the disclosures and fell from 35 to 29 within a week.

88. *Commercial and Financial Chronicle*, January 10, 1885, p. 61; Poor, *Manual of the Railroads of the United States for 1885*, p. 506.

89. *Commercial and Financial Chronicle*, July 26, 1884, p. 96; August 2, 1884, p. 128.

90. Poor, *Manual of the Railroads of the United States for 1885*, pp. 509-511. The new management issued $5,000,000 in bonds and $5,000,000 in new stock, disposing of both issues at a heavy discount. The new resources reduced the floating debt and within a year the financial standing of the company was much improved. *Commercial and Financial Chronicle*, September 6, 1884, p. 264; August 29, 1885, p. 229.

91. Doster, *Alabama's First Railroad Commission*, p. 110.

92. Poor, *Manual of the Railroads of the United States for 1885*, p 511; Poor, *Manual of the Railroads of the United States for 1893*, p. 376.

93. Norton replaced Smith in 1886 at the request of the foreign bondholders who felt that the chief financial officer of the road should be in New York. Norton resigned in 1891 and died two years later. *Commercial and Financial Chronicle*, October 9, 1886, p. 431; February 14, 1891, p. 279.

Louisville and Nashville from 1884 to the year of his death, 1921. Even as vice president to Eckstein Norton, 1886-1891, he was the real boss and the operating head of the road from his headquarters in Louisville.[94] President Smith, unlike James Guthrie, had no great attachment for Louisville. He saw Louisville, not as the master of his railroad, but rather as one of many arms that served the growing system. Smith viewed the entire region south of Louisville and the Ohio River as an economic wilderness created especially as a field of operation for his rail network.[95] Arbitrary, short-tempered, and often impatient, this railroad monarch brooked little interference, whether from a feeble railroad commission, the state legislature over in Frankfort, or Hetty Green who from her private car in the Louisville yards lectured Smith for the extravagant use of brass on his locomotives.[96] Greedy as he was for his company, associated as he was with financial pirates, Smith's own rewards were unusually modest. His salary never rose above $25,000, although he could easily have had it doubled, and he left his widow an estate of but $200,000.[97]

Smith's management brought prosperity to his road. By 1888, the company was able to resume dividends, and during the next six years paid dividends of from 4 per cent to 6 per cent.[98] Several of the early dividends were stock dividends in whole or part.[99] The depression of 1893 caused the company wisely to discontinue

---

[94] A native New Yorker (born in 1836), Smith moved to Illinois at fourteen, but soon was down in Mississippi learning telegraphy and the job of railroading. After dispatching both Confederate and Union trains with equal efficiency, he moved to Louisville after the war. Able and efficient, he rose rapidly and was general freight agent for the L. and N. from 1868 to 1878. After comparable jobs with the B. and O. and the Pennsylvania, he returned to the L. and N. in 1882.

[95] Leighton, *Five Cities*, pp. 67-73.

[96] *Ibid.*, pp. 72-75. Smith, of course, believed in lobbying. He maintained that eminent citizen of Louisville, General Basil Duke, as a company legal counsel. Duke's chief duties were to be on hand in Frankfort with a pocketful of railroad passes.

[97] *Ibid.*, pp. 74-75. Smith believed no railroad president was worth more than $25,000 a year. He lived quietly in Louisville, refused interviews, kept a fast horse, but preferred a nap to recreation.

[98] *Louisville and Nashville Valuation Docket no. 456*, Accounting Report, II, 57, Record Group 134, National Archives.

[99] *Commercial and Financial Chronicle*, December 29, 1888, p. 791; December 28, 1889, p. 842; December 27, 1890, p. 893.

dividend payments, but they were resumed in 1899.[100] During the depression years the L. and N. also introduced the sound and conservative financial practice of charging road betterments to operating expenses, giving up the earlier method of paying for them with additions to the capital account.[101] Earlier the management had also started to retire part of its funded debt through the issuance of new common stock.[102]

The late 1880's and the decade of the 1890's were also years of a changing traffic pattern for the Louisville and Nashville. Smith wanted more long-haul freight, especially industrial freight, and was willing to invest the road's money to get such traffic. While he felt that good dirt roads were often the answer to the transportation needs of rural and agricultural areas, he was always willing to build a spur to the door of any new mine or furnace.[103] As a result of Smith's efforts to build up his freight traffic, the freight ton mileage on his road increased from 687,000,000 ton miles in 1884 to 2,230,000,000 ton miles in 1899. During the same years his total freight revenue nearly doubled from $9,000,000 to $17,000,000, even though the average freight rates were declining from 1.3 to .7 cents per ton mile.[104] On the other hand, President Smith hated passenger traffic, allowed his coaches to become antiques, and cursed a Jim Crow law which forced him to spend money to divide the coaches or buy extra equipment. Smith was supposed to have said of passenger traffic, "You can't make a g– d-- cent out of it."[105] As a result of such an attitude his passenger business increased more slowly than the system itself during the fifteen years and dropped from 28 per cent of the gross earnings in 1884 to but 20 per cent in 1899.[106]

100. *Ibid.*, January 13, 1894, p. 58; *Louisville and Nashville Valuation Docket no. 456*, Accounting Report, II, 57, Record Group 134, National Archives.
101. *Commercial and Financial Chronicle*, October 8, 1898, p. 714.
102. *Ibid.*, September 28, 1889, pp. 387, 402; February 8, 1890, p. 205.
103. Doster, *Alabama's First Railroad Commission*, pp. 135-136; Leighton, *op. cit.*, pp. 74-75.
104. Poor, *Manual of the Railroads of the United States for 1885*, p. 508; H. V. and H. W. Poor, *Manual of the Railroads of the United States for 1900*, p. 422.
105. Leighton, *op. cit.*, p. 74.
106. Poor, *Manual of the Railroads of the United States for 1885*, p. 508; H. V. and H. W. Poor, *Manual of the Railroads of the United States for 1900*,

RAILROADS OF THE SOUTH

In the last fifteen years of the nineteenth century the Louisville and Nashville continued to expand, although at a much slower rate. The system added 1,358 miles in the period, increasing from 3,679 miles in 1884 to 5,037 at the end of the century. Much of this increase was due to the natural growth of the older integral parts of the system. The Nashville, Chattanooga and St. Louis Railway, for example, expanded in the period from 554 to 939 miles. Several new roads were also acquired. The 248-mile Kentucky Central Railway was the most important of the new lines. The L. and N. purchased the entire capital stock of this eastern Kentucky road from C. P. Huntington in December, 1890. Shorter roads acquired during the period were the Alabama Mineral, 125 miles; the Birmingham Mineral, 163 miles; and the Nashville, Florence and Sheffield, 107 miles. All three of these roads served northern Alabama and the area near the mineral district of Birmingham.[107]

At the end of the century the Louisville and Nashville system, extending into eight of the ten southern states (only the Carolinas were untouched), was the second largest system in the South. Its capital structure of $175,000,000 in 1900 was equal to two-thirds the value of all southern railroads in 1859, the year the 185-mile main stem was opened from Louisville to Nashville. In 1900 the system had as many freight cars (21,000) as the entire South during the Reconstruction. As the management celebrated in March, 1900, the fiftieth anniversary of the incorporation of the line, they could look back upon a full half century of solid growth, expanding service, and, by southern standards at least, a remarkable degree of prosperity.

---

p. 422. The L. and N. average passenger rates dropped only slightly during the decade and a half, being 2.32 cents per mile in 1884 and 2.23 cents per mile in 1899.

107. H. V. and H. W. Poor, *Manual of the Railroads of the United States for 1900*, pp. 417-428; Poor, *Manual of the Railroads of the United States for 1885*, pp. 502-503; *Commercial and Financial Chronicle*, December 20, 1890, pp. 851, 876.

CHAPTER 11

THE RICHMOND AND DANVILLE

THE STORY of the Richmond and Danville Railroad, and its associated and related companies, is one of the more complicated and amazing developments in the railroad history of the South. During the Civil War the Richmond and Danville served as one of the major transportation arteries of the beleaguered capital of the Confederacy and at the end of the war was already one of the major lines in the upper South. Early lost to northern control in 1871, the R. and D. soon became the very cornerstone of the vast rail empire being built by Thomas A. Scott's Pennsylvania Railroad and the Southern Railway Security Company. In the decade of the 1880's, a new northern management of the Richmond and Danville rapidly forged together (with the aid of a holding company) a rail empire that accounted for nearly a third of the southern rail mileage in 1890.[1] In the decade that followed, upon the sensational disclosures of the poor management of the past, receivership overtook the jerry-built corporate structure. The outcome of the resulting reorganization managed by J. P. Morgan was the creation of the Southern Railway, a six-thousand-mile system (in 1900) completely dominated by bankers in the North.

When Tom Scott purchased the state-owned common stock in the Richmond and Danville in the summer of 1871 he was confident that his Pennsylvania railroad was on the threshold of a

---

1. Henry V. Poor, *Manual of the Railroads of the United States for 1891* (New York, 1891), pp. 472, xvii. In 1890 the Richmond and West Point Terminal Railway and Warehouse Company (the corporate heir of the R. and D. system) possessed a system of over 8,000 miles. Total rail mileage in the South in 1890 was 29,263 miles.

RAILROADS OF THE SOUTH

successful and profitable southern rail expansion.[2] But neither the Pennsylvania Railroad nor its subsidiary company, the Southern Railway Security Company, found any real profit in the growing southern network. Shortly after the Panic of 1873, the subsidiary holding company initiated a policy of retrenchment and by 1874 the stockholders of the Pennsylvania were investigating with a critical eye the entire southern expansion program.[3] Many of the southern rail securities were disposed of in the middle 1870's, but the Pennsylvania Railroad retained control of the most valuable of the several lines, the Richmond and Danville, until 1880.[4] In the spring of 1880 the Pennsylvania Railroad sold its 24,000 shares of R. and D. stock for a reported $1,200,000 to the W. P. Clyde syndicate, a group of northern and southern capitalists.[5]

The new management was still northern dominated, although it retained a façade of southern control through the presence of several Richmond gentlemen in the board of directors and the retention of A. S. Buford of the same city as president.[6] The Richmond and Danville system in 1880 was still one of very modest proportions, consisting of only 449 miles of owned and leased lines. The original 140-mile main stem from Richmond to Danville had been extended 48 miles to Greensboro, North Carolina, during the Civil War. The major leased line was the 223-mile North Carolina Railroad leased September 11, 1871,

---

2. *Southern Railway Valuation Docket no. 556*, Report of Accounting Section (Richmond and Danville), II, 225, Record Group 134, National Archives; Stuart Daggett, *Railroad Reorganization* (Cambridge, Mass., 1908), pp. 146-147; Nelson M. Blake, *William Mahone of Virginia, Soldier and Political Insurgent* (Richmond, 1935), p. 120. Fairfax Harrison, *A History of the Legal Development of the Railroad System of the Southern Railway Company* (Washington, D. C., 1901), pp. 93-94.

3. Howard W. Schotter, *The Growth and Development of the Pennsylvania Railroad Company* (Philadelphia, 1927), pp. 110-111; George H. Burgess and Miles C. Kennedy, *Centennial History of the Pennsylvania Railroad Company, 1846-1946* (Philadelphia, 1949), pp. 279-281.

4. Burgess and Kennedy, *op. cit.*, p. 281; Schotter, *loc. cit.*

5. Schotter, *loc. cit.*; Harrison, *op. cit.*, p. 246; Daggett, *op. cit.*, p. 149; *Commercial and Financial Chronicle*, June 19, 1880, p. 651.

6. Henry V. Poor, *Manual of the Railroads of the United States for 1881* (New York, 1881), p. 365. *Commercial and Financial Chronicle*, June 19, 1880, p. 651.

THE RICHMOND AND DANVILLE

for 30 years to Tom Scott's Richmond and Danville in a secret board meeting at Company Shops just east of Greensboro.[7]

The Richmond and Danville had acquired in the fall of 1878 a substantial interest in the Charlotte, Columbia and Augusta Railroad, the 191-mile road from Charlotte, North Carolina, to Augusta, Georgia.[8] The latter road retained its separate corporate existence, but several men prominent in the management of the R. and D. were soon included in the board of directors of the South Carolina line.[9] During the middle 1870's the Richmond and Danville management had also established very close traffic arrangements with the Clyde-managed Richmond, York River and Chesapeake Railroad, a short, thirty-eight-mile road from Richmond to West Point on the York River.[10] Although it was a growing system in the late 1870's, the Richmond and Danville had seldom managed to return dividends to its Pennsylvania owners.[11]

The Clyde syndicate was not content with its control of the Richmond and Danville system. The same spring that it purchased the R. and D. from the Pennsylvania, the syndicate obtained from the state legislature of Virginia an act (passed March 8, 1880) incorporating the Richmond and West Point Terminal Railway and Warehouse Company. As a holding company, the new corporation was entitled to acquire by purchase, or otherwise, the securities of railroads in any of the southern states. The new corporation was a necessity to the Clyde group since the Richmond and Danville charter prohibited the leasing of

---

7. *Commercial and Financial Chronicle*, September 23, 1871, p. 402; Cecil Kenneth Brown, *A State Movement in Railroad Development: The Story of North Carolina's First Effort to Establish an East and West Trunk Line Railroad* (Chapel Hill, N. C., 1928), pp. 174-181.

8. *Commercial and Financial Chronicle*, September 14, 1878, p. 280; March 13, 1880, p. 271.

9. Poor, *Manual of the Railroads of the United States for 1881*, pp. 384-386.

10. *Ibid.*, pp. 362, 368-369; Harrison, *loc. cit.* The Clyde-owned Baltimore, Chesapeake and Richmond Steamboat Company was also a party to the traffic agreements.

11. Daggett, *op. cit.*, pp. 147-148; Poor, *Manual of the Railroads of the United States for 1881*, p. 364. Throughout the depression years the R. and D. had kept its funded debt and its fixed charges quite low. Its floating debt was never excessive and its operating ratio was generally quite favorable.

RAILROADS OF THE SOUTH

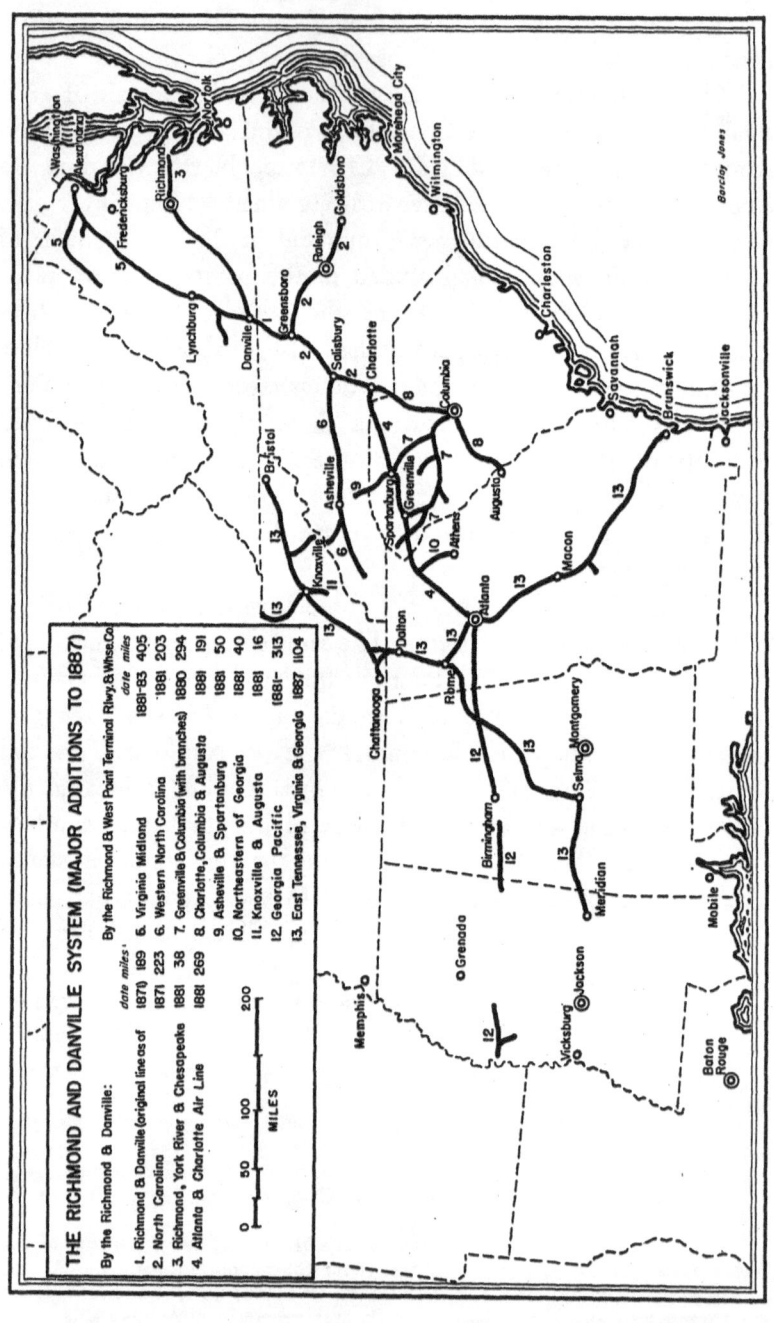

THE RICHMOND AND DANVILLE

any road not directly connected to the parent road. The Terminal Company was an easy way to avoid this limitation. The capital stock of the new company was first set at $3,000,000 but this was soon raised to $5,000,000 and later, April 3, 1882, to $15,000,000. Naturally the R. and D. always held a majority of the outstanding stock. All of the directors of the Richmond and West Point Terminal Company were also directors of the Richmond and Danville, and W. P. Clyde of New York City was president.[12]

The combination of an aggressive management and the new made-to-order holding company permitted an expansion of amazing proportions in the next two years. By mid-1882 the Richmond and Danville had a system in its own right of 827 miles, while the Richmond and West Point Terminal Company controlled an additional 1,248 miles of line.[13]

The Richmond and Danville expanded at both ends of its system, at Richmond and also at Charlotte, North Carolina. On July 1, 1881, the R. and D. leased in perpetuity the thirty-eight-mile Richmond, York River and Chesapeake Railroad. The annual rental paid for the Clyde-controlled line was $85,500.[14] The other and more important extension was the 269-mile road south of Charlotte, the Atlanta and Charlotte Air-Line Railway. This line had been built in the early 1870's by the Richmond and Danville which was supported by the Pennsylvania Railroad.[15] The line was no sooner completed (September, 1873) than the depression brought the familiar sequence of default, receivership, and foreclosure.[16] During 1875 the Pennsylvania Railroad generously relieved the R. and D. of its collateral liabilities incurred

---

12. Henry V. Poor, *Manual of the Railroads of the United States for 1882* (New York, 1882), pp. 385, 388-393; *Commercial and Financial Chronicle*, June 19, 1880, p. 651; Carl Snyder, *American Railways as Investments* (New York, 1907), pp. 670-671; S. F. Van Oss, *American Railroads as Investments* (New York, 1893), pp. 774-775.

13. Poor, *Manual of the Railroads of the United States for 1882*, pp. 380, 389.

14. *Ibid.*, pp. 380, 393-394; *Commercial and Financial Chronicle*, July 16, 1881, p. 66.

15. *Commercial and Financial Chronicle*, September 13, 1873, p. 355; *The Railroad Gazette*, July 23, 1870, p. 391; Harrison, *op. cit.*, p. 202.

16. Harrison, *op. cit.*, pp. 202-203; *Commercial and Financial Chronicle*, September 13, 1873, p. 355; August 15, 1874, p. 167; December 9, 1876, p. 575.

in the original construction of the line.[17] The Richmond and Danville thus had no further financial connections with the reorganized road during the remainder of the decade. However, on March 26, 1881, the Richmond and Danville leased the entire road for an annual rental of $462,500, sufficient to pay the interest on the funded debt and 5 per cent on the capital stock.[18] By the summer of 1881, the Richmond and Danville was operating a main line from tidewater in Virginia to Atlanta.

The expansion in the system achieved through the operations of the Richmond and West Point Terminal Company was considerably more significant. Within two years after the original incorporation of the holding company, it had acquired control over 1,248 miles of southern railway. Several of the additions made to the system by the Richmond and West Point Terminal came through the acquisition of railroads that had experienced receivership during the decade of the 1870's. This was true of the Virginia Midland, the Western North Carolina, and the Columbia and Greenville.

Largest of all the acquisitions was the Virginia Midland, a 405-mile line serving the central part of the state and connecting with the parent road at Danville. The road had been controlled by the Baltimore and Ohio before, during, and immediately after the road's receivership of the late 1870's.[19] The B. and O. sold to the Terminal Company a controlling interest in the Virginia Midland in the late summer of 1881, but negotiations concerning the final transfer of certain securities continued until the first weeks of 1883.[20] A second road, the 203-mile Western North Carolina Railroad, was also acquired in 1881. In the spring of

17. *Commercial and Financial Chronicle*, Februray 19, 1876, p. 180.
18. Poor, *Manual of the Railroads of the United States for 1882*, pp. 426-427; *Commercial and Financial Chronicle*, April 2, 1881, p. 367. When gross earnings reached $1,500,000 a year the rental was to be raised to pay a 6 per cent dividend. A dividend of 7 per cent was due when the gross earnings touched $1,750,000. The R. and D. never paid over the minimum of 5 per cent during the 1880's and the company often failed to have sufficient net earnings to pay the fixed minimum rental.
19. Harrison, *op. cit.*, pp. 475-476; *Commercial and Financial Chronicle*, May 15, 1880, p. 520; December 25, 1880, p. 673.
20. *Commercial and Financial Chronicle*, September 3, 1881, p. 256; February 3, 1883, p. 141; Poor, *Manual of the Railroads of the United States for 1882*, pp. 390-391.

1880, Governor Thomas J. Jarvis had persuaded the state legislature to sell this state-owned road. The railroad had been a problem line ever since its costly experience with the carpetbaggers, Littlefield and Swepson. Jarvis convinced his legislature that they should "stop building railroads and begin building schoolhouses." Unfortunately for the educational system of the state, the sale of the line resulted in a lower tax rate, not more schoolhouses.[21] The state sold the line to William J. Best of New York who soon assigned his interest to the Richmond and Danville holding company.[22] The Greenville and Columbia was the third receivership line acquired. W. P. Clyde, William A. Courtney, Joseph Bryan, and Thomas M. Logan purchased the South Carolina road at a foreclosure sale April 15, 1880, in Charleston.[23] In addition to the 164-mile Greenville and Columbia, which was reorganized as the Columbia and Greenville, the Richmond and West Point Terminal also soon acquired the three short, leased lines that were tributary to the Greenville and Columbia.[24]

The Richmond and West Point Terminal Company also acquired several other roads in 1881 and 1882. Since 1878, the Richmond and Danville had held a substantial portion of the common stock of the 191-mile Charlotte, Columbia and Augusta Railroad. By the fall of 1881, the holding company held 13,024 shares out of the 25,780 shares outstanding.[25] By the end of 1881, the Richmond and West Point Terminal also owned at least majorities of the controlling securities of three additional lines, the fifty-mile Ashville and Spartanburg Railroad, the forty-

---

21. Brown, *A State Movement in Railroad Development*, pp. 226-230; *Commercial and Financial Chronicle*, December 2, 1876, p. 550.

22. *Commercial and Financial Chronicle*, March 6, 1880, p. 249; October 1, 1881, p. 346; November 26, 1881, p. 580; Poor, *Manual of the Railroads of the United States for 1882*, pp. 389-391.

23. *Commercial and Financial Chronicle*, April 17, 1880, p. 408; September 4, 1880, p. 259; October 30, 1880, p. 453; Harrison, *op. cit.*, p. 325.

24. Poor, *Manual of the Railroads of the United States for 1882*, pp. 388-390, 419-421. The three short roads were the Blue Ridge (32 miles), the Laurens (31 miles), and the Spartanburg, Union, and Columbia (68 miles).

25. *Ibid.*, pp. 390, 416-417. About the same time the Charlotte, Columbia and Augusta leased the forty-seven mile Atlantic, Tennessee, and Ohio Railroad, a branch line running from Charlotte to Statesville, North Carolina.

mile Northeastern Railroad of Georgia, and the sixteen-mile Knoxville and Augusta Railroad.[26]

In addition to the roads already in operation, the holding company had ambitious plans for new construction from Atlanta westward to Birmingham, Alabama. The successful promotion of the new line came only after some complicated maneuverings by the Louisville and Nashville, the East Tennessee, Virginia and Georgia, and former Senator John B. Gordon of Georgia. Both the L. and N. and the East Tennessee were interested in acquiring rail entrance into Atlanta, and General Gordon was interested in leaving politics for railroading, specifically a $14,000 a year position offered him by the L. and N.[27] In less than a year after his resignation (May, 1880), however, the L. and N. had succeeded in selling the good General their own recently acquired controlling interest in the projected (but still on paper) Georgia Western Railroad for $50,000.[28] To the amazement and chagrin of the Louisville and Nashville, even before Gordon actually had received the deed from the L. and N., he contracted to sell for $50,000 to President E. W. Cole's East Tennessee, Virginia and Georgia a half interest in a seventeen-mile portion of the projected line.[29] Gordon's next move was to interest the Richmond and West Point Terminal in his remaining rights in the Georgia Western. During the summer of 1881, General Gordon and his Richmond and West Point Terminal associates incorporated the Georgia Pacific Railroad, as successor to the Georgia Western.[30] Gordon became president of the line which was built to Birmingham in 1883 by the Richmond and Danville Extension Company.[31]

26. *Ibid.*, pp. 389-390; *Commercial and Financial Chronicle*, May 13, 1882, p. 550.
27. Harrison, *op. cit.*, pp. 414-424; Raymond B. Nixon, *Henry W. Grady* (New York, 1943), p. 170.
28. Harrison, *loc. cit.* In 1879 and 1880 the L. and N. had bought the projected road for a total of $35,000.
29. *Ibid.* The East Tennessee road wanted the rights possessed by the Georgia Western to use a portion of the right of way of the Western and Atlantic. The road's new president, Colonel Cole, was the same gentleman who had been forced out of the Nashville, Chattanooga and St. Louis by the L. and N. in the spring of 1880.
30. *Ibid.*, 426.
31. Poor, *Manual of the Railroads of the United States for 1882*, pp.

THE RICHMOND AND DANVILLE

By 1883 the Richmond and Danville thus had a 2,200-mile system stretching from tidewater Virginia to central Alabama, with branches serving all the state capitals and most of the principal cities in Virginia, the Carolinas, and Georgia. Throughout the 1880's and down to receivership in 1892, the control of the growing system was essentially northern with only an occasional southerner being included in the board of directors. From 1877 to 1892, seventy-five different men served on the boards of directors of the Richmond and Danville and the Richmond and West Point Terminal Company. Only sixteen of the seventy-five men were from the South. During the fifteen years five men, William P. Clyde, Thomas M. Logan, Calvin S. Brice, Samuel Thomas, and John H. Inman, in general dominated the management of the R. and D. System. Two of the men, Logan and Inman, were native southerners, but Logan early in the postwar years acquired the proper northern spirit, and Inman moved to the North soon after the war.[32]

William P. Clyde dominated the management of the growing system in the early 1880's. He was constantly a director of the Richmond and Danville, from 1881 through 1885, and both director and president of the subordinate holding company, the Richmond and West Point Terminal.[33] Clyde retained A. S. Buford as president of the R. and D., a position he had held with but minor interruption since 1865.[34] A list of presidents for the period will be found on the following page.

Thomas M. Logan, a Confederate Brigadier General at twenty-four, and after the war a rising, young, Richmond business man, was also prominent in the Clyde syndicate. He was a director of the Richmond and West Point Terminal Company during most

---

389-391, 437; *Commercial and Financial Chronicle*, August 20, 1881, p. 201; February 17; 1883, p. 195; November 24, 1883, p. 563. Gordon resigned as president in 1883 and sold his interest for a reported $200,000 profit. Nixon, *op. cit.*, p. 226.

32. William B. Hesseltine, *Confederate Leaders in the New South* (Baton Rouge, Louisiana, 1950), pp. 125-127; Henry Clews, *Fifty Years in Wall Street* (New York, 1915), pp. 557-558.

33. Clyde ceased to be active in the management after 1885, but returned as a director in both companies during the year of receivership, 1892.

34. H. J. Eckenrode, *The Political History of Virginia During the Reconstruction* (Baltimore, 1904), p. 32.

RAILROADS OF THE SOUTH

	Richmond and Danville	Richmond and West Point Terminal Company
1881	A. S. Buford, Richmond	W. P. Clyde, New York
1882	A. S. Buford, Richmond	W. P. Clyde, New York
1883	George S. Scott, New York	W. P. Clyde, New York
1884	A. S. Buford, Richmond	W. P. Clyde, New York
1885	A. S. Buford, Richmond	W. P. Clyde, New York
1886	Alfred Sully, New York	Alfred Sully, New York
1887	George S. Scott, New York	John H. Inman, New York
1888	George S. Scott, New York	John H. Inman, New York
1889	John H. Inman, New York	John H. Inman, New York
1890	John H. Inman, New York	John H. Inman, New York
1891	W. G. Oakman, New York	W. G. Oakman, New York
1892	W. G. Oakman, New York	W. G. Oakman, New York

of its existence and was president of the subsidiary road, the Virginia Midland.[35] Under the early Clyde management the R. and D. was fairly prosperous and paid good dividends in 1881 and 1882.[36] By the fall of 1882, however, a growing floating debt convinced the management that the last quarterly dividend of the year should be passed.[37] The stock of the R. and D. had been unusually active during the year and soon new faces started to appear at the directors' meetings. At the board elections in December, 1882, Robert Harris of New York was elected as a new director, it being generally understood that he represented the interests recently acquired by John D. Rockefeller.[38]

The year 1883 brought more marked changes in the management personnel of the system. Trade in the common stock of the R. and D. continued active during the year and in the summer of 1883, a new syndicate composed of George S. Scott, William P. Clyde, George T. Baker, E. D. Fahnestock, Samuel Thomas, Calvin S. Price, and George I. Seney obtained control of the road.[39] In August and September, 1883, several of the old board mem-

35. *Commercial and Financial Chronicle*, June 19, 1880, p. 651; Clews, *op. cit.*, p. 555.
36. Henry V. Poor, *Manual of the Railroads of the United States for 1885* (New York, 1885), p. 393; *Commercial and Financial Chronicle*, December 16, 1882, p. 707.
37. *Commercial and Financial Chronicle*, November 18, 1882, p. 577.
38. Henry V. Poor, *Manual of the Railroads of the United States for 1883* (New York, 1883), p. 417; *Commercial and Financial Chronicle*, October 21, 1882, pp. 450, 457. The Richmond and Danville stock had sold for 250 early in February, 1882, but by October it had dropped to a low of 57.
39. *Commercial and Financial Chronicle*, July 28, 1883, p. 100; August 4, 1883, p. 111.

THE RICHMOND AND DANVILLE

bers resigned to be replaced by members of the Scott syndicate.[40] Three of the syndicate, General Samuel Thomas, Calvin S. Brice, and George Seney, were in the active management of the East Tennessee, Virginia and Georgia. Calvin S. Brice claimed that greater interchange of business made possible by the common management would greatly increase the prosperity of both roads.[41] Both Thomas and Brice remained active in the management of the Richmond and Danville system until receivership overtook the Richmond and West Point Terminal Company in 1892. The slightly built and talkative Brice was continuously reelected (with the exception of 1885) to the board of directors of the holding company until its collapse in 1892.

In 1885 the Richmond and Danville system consisted of 2,669 miles, of which 853 miles were directly owned and leased by the Richmond and Danville, and 1,816 miles were controlled by the Richmond and West Point Terminal Company. The more than 500 miles added by the holding company since 1882 resulted from the completion of the 313-mile Georgia Pacific and from other minor additions to original portions of the system.[42] In the same year, 1885, the necessity for operating through a holding company was removed when an amendment to its charter gave the Richmond and Danville an unlimited right to hold the stock of the other railroads.[43] Realizing that the Richmond and West Point Terminal Company was superfluous, the R. and D. management in the spring of 1886 quietly began to strip the holding company of its rail securities. Between May and October, it either took long term leases on, or obtained through stock control, railroads totalling over 1,400 miles. In exchange for the $12,000,000 to $13,000,000 of rail securities previously held by the holding company, it gave up $2,500,000 of the holding company's own capital stock. The Richmond and Danville, having

---

40. *Ibid.*, August 11, 1883, p. 151; September 15, 1883, p. 295. At the Richmond stockholders meeting, September 12, 1883, Scott claimed that his group held three-fifths of all the stock outstanding. Scott soon replaced Buford as president.

41. *Ibid.*, August 4, 1883, pp. 111, 128.

42. Poor, *Manual of the Railroads of the United States for 1885*, pp. 390-391.

43. Daggett, *Railroad Reorganization*, pp. 158-160.

RAILROADS OF THE SOUTH

taken the cream of the securities, thus planned to set the holding company completely free of control.[44] The remaining holders of Richmond and West Point Terminal stock protested the whole process, but the Richmond and Danville directors were smugly complacent. Director George S. Scott pointed out in June, 1886, that all the proceedings of the Richmond and Danville had been strictly legal and fair.[45]

Fortunately for the small investors in the Richmond Terminal Company, several wealthy New Yorkers, such as Robert K. Dow, Henry Morrison Flagler, Emanuel Lehman, George F. Stone, and Alfred Sully, at this time became interested in the prospects of the forsaken holding company. Having gained control of the Richmond Terminal Company, the new pool quietly started to buy up Richmond and Danville stock. During the last weeks of the year the R. and D. stock became more and more active and pushed up from 140 in early October to 200 by mid-November.[46] By November 20, 1886, they had turned the tables on the Richmond and Danville management. Instead of the R. and D. controlling the Richmond Terminal Company, the Richmond Terminal Company now controlled the R. and D., holding more than 25,000 shares of R. and D. stock.[47]

At the annual meetings held in December, 1886, many new names appeared on the boards of directors. Ten new men, eight of them from New York, appeared in the list of directors for the now dominant Richmond and West Point Terminal Company.[48]

---

44. *Ibid.; Commercial and Financial Chronicle*, May 15, 1886 p. 604; June 5, 1886, p. 683; June 12, 1886, p. 728. For several years the R. and D. had held $7,510,000 of the $15,000,000 of Richmond and West Point Terminal common stock.

45. *Commercial and Financial Chronicle*, June 12, 1886, p. 728; October 23, 1886, p. 487.

46. Clews, *Fifty Years in Wall Street*, p. 522; *Commercial and Financial Chronicle*, October 9, 1886, p. 427; November 20, 1886, p. 600. The R. and D. stock had been at about 100 in the spring of 1886.

47. Clews, *loc. cit.; Commercial and Financial Chronicle*, November 20, 1886, p. 608; November 27, 1886, p. 635; Daggett, *op. cit.*, p. 160; *Southern Railway Valuation Docket no. 556*, Report of Accounting Section (Richmond and Danville), II, 223, Record Group 134, National Archives. The Richmond Terminal stock became very bullish on the news of the coup. From 39-42 early in November, 1886, it jumped to 70-77 by the end of the month.

48. Henry V. Poor, *Manual of the Railroads of the United States for 1887* (New York, 1887), p. 636.

Alfred Sully of New York, a newcomer with much railroad financial experience in the North, was elected president of the Richmond Terminal Company and the now subordinate R. and D.[49] Several of the veteran directors of previous years, such as Thomas M. Logan and John H. Inman, weathered the upset and were returned to both boards.[50]

Under the new management the Richmond and West Point Terminal Company entered a new phase of extremely rapid expansion and consolidation. Between 1886 and 1890 the total system practically trebled in size, and in 1890 with over eight thousand miles of road, the Richmond and West Point Terminal was one of the largest roads in the nation.[51] The earliest major expansion under the new management was the acquisition of the East Tennessee, Virginia and Georgia Railway. Early in January, 1887, negotiations started between the new management of the Richmond Terminal Company and the officials of the recently reorganized East Tennessee, Virginia and Georgia. By the third week in the month an agreement had been reached whereby the Richmond Terminal Company was to purchase 60,000 shares (a majority) of the East Tennessee First Preferred Stock.[52] A majority of the preferred stock gave the Richmond Terminal Company control, since a provision of the East Tennessee's recent reorganization had withheld control from the common stockholders for five years or at least until the preferred stockholders had received in succession two annual 5 per cent dividends.[53]

As a result of the shifting control, three East Tennessee officials, Calvin S. Brice, Samuel Thomas, and George S. Scott, were returned to membership in the board of the Richmond Terminal Company, and several changes were also made in the East Tennessee board so as to include men from the parent com-

---

49. *Commercial and Financial Chronicle*, December 11, 1886, p. 719; December 18, 1886, p. 738; Clews, *op. cit.*, pp. 553-554.

50. Poor, *Manual of the Railroads of the United States for 1887*, pp. 631, 636.

51. *Commercial and Financial Chronicle*, December 20, 1890, p. 853; Poor, *Manual of the Railroads of the United States for 1891*, p. 472.

52. *Commercial and Financial Chronicle*, January 15, 1887, p. 91; January 22, 1887, p. 119.

53. *Ibid.*, June 2, 1888, p. 708; Daggett, *loc. cit.*; Van Oss, *American Railroads as Investments*, p. 775.

pany.[54] The Richmond Terminal Company continued to control the East Tennessee road until 1892 when both companies went into receivership. In 1887 the East Tennessee voted a 4 per cent preferred stock dividend and a 5 per cent dividend the following year, despite the criticism of minority stockholders that the Richmond Terminal management was keeping the rate intentionally low.[55] Feeling that control through preferred stock alone was inadequate, the Richmond Terminal Company in the fall of 1888 negotiated a ninety-nine-year lease of the East Tennessee road. This proposal, however, was stopped by an adverse judicial decision in November, 1888.[56] In 1889, a second consecutive 5 per cent preferred stock dividend was declared, but the Richmond Terminal Company continued to control the road in spite of the decreased importance of its holdings of preferred stock.[57]

During the spring of 1890, the Brice-and-Thomas-managed East Tennessee road acquired an additional 750 miles of line. In April the East Tennessee acquired major portions of the Erlanger System when it purchased from the English holders a majority of the common stock in both the 336-mile Cincinnati, New Orleans and Texas Pacific Railway, and the 295-mile Alabama Great Southern Railway.[58] The two roads together provided a through

54. *Commercial and Financial Chronicle*, February 5, 1887, p. 184; February 12, 1887, p. 212. The short but broad shouldered Calvin Brice had always been good at getting into things. The son of an Ohio Presbyterian minister he had seen Civil War Service at sixteen, returned home to finish school, gone back to war to become a Lt. Colonel before he was twenty. In the 1870's and 1880's he had been connected with the financing of many northern railroads. In the early 1890's he was a U. S. senator for a short time, and in Washington he quickly gained the reputation for being a lavish host. He engaged in numerous stock market speculations, in one of which he had Grover Cleveland as a partner. Clews, *op. cit.*, p. 554; Arthur Pound and Samuel Taylor Moore, ed., *More They Told Barron, Conversations and Revelations of an American Pepys in Wall Street* (New York, 1931), p. 9; Henry Adams, *The Education of Henry Adams* (New York, 1918), p. 331.

55. *Commercial and Financial Chronicle*, June 2, 1888, p. 708; July 14, 1888, p. 50; September 22, 1888, p. 353.

56. *Ibid.*, September 29, 1888, p. 381; October 6, 1888, p. 410; December 1, 1888, p. 663.

57. *Ibid.*, September 21, 1889, p. 354; October 12, 1889, p. 453; Poor, *Manual of the Railroads of the United States for 1891*, p. 199.

58. Poor, *Manual of the Railroads of the United States for 1891*, p. 194; *Commercial and Financial Chronicle*, February 15, 1890, p. 245; April 19, 1890, p. 560; Harrison, *Legal Development of the Southern Railway*, p. 977.

THE RICHMOND AND DANVILLE

route from Cincinnati to Meridian, Mississippi. The following July 1, 1890, the East Tennessee took possession of the 124-mile Louisville Southern Railroad under a recently negotiated ninety-nine-year lease. The East Tennessee system in mid-1890 thus included nearly 2,600 miles of road.[59]

The other major expansion made by the Richmond Terminal Company in the late 1880's was that extremely prosperous and well-managed property, the Central Railroad of Georgia. This old railroad, chartered in 1835 and completed in 1843, had always been a prosperous line. Between June, 1847, and 1890, it paid a total of seventy-seven dividends, aggregating 345.5 per cent on the capital stock. Throughout the 1880's it had paid regular dividends of from 4 per cent to 8 per cent.[60] The Central system had also expanded in the decade of the 1880's. In 1890 it directly operated 1,312 miles, and had an auxiliary system of an additional 984 miles, which it controlled through lease or stock ownership.[61] The management for twenty years after the Civil War had been clearly southern. In the fall of 1886, a contest for control developed between two Georgia groups, one of which had considerable backing from New York capitalists. The New York-supported General E. P. Alexander gained the presidency of the road at Savannah on January 3, 1887, when the 6,400 votes of Hetty Green of New York gave him 43,000 votes out of a total of 75,000. Alexander succeeded William G. Raoul of Savannah.[62]

During the first year of General Alexander's presidency the Central of Georgia came completely under northern control. In the fall of 1887, a syndicate of New York capitalists, including Alfred Sully, Isaac G. Rice, Emanuel Lehman, John H. Inman, James Swan, and John C. Calhoun, organized under the laws of North Carolina the Georgia Company.[63] The Georgia Com-

---

59. Poor, *Manual of the Railroads of the United States for 1891*, pp. 194-196.

60. *Ibid.*, pp. 91-94.   61. *Ibid.*

62. *Commercial and Financial Chronicle*, November 20, 1886, p. 607; January 8, 1887, p. 59.

63. *Ibid.*, August 13, 1887, p. 210; October 8, 1887, p. 457; December 10, 1887, p. 792; E. G. Campbell, *The Reorganization of the American Railroad System, 1893-1900* (New York, 1938), pp. 97-99. Several of the members of the syndicate such as Sully, Rice, Lehman, and Inman were already directors of the Richmond Terminal or the Richmond and Danville.

pany had the right to hold railroad securities or to operate railroads in North Carolina or any adjoining states. During the fall of 1887, the new corporation purchased 40,000 shares, or a majority, of the capital stock of the Central Railroad of Georgia. Using the $4,000,000 (par value) of Central of Georgia capital stock and $400,000 in cash, subscribed by the syndicate members, as a basis of capitalization, the new Georgia Company next issued $4,000,000 in 5 per cent trust bonds and $12,000,000 of Georgia Company common stock.[64] At the Central of Georgia's annual election of directors in January, 1888, the only ticket of candidates offered was the one supported by the Georgia Company syndicate.[65] General Alexander remained as director and president.

The connection between the Central of Georgia and the Richmond Terminal Company became closer in April, 1888, when John H. Inman, for several years a director in the Richmond Terminal system and also a leader in the Georgia Company syndicate, was elected president of the Richmond Terminal Company.[66] The shrewd John Inman was no man to let a literally golden opportunity slip past. The following fall, in October, 1888, Emanuel Lehman (himself a director of the Richmond Terminal) appeared before the board of the Richmond Terminal Company and offered to sell the entire 120,000 shares of Georgia Company stock at $35 per share and also the $4,000,000 of trust bonds. The Richmond Terminal board, including the president and four directors who would personally profit therefrom, agreed to pay

64. Campbell, *op. cit.*, p. 99; *Commercial and Financial Chronicle*, August 13, 1887, p. 210; December 10, 1887, p. 792. The $4,000,000 of Central of Georgia stock was deposited with the Central Trust Company of New York as security for the new bond issue.

65. *Commercial and Financial Chronicle*, January 7, 1888, p. 37.

66. *Ibid.*, April 7, 1888, p. 449; April 21, 1888, p. 511. Inman replaced Alfred Sully who had resigned early in April. John H. Inman, born on a plantation in eastern Tennessee, preferred a bank clerkship in Georgia to college. After three years in the Confederate army he returned home to find his family ruined by the war. He moved on to New York where he entered his uncle's cotton brokerage firm. He quickly succeeded in the business, organized his own firm in 1870, and was one of the founders of the New York Cotton Exchange. From cotton he moved on to investments in the iron enterprises in Birmingham and railroads throughout the South. Clews, *Fifty Years in Wall Street*, pp. 557-558; Nixon, *Henry W. Grady*, pp. 153, 238; Campbell, *The Reorganization of the American Railroad System, 1893-1900*, pp. 98-99.

$7,500,000 for the securities worth hardly more than half that amount. The cash for the purchase was in part borrowed from the Central Railroad of Georgia ($3,500,000) and from the East Tennessee, Virginia and Georgia, both roads now having managements under the thumb of the Richmond Terminal Company.[67] The swindle was made worse when the Central of Georgia voted Inman and his associates a gratuity of $25,000 for helping to sell the Central of Georgia bonds which permitted that company to make the $3,500,000 loan to the Richmond Terminal Company.[68]

Actually, the addition of the Central of Georgia to the system of the Richmond and West Point Terminal Company was of doubtful value, since the natural interest of the Georgia road was to carry freight to Savannah for water shipment to the North, while it was in the best interest of the Richmond Terminal Company to secure for its own lines the long haul. In a straight mileage sense, however, the addition of the Central of Georgia was important for it permitted the Richmond Terminal Company to boast a network of over seven thousand miles in 1888.[69] The hold over the Central of Georgia was made more complete in the spring of 1891 when the Georgia road was leased to the Georgia Pacific Railway, whose property was already under lease to the Richmond and Danville.[70]

John H. Inman continued to dominate the Richmond and West Point Terminal Company for several years after the acquisition of the Central of Georgia. He remained president and also a director until the year of receivership, 1892.[71] His influence with the board remained so great that he was able to

67. *Commercial and Financial Chronicle,* April 21, 1888, p. 511; October 27, 1888, p. 499; November 24, 1888, p. 625; June 8, 1889, p. 764; Campbell, *op. cit.,* pp. 100-102; Harrison, *Legal Development of the Southern Railway,* pp. 557-558.
68. Campbell, *op. cit.,* p. 101.
69. Daggett, *Railroad Reorganization,* pp. 163-164; *Commercial and Financial Chronicle,* October 27, 1888, p. 486.
70. *Commercial and Financial Chronicle,* March 21, 1891, p. 463; Harrison, *loc. cit.*
71. *Commercial and Financial Chronicle,* March 19, 1892, p. 486; Poor, *Manual of the Railroads of the United States for 1891,* pp. 470, 475. Inman was also president of the Richmond and Danville during the same period.

RAILROADS OF THE SOUTH

dictate to the board the choice of new directors, such as the inclusion of Abram S. Hewitt and R. T. Wilson in December, 1890.[72] No further significant large expansions were made after the purchase of the control of the Central of Georgia in October, 1888. Those increases in mileage that were made were additions to integral portions of the existing system, such as the East Tennessee acquisition in 1890 of the Cincinnati to Meridian route. The Richmond Terminal Company, however, had such a reputation for extravagant expansion that fresh rumors of new expansion plans were often heard. Reports were current from 1887 to 1891 that the Richmond Terminal Company was about to purchase the Baltimore and Ohio.[73] These were false as were the reports in 1891 that Inman's road planned extensions north of the Ohio and west of the Mississippi.[74] Actually, President Inman was positive that the future of his road lay in the South and in July, 1891, he proved as much when he announced that the general headquarters of the company would soon be moved to Atlanta, a city much closer to the center of the entire system.[75]

But financial difficulties were beginning to bother Inman's road during the same year. Throughout the fall of 1891 there were growing reports of large floating debts owed by each of the major portions of the giant system. During September and October, 1891, Inman's board of directors issued confident statements about plans to fund the now admitted debts. Inman admitted the floating debts to be: Richmond Terminal, $530,000; R. and D., $3,200,000; Georgia Central, $3,800,000; and East Tennessee, $1,400,000.[76] The floating debt of the Richmond and Danville was soon to grow larger, chiefly because of the unprofitable operations of its recently leased line, the Georgia Pacific.[77]

72. *Commercial and Financial Chronicle*, December 6, 1890, p. 788.
73. *Ibid.*, March 12, 1887, p. 343; May 17, 1890, p. 703; February 14, 1891, p. 280.
74. *Ibid.*, February 14, 1891, p. 280.
75. *Ibid.*, July 18, 1891, p. 96.
76. Campbell, *op. cit.*, pp. 104-105; *Commercial and Financial Chronicle*, August 15, 1891, p. 224; September 19, 1891, p. 408; October 31, 1891, p. 641. Inman continued to be confident. In August he had claimed that every major part of the system was earning more than its fixed charges.
77. Henry V. Poor, *Manual of the Railroads of the United States for 1893* (New York, 1893), pp. 552, 562; *Commercial and Financial Chronicle*, November 21, 1891, p. 754; December 5, 1891, p. 818.

THE RICHMOND AND DANVILLE

On November 30, 1891, the Richmond Terminal board in its annual report admitted its temporary inability to fund its large floating debt. The result was the appointment of a special stockholders committee headed by Frederick P. Olcutt to consider and work out plans for the reorganization of the entire company.[78] While Olcutt's committee was at work, Inman, possibly fearing what was ahead, resigned the presidency of the Richmond Terminal Company in March, 1892, and was replaced by W. G. Oakman of New York.[79]

During the same month affairs down in Georgia also began to embarrass the Richmond Terminal Company. Mrs. Rowena M. Clarke of Charleston, a minority stockholder who owned fifty shares of Central of Georgia stock, filed suit early in March, 1892, with the United States Circuit Court at Macon, Georgia, claiming that the lease of the Central of Georgia to the Georgia Pacific was invalid since it violated the Georgia Constitution.[80] The court agreed with Mrs. Clarke, declared the lease invalid, appointed General E. P. Alexander temporary receiver for his road, and ordered that the 42,200 shares of Georgia Central stock could not be voted by the Richmond Terminal.[81] In mid-July, 1892, Judge Spear of the United States Circuit Court made the receivership permanent, with H. M. Comer of Savannah as receiver.[82]

The receivership of the Central of Georgia was a real embarrassment to the management of the Richmond Terminal Company. The difficulties in Georgia made it doubly difficult for Olcutt's committee to obtain the necesssary support for its re-

78. *Commercial and Financial Chronicle*, December 12, 1891, p. 878; January 16, 1892, p. 120; March 5, 1892, p. 410; Campbell, *op. cit.*, pp. 93-95.

79. *Commercial and Financial Chronicle*, March 19, 1892, p. 486. Oakman also became president of the East Tennessee, Virginia and Georgia at the same time, replacing S. M. Felton.

80. The Georgia Constitution of 1877 declared illegal and void any contract or agreement between corporations which might defeat or lessen competition in their respective businesses, or encourage monopoly. Harrison, *Legal Development of the Southern Railway*, pp. 557-558.

81. *Ibid.*; *Commercial and Financial Chronicle*, March 12, 1892, p. 443; April 2, 1892, pp. 559-560; April 16, 1892, p. 643; *Central of Georgia Railway Valuation Docket*, no. 60, Accounting Report, I, 82, Record Group 134, National Archives. Alexander resigned as president of the road at the end of March and was replaced by H. M. Comer.

82. *Commercial and Financial Chronicle*, July 23, 1892, p. 145.

funding and reorganization plans. In May, 1892, the Olcutt plan was abandoned and a new committee, consisting of Samuel Thomas, W. E. Strong, and W. P. Clyde, was appointed.[83] The new committee at once requested J. P. Morgan of Drexel, Morgan and Company to examine the Richmond Terminal property with a view to undertaking its reorganization.[84] While Morgan was inspecting the property the situation was complicated by the appointment of receivers for the remaining portions of the system, the Richmond and Danville on June 16, the Richmond Terminal on June 22, and the East Tennessee, Virginia and Georgia on June 24.[85] The inspection of the system made by the representatives of J. P. Morgan showed the whole corporate structure to be hopelessly complex and the physical property to be in poor condition.[86] Even so, Morgan was prepared late in June, 1892, to take on the difficult task of reorganization, provided that the litigation concerning the receivership could be put under his control. When he failed to obtain assurances to that effect, Morgan refused to take over the problem of reorganization.[87]

On August 1, 1892, the Richmond Terminal Company defaulted on some bond interest due, and three weeks later Judge Bond in Baltimore made the company's receivership permanent with W. G. Oakman as receiver.[88] One of Oakman's early acts was to prepare a case against John H. Inman and his associates

---

83. *Ibid.*, March 19, 1892, p. 464; April 16, 1892, p. 643; May 21, 1892, p. 846; May 28, 1892, p. 866; Campbell, *op. cit.*, p. 104. The Olcutt plan would have renamed the system the Southern Railway Company. The details of the plan were quite similar to J. P. Morgan's later actual reorganization, but were too drastic for the security holders of a company that had not yet admitted its own insolvency. Campbell, *op. cit.*, pp. 94-95.

84. *Commercial and Financial Chronicle,* May 28, 1892, p. 888.

85. *Ibid.*, June 11, 1892, p. 965; June 18, 1892, p. 1010; June 25, 1892, p. 1048; July 2, 1892, p. 21. In each case the suits were brought by friends of the company. William P. Clyde claimed that the R. and D. receivership was necessary because the Central of Georgia insisted upon attaching, on one pretext or another, any money which the R. and D. tried to keep in the banks of Atlanta.

86. Campbell, *op. cit.*, pp. 95, 105.

87. *Commercial and Financial Chronicle,* July 2, 1892, pp. 2, 23.

88. *Ibid.*, August 6, 1892, p. 216; August 27, 1892, p. 332. Three weeks later, on September 15, 1892, at a special stockholders meeting, the Richmond Terminal selected an almost entirely new board of directors. William P. Clyde was the only leader of an earlier day who remained in the new group. *Ibid.*, September 17, 1892, p. 463.

alleging fraud in the purchase by the Richmond Terminal Company of the securities of the Georgia Company.[89] Receiver Oakman also endeavored to persuade his large stockholders to capitulate to the stiff terms required by J. P. Morgan. He succeeded in doing so early in 1893, and in a letter of February 2, 1893, Drexel, Morgan and Company agreed to take over the task of reorganization and rehabilitation.[90]

The conditions imposed by J. P. Morgan early in 1893 were such that the security holders virtually accepted in advance any reorganization plan he might suggest. By 1893 the bankers of the North had control of the Richmond Terminal, the Richmond and Danville, and the dozens of associated and related lines. This control was to become nearly permanent for Morgan's reorganization plans were to include a large place in the future management for Morgan-selected directors. The new Southern Railway was to belong to the House of Morgan.

89. *Ibid.*, November 26, 1892, p. 895; December 3, 1892, p. 938; December 24, 1892, p. 1078; March 11, 1893 p. 414. Inman's reply was a masterpiece of ingenious evasion but he did not deny that a gigantic swindle had been put over on the Richmond Terminal. Campbell, *op. cit.*, p. 103.

90. Campbell, *op. cit.*, p. 149; *Commercial and Financial Chronicle*, February 4, 1893, pp. 178, 207.

CHAPTER 12

RECEIVERSHIP AND CONSOLIDATION

THE LAST decade of the nineteenth century, as far as American railroad development was concerned, was in many ways a combination of the two preceding decades. Like the decade following 1870, it was a period early punctuated by numerous railroad defaults and receiverships. At the peak of the rail depression, in mid-1894, a quarter of the nation's railroads were operated by receivers with about $2,500,000,000 of railroad capital affected.[1] As reorganization plans in the last years of the century successfully rehabilitated these stricken roads, several new rail combinations appeared. As in the decade of the 1880's, the drive toward railroad consolidation and monopoly was a growing trend. By 1900 in the South, and most of the nation, a certain rail transportation maturity had been achieved. Most of the present-day large railroad corporations were in existence at the turn of the century.

In at least one respect the decade after 1890 was different from the preceding ten years. In railroad construction the century's last decade produced relatively less new mileage than any other ten-year period since 1850. The percentage increases for past decades had been: 1850 to 1860—240 per cent, 1860 to 1870—73 per cent, 1870 to 1880—76 per cent, and 1880 to 1890—79 per cent. Between 1890 and the end of 1899, the nation's rail mileage increased but 24,016 miles to an 1899 total of 190,833 miles, or an increase of little more than 14 per cent.[2] The decade

1. E. G. Campbell, *The Reorganization of the American Railroad System, 1893-1900* (New York, 1938), pp. 26-27.
2. H. V. and H. W. Poor, *Manual of the Railroads of the United States for 1900* (New York, 1901), pp. xxxix-xl, vi. The mileage decade by decade was: 1850, 9,021 miles; 1860, 30,626 miles; 1870, 52,922 miles; 1880, 93,262 miles; and 1890, 166,817 miles.

254

RECEIVERSHIP AND CONSOLIDATION

of the 1880's had seen three times as much new rail construction as the ten years after 1890. During the rapid construction of the 1880's, only the two worst years, 1884 and 1885, had new mileage figures at all comparable with the best years, 1891 and 1892, of the century's last decade.

As in the preceding decade the southern states had a rate of new rail construction slightly more rapid than the national average. In the years between the end of 1890 and January 1, 1900, the southern states added 5,455 miles of new track to their 1890 network of 29,263 miles. This was an increase of 18.6 per cent as contrasted to a national average of 14.4 per cent. In 1890, the rail mileage in the South accounted for but 17.6 per cent of the nation's total rail mileage, but during the 1890's, 22.7 per cent of the new rail construction occurred in the ten southern states.[3] Four states in the South, Georgia, Louisiana, Florida, and Alabama, each added more new road to their systems in the period than did New England. In fact, the South built almost as much new road in the 1890's as did the ten states of the Trunk Line area (i.e., the Old North West and the Middle Atlantic states). By 1900, the South had rounded out the basic outline of its ultimate railroad system and possessed about three-quarters of its present rail mileage.

Naturally the rate of new construction varied widely among the ten southern states. Georgia, both in new mileage built and in total mileage, was still the leading railroad state. As in the preceding decade, Florida built many new lines in the period, and at the end of the century was in fifth position in rail mileage, as contrasted in tenth place twenty years earlier. Louisiana also built rapidly during the 1890's, adding over nine hundred miles of track, or more than the aggregate for its three neighbors to the north, Mississippi, Tennessee, and Kentucky.[4] The details of the southern construction are reviewed below:

3. In 1900 the South with 34,718 miles of road had 18.2 per cent of the nation's total rail mileage. *Ibid.*, p. vi.

4. *Ibid.;* Henry V. Poor, *Manual of the Railroads of the United States for 1891* (New York, 1891), p. xviii.

RAILROADS OF THE SOUTH

	Total as of Dec. 31, 1890	Rank	Increase in the 9 years	Total as of Dec. 31, 1899	Rank
Va.	3,368	(3)	353	3,721	(3)
N. C.	3,128	(4)	528	3,656	(4)
S. C.	2,297	(9)	495	2,792	(8)
Ga.	4,593	(1)	1,005	5,598	(1)
Fla.	2,489	(7)	745	3,234	(5)
Ala.	3,422	(2)	629	4,051	(2)
Miss.	2,471	(8)	317	2,788	(9)
La.	1,750	(10)	914	2,664	(10)
Tenn.	2,799	(6)	332	3,131	(6)
Ky.	2,946	(5)	137	3,083	(7)
10 states	29,263		5,455	34,718	

The lagging rate of construction both in the South and in the nation as a whole was but a reflection of the general state of depression which dominated the last two-thirds of the decade. Continuing the relative prosperity of the late 1880's the southern lines in 1890 and 1891 were fairly prosperous.[5] In 1890 at least ten major southern lines paid dividends of from 3 per cent to 10 per cent on common or preferred stock.[6] In 1891 and 1892, the southern roads paid cash dividends of over $7,000,000 each year on their capital stock, or an average rate of perhaps 1.1 per cent as compared to the average national railroad dividend rate of 1.9 per cent.[7] But in 1893 southern railroad dividends slumped badly and from 1894 through 1898 southern dividends were no more than from a fifth to a third of the average national rate.[8] The South achieved a moderate recovery by 1899 when its total dividends of $7,200,000 approximated an average of 1 per cent on the total capital stock.[9] The depression was also reflected

5. *Commercial and Financial Chronicle*, July 12, 1890, p. 36; July 11, 1891, p. 37.
6. *Ibid.*, December 27, 1890, p. 893.
7. H. V. and H. W. Poor, *Manual of the Railroads of the United States for 1900*, pp. xiii-xv.
8. *Ibid.* The average dividend rates for the ten southern states and for the nation are reviewed below:

	South	U. S.		South	U. S.
1890	1.0%	1.8%	1895	.3%	1.6%
1891	1.1%	1.9%	1896	.4%	1.5%
1892	1.1%	1.9%	1897	.5%	1.5%
1893	.8%	1.9%	1898	.5%	1.7%
1894	.3%	1.7%	1899	1.0%	1.9%

9. *Ibid.*, pp. xii-xv; *Commercial and Financial Chronicle*, Investor's Supplement, January, 1900, p. 7.

RECEIVERSHIP AND CONSOLIDATION

in the railroad security market, especially after 1893. After fairly good years from 1890 through 1892, the market quotations for railroad common stock slumped roughly 20 per cent in the middle and late 1890's. As in the case of dividends, southern railroad stocks tended to react more violently than the national average. They did, however, achieve a moderate recovery by 1898 and 1899. The following table would indicate this to be true for several southern railroads.[10]

Year	'90	'91	'92	'93	'94	'95	'96	'97	'98	'99
U. S. railroad stock index	49	47	51	43	39	40	40	41	45	56
Average for five southern railroads	47	47	50	45	34	37	36	38	44	52

But the clearest indication of the degree of railroad depression was to be seen in the numerous railroad receiverships that occurred in the 1890's. During the decade, 375 different American railroad companies with a total of 51,619 miles were in receivership. Of these roads, 128 were lines 100 miles or more in length for an aggregate of 42,611 miles.[11] Of the 128 major lines in receivership during the 1890's, 33, or over a quarter of the total companies, were southern lines. In addition to the 15 receiverships associated with the collapse of the 8,000-mile Richmond Terminal system, there were 18 other southern roads with a total length of 4,917 miles also in receivership in the South.[12] The total southern mileage affected was thus 13,000 miles, or nearly half of the mileage of the region in 1890.[13] For the nation, 1893 was by far the worst year for receivership with receivers appointed for over 27,000 miles of road. In the South, however, much of

---

10. *Historical Statistics of the United States, 1789-1945* (Washington, D. C., 1949), p. 281. The five southern lines include the L. and N., the Chesapeake and Ohio, the Mobile and Ohio, the Norfolk and Western, and the Atlanta and Charlotte Air-Line. Average quotations for the five southern roads were listed in the January issues of the *Commercial and Financial Chronicle* from 1890 to 1899.

11. H. V. and H. W. Poor, *Manual of the Railroads of the United States for 1900*, pp. lxxii, xcviii-ci. The longer or major roads accounted for nearly 83 per cent of the total rail mileage in receivership in the decade.

12. *Ibid.*, pp. xcviii-ci.

13. For the nation as a whole, the major lines in receivership (42,611 miles) amounted to little more than a quarter of the nation's total network of 166,817 miles as of 1890.

the difficulty came earlier, in 1892, largely because of the difficulties of the Richmond Terminal Company in that year.[14]

The receivership and reorganization of the Richmond Terminal system was easily the single most important financial development among southern railroads in the mid-1890's. When Drexel, Morgan and Company agreed in early February, 1893, to undertake the financial rehabilitation of this property there was a general feeling of satisfaction in northern financial circles.[15] The properties affected totalled something like six thousand miles of road, the Central of Georgia system not being included because of complicating litigation in which it was involved.[16] Morgan's first step was to call for a deposit of all stocks and bonds with his company. This was an unusual practice, but it was approved by the Richmond Terminal board and by early May, 1893, the great bulk of the securities were in Morgan's possession.[17] While the securities were being deposited with Morgan's firm, the latter's agents had been closely examining the status of the railroad property. The investigation showed much of the property to be badly run down. The Richmond and Danville still had seven hundred miles of light iron rails and its motive power roster included many engines of Civil War vintage. Improper accounting methods were also discovered, such as charging rail renewal to construction accounts rather than to operating expense.[18]

With the assistance of Charles H. Coster, his expert on rail securities, and Francis Lynde Stetson, his favorite corporation attorney, Morgan was able late in May, 1893, to announce the details of his reorganization plan. The plan called for heavy cash assessments upon the junior security holders, the proceeds to be

---

14. H. V. and H. W. Poor, *op. cit.*, pp. lxxii, xcviii-ci.
15. *Commercial and Financial Chronicle*, February 4, 1893, p. 207.
16. Campbell, *The Reorganization of the American Railroad System, 1893-1900*, p. 150.
17. *Commercial and Financial Chronicle*, April 15, 1893, pp. 596, 622; April 22, 1893, p. 669; May 6, 1893, p. 754. This policy was probably necessary since the position of the Richmond Terminal would become extremely vulnerable should foreclosure proceedings be pushed against either the Richmond and Danville or the East Tennessee system.
18. *Ibid.*, May 27, 1893, pp. 858-860. The R. and D. was also guilty of claiming as "assets" certain property destroyed by fires and lost in rail accidents.

RECEIVERSHIP AND CONSOLIDATION

used for property betterment and the payment of the $14,000,000 floating debt. The annual fixed charges were to be reduced from $9,900,000 to less than $7,000,000.[19] The plan was well received and within a month over 90 per cent of the bond and stockholders of the Richmond Terminal Company had approved the reorganization plan.[20] However, the annual reports of the receivers indicated that Morgan's estimates for future earnings were too optimistic. Also, the total of receiver's certificates issued was larger than anticipated. Modifications in the original Morgan plan were thus necessary.[21] The modified plan was submitted in March, 1894. The important changes were the elimination of weaker portions of the system, a reduction in the cash assessments required of security holders, and a somewhat smaller total capital structure.[22] The revised plan was quickly approved and by October, 1894, the new Southern Railway was selecting a board of directors, three of the nine being from Drexel, Morgan and Company.[23] Through a voting trust of the common stock, which his concern received by the terms of reorganization, Morgan was to control the new railway well into the twentieth century.[24]

While the financial control of the new Southern Railway was exclusively northern, the men in top management positions were often southerners. The first president of the new company, Samuel Spencer, as well as the first vice president, Alexander Boyd Andrews, were both born in the South. Born and educated in Georgia, Spencer entered railroad work in 1869 and worked rapidly up through the ranks of the Baltimore and Ohio, becoming the road's president in 1887.[25] As Morgan's railroad ex-

---

19. Campbell, *op. cit.*, pp. 148-149; *Commercial and Financial Chronicle*, May 27, 1893, p. 858.
20. *Commercial and Financial Chronicle*, June 10, 1893, p. 974; June 17, 1893, p. 1016.
21. Campbell, *op. cit.*, p. 153.
22. *Commercial and Financial Chronicle*, February 17, 1894, p. 307; March 3, 1894, pp. 363, 386. Fixed charges were reduced to less than $5,000,000 for the smaller prospective system of 4,600 miles.
23. *Ibid.*, March 24, 1894, p. 514; June 30, 1894, p. 1110; October 27, 1894, p. 739.
24. *Ibid.*, November 10, 1894, p. 836; Campbell, *op. cit.*, p. 160.
25. Edward Hungerford, *The Story of the Baltimore and Ohio Railroad, 1827-1927* (New York, 1928), II, 163-166.

pert after 1889, he was active in the Richmond Terminal receivership and was a natural choice for the presidency of the new company. During his dozen years in the presidency the road increased greatly in length and traffic and trebled its gross earnings. At the time of his death in 1906, he was recognized as a leading figure in the development of the "New South."[26] Spencer's aide, Alexander Andrews, was a North Carolinian who entered railroading shortly after the war. He was reported to have constructed more new rail mileage in North Carolina than any other man. After completing the Western North Carolina Railroad in 1885, he remained prominent in the management of the Richmond and Danville until its receivership in 1892. He was one of the few managers of the old system to be retained in Morgan's reorganized company.[27]

The reorganization of the Central of Georgia was never a part of Morgan's rehabilitation of the Richmond Terminal property. The Georgia Central litigation starting in March, 1892, successfully kept the two reorganizations apart. Throughout the remainder of 1892 and well into 1893, the best efforts at reorganizing the company failed. Receiver (and president) H. M. Comer laid the blame upon the business depression, the poor condition of the property, and the increasing competition of rival lines.[28] In the following year, 1894, Samuel Thomas and Thomas F. Ryan became interested in the reorganization of the line. After several setbacks, the two men finally succeeded in reorganizing the Central of Georgia during the summer of 1895.[29] Once the company was successfully reorganized as the Central of Georgia Railway, both Thomas and Ryan resigned from the board of

---

26. Charles G. Hall, *The Cincinnati Southern Railway, A History* (Cincinnati, 1902), pp. 83-84; *In Memorium, Samuel Spencer* (Atlanta, 1910), pp. 7-11. Spencer was one of seven persons killed in a collision of two passenger trains on his own railroad.

27. Lou Rogers, "A. B. Andrews," *We The People of North Carolina*, VI (July, 1948), 20-23.

28. *Commercial and Financial Chronicle*, October 1, 1892, p. 543; November 12, 1892, p. 805; January 21, 1893, p. 126; July 1, 1893, p. 21.

29. *Ibid.*, June 16, 1894, p. 1034; February 23, 1895, p. 348; October 26, 1895, p. 749. Campbell, *op. cit.*, pp. 155-156; *Central of Georgia Railway Valuation Docket No. 60*, Accounting Report, I., 7-10, Record Group 134, National Archives.

RECEIVERSHIP AND CONSOLIDATION

directors (June 9, 1896).[30] The new organization, now somewhat smaller because of the loss of its share of the lease of the Georgia Railroad, was still indirectly under the control of the new Southern Railway.[31] Early in the twentieth century, however, the Illinois Central acquired a controlling interest in the company.[32] Under both Southern and Illinois Central ownership, the Central of Georgia Railway remained a separate operating unit.

Of the other southern roads in receivership in the 1890's, the Norfolk and Western Railroad was easily the most important.[33] The road had expanded rapidly in the five years prior to the Panic of 1893, and its eventual receivership in 1895 was due much more to this extremely rapid expansion than to any mistakes or scandals on the part of the road's management.[34] With a somewhat strained financial condition due to the rapid expansion, the coal-bearing road was not equal to the extra burden of the depression.[35] In April, 1893, the company failed to vote its usual preferred stock dividend and the following June suffered an embarrassing three-day receivership due to the non-payment of a small, $44,000 debt.[36] During 1893 and 1894, the road operated

30. *Central of Georgia Railway Valuation Docket No. 60*, Accounting Report, I., 13.
31. *Ibid.*, I., 83. Mary G. Cumming, *Georgia Railroad and Banking Company* (Augusta, Georgia, 1945), pp. 90-91; *Commercial and Financial Chronicle*, July 8, 1893, p. 59; January 6, 1894, p. 43; July 7, 1894, p. 28; November 10, 1894, p. 835; June 8, 1895, p. 1008. In 1900, most of the directors were from Georgia, but Samuel Spencer and two other New Yorkers were also included. H. V. and H. W. Poor, *Manual of the Railroads of the United States for 1900*, p. 354.
32. *Central of Georgia Railway Valuation Docket No. 60*, Accounting Report, I., 8, Record Group 134, National Archives.
33. The Norfolk and Western was a 1,328-mile road in the year of its receivership, 1895. The next longest road (other than the various portions of the Richmond Terminal system) that faced receivership in the decade was the Chesapeake, Ohio and Southwestern with 351 miles.
34. Henry V. Poor, *Manual of the Railroads of the United States for 1893* (New York, 1893), p. 859; Campbell, *op. cit.*, pp. 35-37.
35. Campbell, *op. cit.*, p. 36; *Commercial and Financial Chronicle*, April 26, 1890, p. 591; S. F. Van Oss, *American Railroads as Investments* (New York, 1893), p. 755. The Norfolk and Western had extremely low freight rates for its coal traffic. Its average freight ton-mile rate for all freight in 1890 was just above one-half cent.
36. *Commercial and Financial Chronicle*, April 1, 1893, p. 538; June 10, 1893, p. 973.

RAILROADS OF THE SOUTH

with a deficit and a growing floating debt.[37] Anticipating default, the company applied for the appointment of a receiver and a friendly court complied with the request February 6, 1895.[38] The reorganization was not difficult and within fifteen months the plans were complete. The annual fixed charges were scaled down nearly a third to $2,230,000, an amount well below the average net earnings. The new company, the Norfolk and Western Railway, was formally organized September 24, 1896.[39] The control of the road naturally remained in northern hands. Five years later, in 1901, the Pennsylvania Railroad acquired a practical control over the road.[40]

Of the remaining major southern lines in receivership, about half of the mileage (1,784 miles out of 3,589 miles) moved rather quickly from foreclosure and reorganization into the possession of one of the larger southern rail systems. Between 1895 and 1899, the new Southern Railway acquired control over five such roads. The first acquisition was the purchase in June, 1895, of the 105-mile Georgia line, the Atlanta and Florida Railway.[41] The next year, in July, 1896, the Southern took a long-term lease on another short Georgia line recently out of receivership, the 100-mile Georgia Midland Railway.[42] In 1899, three additional roads were acquired, the Atlantic and Yadkin Railway, the Atlantic and Danville Railway, and the Northern Alabama Railway.[43]

Other large southern rail systems also gained control over lines recently in receivership. In 1893, the Illinois Central strengthened the mid-section of its system with the purchase of the Chesapeake, Ohio and Southwestern Railroad.[44] Also, early

---

37. *Ibid.*, March 31, 1894, p. 548; H. V. and H. W. Poor, *Manual of the Railroads of the United States for 1900*, p. 368.
38. *Commercial and Financial Chronicle*, February 9, 1895, pp. 236, 259.
39. *Ibid.*, April 4, 1896, p. 620; Campbell, *op. cit.*, pp. 214-216; H. V. and H. W. Poor, *Manual of the Railroads of the United States for 1900*, p. 366.
40. Carl Snyder, *American Railways as Investments* (New York, 1907), p. 510.
41. *Commercial and Financial Chronical*, June 29, 1895, p. 1148.
42. H. V. and H. W. Poor, *op. cit.*, p. 395.
43. *Ibid.*, pp. 396-399; *Commercial and Financial Chronicle*, May 20, 1899, p. 947.
44. *Commercial and Financial Chronicle*, December 23, 1893, p. 1083; December 30, 1893, p. 1122; December 8, 1894, p. 1006; Carlton J. Corliss, *Main Line of Mid-America, The Story of the Illinois Central* (New York, 1950), pp. 268-270.

RECEIVERSHIP AND CONSOLIDATION

in the depression, in 1894, the Savannah, Florida and Western (the Plant System) gained a controlling interest in the Florida Southern Railroad, a line that had been in receivership between 1890 and 1892.[45] A third line recently in receivership, the Georgia and Alabama Railroad, was one of the several companies included in the Seaboard Air Line Railway late in the 1890's.[46]

At the end of the decade two relatively new major systems, the Atlantic Coast Line and the Seaboard Air Line, rapidly came to the fore as serious competitors for Morgan's Southern Railway.[47] Both systems served the same general region, the South Atlantic States, as did the Southern Railway. Both the Seaboard and Atlantic Coast Line had started as systems in the years after the Civil War, but it was only in the last two years of the century that a solid and rapid consolidation development occurred.

The Atlantic Coast Line Railroad at the turn of the century was the result of the consolidation of over a hundred railroads stretching along the Atlantic Coast from Richmond, Virginia, south to Florida. The sequence of combination and consolidation was slower than for some other systems because of the Panic of 1873 and perhaps also because of the non-railroad interests of some of its northern owners.

The beginning of the system went back to the Reconstruction in North Carolina when Robert Rufus Bridgers, president of the Wilmington and Weldon, persuaded Governor William Holden to permit the sale of state-held stock in both the Wilmington and Weldon Railroad and the Wilmington and Manchester Railroad. On March 31, 1869, William Thompson Walters, Confederate sympathizer and merchant from Baltimore, purchased four thousand shares of Wilmington and Weldon stock and two thousand shares of Wilmington and Manchester stock.[48] Walters, sup-

---

45. H. V. and H. W. Poor, *op. cit.*, pp. 381-382; *Commercial and Financial Chronicle*, October 27, 1894, p. 738.
46. H. V. and H. W. Poor, *op. cit.*, p. 768.
47. Fairfax Harrison, *A History of the Legal Development of the Railroad System of the Southern Railway Company* (Washington, D. C., 1901), p. 22; *Commercial and Financial Chronicle*, May 6, 1899, p. 851.
48. Cecil Kenneth Brown, *A State Movement in Railroad Development: The Story of North Carolina's First Effort to Establish an East and West Trunk Line Railroad* (Chapel Hill, N. C., 1928), pp. 43-44; *Story of the Atlantic Coast Line* (Wilmington, N. C., 1930), pp. 9-10.

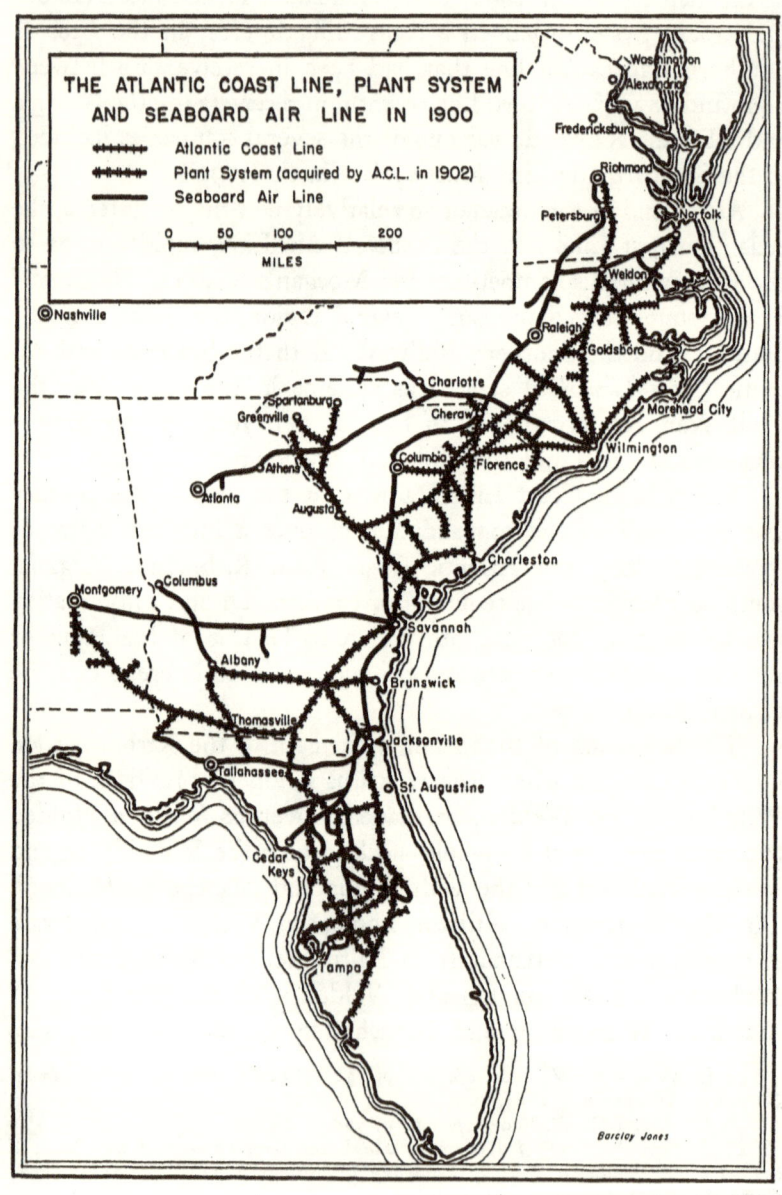

RECEIVERSHIP AND CONSOLIDATION

ported by his able friend and Baltimore banker, Benjamin Franklin Newcomer, soon controlled both lines. Never prosperous in the early postwar years, the Wilmington and Manchester was in receivership by 1868, and two years later was reorganized by the two Baltimore capitalists as the Wilmington, Columbia and Augusta Railroad.[49] Bridgers was president of both lines, Newcomer became vice president, and Walters held the stock.[50] Both roads were included in the Pennsylvania "system" of southern lines in the decade of the 1870's since both Walters and Newcomer were directors of the Southern Railway Security Company. Default and receivership faced the Wilmington, Columbia and Augusta in 1878, but the Baltimore group managed to maintain its control.[51]

Even before the Baltimore men gained control over the two North Carolina roads the coastal rail route from Richmond south to Charleston had been known as the "Weldon Route." In the 1870's the five roads connecting the two cities (Richmond and Petersburg; Petersburg; Wilmington and Weldon; Wilmington, Columbia and Augusta; and the Northeastern of South Carolina) adopted the term Atlantic Coast Line since their route so closely paralleled the Atlantic Ocean. The several companies, though still legally separate, added the route title to their locomotives in addition to their road names.[52]

Soon Walters and Newcomer sought financial control over the connecting roads to the north and south. In late 1884 the Baltimore syndicate purchased the Petersburg Railroad, the line connecting Weldon and Petersburg.[53] About the same time the

49. *The Railroad Gazette*, October 22, 1870, p. 80; Henry V. Poor, *Manual of the Railroads of the United States for 1869-1870* (New York, 1869), pp. 43-44.
50. *The Railroad Gazette*, October 22, 1870, p. 80; December 10, 1870, p. 249.
51. *Commercial and Financial Chronicle*, November 9, 1878, p. 488; October 4, 1879, p. 350; January 24, 1880, p. 84.
52. *Story of the Atlantic Coast Line*, p. 10. Real through service from north to south was helped in the late 1860's by connecting tracks built in Richmond and by bridges at Petersburg and further south. The railroads thus avoided the necessity of transferring passengers and baggage by omnibuses and wagons through the streets of Petersburg and Richmond. Howard Douglas Dozier, *The History of the Atlantic Coast Line* (New York, 1920), pp. 116-118.
53. *Commercial and Financial Chronicle*, January 3, 1885, p. 29. The Petersburg was actually the oldest of the roads in the Atlantic Coast Line since it was chartered in 1830.

Baltimore men were increasing their financial influence over other segments of the route, such as the Richmond and Petersburg, the Northeastern Railroad of South Carolina, and the Cheraw and Darlington.[54]

As a Baltimore commission merchant, Walters was as interested in the rapid northward movement of North Carolina garden truck as in a through passenger service. From small beginnings in the early postwar years the North Carolina garden truck and fruit business expanded until by the middle of the 1880's an improved transportation service northward was an absolute essential. Walters met the requirements by establishing, in conjunction with other northern roads (especially the Pennsylvania Railroad), the Atlantic Coast Despatch, a fast freight service using specially built refrigerator fruit cars. The success of the new service to northern cities soon exceeded the car building facilities of the Wilmington and Weldon shops and in 1889-1890 they purchased three hundred new cars from a Baltimore concern.[55] The Wilmington and Weldon, which in the early postwar years had a traffic that was only 55 per cent freight revenue, by the late 1890's had a freight revenue nearly three times the volume of its passenger business.[56]

Through service south of Wilmington was improved in the spring of 1886 when the five-foot gauge south of the latter city was changed to the narrower standard gauge which was found on all the northern roads of the system. The change in gauge improved the through sleeping car service to Florida.[57] With improvements in both freight and passenger service the whole system prospered, especially the Wilmington and Weldon. In 1885 the Wilmington and Weldon took a ninty-nine year lease on the connecting road to the south, the Wilmington, Columbia and Augusta.[58] The operating ratio on the Wilmington and

54. *Ibid.*, May 23, 1885, p. 624; September 24, 1887, p. 401; December 10, 1887, p. 768.
55. Dozier, *op. cit.*, pp. 122-126.
56. *Ibid.*, pp. 170, 173. By the turn of the century one thousand cars of strawberries were being shipped annually from North Carolina to northern markets.
57. *Story of the Atlantic Coast Line*, p. 10.
58. *Commercial and Financial Chronicle*, June 6, 1885, p. 686.

RECEIVERSHIP AND CONSOLIDATION

Weldon in the 1880's and 1890's averaged under 59 per cent and the *Wall Street Journal* reported that a holder of $10,000 par value Wilmington and Weldon stock would find his investment worth $175,000 by 1902.[59]

The decade of the 1890's brought not only prosperity but also increased financial management of the system by the Baltimore capitalists. In the spring of 1889, the northern control of the growing rail system was made more complete by the incorporation in Connecticut of the Atlantic Coast Line Company. The holding company had its charter amended in 1893 and soon it secured a majority of the stock of many southern roads in the Atlantic Coast Line system.[60] Between 1898 and 1902, the Atlantic Coast Line gained the basic pattern and organization of the present system. On July 16, 1898, the seven-hundred-mile Atlantic Coast Line Railroad of South Carolina was organized to include five roads, the Wilmington, Columbia and Augusta, the Northeastern Railroad of South Carolina, the Cheraw and Darlington, the Manchester and Augusta, and the Florence Railroad. The shareholders of the several lines approved the combination in July, 1898.[61] In the same year a Virginia act permitted the Richmond and Petersburg Railroad and the Petersburg Railroad to consolidate into the one-hundred-mile Atlantic Coast Line Railroad Company of Virginia. Later, Virginia legislation in 1900 gave the new company a shorter name, the Atlantic Coast Line Railroad Company, permitted it a total capitalization of $100,000,000, and gave it the right to purchase other railroads. In April, 1900, the new Atlantic Coast Line Railroad purchased the South Carolina system, the Wilmington and Weldon, and other railroads in the total system.[62] In 1900 the entire system with branches totalled

---

59. Dozier, *op. cit.*, p. 170; Snyder, *American Railways as Investments*, pp. 84-85.
60. Snyder, *loc. cit.*; H. V. and H. W. Poor, *Manual of the Railroads of the United States for 1900*, pp. 341-342; Dozier, *op. cit.*, pp. 140-141.
61. Dozier, *op. cit.*, p. 143; *Story of the Atlantic Coast Line*, p. 13.
62. *Atlantic Coast Line Valuation Docket No. 930*, Accounting Section, I A, 5, Record Group 134, National Archives, Washington, D. C.; Dozier *op. cit.*, pp. 142-143. In August, 1899, the Atlantic Coast Line of South Carolina secured from the L. and N. a half interest in the lease of the Georgia Railroad and Banking Company.

about two thousand miles. Two years later another major southern rail network, the Plant System, was added to the Atlantic Coast Line, providing important extensions into Georgia, Florida, and Alabama.

The Plant System which expanded from two lines purchased in receivership in 1879-1880 to nearly a two-thousand-mile system by the late 1890's was in great measure the work and the property of a single man, Henry Bradley Plant.[63] Plant was a Yankee from Connecticut who moved to the South before the Civil War when his wife's illness caused him to go to Florida in 1853. The next year he became general superintendent for the Adams Express Company for the territory south of the Potomac and Ohio rivers. Fearing confiscation on the eve of the Civil War, the Adams Express Company transferred all of its southern holdings to Plant. Plant reorganized the property as the Southern Express Company with himself as president. Following the war the Adams Express Company brought suit against Plant and his southern concern. The suit was compromised with Plant retaining his Southern Express Company.[64]

Henry B. Plant saw new economic opportunities as southern railroads faced receivership in the depression following the Panic of 1873. While he had a minor interest in the Mobile and Ohio in the late 1870's,[65] his first major venture was with a Georgia line in receivership, the Atlantic and Gulf. Not too greatly damaged by the Civil War this 237-mile line from Savannah to Bainbridge, Georgia, was fairly prosperous in the early postwar years.[66] The depression of the 1870's, however, brought default and receivership to the road and Plant purchased the line at a foreclosure sale in Savannah, November 4, 1879. He paid $300,-

---

63. *Commercial and Financial Chronicle*, April 6, 1895, p. 607; G. Hutchinson Smyth, *The Life of Henry Bradley Plant* (New York, 1898), pp. 132, 138.

64. *Dictionary of American Biography* (New York, 1928-1936), XIV, 646-647; *Commercial and Financial Chronicle*, September 12, 1874, p. 270.

65. Alfred L. Rives to William C. Rives, May 12, 1878, William Rives Papers, Manuscripts Division, Library of Congress, Washington, D. C. Plant was reported in 1878 to be the owner of $300,000 of the first mortgage bonds of the Mobile and Ohio.

66. *Merchants Magazine and Commercial Review*, May, 1868, p. 374; *Commercial and Financial Chronicle*, April 11, 1868, p. 456.

RECEIVERSHIP AND CONSOLIDATION

000 for the line, subject to mortgages amounting to $2,710,000. In the winter of 1879-1880 the new property was organized as the Savannah, Florida and Western Railway with Plant as president.[67] The Savannah and Charleston, the second road acquired by Plant, was left at the war's end with little more than a right of way and a road bed. Its recovery after the war was slow and in 1873-1874 Edward King remarked after a trip on the line that " . . . it is a penance to ride over it."[68] The road was in default in 1873 and after a long receivership was sold in Charleston, June 7, 1880. Plant was the high bidder and acquired the line for $300,200. He reorganized his purchase as the Charleston and Savannah Railway with himself as president and with a board of directors including W. T. Walters and B. F. Newcomer, both of Baltimore.[69]

Two years later, in 1882, with the assistance of W. T. Walters and other northern capitalists, including Morris K. Jesup and Henry Morrison Flagler, Plant organized the Plant Investment Company. The new company soon expanded its rail holdings, using the Savannah, Florida and Western as the keystone of the system. In 1884 the Plant Investment Company purchased from the German owners the controlling interest in the Brunswick and Western, a road that served the southern portion of Georgia.[70] In the same year the Plant interests also acquired the South Florida Railroad, a new line that was being constructed from Sanford, Florida, to Tampa.[71] The Plant system in 1890 gained its fifth line by purchasing a controlling interest in the Alabama Midland, a two-hundred-mile road connecting the western terminal of the Savannah, Florida and Western with Montgomery, Alabama.[72]

During the next decade the expansion continued. Early in 1895 Plant acquired, in Florida, the 48-mile St. Johns and Lake

---

67. *Commercial and Financial Chronicle*, November 8, 1879, p. 488; December 6, 1879, p. 608; Dozier, *op. cit.*, pp. 132-133.
68. Edward King, *The Great South* (Hartford, 1875), p. 364.
69. *Commercial and Financial Chronicle*, June 12, 1880, p. 625; Dozier, *op. cit.*, pp. 133-134.
70. Dozier, *op. cit.*, pp. 134-135; *Commercial and Financial Chronicle*, August 30, 1884, p. 233; October 10, 1885, p. 419; *The Manual of Statistics, Railroad, Grain and Produce, Cotton, Petroleum, Mining Dividends and Production* (n. p., 1885), p. 21 (hereafter cited as *The Manual of Statistics*).
71. Poor, *Manual of the Railroads of the United States for 1891*, p. 529.
72. *Commercial and Financial Chronicle*, July 12, 1890, p. 50.

RAILROADS OF THE SOUTH

Eustis Railroad, and the 152-mile, narrow-gauge Sanford and St. Petersburg Railway.[73] By this time the various railroad properties together with certain steamship lines belonging to the Plant Investment Company were merged for operating purposes under the name of the Plant System.[74] In the 1890's Plant also was associated with both Walters and Newcomer in their control of the Wilmington and Weldon, the Wilmington, Columbia and Augusta, and the Northeastern Railroad of South Carolina.

Henry Bradley Plant's death, June 23, 1899, found the Plant System consisting of 14 railroads totalling 2,100 miles plus subordinate but large holdings in southern steamship lines and hotels.[75] Just before his death Plant had tried to regain his Connecticut citizenship in order to validate a provision in his will which would prohibit any partition of his railroad empire prior to the majority of his four-year-old great grandson. The will was contested by his widow, he was declared a citizen of New York, and there remained no legal hinderance to the disposal and consolidation of the railroad property. In April, 1902, the Atlantic Coast Line completed negotiations providing for the acquisition of the entire Plant Railroad System. The consolidation of the two large networks was a natural one and created a rail empire of about four thousand miles streaching from Virginia to Florida and the Gulf.[76]

By the end of the century another major rail system, the Seaboard Air Line Railway, also achieved its basic organization. The system started shortly after the Civil War when northerners from Philadelphia and Baltimore controlled the Seaboard and Roanoke Railroad, a line running eighty miles from Portsmouth, Virginia, to Weldon, North Carolina, on the Roanoke River.[77] Under the management of President and General Superintendent John M. Robinson of Baltimore, the road had a low funded debt, a favorable operating ratio, and paid regular dividends of as high as 8

---

73. *Ibid.*, March 23, 1895, p. 523; April 6, 1895, p. 607.
74. *Atlantic Coast Line Valuation Docket No. 930*, Accounting Section, I A, 226, Record Group 134, National Archives, Washington, D. C.
75. *Railroad Gazette*, June 30, 1899, p. 481.
76. Dozier, *op. cit.*, pp. 145-146; *Story of the Atlantic Coast Line*, pp. 12-13; Snyder, *American Railways as Investments*, pp. 84-85.
77. Poor, *Manual of the Railroads of the United States for 1869-1870*, p. 281.

RECEIVERSHIP AND CONSOLIDATION

per cent, even during the depression years of the mid-1870's.[78] During the same depression years, Robinson acquired a growing influence over the Raleigh and Gaston Railroad, a ninety-seven-mile line connecting Weldon and Raleigh, the capitol of the state. By 1876 he was president of both the Raleigh and Gaston and a new road being built towards Columbia, South Carolina, the Raleigh and Augusta Air Line.[79] Neither line was as prosperous as the Seaboard and Roanoke, since the Raleigh and Gaston had financially extended itself to aid in the extension towards Augusta, and the new Raleigh and Augusta Air Line gained only a modest traffic during the depression of the 1870's. Nevertheless, Robinson and his associates were in control of a standard gauge, fairly direct, 280-mile line running from Portsmouth across North Carolina toward Atlanta.

During the 1880's Robinson expanded his system further to the west and south. In 1881 his Seaboard and Roanoke became a large stockholder in the Carolina Central, a 242-mile line running west from Wilmington, North Carolina, to connect with the Raleigh and Augusta Air Line at Hamlet. By the summer of 1883 Robinson's three original roads held a controlling interest in the stock of the Carolina Central.[80] During the decade the Seaboard and Roanoke had a favorable operating ratio and paid regular dividends of from 7½ to 10 per cent. At the end of the decade, on July 1, 1889, the two northern lines, the Seaboard and Roanoke and the Raleigh and Gaston, leased (for the term of its corporate existence) the projected and partially built Georgia, Carolina and Northern Railway.[81] The lease of the latter road gave Robinson's growing system entry into Atlanta when the line was completed in the spring of 1892.

By 1891 the entire system of five roads and over eight-hundred miles was known as the Seaboard Air Line and furnished through

---

78. Henry V. Poor, *Manual of the Railroads of the United States for 1874-1875* (New York, 1874), p. 231.
79. Henry V. Poor, *Manual of the Railroads of the United States for 1877-1878* (New York, 1877), pp. 214, 651.
80. *Commercial and Financial Chronicle*, November 19, 1881, p. 559; August 4, 1883, p. 128; *The Manual of Statistics*, p. 26.
81. H. V. and H. W. Poor, *Manual of the Railroads of the United States for 1895* (New York, 1895), p. 759.

service from tidewater at Portsmouth and Norfolk, Virginia, to Atlanta. Robinson was president of the Seaboard Air Line and also headed four of the five major component lines. Connecting steamer service north to Baltimore and New York was provided by the Baltimore Steam Packet Company and by the Old Dominion Steamship Company.[82] In the summer of 1896, the new Seaboard Air Line started a serious freight rate war with the newly organized Southern Railway. The dispute was finally ended when third parties applied to the courts for injunctions which effectively restrained the two railroads.[83]

Between 1898 and 1900, the Seaboard Air Line gave its name to a much expanded system which included nearly 1,500 new miles of trackage chiefly in Alabama, Florida and Georgia. In December, 1898, John L. Williams and Sons of Richmond and Middendorf, Oliver and Company of Baltimore, already owners of the 450-mile Georgia and Alabama Railway, purchased for themselves and associates a controlling interest in the Seaboard Air Line system.[84] The Georgia and Alabama had been organized in 1895 as a successor to the Savannah, Americus and Montgomery Railway, a line built and completed in the years just prior to the Panic of 1893. The main line of the Georgia and Alabama ran from Savannah to Montgomery and thus gave the Seaboard new connections to the west.

Two months later, in February, 1899, the new owners of the Seaboard added another important system when they purchased from W. Bayard Cutting and R. Fulton Cutting, both of New York City, a majority of the shares of the 940-mile Florida, Central and Peninsular Railroad.[85] Located principally in Florida, the new purchase gave the consolidated system connections to all

---

82. Henry V. Poor, *Manual of the Railroads of the United States for 1892* (New York, 1892), p. 575; Van Oss, *American Railroads as Investments*, p. 796.
83. Emory R. Johnson and Thurman W. Van Metre, *Principles of Railroad Transportation* (New York, 1919), pp. 545-547.
84. H. V. and H. W. Poor, *Manual of the Railroads of the United States for 1900*, p. 768.
85. *Ibid.*, p. 761; *Railroad Gazette*, March 10, 1899, p. 182. The Florida Central and Peninsular had been organized in 1889 following the foreclosure sale of the predecessor line, the Florida Railway and Navigation Company. *Commercial and Financial Chronicle*, April 7, 1888, p. 448; May 12, 1888, p. 609; July 7, 1888, p. 21.

RECEIVERSHIP AND CONSOLIDATION

parts of Florida except in the southern and western extremities. One of the most strategically located branches of the new line ran from Savannah north to Columbia, South Carolina.[86] Two other short connecting lines were added to the system to give a new through route from Richmond south to Florida. At the northern end of the route the newly constructed, 102-mile Richmond, Petersburg and Carolina improved the service between Richmond and Raleigh. In South Carolina a fifty-five-mile link between Columbia and Cheraw completed the direct route to the south.[87] In October, 1899, the Seaboard Air Line concluded negotiations with the Richmond, Fredericksburg and Potomac Railroad and the Pennsylvania Railroad to acquire trackage rights to Washington, D. C. and New York City. The Seaboard owners claimed their new through service to Tampa was seventy-five to one hundred miles shorter than competing lines.[88] The new system also expected an increased freight business for they ordered two thousand new freight cars in 1900.

The final step came in April, 1900, when the Baltimore and Richmond financiers organized a new corporation, the Seaboard Air Line Railway, to effect a complete consolidation of the three railroad systems. The new network included 20 different, separate companies consisting of 2,600 miles of line.[89] John Skelton Williams, a young Richmond banker of thirty-five, and son of John L. Williams, was president of the new company. The president was a southerner, but seven of the nine directors were from the North.[90]

Southern railroad development in the century's last decade followed a varied pattern. The modest prosperity of the early 1890's was soon broken by record-breaking receiverships. New rail construction in the 1890's was relatively very slow, but still at the century's end the southern rail network was basically com-

86. *Commercial and Financial Chronicle*, October 7, 1893, p. 595.
87. H. V. and H. W. Poor, *Manual of the Railroads of the United States for 1901* (New York, 1901), p. 770; *Railroad Gazette*, April 21, 1899, p. 291.
88. *Railroad Gazette*, October 27, 1899, p. 754.
89. *Ibid.*, October 5, 1900, p. 680; H. V. and H. W. Poor, *Manual of the Railroads of the United States for 1901*, p. 770.
90. H. V. and H. W. Poor, *Manual of the Railroads of the United States for 1900*, p. 760.

plete. Perhaps most important, the only workable solution to many of the region's (and to the nation's) rail receiverships proved to be reorganizations planned and managed by the bankers of the North. At the end of the century two new major systems were completed, largely with northern men in positions of control. In both reorganization and consolidation the end of the century found northern money and management triumphant.

CHAPTER 13

SOUTHERN RAILROADS AND NORTHERN FINANCE IN 1900

IN THE three and a half decades after the Civil War, southern railroads had developed a transportation system which quite adequately served the industrial and agricultural requirements of the "New South." By the end of the century the rail network in mileage, corporate arrangement, and services performed had achieved much of the general pattern and outline found in the railroad maturity of the twentieth century.

In expanding from 9,000 miles of line in 1865 to nearly 35,000 miles in 1900 the ten southern states had gained the general physical outline of their ultimate rail network. The 35,000 miles in existence in 1900 equalled three-fourths of the total southern mileage in existence during the peak mileage years of the 1920's. At the end of the century all the southern states, with the exception of Florida and Louisiana, had built the great bulk of their eventual rail mileage. Also by 1900 most of the present-day railroad corporations had appeared. The Southern Railway, the L. and N., the Atlantic Coast Line (including the Plant System after 1902), the Seaboard Air Line, and the Illinois Central (south of Cairo) were all in existence and with their aggregate of 20,000 miles of line accounted for three-fifths of the total mileage in the south. Smaller major lines such as the Chesapeake and Ohio, the Norfolk and Western, the Central of Georgia, and the Mobile and Ohio made up an additional 5,000 miles of road.[1]

During the generation following the Civil War, southern rail-

---

1. Fairfax Harrison, *A History of the Legal Development of the Railroad System of the Southern Railway Company* (Washington, D. C., 1901), p. 22.

roads also made real gains towards an integration with the railroads of the rest of the nation. At the time of the Civil War, southern railroads were physically separated from all northern lines since not a single permanent railroad bridge was in existence across either the Ohio or the Potomac. A free and easy interchange of traffic between the two sections was also made difficult by long and slow river ferry boat service, by the difference in gauge, and by a notable reluctance of all roads to see their rolling stock leave their own lines. In the South, through rail traffic within the region itself was embarrassed by the lack of adequate terminal facilities.

Physical rail connections with the North came fairly early in the postwar period. Albert Fink's bridge across the Ohio for the L. and N. was completed in 1870, the Cincinnati Southern spanned the same river in 1877, and the Illinois Central's Cairo bridge was completed in 1889.[2] Rail service to and from the North was also improved with the acceptance of standard gauge by southern railroads. Some few roads were changing to the standard 4 feet 8½ inches by 1880 and the remainder of the southern roads did so early in the summer of 1886.[3] Integration into the national system was also aided as the Illinois Central acquired a line to New Orleans and as Virginia lines like the Chesapeake and Ohio and the Norfolk and Western built lines through West Virginia into Ohio.

As fast freight lines appeared, like the "Green Line" and the Atlantic Coast Despatch System, southern railroads became more concerned with better terminal facilities and a more efficient interchange of traffic.[4] In 1875 southern railroad cooperation was so successful in the newly formed Southern Railway and Steamship Association that favorable northern comment soon resulted in the Association's first commissioner, Albert Fink, being called to New

---

2. Ellis Merton Coulter, *The Cincinnati Southern Railroad* (Chicago, 1922), pp. 45-46; Henry V. Poor, *Manual of the Railroads of the United States for 1877-1878* (New York, 1877), p. 386; Carlton J. Corliss, *Main Line of Mid-America, The Story of the Illinois Central* (New York, 1950), p. 226.

3. *Commercial and Financial Chronicle*, May 29, 1886, p. 649.

4. Robert Selph Henry, *The Story of Reconstruction* (Indianapolis, 1938), pp. 246-247; Howard Douglas Dozier, *The History of the Atlantic Coast Line* (New York, 1920), pp. 124-126.

York to manage pooling operations for the trunk lines.[5] Even as consolidation became the rule in the 1890's a considerable cooperation continued. Just after the turn of the century, six eastern lines, the Pennsylvania, the Baltimore and Ohio, the Southern, the Atlantic Coast Line, the Seaboard, and the Chesapeake and Ohio, joined together to operate as a "union" line the short but strategically located Richmond, Fredericksburg and Potomac Railroad.[6]

Also during the postwar generation, southern lines achieved marked improvements in service, schedules, and economy of transportation. Rates had been universally high during the years of rehabilitation following the war, with freight ton-mile rates sometimes even higher than passenger mile rates.[7] Competition in the 1870's brought freight rates down to one and one-half to three cents per ton-mile and passenger rates to four to five cents per mile.[8] During the 1880's many southern states established state railroad commissions whose activity often resulted in a further lowering of rates. This was especially true in Alabama, Georgia and South Carolina, where a three or three and one-half cent passenger rate soon became normal.[9] Most of the railroads protested violently concerning this maximum rate regulation, but passenger rates continued to decline, and a two and one-half cents per mile passenger rate was typical in the 1890's[10] As the rates de-

---

5. Charles Francis Adams, Jr., *Railroads, Their Origin and Problems* (New York, 1880), pp. 172-173; George H. Burgess and Miles C. Kennedy, *Centennial History of the Pennsylvania Railroad Company, 1846-1946* (Philadelphia, 1946), p. 360.

6. *Atlantic Coast Line Valuation Docket No. 930*, Accounting Section, IA, 38, Record Group 134, National Archives; Frederick A. Cleveland and Fred Wilbur Powell, *Railroad Finance* (New York, 1923), pp. 315-316.

7. *DeBow's Review*, February, 1866, pp. 217-219; February, 1867, p. 216; March, 1870, pp. 237-253. *Merchant's Magazine and Commercial Review*, December, 1866, p. 431; October, 1868, p. 287.

8. James F. Doster, *Alabama's First Railroad Commission, 1881-1885* (University, Alabama, 1949), p. 53; Maxwell Ferguson, *State Regulation of Railroads in the South* (New York, 1916), pp. 99-100; S. F. Van Oss, *American Railroads As Investments* (New York, 1893), p. 745; Fred A. Shannon, *The Farmer's Last Frontier* (New York, 1945), p. 296.

9. Doster, *loc. cit.*; Ferguson, *op. cit.*, pp. 43-44, 88-90, 99-100.

10. Ferguson, *op. cit.*, pp. 100-101; *Commercial and Financial Chronicle*, September 19, 1885, p. 321; December 26, 1891, p. 955; H. V. and H. W. Poor, *Manual of the Railroads of the United States for 1900* (New York, 1901), p. x.

clined the service actually improved with the standardization of gauge, the introduction of through trains, and the appearance of the passenger vestibule car. On January 9, 1888, the first all-Pullman vestibule train left Jersey City for Jacksonville, Florida. The trip was made in less than thirty hours. Freight rates in the South consistently averaged higher than for the North, but here, too, real reductions were made. By the 1890's the average southern railroad freight rate was down to one cent or less per ton-mile. In 1900 the South Atlantic states had average freight rates lower than the national average, being bettered only by the Middle Atlantic states.[11]

In general, the change and development in railroad equipment and rolling stock did not keep pace with the reduction in rates. As in the rest of the nation, 90 per cent or more of the southern mileage was laid with steel rail by 1900, but the rolling stock that ran on the improved track was still largely wooden. With the exception of improved lighting, added interior ornamentation, and safer brakes, the wooden passenger cars of 1900 were really very little different from the cars of 1865 and 1870. The average new passenger car built in the 1890's in fact cost no more ($4,000 to $5,000) than those of a quarter of a century before.[12] Much of the motive power also had changed very little. The locomotive of 1900, using coal instead of wood, had, of course, lost the balloon stack of an earlier day. Motive power at the turn of the century was also minus much of the earlier shining brass and bright paint, and by 1900 most locomotives were listed on equipment rosters by number rather than by name. But the American-type locomotive (4-4-0 wheel arrangement), so typical of the Civil War era, was still the standard for passenger train motive power in 1900.[13]

11. H. V. and H. W. Poor, *op. cit.*, pp. xi-xiii; A. K. McClure, *The South, Its Industrial, Financial and Political Condition* (Philadelphia, 1886), p. 102; Shannon, *op. cit.*, p. 297. H. V. and H. W. Poor, *Manual of the Railroads of the United States for 1901* (New York, 1901), pp. xi-xiii.

12. *Commercial and Financial Chronicle*, October 7, 1893, p. 597; August 9, 1879, p. 147. *Quiz on Railroads and Railroading* (Washington, D. C., 1950), question 44, question 170. Passenger coaches by the early 1950's were costing nearly $100,000 per car.

13. The speed record at the century's end was held by an American-type locomotive, the New York Central No. "999," which on May 10, 1893, had reached a speed of 112.5 miles per hour. In the 1890's first class locomotives

NORTHERN FINANCE IN 1900

As it had been ever since the Civil War, the southern rail system in 1900 was in a weak financial position. The lightly built and equipped railroads of the ten southern states had an average total capitalization of $42,000 per mile of road, about 40 per cent below the national figure. The economy of the South provided this inferior railroad network with a light traffic density and both freight and passenger revenue per mile of road lagged nearly a third below the rest of the nation. In 1900 the southern railroads accounted for nearly a fifth of the national mileage and over an eighth of the total railroad property valuation, but in total dividend payments they paid only 6 per cent of the national total. While the average northern or western line was paying dividends of over 2½ per cent, the typical southern line was paying dividends of slightly over 1 per cent on its capital stock.[14]

As for northern financial influence over southern railroads, the situation at the end of the century represented a natural continuation of the trends already well established in the decade of the 1880's. In 1890, while only 47 per cent of the total director group for fifty-eight major southern lines (over 100 miles in length) came from the North, northern influence was actually dominant in forty-three of the fifty-eight companies, and in 88 per cent of the total rail mileage concerned (21,560 miles).

The degree of rail consolidation achieved between 1890 and 1900 is well illustrated by the fact that while there were 58 lines in 1890 over 100 miles in length, by 1900 the number had been reduced to but 31 roads. In 1890 the 58 roads accounted for 74 per cent of the total mileage of the region, but in 1900 the 31 major lines totalled 30,105 miles, or 87 per cent of the region's total of 34,718 miles.[15]

In 1900 these 31 major southern railroads had official boards

---

(both passenger and freight) cost $10,000 to $12,000 each, or no more than locomotives of 1865. *Commercial and Financial Chronicle,* October 7, 1893, p. 597; E. W. Cole to War Department, November 18, 1868, Library of the Bureau of Railway Economics, Washington, D. C.

14. H. V. and H. W. Poor, *Manual of the Railroads of the United States for 1901,* pp. ii-xv. In two respects, operating ratio and stock-bond ratio, southern lines were very close to the national average in 1900.

15. The extent of consolidation can be seen by the fact that in 1890 the typical major southern line averaged 372 miles in length. By 1900, the 31 major lines averaged 971 miles in length.

of directors totalling 311 members. Over three-fifths of these directors, or 193, came from the North. As in the past, the great majority of the northern directors, 121 or 63 per cent, came from New York City. Baltimore was in second place with eleven men, enough directors, however, to control two of the really large systems, the Atlantic Coast Line and the Seaboard Air Line. Every one of the southern states was represented in the group of 118 directors which came from the South. Georgia with fifty-two directors had nearly as many as all of the other states combined. Atlanta and Savannah each had more directors listed than were to be found in all the four neighboring states of South Carolina, Florida, Alabama, and Tennessee.[16]

When the thirty-one major lines are examined according to the degree of northern financial management and the size of the company, they fall easily into three classes or groups. Most important were the ten really large systems, all of which were northern dominated in 1900. Next would be a group of thirteen somewhat shorter lines (all under 500 miles) which were also dominated by northern money and influence. Finally, a third group consisted of eight rather short lines where northern control was either lacking or less than complete.

The ten large systems in 1900 included the Southern Railway (5,958 miles), the Louisville and Nashville (5,038 miles), the Seaboard Air Line (2,600) miles), the Illinois Central (2,310 miles south of Cairo), the Atlantic Coast Line (2,101 miles), the Plant System (2,013 miles), the Central of Georgia (1,581 miles), the Norfolk and Western (1,550 miles), the Chesapeake and Ohio (1,445 miles), and the Mobile and Ohio (876 miles). All but one of these lines possessed well over 1,000 miles of road, and in aggregate the ten totalled 25,472 miles, or over five-sixths of the mileage for the 31 companies (and 73 per cent of the total southern mileage). Of the 120 directors listed by the companies, 83 came from the North and only 37 were southerners. Five of the

16. All the figures and statistics on directorships and railroad mileage are based on the several company records in Henry V. Poor, *Manual of the Railroads of the United States for 1891* (New York, 1891); H. V. and H. W. Poor, *Manual of the Railroads of the United States for 1900*; H. V. and H. W. Poor, *Manual of the Railroads of the United States for 1901.*

ten presidents did give southern addresses. However, such "southern" presidents as Milton H. Smith in Louisville, E. L. Russell down in Mobile, and John Skelton Williams of Richmond were always under the effective control of the New York or Baltimore owners of the L. and N., the Mobile and Ohio, and the Seaboard.

Thirteen shorter roads ranging in length from the 103-mile Norfolk and Southern Railroad to the 474-mile Florida East Coast Railway were also under the financial management of northern men and money.[17] The mileage of these lines (3,334 miles) added to the ten larger systems gave a total of 28,806 miles dominated by the North or nearly 96 per cent of the mileage of the major southern lines. The extent of northern financial control over the 13 railroads is indicated by the presence of 89 northern directors out of a total of 125.[18] Four of the thirteen roads were without a single southerner in their official boards, and three other lines had only one southern representative per board of directors. One of the most completely controlled was Henry Morrison Flagler's Florida East Coast Railway, a road connecting Jacksonville with the small village of Miami. Although a majority of the directors of the line were from Florida, Flagler really owned the road by himself.[19]

In the remaining eight major southern lines, northern financial influence was either weak or at least something less than com-

---

17. The thirteen roads in this group were: the Alabama Great Southern Railroad, the Alabama and Vicksburg Railway, the Cincinnati, New Orleans and Texas Pacific Railway, the East and West Railroad (in Alabama), the Florida East Coast Railway, the Georgia Railroad, the Gulf and Ship Island Railroad, the New Orleans and Northeastern Railroad, the Norfolk and Southern Railroad, the South Carolina and Georgia Extension Railway, the Southern Pacific Railroad (465 miles in Louisiana), the Texas and Pacific Railway (326 miles in Louisiana), and the Vicksburg, Shreveport and Pacific Railroad.

18. Of the thirty-six southern directors, seventeen were from a single line, the Georgia Railroad. This line had been originally leased to the Central of Georgia in 1881, but in 1900 the lease was shared equally by the L. and N. and the Atlantic Coast Line. Mary G. Cumming, *Georgia Railroad and Banking Company* (Augusta, Georgia, 1945), pp. 90-91.

19. H. V. and H. W. Poor, *Manual of the Railroads of the United States for 1900*, p. 408. Between 1870 and 1883, Flagler was one of the principal figures associated with John D. Rockefeller's Standard Oil Company. In 1883 he retired from an active role in the oil business and turned to Florida. The last thirty years of his life were intimately connected with the eastern coast of that state.

RAILROADS OF THE SOUTH

plete.[20] The eight roads were all short, six of them being under two hundred miles in length. The aggregate length was but 1,299 miles, or little more than 4 per cent of the total mileage of the 31 major companies. While five of the eight railroad presidents were from the North, southern directors outnumbered northern men forty-five to twenty-one. Again railroad men in Georgia were prominent in the list, as twenty-eight of the southern directors came from that state. This was but natural, however, since five of the eight roads were located at least partially in Georgia.

Northern financial management over southern railroads was thus nearly complete in 1900. The development of this influence had been gradual, starting with the early postwar years and continuing alike through both periods of depression and prosperity. This gradual development from Civil War to 1900 is summarized for major southern railroads (100 miles or more in length) in the following table:[21]

	1870	1880	1890	1900
Southern Railroads	43	34	58	31
Southern Presidents	36	18	22	13
Northern Presidents	7	16	36	18
Northern Presidents	16%	47%	62%	58%
Southern Directors	345	210	302	118
Northern Directors	81	125	269	193
Northern Directors	19%	37%	47%	63%
Northern-controlled Mileage	21%	48%	88%	96%

Ruined and devastated by war, southern railroads in 1865 were anxious for help and assistance, wherever it could be found, whether it be local, northern or foreign. But in the early Reconstruction, northern men were not overly anxious to comply with the southern pleas and entreaties for northern capital and

---

20. The eight roads were: the Atlanta, Knoxville and Northern Railway, the Atlantic, Valdosta and Western Railway, the Chattanooga, Rome and Southern Railroad, the Georgia Southern and Florida Railway, the Louisville, Henderson and St. Louis Railway, the Macon and Birmingham Railway, the New Orleans and Northwestern Railway, and the Western Railway of Alabama.

21. The figures and estimates for 1870, 1880, and 1890 in the above table are based on the director and mileage surveys reviewed in chapters 7 and 9. The decline in the number of roads listing directors from 1870 to 1880 is caused by the fact that many of the receivership roads of the late 1870's were still in the process of reorganization in 1880.

financial assistance. Nevertheless, some northern money was venturing south in the late 1860's. In 1870 a degree of northern influence over southern railroads had been created by a variety of methods. Some of the northern-controlled mileage, like C. P. Huntington's Chesapeake and Ohio, had been gained by northerners as they brought in outside capital to complete and rehabilitate unfinished lines. A few southern roads, often the shorter and newer lines, were lost to outside management during the era of the carpetbagger. The activities of the Stanton brothers in Alabama, Hannibal Kimball in Georgia, and General Milton Littlefield in North Carolina would be excellent illustrations of this second method. Still a third technique was that illustrated by William T. Walters' purchase in 1869 of the North Carolina-held stock in the Wilmington and Weldon, and the Wilmington and Manchester railroads. Shortly after 1870, Tom Scott, of the Pennsylvania Railroad and the Southern Railway Security Company, used the same general method to put together a portion of his growing rail empire in the South.

In the decade of the 1870's most of the expansion of northern financial influence was caused by the numerous southern railroad receiverships. The increase in the degree of northern control and management, from perhaps a sixth of the southern mileage in 1870 to nearly a half in 1880, grew out of the sequence of receivership and reorganization faced by over half of the major southern lines. When northern and foreign bondholders took over the active management of locally owned lines as the southern officials and directors were forced into default, railroad after railroad quietly moved toward northern and outside domination. In Virginia, William Mahone's recently consolidated and locally controlled Atlantic, Mississippi and Ohio Railroad suffered default, receivership and eventually a foreclosure sale in 1881, being purchased by New York and Philadelphia capitalists. Down in New Orleans, Colonel McComb, a northerner who had some southern assistance in running his New Orleans to Cairo road, lost his line to the expanding Illinois Central. Towards the end of the decade, many other southern lines moved from receivership into the hands of northerners as their reorganization process brought inclusion in such expanding systems as the East Tennessee, Virginia and Georgia, and the new rail network being built by Henry Bradley Plant.

This trend towards consolidation and combination was a dominant characteristic of the more prosperous decade of the 1880's. By the end of the decade, every one of the really large southern roads experiencing expansion in the period was under northern financial management. A group of northern men, such as Samuel Thomas, Calvin Brice, and George Seney for the East Tennessee, Virginia and Georgia, C. C. Baldwin, Eckstein Norton, and Milton Smith for the L. and N., and W. P. Clyde and John Inman for the Richmond and Danville, were predominantly responsible for this extensive rail expansion and consolidation. During the decade, these men, and others like them, more than trebled the mileage of northern-controlled southern railroads. By 1890, using a variety of methods, including outright purchase, large scale new construction, and long term leases, they had achieved a working financial control over the vast majority of all southern railroads.

In the last decade of the nineteenth century, another period of widespread rail receivership failed to slow this inevitable movement towards larger and larger rail systems. By the end of the century, two relatively new combinations were serving the coastal states of the South, the Seaboard Air Line and the Atlantic Coast Line. These combinations, like all other large systems, and most smaller roads, were northern controlled. The end of the century found northern men, money and management firmly placed in positions of dominance over the railroads of the South.

BIBLIOGRAPHY

PRIMARY WORKS

Ackerman, William K. *Historical Sketch of the Illinois Central Railroad.* Chicago, 1890.

——. Letters, 1876-1878. Illinois Central Archives. Newberry Library, Chicago.

Andrews, Sidney. *The South Since the War.* Boston, 1866.

Annual Reports, 1855-1890. Illinois Central Archives. Newberry Library, Chicago.

Atlantic Coast Line Valuation Docket, Number 930. National Archives.

Avary, Myrta Lockett. *Dixie After the War.* New York, 1906.

Beauregard, P. G. T. Papers. Library of Congress.

Breckinridge, John C. Papers. Library of Congress.

Butler, Benjamin F. Papers. Library of Congress.

Campbell, George. *White and Black, the Outcome of a Visit to the United States.* New York, 1879.

Central of Georgia Valuation Docket, Number 60. National Archives.

Clarke, James C. Out Letters, 1875. Illinois Central Archives, Newberry Library, Chicago.

Clews, Henry. *Fifty Years in Wall Street.* New York, 1915.

——. *The Wall Street Point of View.* New York, 1900.

Cole, E. W. Letter to War Department, November 18, 1868. Library of the Bureau of Railway Economics in Washington, D. C.

Commercial and Financial Chronicle, 1865-1900.

De Bow's Review.

Depew, Chauncey. Papers. Library of Congress.

Dilke, Charles Wentworth. *Greater Britain, A Record of Travels in English Speaking Countries During 1866-1867.* London, 1872.

Douglas, John M. In Letters, 1875. Illinois Central Archives. Newberry Library, Chicago.

RAILROADS OF THE SOUTH

Eighth Census of the United States, 1860. Mortality and Property. Washington, D. C., 1866.

Eleventh Census of the United States, 1890. Population. Washington, D. C., 1895.

Fink, Albert. *Cost of Railroad Transportation, Railroad Accounts and Governmental Regulation of Railroad Tariffs.* Louisville, 1875.

Flint, Henry M. *Railroads of the United States, Their History and Statistics.* Philadelphia, 1868.

Georgia Railroad and Banking Company, Reports of Directors, 1861-1865.

Georgia Railroad Valuation Docket, Number 312. National Archives.

Historical Statistics of the United States, 1789-1945. Washington, D. C., 1949.

Illinois Central Minute Book (vols. II and III). Illinois Central Archives. Newberry Library, Chicago.

Illinois Central Newspaper Clipping Scrap Book (vol. I). Illinois Central Archives. Newberry Library, Chicago.

Illinois Central, Supporting Papers, Board Minutes, 1875. Illinois Central Archives. Newberry Library, Chicago.

Illinois Central, Supporting Papers, Board Minutes, 1876. Illinois Central Archives. Newberry Library, Chicago.

Kelley, William D. *The Old South and the New.* New York, 1888.

Kennaway, John H. *On Sherman's Track: or the South After the War.* London, 1867.

King, Edward. *The Great South.* Hartford, 1875.

Louisville and Nashville Valuation Docket, Number 456. National Archives.

McClure, A. K. *The South, Its Industrial, Financial and Political Condition.* Philadelphia, 1886.

McComb, H. S. Papers and Letters, 1870. Illinois Central Archives. Newberry Library, Chicago.

Manual of Statistics, Railroad, Grain and Produce, Cotton, Petroleum, Mining Dividends and Production, The. n. p., 1885.

Merchants' Magazine and Commercial Review.

Mississippi Central Annual Report, 1867. Illinois Central Archives. Newberry Library, Chicago.

Mississippi Central Miscellaneous Legal Records Book. Illinois Central Archives. Newberry Library, Chicago.

Mississippi Central Record Book, 1863-1870. Illinois Central Archives. Newberry Library, Chicago.

BIBLIOGRAPHY

Mobile and Ohio Valuation Docket, Number 149. National Archives.
Nashville, Chattanooga and St. Louis Valuation Docket, Number 367. National Archives.
New Orleans, Jackson and Great Northern Minute Book (vols. I, II and III). Illinois Central Archives. Newberry Library, Chicago.
Nordhoff, Charles. *Cotton States in the Spring and Summer of 1875.* New York, 1876.
Norfolk and Western Valuation Docket, Number 343. National Archives.
Noyes, Alexander Dana. *The Market Place, Reminiscences of a Financial Editor.* Boston, 1938.
Pennsylvania Charter, with Supplements, The. Pittsburgh, 1875.
Peto, Samuel M. *The Resources and Prospects of America.* London, 1866.
Pike, James S. *The Prostrate State, South Carolina Under Negro Government.* New York, 1874.
Poor, Henry V. *Manual of the Railroads of the United States.* New York, 1868-1900.
Pound, Arthur, and Samuel Thomas Moore (eds.). *More They Told Barron, Conversations and Revelations of an American Pepys in Wall Street.* New York, 1931.
Prices of Railroad Stocks for Thirty-two Years, 1854-1886. New York, 1886.
Railroad Gazette.
Railway Age.
Reid, Whitelaw. *After the War: A Southern Tour.* Cincinnati, 1866.
Reports of the Committees of the House of Representatives. 39th Congress, 2nd Session, No. 34.
Richmond and Danville Railroad Company, 24th Annual Report. Richmond, 1871.
Richmond and Danville Railroad Company, 27th Annual Report. Richmond, 1874.
Rives, William. Papers. Library of Congress.
Sherman, W. T. *Memoirs of General W. T. Sherman.* New York, 1891.
Somers, Robert. *The Southern States Since the War, 1870-1871.* London, 1871.
Southern Railway Valuation Docket, Number 556. National Archives.
Tenth Census of the United States, 1880. Transportation. Washington, D. C., 1883.

RAILROADS OF THE SOUTH

Trowbridge, J. T. *The South: A Tour of Its Battlefields and Ruined Cities.* Hartford, 1866.

Washburn, Elihu. Papers. Library of Congress.

SECONDARY WORKS

Adams, Charles Francis, Jr. *Railroads, Their Origin and Problems.* New York, 1880.

Adams, Henry. *The Education of Henry Adams.* New York, 1931.

Ambler, Charles H. *Francis H. Pierpont.* Chapel Hill, 1937.

———. *A History of the Transportation in the Ohio Valley.* Glendale, Calif., 1932.

American Railway, The: Its Construction, Development, Management and Appliances. New York, 1892.

Belcher, Wyatt Winton. *The Economic Rivalry Between St. Louis and Chicago, 1850-1880.* New York, 1947.

Black, Robert C. "The Railroads of Georgia in the Confederate War Effort," *The Journal of Southern History,* 13 (November, 1947), 510-534.

———. *The Railroads of the Confederacy.* Chapel Hill, 1952.

Blake, Nelson M. *William Mahone of Virginia, Soldier and Political Insurgent.* Richmond, 1935.

Brown, Cecil Kenneth. *A State Movement in Railroad Development: The Story of North Carolina's First Effort to Establish an East and West Trunk Line Railroad.* Chapel Hill, 1928.

Buck, Paul H. *The Road to Reunion, 1865-1900.* Boston, 1938.

Burgess, George H., and Miles C. Kennedy. *Centennial History of the Pennsylvania Railroad Company.* Philadelphia, 1949.

Burt, Jesse C., Jr. "Four Decades of the Nashville, Chattanooga and St. Louis Railway, 1873-1916," *Tennessee Historical Quarterly,* 9 (March, 1950), 99-130.

Campbell, E. G. "Indebted Railroads, A Problem of Reconstruction," *The Journal of Southern History,* 6 (May, 1940), 167-188.

———. *The Reorganization of the American Railroad System, 1893-1900.* New York, 1938.

Capers, Gerald M., Jr. *The Biography of a River Town, Memphis: Its Heroic Age.* Chapel Hill, 1939.

Caskey, Willie Malvin. *Secession and Restoration of Louisiana.* Baton Rouge, 1938.

Chapman, John Will. *Railroad Mergers.* New York, 1934.

Clark, George T. *Leland Stanford.* Stanford University, 1931.

Clark, Thomas D. *The Beginning of the L. and N.* Louisville, 1933.

BIBLIOGRAPHY

———. *A Pioneer Southern Railroad.* Chapel Hill, 1936.
Clark, William H. *Railroads and Rivers.* Boston, 1939.
Cleveland, Frederick A., and Fred Wilbur Powell. *Railroad Finance.* New York, 1923.
———. *Railroad Promotion and Capitalization in the United States.* New York, 1909.
Cochran, Thomas C. *Railroad Leaders, 1845-1890.* Cambridge, 1953.
Corliss, Carlton J. *Main Line of Mid-America, The Story of the Illinois Central.* New York, 1950.
Cotterill, Robert S. "Southern Railroads, 1850-1860." *The Mississippi Valley Historical Review,* 10 (March, 1924), 396-405.
Coulter, E. Merton. *The Confederate States of America, 1861-1865.* Baton Rouge, 1950.
———. *The Cincinnati Southern Railroad and the Struggle for Southern Commerce.* Chicago, 1922.
———. *The South During Reconstruction, 1865-1877.* Baton Rouge, 1947.
———. *William G. Brownlow.* Chapel Hill, 1937.
Couper, William. *Claudius Crozet, Soldier, Scholar, Educator, Engineer.* Charlottesville, 1936.
Cumming, Mary G. *Georgia Railroad and Banking Company.* Augusta, 1945.
Daggett, Stuart. *Railroad Reorganization.* Cambridge, Mass., 1908.
Daniels, W. M. *American Railroads, Four Phases of Their History.* Princeton, 1932.
Derrick, Samuel M. *Centennial History of the South Carolina Railroad.* Columbia, S. C., 1930.
Dictionary of American Biography. New York, 1928-1936.
Doster, James F. *Alabama's First Railroad Commission, 1881-1885.* University, Ala., 1949.
———. "Trade Centers and Railroad Rates in Alabama, 1873-1885," *The Journal of Southern History,* 18 (May, 1952), 169-192.
Dozier, Howard Douglas. *The History of the Atlantic Coast Line.* New York, 1920.
Du Bose, John Witherspoon. *Alabama's Tragic Decade.* Birmingham, 1940.
Eckenrode, H. J. *The Political History of Virginia During the Reconstruction.* Baltimore, 1904.

RAILROADS OF THE SOUTH

Ferguson, E. A. *Founding of the Cincinnati Southern Railway.* Cincinnati, 1905.

Ferguson, Maxwell. *State Regulation of Railroads in the South.* New York, 1916.

Fish, Carl Russell. "The Northern Railroads, April 1861," *The American Historical Review,* 22 (July, 1917), 778-793.

———. *The Restoration of the Southern Railroads.* Madison, 1919.

Fleming, Howard. *Narrow Gauge Railways in America.* Oakland, 1949.

Fleming, Walter L. *Civil War and Reconstruction in Alabama.* Cleveland, 1911.

Freed, Clyde H. *The Story of Railroad Passenger Fares.* n.p., 1942.

Garner, James Wilford. *Reconstruction in Mississippi.* New York, 1901.

Garrett, William. *Reminiscences of Public Men in Alabama.* n.p., 1872.

Gates, Paul Wallace. *The Illinois Central and Its Colonization Work.* Cambridge, Mass., 1934.

Grodinsky, Julius. *Railroad Consolidation, Its Economics and Controlling Principles.* New York, 1930.

Hall, Charles G. (ed.). *The Cincinnati Southern Railway, A History.* Cincinnati, 1902.

Hamilton, J. G. de Roulhac. *Reconstruction in North Carolina.* New York, 1914.

Hampton, Taylor. *The Nickel Plate Road.* Cleveland, 1947.

Haney, Lewis Henry. *A Congressional History of Railways in the United States to 1850.* Madison, 1908.

Harlow, Alvin F. *The Road of the Century, The Story of the New York Central.* New York, 1947.

Harrison, Fairfax. *A History of the Legal Development of the Railroad System of the Southern Railway Company.* Washington, D. C., 1901.

Harvey, George. *Henry Clay Frick, the Man.* New York, 1928.

Henry, Robert Selph. *The Story of the Confederacy.* New York, 1936.

———. *The Story of Reconstruction.* Indianapolis, 1938.

———. *This Fascinating Railroad Business.* Indianapolis, 1942.

Herbert, Hilary A. and others. *Why the Solid South, or Reconstruction and Its Results.* Baltimore, 1890.

Hesseltine, William B. *Confederate Leaders in the New South.* Baton Rouge, 1950.

BIBLIOGRAPHY

———. *The South in American History.* New York, 1943.
Hidy, Ralph W. *The House of Baring in American Trade and Finance.* Cambridge, 1949.
Hillyard, M. B. *The New South.* Baltimore, 1887.
Holbrook, Stewart H. *The Story of American Railroads.* New York, 1947.
Hollander, J. H. *The Cincinnati Southern Railway, A Study in Municipal Activity.* Baltimore, 1894.
———. *The Financial History of Baltimore.* Baltimore, 1899.
Hovey, Carl. *The Life Story of J. Pierpont Morgan.* London, 1912.
Hultgren, Thor. *American Transportation in Prosperity and Depression.* New York, 1938.
Hungerford, Edward. *The Story of the Baltimore and Ohio Railroad, 1827-1927.* New York, 1928.
In Memorium, Samuel Spencer, Atlanta, 1910.
Johnson, Emory R. *American Railway Transportation.* New York, 1914.
Johnson, Emory R. and Thurman W. Van Metre. *Principles of Railroad Transportation.* New York, 1919.
Johnston, James Houstoun. *Western and Atlantic Railroad of the State of Georgia.* Atlanta, 1931.
Josephson, Matthew. *The Robber Barons.* New York, 1934.
Joubert, William H. *Southern Freight Rates in Transition.* Gainesville, Fla., 1949.
Kamm, Samuel Rickey. *The Civil War Career of Thomas A. Scott.* Philadelphia, 1940.
Lane, Wheaton J. *Commodore Vanderbilt.* New York, 1942.
Larson, Henrietta. *Jay Cooke, Private Banker.* Cambridge, 1936.
Leighton, George R. *Five Cities, the Story of Their Youth and Old Age.* New York, 1939.
Lewis, Oscar. *The Big Four, The Story of Huntington, Stanford, Hopkins, and Crocker, and of the Building of the Central Pacific.* New York, 1945.
Loree, L. F. *Railroad Freight Transportation.* New York, 1922.
MacGill, Caroline. *A History of Transportation in the United States Before 1860.* Washington, D. C., 1917.
McGrane, Reginald C. *Foreign Bondholders and American State Debts.* New York, 1935.
McMeekin, Isabel McLennon. *Louisville, the Gateway City.* New York, 1946.

Middleton, P. Harvey. *Railways and Public Opinion, Eleven Decades.* Chicago, 1941.

Moore, Albert B. "Railroad Building in Alabama During the Reconstruction Period," *The Journal of Southern History*, I (November, 1935), 421-441.

Murphey, Herman K. "The Northern Railroads and the Civil War," *The Mississippi Valley Historical Review*, 5 (December, 1918), 324-338.

Mutual Magazine, The. Pennsylvania Railroad Centennial Souvenir Edition. April, 1946.

Meyers, Gustavus. *History of the Great American Fortunes.* New York, 1907.

National Cyclopedia of American Biography. New York, 1898-1904.

Nelson, James Poyntz. *The Chesapeake and Ohio Railway.* Richmond, 1927.

Nixon, Raymond B. *Henry W. Grady.* New York, 1943.

Oberholtzer, Ellis Paxson. *Jay Cooke, Financier of the Civil War.* Philadelphia, 1907.

Owen, Thomas M. *History of Alabama and Dictionary of Alabama Biography.* n.p., n.d.

Pangborn, J. G. *Picturesque B. and O., Historical and Descriptive.* Chicago, 1882.

Patton, James Welch. *Unionism and Reconstruction in Tennessee, 1860-1869.* Chapel Hill, 1934.

Pearson, Henry Greenleaf. *An American Railroad Builder, John Murray Forbes.* New York, 1911.

Phillips, U. B. *A History of Transportation in the Eastern Cotton Belt to 1860.* New York, 1913.

———. "Railroad Transportation in the South," *South in the Building of the Nation.* Richmond, 1909. Vol. VI, 305-316.

Pierce, Harry H. *Railroads of New York, A Study of Government Aid, 1826-1875.* Cambridge, Massachusetts, 1953.

Pratt, Edwin. *American Railways.* London, 1903.

Public Aids to Transportation. Washington, D. C., 1938.

Ramsdell, C. W. "The Confederate Government and the Railroads," *The American Historical Review*, 22 (July, 1917), 794-810.

Randall, J. G. *The Civil War and Reconstruction.* Boston, 1937.

Reed, Wallace P. (ed.). *History of Atlanta, Georgia.* n.p., 1889.

Riegel, R. E. "Federal Operation of Southern Railroads," *The Mississippi Valley Historical Review*, 9 (September, 1922), 126-138.

BIBLIOGRAPHY

———. "Trans-Mississippi Railroads During the Fifties," *The Mississippi Valley Historical Review*, 10 (September, 1923), 153-172.
Ripley, William Z. (ed.) *Railway Problems*. New York, 1913.
Rogers, Lou. "A. B. Andrews," *We the People of North Carolina*. 6, No. 3 (July, 1948), 20-23.
Sanborn, John Bell. *Congressional Grants of Land in Aid of Railways*. Madison, 1899.
Satterlee, Herbert L. *J. Pierpont Morgan, An Intimate Portrait*. New York, 1939.
Schotter, Howard W. *Growth and Development of the Pennsylvania Railroad Company*. Philadelphia, 1927.
Shannon, Fred A. *The Farmer's Last Frontier*. New York, 1945.
Sheldon, Addison E. *Land Systems and Land Policies in Nebraska*. Lincoln, 1936.
Simkins, Francis Butler and Robert Hilliard Woody. *South Carolina During Reconstruction*. Chapel Hill, 1932.
Sipes, William B. *The Pennsylvania Railroad: Its Origins, Construction, Condition, and Connections*. Philadelphia, 1875.
Smyth, G. H. *Life of Henry Bradley Plant*. New York, 1898.
Snyder, Carl. *American Railways as Investments*. New York, 1907.
Stimson, A. L. *History of the Express Business*. New York, 1881.
Story of a Pioneer, A Brief History of the Florida East Coast Railway, The. n.p., 1946.
Story of the Atlantic Coast Line, The. Wilmington, N. C., 1930.
Summers, Festus P. *The Baltimore and Ohio in the Civil War*. New York, 1939.
Taylor, George Rogers. *The Transportation Revolution, 1815-1860*. New York, 1951.
Thompson, C. Mildred. *Reconstruction in Georgia, Economic, Social, Political, 1865-1872*. New York, 1915.
Turner, Charles W. "The Richmond, Fredericksburg and Potomac Railroad at War, 1861-1865," *The Historian* (Spring, 1946), pp. 111-130.
———. "The Virginia Central Railroad at War, 1861-1865," *The Journal of Southern History*, 12 (November, 1946), 510-533.
———. "Virginia Railroad Development, 1845-1860," *The Historian* (Autumn, 1947), pp. 43-62.
Turner, George Edgar. *Victory Rode the Rails*. Indianapolis, 1953.
Van Oss, S. F. *American Railroads As Investments*. New York, 1893.

RAILROADS OF THE SOUTH

Weber, Thomas. *The Northern Railroads in the Civil War.* New York, 1952.
Who Was Who in America, 1897-1942. Chicago, 1942.
Woodward, C. Vann. *Reunion and Reaction.* Boston, 1951.
Yulee, C. Wickliffe. *Senator Yulee of Florida.* n.p., 1917.

INDEX

Ackerman, William K., 170, 171, 176, 176n., 179, 185
Adams Express Co., 54, 102-103, 103n., 138n., 268
Alabama, New Orleans, Texas & Pacific Junction Railways Co., 136-137, 137n.
Alabama, railroad building, 5, 61, 62, 88, 88n., 191, 193, 255-256; railroad mileage, 5, 7-8, 32, 61, 88, 193, 255-256; financing of railroads, 32-33, 88-94, 217; destruction of railroads, 44; railroad carpetbaggers, 62, 88-94; restoration of railroads, 88; state debt in early 1870's, 94; leader in iron production, 193-194; mentioned, 26, 53, 137, 155, 277
Alabama & Chattanooga R.R., 82n., 89-93, 98, 117, 130, 130n., 131 (map), 133, 135, 136-137, 193
Alabama & Florida R.R., 88
Alabama & Tennessee River R.R., 33, 128
Alabama & Vicksburg R.R., 281n.
Alabama Central R.R., 199
Alabama Great Southern R.R., 92, 136, 202, 246, 281n.
Alabama Midland R.R., 205, 269
Alabama Mineral R.R., 232
Alabama River, 17
Alexander, E. P., 223, 247, 248, 251, 251n.
Alexander, Junius B., 174, 175, 176, 178, 178n.
Alexandria, Va., 11, 144
Alexandria & Fredericksburg R.R., 105, 106 (map), 118
American Bible Society of New York, 27n.

American Railroad Journal, 24
Ames, Oakes, 147n.
Anderson, Gen. Richard H., 57
Andrews, Alexander Boyd, 259, 260
Andrews, Sidney, 39, 39n., 41, 42, 43, 48, 58
Arkansas, 4n.
Asheville, N. C., 71
Asheville & Spartanburg R.R., 236 (map), 239
Aspinwall, William H., 127n.
Atlanta, Ga., rail center of Ga., 10, 280; and Western & Atlantic R.R., 10, 32; a prosperous city, 10-11, 10n., 58, 58n., 81, 187, 187n.; railroad destruction, 43, 43n.; absence of depots after Civil War, 48; H. I. Kimball in, 81, 81n., 87-88; mentioned, 11n., 28, 40, 101n., 107, 110, 112, 192, 199, 240, 250
Atlanta, Knoxville & Northern R.R., 282n.
Atlanta & Charlotte Air-Line Railway, 113n., 145-146, 146n., 236 (map), 237-238, 257n.
Atlanta & Florida R.R., 208n., 262
Atlanta & Richmond Air-Line, 82, 106 (map), 111, 112-113, 113n., 114, 118, 130n., 131 (map), 145-146
Atlanta & West Point R.R., 27, 80
Atlanta *Constitution*, 84n., 226n.
Atlantic, Mississippi & Ohio R.R., xvii, 67, 67n., 68, 68n., 108, 109, 109n., 116n., 130n., 131 (map), 132, 132n., 137-139, 283
Atlantic, Tennessee & Ohio R.R., 111n., 239n.
Atlantic, Valdosta & Western R.R., 282n.

295

INDEX

Atlantic & Danville R.R., 262
Atlantic & Great Western R.R., 194n.
Atlantic & Gulf R.R., 32, 57, 130n., 131 (map), 146, 205, 268
Atlantic & North Carolina R.R., 27, 29, 31, 31n.
Atlantic & Yadkin R.R., 262
Atlantic Coast Despatch, 266, 276
Atlantic Coast Line, 121, 205n., 263-268, 264 (map), 270, 275, 277, 280, 281n., 284
Atlantic Coast Line Company, 267
Augusta, Ga., 11, 17, 113

Baggage, checking, 12, 48, 103
Bainbridge, Cuthbert & Columbus R.R., 82, 83
Baker, George T., 242
Baldwin, Christopher Columbus, and L. & N. R.R., 220, 221, 222, 228-229, 284
Baltimore, Chesapeake & Richmond Steamboat Co., 235n.
Baltimore, Md., supports ambitions of B. & O. in Virginia, 65, 66; financial control over southern railroads, 130, 136, 147, 153, 207, 280; Atlantic Coast Line, 265-267; Seaboard Air Line, 270, 272, 273; mentioned, 102, 103
Baltimore & Ohio R.R., interests in railroads of Virginia, 65, 67, 144, 238; conflict with Pennsylvania R.R., 103-104, 104n., 108-110, 120; mentioned, 5, 9, 126, 168, 250, 277
Baltimore & Potomac R.R., 103-104
Baltimore Steam Packet Co., 272
Banking privileges, given railroad companies, 29, 53
Barbour, John S., 144
Baring, House of (England), 35, 35n.
Baton Rouge, Grosse Tete & Opelousas R.R., 33
Beaufort, N. C., 46
Beauregard, Gen. P.G.T., and New Orleans, Jackson & Great Northern R.R., 58, 159-164; business interests, 161; and Col. McComb, 161-164; mentioned, xvi, 54, 67n., 172n.
Benjamin, Judah P., 8
Best, William J., 145, 239
Big Four R.R., 203
Birmingham, Ala., 193, 194n., 206, 217, 218, 218n., 232, 240

Birmingham Mineral R.R., 232
Blodgett, Foster, 80, 84, 84n.
Blue Freight Line, 49
Blue Ridge, 28
Blue Ridge R.R. (S.C.), 32n., 34, 76, 77, 77n., 78, 79, 239n.
Blue Ridge R.R. (Va.), 126
Bonds, railroad, 23, 23n., 29, 32, 33, 35, 36, 50, 55, 70, 97, 98, 123, 124, 132-133, 134, 138, 159, 171, 189, 197, 201, 228, 283
Boston, Mass., 55, 130, 207
Boxcars, used as passenger equipment after Civil War, 46
Bragg, Gen. Braxton, 45
Bragg, Thomas, 111
Brawley, W. H., 140
Breckinridge, Gen. John. C., investments in northern railroads, 55n.; and railroads in Kentucky, 56n., 97; and Cincinnati Southern R.R., 213, 213n.
Bribery, during era of railroad carpetbaggers, 67, 69, 69n., 70n., 73, 74n., 78, 78n., 81, 81n., 83, 83n., 84, 86, 86n., 87, 89, 90n., 91, 91n., 96, 97
Brice, Calvin S., and the East Tennessee, Virginia & Georgia R.R., 198, 200, 202, 202n., 245, 246; and Richmond & Danville R.R., 241, 243, 245; early career, 246n.; mentioned xvii, 246n., 284
"Bridge Burners," of East Tennessee, 20
Bridgers, Robert Rufus, 72-73, 136, 263, 265
Bridges, railroad, lack of connecting bridges to North, 11, 276; destruction of during Civil War, 15, 39, 40, 41, 44, 45, 158; lack of during early Reconstruction, 47, 47n., 48, 57; repaired and built, 159; mentioned, 11n., 20, 104, 167, 167n., 182, 214n., 265n.
Bristol, Va., 9, 11, 17, 41, 47, 67, 110n., 114, 197
Brown, Gov. Joseph E., and Western & Atlantic R.R. lease, 85-87, 86n.; mentioned, 21n., 49, 227
Brownlow, Gov. "Parson" William G., 96, 215
Brunswick & Albany R.R., 82-83 83n., 130, 130n., 131 (map), 137, 140-141

296

INDEX

Brunswick & Florida R.R., 82
Brunswick & Western R.R., 205, 269
Bryan, Joseph, 145, 239
"Bucktails," 109
Bucktail Swindle, 109
Buford, A.S., 64, 67n., 113, 145, 234, 241, 242, 243n.
Bullock, Gov. Rufus B., and railroad carpetbaggers in Georgia, 79-80, 82-88; and H. I. Kimball, 81, 83; and the Western & Atlantic R.R. lease, 83-87; mentioned, 103n.
"Bummers," Sherman's, 40
Butler, Benjamin F., 62

Cairo, Ill., 155, 156, 169, 170
Cairo Extension, 160 (map), 166-167, 168, 172, 177-178
Caldwell, Gov. Todd R., 111, 111n.
Calhoun, John C. (of N.Y.), 247
Calhoun, John C. (of S.C.), 9
Callaway, Col. Thomas H., 114, 115
Cameron, James Donald, and Southern Railway Security Co., 102, 102n., 107n., 119n.
Cameron, Senator Simon B., 74, 85, 86n., 102, 104, 104n., 115
Campbell, George, 186n.
Campbell, Judge John A., 173, 174, 179
Canton, Miss., 8, 58, 156
Cape Fear & Yadkin R.R., 208n.
Capital structure, of southern railroads, 35, 35n., 123, 132, 132n., 134, 232, 279, 279n.
Cardozo, F. L., 75, 76n.
Car ferry, railroad, 167
Carolina Central R.R., 130n., 131 (map), 137, 139-140, 271
Carpetbaggers, and southern railroads, xv, xvi, 61-65, 69-98, 145, 161-165, 283
Cartersville & Van Wert R.R., 82, 82n., 83, 84
Car wheels, 16
Cass, George Washington, and Southern Railway Security Co., 102, 104, 119n.
Cass, Lewis, 102
Cavalry, and destruction of railroads, 40-41, 40n., 41n.
Cecilia branch, 216 (map), 219
Cedar Keys, Fla., 11
Central Mississippi R.R., 180

Central Pacific R.R., 127
Central R.R. of Georgia, 18, 26, 27, 28, 34, 44, 53, 56, 79, 85, 133, 133n., 134n., 149-150, 188n., 189n., 197, 205-206, 208n., 209, 221, 222, 225, 227, 247-250, 251, 251n., 252n., 258, 260-261, 261n., 275, 280, 281n.
Central Southern R.R., 217
Chamberlain, Daniel Henry, 75, 76n., 79
Charleston, S. C., financing of railroads, 9, 26, 34, 77, 78n., 140; mentioned, 11, 39, 48, 112, 117
Charleston & Hamburg R.R., 26
Charleston & Savannah R.R., 23, 34, 147, 205, 209
Charleston Mercury, 54
Charlotte, Columbia & Augusta R.R., 106 (map), 111, 112, 113, 114, 118, 188n., 209, 235, 236 (map), 239, 239n.
Charlotte, N. C., 10, 111, 112
Charlotte & South Carolina R.R., 26, 113
Charlottesville, Va., 11
Chase, Chief Justice Salmon P., 44n., 46
Chatham R.R., 70
Chattanooga, Rome & Columbus R.R., 208n.
Chattanooga, Rome & Southern R.R., 282n.
Chattanooga, Tenn., Memphis & Charleston R.R., 9, 45, 116; Nashville & Chattanooga R.R., 9; East Tennessee and Georgia R.R., 9-10; Western & Atlantic R.R., 32; Alabama & Chattanooga R.R., 89; East Tennessee, Virginia & Georgia R.R., 114, 199; mentioned, 11, 16n., 17, 20, 43, 43n., 46n., 57, 91, 115, 213
Cheraw & Darlington R.R., 106 (map), 117, 118, 266, 267
Cherokee R.R., 82, 82n., 83
Chesapeake, Ohio & Southwestern R.R., 143, 160 (map), 183, 185, 261n., 262
Chesapeake & Ohio R.R., xvii, 27, 48, 109, 126-128, 130n., 131, 131 (map), 133, 135, 148, 188n., 194, 197, 203-204, 257n., 275, 276, 277, 280, 283
Chicago, Ill., 58, 156
Chicago, St. Louis & New Orleans R.R.,

297

INDEX

180-183, 194, 197, 203, 203n., 223, 223n.
Chicago & Eastern Illinois R.R., 224
Chicago Fire, 87
Chinese, used as railroad labor, 90
Cincinnati, New Orleans & Texas Pacific R.R., 202, 214-215, 246, 281n.
Cincinnati, Ohio, and Cincinnati Southern R.R., 212-215; mercantile losses to Louisville, 212-213, 212n.; mentioned, 126, 204
Cincinnati & Georgia R.R., 199
Cincinnati Southern R.R., 56n., 137n., 212-215, 276
Cipher code, used by the Illinois Central, 173-174
Cities, southern, and railroad finance, 7, 9, 10, 23, 25, 26, 31, 34-35, 78n., 88, 89, 162-163, 163n.
City Point, Va., 21
Clark, Clarence H., and Norfolk & Western R.R., 139, 139n.
Clarke, James C., 169, 169n., 173, 175, 176, 178, 180, 181, 181n., 182, 183n., 184, 185, 223
Clarke, Leverett H., 171
Clarke, Mrs. Rowena M., 251
Cleveland, Grover, 246n.
Clews, Henry, 55, 55n., 62, 87, 90, 201n.
Clyde, W. P., and Richmond & Danville R.R., 145, 234, 237, 239, 241, 241n., 242, 252, 252n., 284
Clyde Syndicate, 120, 121, 139, 234, 235, 241
Coal, large deposits in W. Va., 127, 127n.; low rates for, 261n.; mentioned, 16
Cole, Col. Edwin W., and the East Tennessee, Virginia & Georgia R.R., 197, 198, 226n., 240, 240n.; and the Nashville, Chattanooga & St. Louis R.R., 224-226, 227; mentioned, xvii, 52, 86n.
Collinson, John, 137-138
Colquitt, Gov. Alfred, 227
Columbia, S. C., 42, 42n., 56, 88
Columbia & Augusta R.R., 114, 114n.
Columbia & Greenville R.R., 23, 209, 238, 239
Columbus, Ky., 6, 11, 156, 157, 170
Comer, H. M., 251, 251n., 260
Commercial and Financial Chronicle, 36-37, 54

Company Shops, N. C., 111
Confederate Congress, and railroad construction, 17
Confederate Government, railroad construction, 17; rail equipment, 18, 82; maintenance of railroads, 19; railroad policy, 19; transportation payments, 42n., 158n.; destruction of railroads, 43
Confederate troops, abuse of rolling stock, 18, 19-20; railroad destruction, 21, 41
Confederate veterans, free transportation back home, 48; as railroad labor, 57
Congress (U.S.), 51-52
Conservatives, southern, and exposure of carpetbaggers, 62, 97; and Gen. Littlefield, 69; control Georgia legislature, 84; mentioned, 64, 69n., 119n.
Consolidation, of railroads, during the 1880's, 186, 195-209, 284; by the L. & N., 210, 215-228, 232; by the Richmond & Danville, 233-253; during the 1890's, 254, 263-274, 277, 279, 284; mentioned, 58, 99, 121
Construction, of railroads, 3-11, 17, 25 (map), 56, 59-61, 122, 122n., 125, 152, 186, 189-193, 192 (map), 196, 196n., 207, 254-256, 273, 275
Convicts, 145
Cook, George, 86, 86n.
Cooke, Jay, & Company, 122, 137
Corinth, Miss., 42
Coster, Charles H., 258
Cost of railroad construction, 5-6, 10, 57, 127, 131-132, 132n., 134
Cotton, 53, 192-193
Counties, southern, and railroad finance, 25-26, 34, 88, 89
Courtney, William A., 145, 239
Covington & Macon R.R., 208n.
Covington & Ohio R.R., 126
Cowan, R. H., 72
Credit Mobilier, 162n.
Crescent Line, 150n.
Crews, Joseph, 76n.
Cross ties, 12, 39, 40
Cutting, R. Fulton, 272
Cutting, W. Bayard, 272

INDEX

Dalton, Ga., 114
Dan River & Coalfield R.R., 111n.
Danville, Va., 17, 107, 144
Davies, J. S., 149
Davis, Jefferson, 17
De Bow, James, quoted, 7, 19, 27, 48, 54, 55, 58
Decatur, Ala., 43, 217
Default, on bond interest, 122-125, 124n., 130, 152, 201, 254
Delano, F. H., 128
Delano, John S., 86, 86n.
Depots, railroad, during Civil War, 39, 40, 41, 43, 44; after Civil War, 47-48; repaired, 159, 181
Depression of 1884, 187
d'Erlanger, Baron Emile, of Paris, 161, 161n.
Destruction of railroads, 20-22, 39-45, 142, 146, 158
De Weese, John T., and railroad ring in North Carolina, 69-73; mentioned, 61, 62n.
Dining cars, absence of in 1860, 12
Dinsmore, William B., 86n.
Directors, of southern railroads, 1867-1868, 37-38, 38n.; 1870-1871, 129-130, 133, 134; 1880-1881, 153-154; 1890, 206-209; 1900, 279-282; mentioned, 127, 128, 139, 150, 162n., 164, 168, 180n., 198, 220, 241, 244, 259, 261n., 273
Discrimination, against large stockholders, 28-29, 115
Dividends, railroad, 10, 15, 16, 27, 58, 79, 97, 100, 111n., 116, 119, 123-124, 133-134, 134n., 146n., 149, 149n., 158, 158n., 188-189, 197, 205, 206, 210-211, 219, 219n., 224, 228, 230, 235, 238n., 242, 245, 247, 256-257, 270, 271, 279
Dodge, Gen. Grenville M., 118n.
Douglas, John M., 166, 170, 172, 173, 174, 176, 176n.
Douglas, Senator Stephen A., 7, 155, 185
Dow, Robert K., 244
Drexel, Morgan & Co., 203, 252, 253, 258, 259
Duke, Gen. Basil, 230n.
Duncan, William Butler, 142-143, 170

East Alabama & Cincinnati R.R., 89, 93, 93n.

East & West Railroad of Alabama, 209, 281n.
East Cairo, Ky., 166
East Tennessee, Virginia & Georgia R.R., xvii, 72n., 92n., 106 (map), 110n., 114-116, 117, 118, 119n., 120, 128, 129, 137, 153n., 188n., 189n., 196-203, 204, 226n., 236 (map), 240, 240n., 243, 245-247, 249, 250, 251n., 252, 258n., 284
East Tennessee & Georgia R.R., 10, 15, 33n., 45, 51, 51n., 114, 115, 115n.
East Tennessee & Virginia R.R., 9, 45, 114, 115
Edgar, S. H., 178n.
Editors, and railroad promotion, 24
Elizabethtown, Lexington & Big Sandy R.R., 56n., 209
Elizabethtown & Paducah R.R., 130n., 137, 142, 143
Ellison, H.H., 107n.
Embargo, railroad, on L. & N., 16
Emory College, and railroad securities, 26
Employees, railroad, 13, 18n.
English investments, in southern railroads, 18, 23, 35, 67, 137-138, 147, 157, 159, 215, 229, 246
English rail manufacture, 18-19, 137n., 157
Equipment and supplies, railroad, during Civil War, 16, 17, 19
Erie R.R., 5, 168, 194n.
Erlanger, Emile, of London, 92, 136-137
Erlanger System, 246
European investments in southern railroads, 23, 35, 88, 126, 141, 143, 161n.
Evans, Thomas W., 225
Exchange Hotel, Montgomery, Ala., 91, 217

Fahnestock, E. D., 242
Fares, passenger, 46, 46n., 48, 169, 277
Fast freight lines, 49, 150-151, 195, 266, 276
Federal Treasury, surplus, 31
Felton, S. M., 251n.
Ferguson, E. A., 213
Ferryboat, service, 47, 156, 276
Fillmore, President Millard, 155
Finance, railroad, 1865, 23-38; early 1870's, 100, 131-133; 1900, 279

299

INDEX

Financial assistance, by states to railroads, 29-34
Financial loss, due to southern rail destruction, 39, 42, 42n., 45n., 53
Fink, Albert, and L. & N. bridge at Louisville, 11, 276; and Southern Railway & Steamship Association, 150-151, 276-277; mentioned, 218
Fink, Henry, 138, 201, 202
Fiscal agents, 38, 38n.
Fish, Stuyvesant, 184, 185
Fisk, Jim, 72, 91n.
Fisk, Pliny, 127n.
Fisk & Hatch (New York banking firm), 127
Flagler, Henry Morrison, xvii, 205, 244, 269, 281, 281n.
Florence, S. C., 11, 117n.
Florence R.R., 267
Florida, Central & Peninsular R.R., 272, 272n.
Florida, Central & Western R.R., 141
Florida, railroad building, 4, 5, 61, 94, 191, 193, 255-256; railroad mileage, 5, 32, 61, 191, 193, 255-256; financing of railroads, 32, 95; railroad carpetbagger activity, 94-95; railroads after Civil War, 94-95; mentioned, 19, 62, 69, 71, 281, 281n.
Florida Central R.R., 141
Florida East Coast Railway, xvii, 281, 281n.
Florida Railway & Navigation Co., 141, 141n., 272n.
Florida R.R., 27
Florida Southern R.R., 263
Forbes, John Murray, 36, 36n.
Foreclosure sales, of railroads, 130
Foreign investments, in American railroads, 18, 23, 35, 36-38, 67, 137-138, 141, 147, 157, 159, 205, 215, 229, 246, 269
Forrest, Gen. Nathan Bedford, and railroad raids, 40, 40n.; president of Selma, Marion & Memphis R.R., 93
Forstall, E. J., 164n., 178, 178n.
Freedman's Bureau, 74
Freight cars, after Civil War, 49; in South in 1872, 100n.; refrigerator cars, 266; mentioned, 21n., 151, 169, 232
Freight rates, after Civil War, 48-49, 277; pooling arrangements, 150-152;
during 1880's, 189, 231; during 1890's, 261n., 272; mentioned, 218n., 222-223, 278
Freight service, importance, 13; improvement, 49, 277; fast freight, 150-151, 165; mentioned, 175, 185, 231, 266
Frost, Col. E. D., 165, 165n., 169
Fuel, shortage of, 19, 19n., 48n.
Funded Debt. See Bonds, railroad

Galt House, Louisville, Ky., L. & N. conference at, 218, 218n.
Garden truck, shipment north, 195, 266, 266n.
Garrett, John W., 65, 104, 104n., 108
Garrett, Robert, 66, 144
Gauge, railroad, variation of, 11-12, 12n., 167n., 195, 276; standardization of, 58, 182, 182n., 194-195, 194n., 266, 276, 278; mentioned, 112, 112n.
General merchandise stores, appearance of after Civil War, 212
Georgia, Carolina & Northern R.R., 271
Georgia, railroad building, 4, 5, 32, 61, 62, 79, 79n., 82, 82n., 191, 193, 255-256; railroad mileage, 5, 61, 79, 96n., 191, 193, 255-256; safety record of, 6n.; financing of railroads, 10, 29, 32, 78-83, 91,113n., 128; and Sunday trains, 12n.; destruction of railroads, 21, 40, 43-44, 43n., 44n.; restoration of railroads, 53, 58; railroad carpetbaggers, 62, 79-88; has prosperous railroads, 79; Western & Atlantic R.R. lease, 83-87, 104, 104n.; local control of railroads, 144, 280, 282; mentioned, 19, 20, 21, 27, 45, 46n., 51, 52, 227, 251, 251n., 277
Georgia, Southern & Florida R.R., 208n., 282n.
Georgia & Alabama R.R., 263, 272
Georgia Company, 247-248, 253
Georgia Midland R.R., 262
Georgia Pacific R.R., 196, 208n., 236 (map), 240, 243, 249, 250, 251
Georgia R.R., 15, 26, 27, 34, 43, 47, 49, 53, 79, 101, 134, 134n., 149, 188n., 208n., 222n., 227-228, 261, 267n., 281n.
Georgia Western R.R., 240, 240n.

300

INDEX

German investments, in southern railroads, 141, 205, 269
Gilmer, Francis M., 217
Gindrat, Col. John H., 92
Goldsboro, N. C., 10, 31, 42, 112
Goodman, Walter, 156, 157, 161
Gordon, Gen. John B., 52, 227, 240, 241n.
Gordon, W. A., 164n.
Gould, Jay, 119n., 220, 229
Grady, Henry, 84n., 87, 186, 193, 226n.
Grand Junction, Tenn., 47-48
Grant, Gen. U. S., supply lines disrupted, 41n.; mentioned, 21, 22n., 47n., 67n.
Green, Edward H., xvii, 149, 149n., 220
Green, Hetty, 220, 230, 247
Green, John F., 229
Green Line Transportation Co., 49, 150-151, 150n., 276
Greensboro, N. C., 10, 17, 107, 111
Greenville, S. C., 76
Greenville & Columbia R.R., 26, 32, 75, 76-78, 97, 130n., 131 (map), 145, 236 (map), 239
Gulf & Ship Island R.R., 281n.
Guthrie, James, and the L. & N. R. R., 8-9, 16n., 46n., 148-149, 211, 212, 215, 219, 230; as a railroad investor, 24

"Hairpins," Sherman's, 40, 47
Harmon, Col. M. J., 66
Harpers Ferry, Va., 20
Harriman, Edward H., 184, 185
Harris, A. L. "Fatty," 80, 84
Harris, Robert, 242
Hatch, A. S., 135
Hatch, William B., 127n.
Haupt, Herman, 49
Hayes, Rutherford B., 118n.
Hazlehurst, George H., 128n.
Henderson branch, 216 (map), 219
Henning, B. S., 141
Hewitt, Abram S., 194n., 250
Hill, Benjamin H., 86n.
Hinds, J. J., 93
Holden, Gov. William W., 69, 71, 73, 73n., 263
Holland, D. P., 141
Holt, William S., 86n.
Hotchkiss, N. P., 84

Houston, L. E., 164n.
Hugbart, William, 119
Huntington, C. P., and Chesapeake & Ohio R.R., 127, 128n., 133, 135, 203-204, 283; and Chesapeake, Ohio & Southwestern R.R., 143, 185; mentioned, xvii, 109, 184, 232
Huntington, W. Va., 127
Hurlburt, Col. Ed., 80, 80n., 84, 84n.
Hurley, Timothy, 76n.

Illinois, railroad building in, 3, 59
Illinois Central R.R., xvi, xvii, 6, 7, 129, 155-156, 157, 158, 160 (map), 165-185, 223, 261, 262, 275, 276, 280, 283
Indiana, 3
Inflation, and Confederate railway operation, 16
Ingalls, Melville E., 203, 204
Inman, John H., and Richmond & Danville R.R., 241, 242, 245, 247, 247n., 248, 248n., 249, 249n., 250, 250n., 251, 252, 253n., 284
International Cotton Exposition (1881), 193
Investors, railroad, 24
Iron ore deposits, on line of the Illinois Central, 168n.
Iron production, in the South, 193-194, 218

Jackson, Gen. Thomas J. (Stonewall), 20
Jackson, Tenn., 11, 41n., 157, 162
Jacksonville, Fla., 11, 102n.
Jacksonville, Pensacola & Mobile R.R., 95, 130n., 131 (map), 137, 140, 141
Jacob, Charles D., 149n., 220
James, D. Willis, 107n., 119n.
Jaques, Joseph, 116
Jarvis, Gov. Thomas J., 239
Jesup, M. K., 119n., 205, 269
Johnson, President Andrew, 51
Johnston, Gen. Joseph E., 21n., 64, 161n.
Johnston, William, 114n.
Jones, Andrew Jackson, 70n., 72, 73

Kennaway, John, 42, 46, 47, 48n.
Kentucky, railroad building, 4, 5, 33, 60, 60n., 61, 191, 193, 256; railroad mileage, 5, 60-61, 193, 256; financ-

301

INDEX

ing of railroads, 34; mentioned, 28, 77n., 97, 213-214
Kentucky Central R.R., 232
Kimball, Frederick J., 204
Kimball, Hannibal I., as railroad promoter, 24; railroad carpetbagger acvitities in Georgia, 80-88, 97, 283; sleeping car promoter, 81, 84; real estate ventures, 81, 81n.; and Western & Atlantic R.R. lease, 83-87; vindicated, 87-88; mentioned, 87n., 91n., 141, 193
Kimball House, Atlanta, Ga., 81, 81n., 87
Kimpton, H. H., and railroad ring in S. C., 75n., 76, 76n., 77, 78
King, Edward, 55n., 92, 92n., 146, 269
King, Edward (President of Union Trust Co.), 139
King, John P., president of Georgia R.R., 16, 80, 85
King, Senator William R., 7, 155
Knoxville, Tenn., 11, 17, 20, 27, 32n., 77, 114, 213
Knoxville & Augusta R.R., 236 (map), 240
Knoxville & Kentucky R.R., 26-27
Kosciusko branch, 177-178

Labor, railroad, 57, 145
"Ladies Car," 48n.
"Lady Davis," 20n.
Land grants, Federal, 7, 7n., 63, 63n., 155; state, 63
Laurens R.R., 76n., 239n.
Lawyers, railroad, 86, 175
Lee, Gen. Robert E., supply problem, 17, 20; president of the Valley R.R., 65-66
Lehman, Emanuel, 244, 247, 247n., 248
Leslie, C. P., 76n.
Lincoln, Abraham, 21
Lindsay, Gov. Robert, 91, 92n., 93, 94
Littlefield, Gen. Milton S., leader of railroad ring, 69; and N. C. railroads, 69-73, 145, 239, 283; and Fla. railroads, 95, 141; mentioned, 61, 97, 117
Local capital, and southern railroads, after Civil War, 52-54; 1890, 208-209; 1900, 280, 281, 282; mentioned, 23-38
Locomotives, American-type, 12, 278n.; cost of, 12n., 52n., 278n.; manufacture of, 18; raids during the Civil War, 20, 21; losses by Confederacy, 44, 44n., 50n.; condition after Civil War, 46, 46n.; sale by Federal Government, 52, 52n.; number in South in 1872, 100n.; types in use in 1900, 278, 278n.; mentioned, 175, 211, 258, 265
Logan, Gen. Thomas M., and the Richmond & Danville R.R., 139, 139n., 145, 239, 241, 245
Long Bridge, 104, 105
Lord, Samuel, 140
Louisiana, railroad building in, 5, 61, 95, 191, 193, 255-256; railroad mileage in, 5, 61, 193, 255-256; financing of railroads, 33, 95, 163; railroad destruction, 39, 44; railroad carpetbagger activity, 94, 95, 163
Louisiana Jockey Club, 178n.
Louisville, Cincinnati & Charleston R.R., 26, 31
Louisville, Cincinnati & Lexington R.R., 130n., 131 (map), 148, 148n., 216 (map), 224
Louisville, Henderson & St. Louis R.R., 282n.
Louisville, Ky., and the L. & N. R.R., 8-9, 35, 148-149, 149n., 210, 212, 215, 218, 219, 220, 222, 229, 230; railroad bridge, 11, 11n.; financing of railroads, 35, 220; mentioned, 43n., 143, 214
Louisville, New Albany & Chicago R.R., 224
Louisville, New Orleans & Texas R.R., 160 (map), 183, 184, 196
Louisville, Paducah & Southwestern R.R., 130n., 131 (map), 219
Louisville, St. Louis & Texas R.R., 208n.
Louisville & Nashville R.R., xvi, xvii, xviii, 4n., 8-9, 9n., 16, 21, 24, 28, 46n., 49, 53, 93n., 132, 132n., 134, 134n., 143, 144, 147-149, 151, 153n., 162, 188n., 196, 197, 210-232, 216 (map), 240, 240n., 257n., 267n., 275, 276, 280, 281, 281n., 284
Louisville Southern R.R., 202, 247
Lubricating oil, 16
Lynchburg, Va., and the Virginia & Tennessee R.R., 9; railroad destruc-

302

INDEX

tion, 41; mentioned, 11, 17, 47, 55n., 109
Lynchburg & Danville R.R., 144
Lynchburg & Durham R.R., 209n.
Lyon, John M., 109

McClellan, George B., 157
McComb, Col. Henry S., as railroad promoter, 24; and New Orleans, St. Louis & Chicago R.R., 133, 168-174, 283; and Mississippi Central R.R., 161-162; and New Orleans, Jackson & Great Northern R.R., 161-168; and Mississippi & Tennessee R.R., 162n., 183-184; and northern railroads, 162n.; and Illinois Central R.R., 165-179; charges of fraud against, 177-179; mentioned, xvi
"McComb, H. S.," 167, 170
McComb City, Miss., 167, 177, 177n.
McGhee, Charles M., 115-116
Machine shops, railroad, 43, 43n.
Macon, Ga., Southwestern R.R. of Georgia, 10; Western & Atlantic R.R., 85-86; mentioned, 28, 43, 44, 128, 198
Macon & Augusta R.R., 82
Macon & Birmingham R.R., 282n.
Macon & Brunswick R.R., 82n., 126, 128, 130n., 131 (map), 135, 137, 198, 198n.
Macon & Western R.R., 28, 44, 85
Madison, Ind., 8
Magrath, William J., 140
Mahone, William, and Norfolk & Petersburg R.R., 41, 66; "railroad Bismarck" of Virginia, 66, 66n.; and South Side R.R., 66; and Virginia & Tennessee R.R., 66; and Atlantic, Mississippi & Ohio R.R., 67, 67n., 109-110, 110n., 137-139, 283; and southern ambitions of Pennsylvania R.R., 107, 108, 109-110, 109n., 115-116, 116n.; mentioned, 138n., 161n.
Mail, U. S., 44n., 158
Manchester & Augusta R.R., 267
Mansfield, Josie, 72
Marietta & North Georgia R.R., 208n.
Maryland, and railroad construction, 60, 60n.
Matthews, Edward, 140
Maysville & Big Sandy R.R., 204
Memphis, Clarksville & Louisville R.R., 215, 215n., 216 (map)

Memphis, Paducah & Northern R.R., 143
Memphis, Tenn., L. & N. R.R., 9, 215, 217; Mississippi & Tennessee R.R., 162n.; mentioned, 11, 45, 116n., 187, 187n., 199
Memphis & Charleston R.R., 9, 13, 45, 51, 51n., 57, 106 (map), 116-117, 116n., 118, 119, 119n., 188n., 199-200
Memphis & Ohio R.R., 215, 216 (map)
Memphis Appeal, 54
Mercer University, 26
Meridian, Miss., Confederate rail construction, 17; mentioned, 44, 89, 92, 199
Metropolitan Bank of New York, 198, 201
Miami, Fla., 281
Michigan Central R.R., 36
Middendorf, Oliver & Co., 272
Middle Atlantic States, railroad building in, 191
Mileage, of railroads, 3-6, 59-61, 59n., 60n., 122, 122n., 124, 125, 189-193, 207-209, 210n., 233n., 254-256, 275, 279
Military Railway Department (U.S.), 21, 50
Milner, John T., 193
Mississippi, railroad building, 4, 5, 61, 66, 95, 95n., 191, 193, 256; railroad mileage in, 5, 32, 61, 193, 256; railroad financing, 8, 33, 163; railroad destruction, 44-45; railroad carpetbagger activity, 94, 95; mentioned, 155
Mississippi & Tennessee R.R., 160 (map), 162n., 183-184, 184n.
Mississippi Central & Tennessee R.R., 157
Mississippi Central R.R., 8, 45, 117, 156-157, 158, 160 (map), 161, 162, 163, 165, 165n., 166, 168, 171, 171n., 174-177, 178, 180, 181, 183
Mississippi River traffic, importance in 1860, 13; importance after Civil War, 49
Mobile, Ala., projected Mobile & Ohio R.R., 7-8, 35; financing of railroads, 34-35; railroad destruction, 44; mentioned, 11
Mobile & Alabama Grand Trunk R.R., 93n.

INDEX

Mobile & Birmingham R.R., 202
Mobile & Girard R.R., 206
Mobile & Montgomery R.R., 93, 93n., 130n., 131 (map), 147, 216 (map), 221
Mobile & Ohio R.R., 6, 7, 9, 33, 34-35, 36, 37, 44, 92n., 130n., 131 (map), 137, 142-143, 155-156, 156n., 157, 158, 158n., 166, 169, 170, 194, 197, 199, 203, 223, 223n., 257n., 268, 268n., 275, 280, 281
Montgomery, Ala., Confederate railroad rate convention, 16n.; mentioned, 11, 90, 206, 217, 218
Montgomery & Eufaula R.R., 93n., 206, 221
Montgomery & West Point R.R., 44, 44n., 48
Morehead City, N. C., 31
Morgan, Charles, 129, 133n.
Morgan, E. D., 147n.
Morgan, J. Pierpont, xvii, 140n., 233, 252, 252n., 253, 258, 259
Morgan's Louisiana & Texas R.R., 126, 129, 133n.
Morgan's Raiders, 20-21
Murdock, Abraham, 49, 142, 143

Nash, Senator Beverly, 78n.
Nashville, Chattanooga & St. Louis R.R., 188n., 189n., 197, 199, 208n., 209, 216 (map), 223, 224-227, 232, 240n.
Nashville, Florence & Sheffield R.R., 232
Nashville, Tenn., L. & N. R.R., 9, 215, 215n., 217, 224, 227n.; mentioned, 11, 27, 43n.
Nashville & Chattanooga R.R., 9, 27, 28, 34, 45, 45n., 51n., 52, 52n., 86n., 116
Nashville & Decatur R.R., 23, 45, 216 (map), 217-218
Natchez & Jackson R.R., 35
Neagle, John L., 75, 76
Neely, Gen. Rufus Polk, 175, 176
Negroes, segregation of, on trains, 46, 46n., 231; during Reconstruction, 56; as railroad labor, 42n., 57, 57n., 67n.; control of votes of, 67n., 85n., 89, 89n.; and railroad carpetbaggers, 69, 69n., 74-75, 80, 81n., 89, 96; slave labor used to pay stock subscriptions, 157; mentioned, 40

Newcomb, H. D., and L. & N. R.R., 148, 212, 215, 217, 218, 219
Newcomb, Horatio Victor, and L. & N. R.R., 148, 149, 219, 220, 225, 225n., 226n., 227, 227n.
Newcomer, Benjamin Franklin, and Southern Railway Security Co., 102, 107, 107n., 114, 119n., 120; and Wilmington, Columbia & Augusta R.R., 136, 265; and Wilmington & Weldon R.R., 265; mentioned, 73n., 147n., 205, 269, 270
Newell, John, 178
New England, railroad building in, 59, 191
New Jersey, 4
New Orleans, Jackson & Great Northern R.R., xvi, 6, 8, 9, 33, 36, 44, 44n., 51, 52, 54, 156, 157, 158-168, 160 (map), 171, 174, 176, 178, 179
New Orleans, Jackson & Northern R.R., 179, 180
New Orleans, La., railroad conventions, 8, 156; financing railroads, 9; New Orleans, Jackson & Great Northern R.R., 156, 159, 163; mentioned, 11, 57, 58, 113n., 157, 166, 187n., 222
New Orleans, Mobile & Chattanooga R.R., 95
New Orleans, Mobile & Texas R.R., 95, 147, 147n.
New Orleans, Opelousas & Great Western R.R., 33, 129
New Orleans, St. Louis & Chicago R.R., xvi, xviii, 130n., 131 (map), 133, 137, 142, 143n., 155, 162, 168-174, 176n.
New Orleans & Carrollton R.R., 161, 161n.
New Orleans & Mobile R.R., 130n., 131 (map), 147-148, 147n., 216 (map), 221
New Orleans & Northeastern R.R., 281n.
New Orleans & Northwestern R.R., 137n., 282n.
New Orleans & Selma R.R., 93n.
Newport News, Va., 203
New York, 4
New York Central R.R., 5, 168
New York City, finance and southern railroads, 28, 55, 126-127, 128, 129-130, 139, 140, 143, 146, 147, 147n., 148-149, 150, 153, 207, 219-220,

304

INDEX

226, 229, 242, 244, 247, 280, 283; mentioned, 66n., 69, 77, 113n., 203
Nickel Plate R.R., 200
Norfolk, Va., 34, 109, 109n., 199
Norfolk & Great Western R.R., 109
Norfolk & Petersburg R.R., 41, 66, 67
Norfolk & Southern R.R., 281
Norfolk & Western R.R., 67n., 139, 189n., 197, 199, 202, 203, 204-205, 257n., 261-262, 261n., 275, 276, 280
North Carolina, railroad building, 4, 5, 61, 62, 68, 68n., 191, 193, 256; railroad mileage, 5, 30n., 31, 61, 68, 68n., 193, 256; financing of railroads, 10, 26, 29, 30-31, 68-74, 110; destruction of railroads, 21, 40, 42; railroad carpetbaggers, 62, 68-74, 95; disposal of railroad securities, 72-73, 263; North Carolina R.R., 110-111, 112; Western North Carolina R.R., 145, 239; mentioned, 20, 45, 75, 107, 266
North Carolina R.R., 10, 26, 31, 31n., 42, 52, 69n., 106 (map), 110-112, 112n., 118, 133, 134n., 153, 234-235, 236 (map)
North-East & South-West Alabama R.R., 89, 90
Northeastern R.R. of Georgia, 236 (map), 240
Northeastern R.R. of South Carolina, 106 (map), 117, 118, 205, 265, 266, 267, 270
Northern Alabama R.R., 262
Northern capital, and southern railroads, 23, 27, 28, 50, 53, 54, 55, 64, 88, 89, 126, 149, 186, 198, 202, 206, 273; in South, 55-56; before 1873, 126, 129-130, 133; 1880-1881, 153-154; 1890, 206-209; L. & N., 210, 219-220; Richmond & Danville R.R., 233, 234, 241, 252-253, 259; 1900, 279-282; mentioned, 143
Northern Central Railway, 102, 103, 104
North Louisiana & Texas R.R., 95
Northwest, railroad building in, 191
Norton, Eckstein, 229, 229n., 230, 284

Oakman, W. G., 242, 251, 251n., 252
Ohio, 3, 194, 213
Ohio Extension (Norfolk & Western), 204n.

Ohio River, as trade artery, 213
Okolona, Miss., 44
Olcutt, Frederick P., 251, 252, 252n.
Old Dominion Steamship Co., 203, 272
Operating ratio, of railroads, 15, 15n., 83, 123, 132, 134, 189, 197, 211, 266-267, 279n.
Orange, Alexandria & Manassas R.R., 65, 108-109, 144
Orange & Alexandria R.R., 57, 65
Orange Belt R.R., 208n.
Orangeburg, S. C., 43
Ordnance production, 18
Orr, James L., 76
"Osborn, W. H.," 167
Osborn, William H., 157, 166, 172, 173, 174, 176n., 177, 178, 179, 180, 181, 183n., 185
Owensboro & Nashville R.R., 225, 226

Paducah & Elizabeth R.R., 143
Panic of 1837, 35
Panic of 1857, 3, 120n., 156
Panic of 1873, xv, 60, 94, 98, 100, 113, 116, 119, 120, 122-124, 126, 127, 132, 153, 168, 195, 219, 234, 263, 268
Panic of 1893, 230, 256-257, 261
Parker, Miles G., and railroad ring in South Carolina, 74, 75, 76n.
Passenger service, cars, 12; night travel, 12; Sunday service, 12, 12n.; coupon tickets, 12; speed, 13, 113n., 165, 277, 278; during Civil War, 19-20; during Reconstruction, 46-48; rates, 189, 232n., 277; rate war, 223; cost of passenger cars, 278, 278n.; mentioned, 151n., 182, 231, 265n., 266, 277
Passes, railroad, 85, 85n., 230n.
Patterson, "Honest John," 74-79, 97
Patton, ex-Governor (of Ala.), 90, 90n.
Peabody, George, 157
Pennington, J. L., 93
Pennsylvania, rolling stock manufacture as compared to South, 18; control of politics in, 102; mentioned, 4, 194
Pennsylvania Company, 102
Pennsylvania R.R., interests in Virginia railroads, 65, 65n., 67, 68; southern ambitions in the 1870's, 99-121, 233, 234, 235, 237, 265; before

305

INDEX

and during Civil War, 100; mentioned xv, 5, 49, 148, 148n., 168, 172n., 195, 262, 266, 273, 277
Pensacola & Atlantic R.R., 209, 222
Pensacola & Georgia R.R., 95
Pensacola & Selma R.R., 216 (map), 222
Pensacola R.R., 216 (map), 222
Perkins, Charles L., 138
Petersburg, Va., 42
Petersburg R.R., 15, 26, 41, 53, 56, 265, 265n., 267
Peto, Sir Morton, 36
Philadelphia, Pa., control over southern railroads, 153, 207, 270
Philadelphia, Wilmington & Baltimore R.R., 13
Piedmont Air-Line Route, 113n.
Piedmont R.R., 110
Pierpont, Gov. Francis H., 30, 54, 64, 67
Pittsburgh, Fort Wayne & Chicago Railway, 102
Plant, Henry Bradley, and Southern Railway Security Co., 102, 102n., 103, 103n., 104, 119n., 120; and Savannah, Florida & Western R.R., 146, 269; and Charleston & Savannah R.R., 146-147, 269; and Plant System, 205, 268-270; mentioned, 86n., 144, 147n., 284
Plant Investment Co., 205, 269, 270
Plant System, 146, 203, 205, 205n., 263, 264 (map), 268-270, 275, 280
Poe, Col. Orlando M., 40
Pollard, Charles T., 147
Pooling, railroad, 150-152, 276-277
Pope's Creek, Md., 103-104
Porter, James D., 226
Porter, Thomas K., 177n.
Port Royal, S. C., 55, 149
Port Royal & Augusta Railway, 150, 209
Port Royal & Western Carolina R.R., 209
Port Royal R.R., 130n., 131 (map), 149-150
Presidencies, of southern railroads, 130, 153, 208, 282
Promoters, railroad, 24, 60, 89, 99
Prosperity, railroad, before the Civil War, 27; during Civil War, 15, 16, 157; after the Civil War, 60,

60n.; in Georgia after Civil War, 79; during 1870's, 132-134, 152; during the 1880's, 186-189, 196, 206; during the 1890's, 256, 267, 273; mentioned, 247
Pullman, George M., 81
Pullman Palace Car Co., 182n.

Rail, types in use by 1860, 12, 12n.; English production, 18-19; southern production, 19, 57; destruction during Civil War, 20-22, 20n., 22n., 39, 40, 42, 43, 44; reuse of bent rails, 47, 47n., 56, 92n.; steel rail, 278; mentioned, 13, 43n., 53, 157, 171, 175, 258
Railroad conventions, 7, 24-25, 150, 156
Railroad guides (Time Tables), 12-13
Raleigh, N. C., 10, 88
Raleigh & Augusta R.R., 209n., 271
Raleigh & Gaston R.R., 110, 209n., 271
Randolph, Lewis V. F., 172, 179
Ransier, A. J., 75
Raoul, Willliam G., 247
Rates, during Civil War, 16, 16n.; during Reconstruction, 48-49, 58; rate competition, 150-152, 168, 272, 277; during 1880's, 189; rate discrimination, 212, 214n., 222-223; during 1890's, 261n.; maximum rate regulation, 277; mentioned, 69n., 169, 211, 211n., 231, 232n.
Receivership, of railroads, 91-92, 113, 122-125, 129-150, 174-180, 186, 201, 203, 254, 257-263, 268, 273, 283, 284
Reconstruction (political), and state railroad aid programs, 63; mentioned 56, 64, 97
Reed, J. P., 76
Reid, Whitelaw, 44, 44n., 46, 46n., 47, 47n., 53, 54, 55, 55n., 57, 58n.
Restoration of southern railroads, after Civil War, 49-58, 59, 60, 158-159, 162n.
Rice, Isaac G., 247, 247n.
Richmond, Fredericksburg & Potomac R.R., xv, 27, 105, 273, 277
Richmond, Petersburg & Carolina R.R., 273
Richmond, Va., Richmond & Danville R.R., 10, 233, 234; fire of April 2, 1865, 42; Pennsylvania R.R., 105,

306

INDEX

110; mentioned, 11, 15, 17, 20, 41, 55, 57, 58, 64, 127, 187n., 263, 265n.
Richmond, York River & Chesapeake R.R., 235, 236 (map), 237
Richmond & Alleghany R.R., 204
Richmond & Danville Extension Co., 240
Richmond & Danville R.R., xvi, xvii, xviii, 10, 31n., 49, 64, 67n., 68, 72n., 105-108, 106 (map), 110-113, 114, 117, 118, 119, 119n., 120, 121, 139, 144-146, 153n., 196, 197, 202, 202n., 233-253, 236 (map), 257, 258-260, 284
Richmond & Petersburg R.R., 41, 105 106 (map), 107, 118, 265, 266, 267
Richmond & West Point Terminal Railway & Warehouse Co., 121, 144-146, 202, 202n., 204, 206, 233, 233n., 235, 237-253, 257, 258-260
River competition, for railroads, 49
Rives, Alfred L., 142, 142n., 223n.
Roadbed, value of, 56
Robb, James, 8, 36, 156
Roberts, Dr. Charles H., 140
Robinson, John M., and Seaboard Air Line, 270-272
Rockefeller, John D., 242, 281n.
Rolling mills, at Chattanooga, 57
Rolling stock, types used in 1860, 12; during Civil War, 15, 18, 39, 41, 42, 44, 44n., 45, 45n., 158; on loan, 17, 276; during Reconstruction, 46; purchased from Federal Government, 50-51, 50n., 51n., 158-159; Western & Atlantic R.R., 85; freight cars in South in 1872, 100n.; new passenger types in 1890's, 278; cost of passenger equipment, 278, 278n.; mentioned, 142, 167n., 182, 195, 232
Roosevelt, James, 102, 102n., 119, 119n.
Roundhouses, railroad, 43
Routes, major southern railroads, 11, 11n., 118
Russell, E. L., 281
Ryan, Thomas Fortune, 220, 229, 260

Sage, Russell, 217, 220
St. Johns & Lake Eustis R.R., 270
St. Louis & Southeastern R.R., 130n., 131 (map), 148, 219

Salaries, of railroad officials, 67, 67n., 138, 139n., 159, 159n., 178n., 180n., 181, 226n., 230, 230n.
Salisbury, N. C., 71
Sanford & St. Petersburg R.R., 270
Savannah, Americus & Montgomery R.R., 209n., 272
Savannah, Florida & Western R.R., 146, 197, 205, 263, 269
Savannah, Ga., and the Southwestern R.R. of Georgia, 10; financing of railroads, 34; mentioned, 11, 17, 21, 32, 39, 42, 43, 112, 249, 280
Savannah & Charleston R.R., 43, 130n., 131 (map), 146-147, 269
Savannah & Memphis R.R., 93n.
Savannah & Western Railway, 206
Schedules, of trains, during Civil War, 17, 20; after Civil War, 48, 159n.; improved by 1867, 58; mentioned, 13, 92n., 113n., 165, 167n., 182, 277, 278, 278n.
Schreiber, A., 164n., 170n., 174
Scioto Valley & New England R.R., 204
Scott, George S., 202, 242, 243n., 244, 245
Scott, Gov. Robert K., 74, 78, 79
Scott, Thomas A., and Richmond & Danville R.R., 68, 233, 235; and Western & Atlantic R.R. lease, 85-86, 86n., 115; and Pennsylvania R.R., 101-121, 283; description of, 101-102; mentioned, 148n., 172n., 177n.
Scott Syndicate, 243, 243n.
Screven, John, 146
Seaboard Air Line, xv, 263, 264 (map), 270-273, 275, 277, 280, 281, 284
Seaboard & Roanoke R.R., xv, 140, 270, 271
Segregation, racial, on railroads, 46, 46n.
Selma, Ala., 17, 197, 223
Selma, Marion & Memphis R.R., 89, 93, 93n.
Selma, Rome & Dalton R.R., 126, 128-129, 130n., 131 (map), 135, 137, 197, 198, 199
Selma & Gulf R.R., 93n.
Selma branch, 216 (map), 222-223
Seney, George I., and the East Tennessee, Virginia & Georgia R.R., 198,

INDEX

200, 201, 201n., 202n., 243, 284; mentioned, xvii, 242
Shackleford, Judge C. C., 158, 159
Shenandoah Valley R.R., 65, 204
Sherman, Gen. William T., destruction of railroads, 20n., 21-22, 21n., 22n., 40, 42-44, 45, 92, 158; supply problem, 43n., 46n.
Shops, railroad, 39
Shovels, 16
Sinking Fund Commission (of S. C.), 77
Sleeping cars, 12, 12n., 81, 84, 266
Slidell, John, 8
Sloan, Dr. William, 72
Sloan, Samuel, 140n.
Sloss, James Withers, 217-218, 218n.
Smith, Gov. William H., and railroad carpetbaggers in Alabama, 89-91, 93
Smith, Milton H., and L. & N. R.R., 218n., 221, 229-231, 281, 284
Smith, Sidney, 8, 36
Smith, W. A., 69n., 110
Smith, Williamson, 164n.
Social Circle, Ga., 43
Somers, Robert, 53, 142, 142n.
South & North Alabama R.R., 93, 93n., 193, 216 (map), 217-218
South Carolina, railroad building, 4, 5, 61, 62, 74, 191-193, 256; railroad mileage, 5, 61, 74n., 193, 256; financing of railroads, 31-32, 74, 75, 75n., 76-79; destruction of railroads, 39, 40, 42-43; railroad carpetbaggers, 62, 73-79; state debt, 75; mentioned, 18, 20, 26, 45, 55, 77n., 107, 277
South Carolina & Georgia Extension R.R., 281n.
South Carolina R.R., xvii, 19, 28, 32, 34, 36, 37, 42-43, 42n., 48, 53, 56, 57, 77, 130n., 131 (map), 137, 140, 140n.
South-East & St. Louis R.R., 216 (map), 223, 225, 226
Southern Express Co., 54, 80, 86n., 103n., 146, 268
Southern Pacific Co., 129
Southern Pacific R.R., 281n.
Southern Passenger Association, 151n.
Southern Railroad Association, 162, 165n., 168, 179
Southern Railway, xvi, xvii, 112n., 233, 252n., 253, 259-260, 261, 262, 263, 272, 275, 277, 280
Southern Railway & Steamship Association, 151-152, 196, 276
Southern Railway Security Company, xv, 72n., 92n., 99, 101-107, 112-121, 129, 199, 233, 234, 265, 283
South Florida R.R., 205, 269
South Georgia & Florida R.R., 82n.
South Side R.R., 41, 66, 67
Southwestern R.R. of Georgia, 10, 27, 85, 133, 133n., 134n., 206
Soutter & Co., 71, 90
Spartanburg & Union R.R., 76n., 239n.
Speculation, in railroad securities, 25, 28
Speed, of trains, 13, 48, 48n., 159, 165, 167, 175
Spencer, Samuel, 259-260, 260n., 261
Stage coaches, after Civil War, 47
Standard Time, 195
Standiford, E. D., 221
Stanton, Daniel C., 89, 91n., 97, 136, 283
Stanton, John C., railroad promoter, 24; in Alabama, 89-93, 97, 136, 283; real estate holdings in Chattanooga, 91; votes 900 of his railroad employees, 91; mentioned, 117, 133, 193, 218
Stanton House, hotel in Chattanooga, owned by John Stanton, 91, 91n.
State aid programs for railroads, and carpetbagger activity, 63, 70-73, 79-83, 88-94
State railroad commissions, 277
States, southern, and railroad finance, 8-10, 23-26, 29-34, 63, 162-163, 163n.
Steamer connections, south of Cairo, Ill., with southern railroads, 156, 166, 167, 167n., 170
Stephens, Alexander H., and Western & Atlantic R.R. lease, 86, 86n.
Stetson, Francis Lynde, 258
Stevenson, Vernon K., 200, 217, 225
Stockholders Investigation Committee (Pennsylvania R.R.), 116, 119
Stocks, railroad, quotations of, 152, 187-188, 242n., 244, 244n., 257; mentioned, 23n., 29-34, 35, 37-38, 60, 60n., 115, 132, 149, 149n., 157, 162-163, 163n., 186, 189, 201, 226n., 229n., 237, 242, 259, 267

308

INDEX

Stone, George F., 244
Stoneman, Gen. George, 67n.
Strawberries, shipped north by rail, 266n.
Strong, W. E., 252
Subscription, to railroad securities, 24, 26-29, 31
Sullivan, D. F., 222
Sully, Alfred, 242, 244, 245, 247, 247n.
Swan, James, 247
Swann, John, 136
Swepson, George W., and railroad ring in North Carolina, 69-73, 97, 239; and railroads in Florida, 95; mentioned, 117, 145
Switches, railroad, 40

Taft, Judge Alphonso, 213n.
Tallahassee R.R., 95
Tampa, Fla., 205
Tate, Sam, 51
Tate, Samuel McD., 71
Tennessee, railroad building, 4, 5, 33, 61, 191-193, 256; railroad mileage, 5, 33, 61, 96n., 193, 256; financing of railroads, 8, 9, 33-34, 33n., 96, 115, 181; railroad destruction, 45; carpetbagger railroad activity, 94, 96; state debt, 96; mentioned, 18, 51, 118, 175, 213
Tennessee & Alabama Central R.R., 217
Tennessee & Alabama R.R., 217
Tennessee Midland R.R., 209n.
Tennessee Pacific R.R., 27
Terminal facilities, during Civil War, 17, 276; on "Weldon Route," 265n.; mentioned, 58
Texas, 4n., 19
Texas & Pacific R.R., 118n., 281n.
Textile production, in the South, 192-193
Thomas, Samuel, and the East Tennessee Virginia & Georgia R.R., 198, 199n., 200, 202, 202n., 245, 246; and Richmond & Danville R.R., 241, 243, 245, 252; mentioned, xvii, 260, 284
Thomson, John Edgar, 66, 100-101
Tombigbee River, 17
Tomlinson, Reuben, 76n.
Track, maintenance, 17; after Civil War, 47, 47n.; change of gauge in 1886, 194-195; mentioned, 11, 12, 57, 171n., 181-182
Transfer points, railroad, 17, 265n., 276
Trowbridge, J. T., 44, 44n., 46, 47, 47n., 56
Tucker, John, 129, 129n.
Tunstall, W. P., 10

Union Army, and southern railroads, 20-22
Union City, Tenn., 44
Union Line, 150n.
Union Pacific R.R., 118n., 162n.
Union Trust Co., 139, 150

Valley R.R., 65, 66, 66n.
Valuation, assessed, in the South in the 1860's, 60
Vanderbilt, W. H., 200
Vicksburg, Miss., 17
Vicksburg, Shreveport & Pacific R.R., 281n.
Vicksburg, Shreveport & Texas R.R., 33
Vicksburg & Meridian R.R., 137n.
Virginia, railroad building, 4, 5, 9, 61, 65n., 66, 66n., 191-193, 256; railroad mileage, 5, 30n., 61, 65n., 96n., 193, 256; financing of railroads, 10, 28, 29-30, 31, 64, 126; railroad destruction, 39, 41-42; railroad restoration, 54, 57; carpetbagger activity, 64-65; consolidation of railroads, 66-67; sale of state-owned railroad securities, 67-68, 105-110; debts owed by railroads, 67, 67n.; mentioned, 18, 20, 51, 75, 104, 126n., 235
Virginia & Kentucky R.R., 67
Virginia & Tennessee R.R., 9, 30, 41, 66, 67
Virginia Central R.R., 126
Virginia Midland R.R., 144, 197, 209, 236 (map), 238, 242

Wadley, William M., 149, 161n., 206, 227
Wages, for railroad personnel, 16, 57n., 67, 67n., 90, 138, 171, 173
Walker, Gov. Gilbert C. (of Virginia), 64, 108
Walker, James, 108
Walker, T. A., 129, 129n.

309

INDEX

Wallace, Major Campbell, 83
Wall Street Journal, quoted, 267
Walter, Harvey W., 156
Walters, William Thompson, and Southern Railway Security Co., 102, 104, 107, 107n., 114, 119n., 120; and Wilmington, Columbia & Augusta R.R., 136; and Wilmington & Weldon R.R., 73, 263-265; and Atlantic Coast Line, 266-267; mentioned 72, 86n., 115, 147n., 205, 269, 270, 283
Walthall, Gen. Edward, 174
Warmoth, Gov. Henry Clay, 163
Washington, D. C., 57, 103-104, 105, 108
Washington & Richmond R.R., 105
Washington City, Virginia Midland & Great Southern R.R., 130n., 131 (map), 144
Waterman, George W., 76, 76n.
Water tanks, railroad, 40
Waycross, Ga., 11
Weldon, N. C., 11
"Weldon Route," 265
West, Gen. Absolom M., 161, 162
Western & Atlantic R.R., 10, 19, 32, 43, 43n., 49, 51, 52, 83-87, 104, 104n., 106 (map), 115, 118, 209n., 225, 227
Western North Carolina R.R., 26, 31, 31n., 70-71, 71n., 72n., 97, 117, 130n., 131 (map), 145, 153, 202, 236 (map), 238-239, 260
Western R.R. of Alabama, 130n., 131 (map), 149, 209, 222, 282n.
Western states, railroad building in, 191
West Point, Ga., 44n.
West Virginia, 127, 127n.
White Line, 150n.

Whitney, C. A., 129
Wickham, Gen. William C., and Chesapeake & Ohio R.R., 126-127, 127n., 135
Williams, John L., 272, 273
Williams, John Skelton, 273, 281
Williamston & Tarboro R.R., 70
Wills Valley R.R., 90
Wilmington, Charlotte & Rutherford R.R., 72, 139
Wilmington, Columbia & Augusta R.R., 73, 102, 106 (map), 107, 107n., 112, 117n., 118, 119, 119n., 121, 130n., 131 (map), 135-136, 136n., 189n., 205, 205n., 265, 266, 267, 270
Wilmington, N. C., 11, 28, 34, 72, 86n., 112
Wilmington & Manchester R.R., 73, 263, 265, 283
Wilmington & Raleigh R.R., 31
Wilmington & Weldon R.R., 16, 28, 28n., 31, 42, 72-73, 102, 106 (map), 107, 107n., 112, 118, 119, 119n., 121, 136, 189n., 205, 205n., 209, 263, 265, 266, 267, 270, 283
Wilson, Richard T., and the B. & O. R.R. in Virginia, 67; and Southern Railway Security Co., 103, 115-117, 119n.; and the East Tennessee, Virginia & Georgia R.R., 115-117, 120, 128, 129, 137; and Macon & Brunswick R.R., 128, 137, 198; and Selma, Rome & Dalton R.R., 129, 137; mentioned, 184, 250,
Wilson's Raiders (Gen. James H.), 44
Winchester, Va., 20
Wrecks, 20, 47, 260n.

Yellow fever epidemics, 182n., 199

www.ingramcontent.com/pod-product-compliance
Lightning Source LLC
Chambersburg PA
CBHW032221010526
44113CB00032B/195